MANDEVILLE'S FABLE

Mandeville's Fable

PRIDE, HYPOCRISY, AND SOCIABILITY

ROBIN DOUGLASS

PRINCETON UNIVERSITY PRESS

PRINCETON & OXFORD

Published by Princeton University Press
41 William Street, Princeton, New Jersey 08540
99 Banbury Road, Oxford OX2 6JX

press.princeton.edu

All Rights Reserved

ISBN 9780691218670
ISBN (pbk.) 9780691219172
ISBN (e-book) 9780691224695

British Library Cataloging-in-Publication Data is available

Editorial: Ben Tate and Josh Drake
Production Editorial: Jaden Young
Jacket/Cover Design: Karl Spurzem
Production: Lauren Reese
Publicity: Alyssa Sanford and Charlotte Coyne
Copyeditor: Catja Pafort

Jacket image: Title page from The Fable of The Bees: or, Private Vices, Publick Benefits by Bernard Mandeville. (1714). History and Art Collection / Alamy Stock Photo.

This book has been composed in Arno Pro

10 9 8 7 6 5 4 3 2 1

He took uncommon Pains to search into human Nature, and left no Stone unturn'd, to detect the Pride and Hypocrisy of it, and among his intimate Friends to expose the Stratagems of the one, and the exorbitant Power of the other.

—BERNARD MANDEVILLE, *THE FABLE OF THE BEES. PART II*

CONTENTS

Preface xi

Conventions xv

Introduction   1

A pride-centred theory of sociability   4

Satire and philosophy   12

'Private Vices, Publick Benefits' and the origins of sociability   17

A brief roadmap   22

PART I. MORAL PSYCHOLOGY   25

1. Pride and Human Nature   27

   The place of pride in Mandeville's psychology   29

      Pride, fear, and self-preservation   32

      Self-love and self-liking   35

      Pride and shame   38

   Criticisms of Mandeville's psychology   41

      Objections to psychological egoism   42

      Pride vs. praiseworthy motives   47

   Conclusion   55

2. The Morality of Pride   57

   The vice of pride   59

      Definitional complexities   60

      The morality of self-liking   62

The problem of sincerity   67

  An Augustinian view of pride?   69

  A satire upon morality?   75

Is pride really that bad?   80

  Pride vs. a well-regulated desire for esteem   83

Conclusion   89

3. Sociability, Hypocrisy, and Virtue   92

  Enter Shaftesbury   94

    Shaftesbury on sociability, virtue, and beauty   98

    A digression on the 'Pulchrum & Honestum'   101

  Virtue, self-denial, and hypocrisy   103

    Why 'a vast Inlet to Hypocrisy'?   105

    Social utility and 'counterfeited' virtue   109

  Sociability and hypocrisy   114

    The use and abuse of hypocrisy   114

    Hypocrisy and the origin of virtue   118

    Should hypocrisy be unmasked?   123

  Conclusion   129

PART II. HISTORICAL NARRATIVES   133

4. The Desire of Dominion and Origin of Society   135

  Mandeville's origin stories   138

    The role of human contrivance (1714–23)   141

    Mandeville's historical turn   147

  Sociability and the steps towards society   151

    On 'the Sociableness of Man'   154

    Mandeville vs. Temple on the savage family   157

    The first two steps   164

    The third step and the origin of language   168

    Addendum on whether Cleomenes and Horatio switch roles   171

Conclusion		175
	A theory of social evolution?	175
	A theory of political authority?	179
5.	Honour, Religion, and War	183
	The origins of virtue and honour, revisited	185
	Virtue and honour	187
	Modern honour	190
	The origin of honour	196
	Christian virtue	199
	The passions of war	203
	Duelling, honour, and politeness	204
	Love of country and religious enthusiasm	211
	Conclusion	217
	Conclusion	220
	Pride in the economic sphere	222
	Was Mandeville right?	226

Bibliography   231

Index   247

PREFACE

WHY A BOOK ON MANDEVILLE? I offer some more scholarly reasons in what follows, yet as is often the case, the deeper truth is more personal. Mandeville divides people and most who stick with him (so my anecdotal evidence suggests) do so, in part at least, because he gets under their skin. There is something unsettling about reading Mandeville. He leaves you questioning yourself in a way that is true of much of the psychologically richest philosophy and literature. You can go away and read Adam Smith's *The Theory of Moral Sentiments* and feel a bit better about yourself, but when you come back to Mandeville the doubts soon return. Such is my experience, anyway, and if I have managed to capture something of why that is the case in writing this book, then I will count it a success.

I also find Mandeville very enjoyable to read (again, this divides people), not least because of his withering criticisms of the moralism of his day and his willingness to say of his contemporaries many things that I would never dare to say publicly of mine. One of the consequences of spending a lot of time with Mandeville is that it helps you to recognise some of the pathologies of taking yourself and what you do too seriously. He was particularly scathing of the 'great Opinion Scholars have of themselves', especially those who regard their vocation as more noble or valuable than most other professions.[1] Although the scholars he had in mind are not quite the same as the academics that inhabit universities today, the latter are certainly not immune from his charge. I suspect that working in academia has heightened my sense that Mandeville still speaks to us now.

My title closely resembles that of a fine article by Laurence Dickey that (unsurprisingly) addresses similar themes, albeit from a much more historical

---

1. *Female Tatler*, no. 66: 109–12.

perspective.[2] I noticed the similarity only after having settled on the title, even though I must have first read Dickey's article many years earlier, so perhaps it subconsciously influenced my choice. In any case, this book is about Mandeville's theory of sociability, at the heart of which is the passion of pride. Pride and hypocrisy are very closely related, although hypocrisy is not as central to my analysis as pride and its place within the title is as much explained by aesthetic considerations as by substantive ones.

I have incurred many debts in writing this book. One is to my students. I have been teaching *The Fable of the Bees* at King's College London since 2012 and I have endeavoured to write the type of book that my students might find helpful. Some books should be written for a specialist audience alone. This is not one of them. Striking the right balance between scholarly rigour and accessibility is no easy task, but in so far as I have succeeded then it is because teaching keeps us honest: the vast majority of the conversations I have had about Mandeville are with undergraduate students grappling with his ideas for the first time, and my approach in this book has been influenced at least as much by those conversations as it has by the state of specialist debates within the academic literature.

During the summer of 2019, Sofia Pesce, then an undergraduate student at King's College London, conducted a literature review of the Italian scholarship on Mandeville for me. Some of the best recent research on Mandeville has been published in Italian and, while I have been unable to engage with it fully, Sofia's work allowed me to draw upon and acknowledge several of the most important contributions. I would like to thank Sofia for carrying out the review so thoroughly, and the King's Undergraduate Research Fellowship scheme for providing funding.

Parts of this book build on articles that I have published previously, and I thank the publishers of those journals for permitting me to reuse that material here. Chapters 1 and 2 draw from, revise, and considerably expand upon arguments that I first set out in 'The Dark Side of Recognition: Bernard Mandeville and the Morality of Pride', *British Journal for the History of Philosophy* (online first, 2021), and Chapter 3 similarly develops ideas from 'Bernard Mandeville on the Use and Abuse of Hypocrisy', *Political Studies* 70, no. 2 (2022): 465–82. I have also borrowed odd passages from 'Morality and Sociability in Commercial Society: Smith, Rousseau—and Mandeville', *The Review of*

---

2. Laurence Dickey, 'Pride, Hypocrisy and Civility in Mandeville's Social and Historical Theory', *Critical Review* 4, no. 3 (1990): 387–431.

Politics 79, no. 4 (2017): 597–620; and 'Mandeville on the Origins of Virtue', *British Journal for the History of Philosophy* 28, no. 2 (2020): 276–95.

I have presented my work-in-progress on Mandeville to audiences at Brown, Cambridge, Groningen, King's College London, and Oxford. I am very grateful for the instructive feedback that I received on each occasion. A number of people have discussed my ideas on Mandeville with me in greater depth, in some cases generously taking the time to comment on drafts of my work. I would particularly like to thank Adrian Blau, Christopher Brooke, John Callanan, Elad Carmel, Ross Carroll, Alexandra Chadwick, Julia-Anne Costet, Jack Edmunds, Charles Griswold, Heikki Harra, Mark J. Hill, Kinch Hoekstra, Steven Klein, Robert Lamb, Antong Liu, Daniel Luban, Christian Maurer, John Meadowcroft, Carmen Pavel, Mark Pennington, Max Skjönsberg, and Adam Tebble, along with all the referees that have reviewed my work on Mandeville. At Princeton University Press, it has been a pleasure working with Ben Tate and I very much appreciate the enthusiasm he has shown for this project from the outset.

Three people deserve special mention. I had the good fortune to be writing this book at the same time as my colleague, Paul Sagar, was writing a book on Adam Smith. Paul has been the ideal interlocutor, always willing to play Smith (and sometimes Hume) to my Mandeville, and my ideas have benefitted immeasurably from our many conversations and the incisive feedback he has offered on drafts of everything that I have written on Mandeville. Johan Olsthoorn and Tim Stuart-Buttle have likewise been unfailingly sharp readers of several drafts of my work, and both provided me with extensive feedback on the final draft of this book. I am greatly indebted to Johan, Paul, and Tim for so often pointing out ways to improve my interpretation and arguments, and for pressing me to think far more carefully about the central topics of this book than I would have otherwise.

The following short titles are used for citations to Mandeville's works:

Fable   *The Fable of the Bees: or, Private Vices, Publick Benefits*, ed. F. B. Kaye in 2 vols. (Indianapolis: Liberty Fund, 1988).

Female Tatler   *By a Society of Ladies: Essays in the Female Tatler*, ed. Maurice M. Goldsmith (Bristol: Thoemmes Press, 1999).

Free Thoughts   *Free Thoughts on Religion, the Church, and National Happiness*, ed. Irwin Primer (London and New York: Routledge, 2017).

Letter to Dion   *A Letter to Dion, Occasion'd by his Book call'd Alciphron, or The Minute Philosopher* (London: J. Roberts, 1732).

Mischiefs   *The Mischiefs that ought Justly to be Apprehended from a Whig-Government* (London, 1714).

Modest Defence   *Bernard Mandeville's 'A Modest Defence of Publick Stews': Prostitution and Its Discontents in Early Georgian England*, ed. Irwin Primer (New York: Palgrave Macmillan, 2006).

Origin of Honour   *An Enquiry into the Origin of Honour, and the Usefulness of Christianity in War* (London, 1732).

Pamphleteers   *The Pamphleteers: A Satyr* (London, 1703).

Treatise   *A Treatise of the Hypochondriack and Hysterick Diseases (1730)*, ed. Sylvie Kleiman-Lafon (Cham: Springer, 2017).

Tyburn   *An Enquiry into the Causes of the Frequent Executions at Tyburn: and A Proposal for some Regulations concerning Felons in Prison, and the good Effects to be Expected from them* (London: J. Roberts, 1725).

Virgin Unmask'd   *The Virgin Unmask'd: or Female Dialogues Betwixt an Elderly Maiden Lady, and her Niece, On Several Diverting Discourses on Love, Marriage, Memoirs, Morals, &c. of the Times* (London: J. Morphew and J. Woodward, 1709).

All citations to the *Fable* are given by volume and page number to the Kaye edition (e.g. *Fable* I, 2). In the text itself I often differentiate further between the 1714 and enlarged 1723 editions of the first volume, and I use *Fable II* as shorthand for *The Fable of the Bees. Part II*. Citations to Mandeville's other works are given by page number alone, except for the *Female Tatler* where I also provide the number of the entry. For other primary sources, I sometimes cite the page number and sometimes that of the book, part, chapter, section, or equivalent, where this is either standard scholarly practice or facilitates easier comparison with other editions.

Spelling, capitalisation, and punctuation generally follow the conventions of the edition cited, although I have modernised the long 's' and the rounded and pointed forms of 'u' and 'v' when quoting from early modern sources. I have also removed the italics when quoting from lengthy passages that are entirely italicised, such as prefaces, reversing the typeface where necessary to preserve the original emphasis.

MANDEVILLE'S FABLE

Introduction

BERNARD MANDEVILLE'S *The Fable of the Bees: or, Private Vices, Publick Benefits* was one of the most notorious books of eighteenth-century Europe. The subtitle itself, protested one critic, 'implies a Libel upon Virtue, and an Encomium upon Vice', a complaint echoed by others who charged Mandeville with exposing '*moral Virtue*, as a Fraud and Imposition', or with representing 'Virtue as base and contemptible in Theory, and mischievous in Practice'.[1] While many attacked the *Fable* as a subversive apology for vice, irreligion, and decadence, some of the finest minds of the period discerned a greater seriousness of purpose. In the preface to her French translation, for example, Emilie Du Châtelet commended the *Fable* as 'the best book of ethics ever written, that is to say, the one that leads men to the true source of the feelings to which they abandon themselves almost all without examining them.'[2] Even if it was rare

---

1. See, respectively, John Dennis, *Vice and Luxury, Public Mischiefs: or, Remarks On a Book Intituled, The Fable of the Bees; or, Private Vices Publick Benefits* (London, 1724), 12; William Law, *Remarks upon A Late Book, entituled, The Fable of the Bees, or Private Vices, Publick Benefits* (London, 1724), 1; George Bluet [or Blewitt], *An Enquiry whether A general Practice of Virtue tends to the Wealth or Poverty, Benefit or Disadvantage of a People?* (London, 1725), 23. These and other contemporary responses are helpfully collected in J. Martin Stafford (ed.), *Private Vices, Publick Benefits? The Contemporary Reception of Bernard Mandeville* (Solihull: Ismeron, 1997).

2. Emilie Du Châtelet, 'Translator's Preface for *The Fable of the Bees*', in her *Selected Philosophical and Scientific Writings*, ed. Judith P. Zinsser (Chicago and London: The University of Chicago Press, 2009), 50. For discussions of how Du Châtelet's translation reworked Mandeville's ideas, see Judith P. Zinsser, 'Entrepreneur of the "Republic of Letters": Emile de Breteuil, Marquise Du Châtelet, and Bernard Mandeville's *Fable of the Bees*', *French Historical Studies* 25, no. 4 (2002): 595–624; Felicia Gottmann, 'Du Châtelet, Voltaire, and the Transformation of Mandeville's *Fable*', *History of European Ideas* 38, no. 2 (2012): 218–32; Elisabeth Wallmann, 'The Human-Animal Debate and the Enlightenment Body Politic: Emile Du Châtelet's Reading of Mandeville's *Fable of the Bees*', *Early Modern French Studies* 42, no. 1 (2020): 86–103.

to encounter such exalted praise in print—Du Châtelet's translation remained unpublished—Mandeville's philosophical importance was more widely acknowledged. David Hume listed him amongst the 'late philosophers in *England*, who have begun to put the science of man on a new footing', with Adam Smith placing Mandeville in similar company.[3]

Mandeville is no longer a household name and where the *Fable* does occupy a place in the public imagination it is, regrettably, because it has come to be regarded as an early iteration of laissez-faire capitalism. Writing in *Prospect Magazine*, for instance, Julian Baggini declaims the 'radical wrongness' of 'Mandevillian laissez-faire', informing us that the 1705 verse, *The Grumbling Hive: or, Knaves Turn'd Honest* (later incorporated into the *Fable*), set out 'the most enduring argument for the value of the free market.'[4] Tomas Sedlacek similarly reads Mandeville as 'a key proponent of the *need for greed* philosophy' and accords him the dubious honour of being 'the very first modern economist.'[5] It is no surprise, then, that more nuanced discussions feel the impetus to correct those who 'have taken Mandeville to be the first uber-capitalist.'[6]

This caricature of Mandeville builds upon what his contemporaries found most scandalous about his ideas—typically updated to reflect the malaises of twenty-first century capitalism—rather than what remains of greatest philosophical interest today. I instead follow the likes of Du Châtelet, Hume, and Smith in taking his philosophical credentials more seriously. Within specialist circles, Mandeville is increasingly recognised as a central figure for many debates in early modern European philosophy,[7] and some of the most important

---

3. David Hume, *A Treatise of Human Nature* [1739–40], ed. David Fate Norton and Mary J. Norton (Oxford: Oxford University Press, 2000), Intro.7; Adam Smith, 'Letter to the *Edinburgh Review*' [1756], in his *Essays on Philosophical Subjects*, ed. W. P. D. Wightman and J. C. Bryce (Indianapolis: Liberty Fund, 1982), 250.

4. Julian Baggini, 'The radical wrongness of Bernard Mandeville: the free marketeer whose bee analogy came back to sting him', *Prospect*, May 10 2020: https://www.prospectmagazine. co.uk/philosophy/bernard-mandeville-free-market-economics-fable-bees (accessed May 27, 2022).

5. Tomas Sedlacek, *Economics of Good and Evil: The Quest for Economic Meaning from Gilgamesh to Wall Street* (New York: Oxford University Press, 2011), 183–90.

6. Callum Williams, *The Classical School: The Turbulent Birth of British Economics in Twenty Extraordinary Lives* (London: Profile Books, 2020), 27.

7. In the past few years alone, see Daniel J. Kapust, *Flattery and the History of Political Thought: That Glib and Oily Art* (Cambridge: Cambridge University Press, 2018), 132–69; Elena Muceni, *Apologia della virtù sociale: L'ascesa dell'amor proprio nella crisi della coscienza europea*

studies of his thought have considerably improved our understanding of the intellectual context in which his ideas were both conceived and received.[8] This book focuses less on the historical impact of his ideas and more on their philosophical strengths and weaknesses. I endeavour to do for *The Fable of the Bees* what countless scholars have done for canonical texts in the history of moral and political thought; that is, to analyse it philosophically, first and foremost, by attempting to make sense of and evaluate Mandeville's ideas and arguments on their own terms. I hope to show that one of the many ways we can profitably read the *Fable* is by taking Mandeville at his word when he claimed that it was largely 'a Philosophical Disquisition into the Force of the Passions, and the Nature of Society'.[9]

This quotation also sets the scene for what follows by drawing attention to Mandeville's theory of sociability, a strand of his thought that spans topics now associated with the fields of moral psychology, social theory, and political philosophy, amongst others. The main aim of this book, in short, is to offer a sympathetic interpretation and qualified defence of Mandeville's pride-centred theory of sociability. In the remainder of this chapter, I introduce the book's central themes and justify my approach in greater detail. This involves,

(Milan: Mimesis, 2018), 133–80; Paul Sagar, *The Opinion of Mankind: Sociability and the Theory of the State from Hobbes to Smith* (Princeton and Oxford: Princeton University Press, 2018), 39–49, 81–93; Roger Crisp, *Sacrifice Regained: Morality and Self-Interest in British Moral Philosophy from Hobbes to Bentham* (Oxford: Oxford University Press, 2019), 60–73; Christian Maurer, *Self-love, Egoism and the Selfish Hypothesis: Key Debates from Eighteenth-Century British Moral Philosophy* (Edinburgh: Edinburgh University Press, 2019), 58–85; Tim Stuart-Buttle, *From Moral Theology to Moral Philosophy: Cicero and Visions of Humanity from Locke to Hume* (Oxford: Oxford University Press, 2019), 118–48; Samuel Hollander, *A History of Utilitarian Ethics: Studies in Private Motivation and Distributive Justice, 1700–1875* (London and New York: Routledge, 2020), 47–54.

8. For book-length studies, see Thomas A. Horne, *The Social Thought of Bernard Mandeville: Virtue and Commerce in Early Eighteenth-Century England* (London and Basingstoke: Macmillan, 1978); Maurice M. Goldsmith, *Private Vices, Public Benefits: Bernard Mandeville's Social and Political Thought* (Cambridge: Cambridge University Press, 1985); Edward J. Hundert, *The Enlightenment's Fable: Bernard Mandeville and the Discovery of Society* (Cambridge: Cambridge University Press, 1994). For Mandeville's life and background, see additionally Rudolph Dekker, '"Private Vices, Public Virtues" Revisited: The Dutch Background of Bernard Mandeville', trans. Gerard T. Moran, *History of European Ideas* 14, no. 4 (1992): 481–98; Harold J. Cook, 'Bernard Mandeville', in *A Companion to Early Modern Philosophy*, ed. Steven Nadler (Malden, MA: Blackwell, 2002), 469–82; Mauro Simonazzi, *Le favole della filosofia: Saggio su Bernard Mandeville* (Milan: Franco Angeli, 2008), 33–69.

9. *Letter to Dion*, 54–55.

first, outlining Mandeville's theory of sociability and highlighting its distinctiveness in comparison to those of several other early modern philosophers; second, discussing the relationship between satire and philosophy to address some doubts about reading the *Fable* philosophically; third, explaining how the focus on what I call Mandeville's 'origins of sociability' thesis departs from the more familiar 'private vices, public benefits' paradox; and, finally, providing a brief roadmap of how my arguments unfold in subsequent chapters.

A pride-centred theory of sociability

What do I mean by a pride-centred theory of sociability? A theory of sociability seeks to explain why humans associate with one another and how they continue to live together in various forms of social organisation. Plausible theories will typically have something to say about the basis of our social or moral norms and may also accord a central role to formal institutions, such as government or the law, in coordinating and regulating human interaction. Humans associate very differently in a wide range of social contexts and settings. The social norms we observe in families, for example, differ in both intensity and kind from those that predominate in largescale political societies. A theory of sociability should be attentive to these differences, but Mandeville's focus throughout much of his work is on largescale society. From his earliest discussions of the notion 'that *Man is a Sociable Creature*', he casts the problem in terms of how 'even the greatest Numbers may . . . compose a lasting Society.'[10] In taking this approach he was in good company. All eighteenth-century debates on sociability had to grapple with Thomas Hobbes's famous repudiation of the Aristotelian assumption 'that Man is an animal born fit for Society', which involved distinguishing between the initial factors that drive humans to associate and the basis of a 'large or lasting society.'[11]

10. *Female Tatler*, no. 62: 99; see also *Fable* I, 4, 347; *Fable* II, 183.

11. See Thomas Hobbes, *On the Citizen* [1642], ed. and trans. Richard Tuck and Michael Silverthorne (Cambridge: Cambridge University Press, 1998), i.2. On the importance of the 'large or lasting' condition to Hobbes's theory and subsequent debates, see Sagar, *Opinion of Mankind*, 30 and *passim*. On Hobbes's response to Aristotle in this passage, see Nicholas Gooding and Kinch Hoekstra, 'Hobbes and Aristotle on the Foundation of Political Science', in *Hobbes's On the Citizen: A Critical Guide*, ed. Robin Douglass and Johan Olsthoorn (Cambridge: Cambridge University Press, 2020), 31–50, which shows that Aristotle's position was more complex than Hobbes suggested.

Explaining sociability in large and lasting societies is a complex task and we should not assume that it can be reduced to any single quality, such as pride. Mandeville's pride-*centred* theory does not hold that pride is the *only* passion or quality relevant to explaining human sociability; it maintains, rather, that it is the *predominant* one.[12] I shall say a lot more about how Mandeville understands pride throughout the book, but provisionally it helps to focus on his claim that the 'true Object of Pride or Vain-glory is the Opinion of others', from which we desire to 'be well thought of, applauded, and admired by the whole World, not only in the present, but all future Ages.'[13] Pride is a passion that leads us to care about how other people think of us. We conform to societal norms and perform actions that appear virtuous because we expect other people to think more highly of us for doing so and lowly of us for not doing so (the latter gives rise to shame). Crucially, for Mandeville, we are not always aware of the myriad ways in which pride regulates our behaviour. We learn to internalise social norms requiring us to conceal pride from a young age, which is one reason why it should be regarded as 'the *hidden* Spring' behind so much of what we do.[14]

Why should our desire for the good opinion of others be regarded as a form of pride? Philosophers sometimes use terms like the desire for esteem or recognition,[15] or, for those who approach the problem via Jean-Jacques Rousseau, *amour-propre*.[16] While fine-grained distinctions between these terms can

12. See, for example, *Fable* II, 75–77, where Mandeville refers to pride as our 'predominant Passion', which is capable of (but does not always succeed in) governing the rest. See also Malcolm Jack, 'Men Become Sociable by Living Together in Society: Re-assessing Mandeville's Social Theory', in *Bernard de Mandeville's Tropology of Paradoxes: Morals, Politics, Economics, and Therapy*, ed. Edmund Balsemão Pires and Joaquim Braga (New York, Dordrecht, and London: Springer, 2015), 5–6.

13. *Fable* II, 64.

14. *Fable* II, 79 (emphasis added).

15. On Mandeville as a theorist of recognition, see Simonazzi, *Le favole della filosofia*, especially 159–81; idem., 'Reconnaissance, *Self-liking* et contrôle social chez Mandeville', in *La reconnaissance avant la reconnaissance: Archéologie d'une problématique moderne*, ed. Francesco Toto, Théophile Pénigaud de Mourgues and Emmanuel Renault (Lyon: ENS Éditions, 2017), 127–44; Bjorn Wee Gomes, 'The Desire and Struggle for Recognition' (Columbia University PhD thesis, 2017), 24–164; Robin Douglass, 'The Dark Side of Recognition: Bernard Mandeville and the Morality of Pride', *British Journal for the History of Philosophy* (2021), online first.

16. See, at greatest length, Frederick Neuhouser, *Rousseau's Theodicy of Self-Love: Evil, Rationality, and the Drive for Recognition* (Oxford: Oxford University Press, 2008); and, more succinctly, idem., 'Rousseau and the Human Desire for Recognition (*Amour Propre*)', in *The*

be drawn, they all highlight the fact that we care deeply about our reputation and social standing. These are intersubjective social phenomena, which is to say that how we think about ourselves depends on the views that other people hold of us. Unlike our desire for esteem or recognition, however, the term pride has negative moral connotations, having long been associated with Original Sin in Christian and especially Augustinian thought. Scholars are divided over Mandeville's relationship with this tradition and (to anticipate Chapter 2) my view is that his moral psychology lends support to many of the reasons why pride has traditionally been considered a vice. Whether or not my reading proves persuasive, it remains the case that pride is the term that Mandeville regularly used, fully aware of its association with vice and sin, and any plausible interpretation should have something to say about his reasons for doing so.

The foregoing remarks provide a preliminary sketch of Mandeville's pride-centred theory of sociability, with more details and nuances to be added in due course. To start teasing out the distinctiveness of that theory, it may also be helpful to offer some brief comparisons with several other prominent philosophers from the period.[17] Indeed, although this book is not a comparative study, I hope at least to motivate the claim that Mandeville articulates the most sophisticated version of a pride-centred theory of sociability in early modern European philosophy (and perhaps beyond). The plausibility of this claim will largely depend on whether I succeed in presenting his theory as worth taking seriously in its own right, yet we cannot assess the comparative dimension of the claim without some idea of the competition.

Connections have long been drawn between Hobbes and Mandeville, and Hobbes could be viewed as the first philosopher to place questions of pride and recognition at the heart of debates on sociability. In his posthumously published lectures on Rousseau and Smith, István Hont declared that 'the politics of recognition was Hobbes's—not Rousseau's or Smith's—invention.'[18]

Philosophy of Recognition: Historical and Contemporary Perspectives, ed. Hans-Christoph Schmidt am Busch and Christopher F. Zurn (Lanham, MA and Plymouth: Lexington Books, 2010), 21–46.

17. For a recent and more wide-ranging survey focusing on the desire for esteem in early modern philosophy, see Andreas Blank, 'Esteem and Self-Esteem in Early Modern Ethics and Politics. An Overview', *Intellectual History Review* 32, no. 1 (2022): 1–14, along with the subsequent articles in the special issue that Blank's piece introduces.

18. István Hont, *Politics in Commercial Society: Jean-Jacques Rousseau and Adam Smith*, ed. Béla Kapossy and Michael Sonenscher (Cambridge MA and London: Harvard University Press,

Hobbes certainly thought that the desire for self-esteem is central to human psychology, going so far as to claim that every 'pleasure of the mind is either glory (or a good opinion of oneself), or ultimately relates to glory'. While all society 'exists for the sake either of advantage or of glory', he denied that 'large or lasting society can be based upon the passion for glory'. Pride is central to explaining human conflict, but for that very reason our desire for pre-eminence must be tamed by mutual fear in largescale societies.[19] Even amongst commentators who see in Hobbes's theory the potential to harness pride for social stability,[20] none would attribute to him the view that there is no other passion 'so beneficial to Society'.[21]

If not Hobbes, then perhaps we could look to some of Mandeville's other predecessors for rival pride-centred theories of sociability. As has been extensively documented, Mandeville owed much to seventeenth-century French moralists, for whom pride, or *amour-propre*, was key to understanding human nature, at least in our fallen state.[22] These debts were not missed by Mandeville's contemporaries, who highlighted the influence of François de la Rochefoucauld, Jacques Esprit, and Pierre Bayle, amongst others.[23] Mandeville

---

2015), 12. For doubts about Hont's claim, see Axel Honneth, *Recognition: A Chapter in the History of European Ideas*, trans. Joseph Ganahl (Cambridge: Cambridge University Press, 2021), 10–12.

19. Hobbes, *On the Citizen*, i.2.

20. For a recent example, see S. A. Lloyd, 'All the Mind's Pleasure: Glory, Self-Admiration, and Moral Motivation', in *Hobbes's* On the Citizen: *A Critical Guide*, 51–70. For analysis of how Mandeville's ideas of pride and sociability build upon and depart from Hobbes, see Sagar, *Opinion of Mankind*, 27–49.

21. *Fable* I, 124.

22. See F. B. Kaye, 'Introduction' [1924], to *Fable* I, lxxix–lxxxiv; Arthur O. Lovejoy, *Reflections on Human Nature* (Baltimore: The John Hopkins Press, 1961), 153–79; Horne, *Social Thought*, 19–31; Dickey, 'Pride, Hypocrisy and Civility'; Hundert, *Enlightenment's Fable*, 30–38; Jean Lafond, *L'homme et son image: Morales et littérature de Montaigne à Mandeville* (Paris: Champion, 1996), 441–58; John M. Parrish, *Paradoxes of Political Ethics: From Dirty Hands to the Invisible Hand* (Cambridge: Cambridge University Press, 2007), 185–231; Michael Locke McLendon, *The Psychology of Inequality: Rousseau's Amour-Propre* (Philadelphia: University of Pennsylvania Press, 2019), 84–92. For the argument that the French influence has been overstated to the neglect of Dutch sources (especially Johan and Pieter de la Court), see Rudi Verburg, 'The Dutch Background of Mandeville's Thought: Escaping the Procrustean Bed of Neo-Augustinianism', *Erasmus Journal for Philosophy and Economics* 9, no. 1 (2016): 32–61.

23. See, for example, Richard Fiddes, *A General Treatise of Morality, Form'd upon the Principles of Natural Reason only* (London, 1724), lxxvi, xc–xciv; Bluet, *Enquiry*, 'Preface', 90–91, 98, 121–22, 127–34; Law, *Remarks*, 53–54; William Warburton, *A Critical and Philosophical Enquiry into the*

clearly follows this tradition in unearthing the hidden depths of pride and showing how our vices can be masked to give the outward appearance of virtue. La Rochefoucauld's memorable epigraph, 'Our virtues are, most often, only vices in disguise', could have easily adorned the *Fable*,[24] and Bayle—probably the single greatest influence on Mandeville—underscored the 'falseness of the majority of human virtues' when advancing his infamous argument that a society of atheists could subsist just as peacefully as a society of pagans, or even Christians.[25] Central to this tradition is the notion that pride is the one vice, above all others, that governs our conduct. Consider Esprit: 'Pride is so much the absolute Master of Man, that it is the Prince of all his Internal Inclinations, and of all his Actions.'[26] Or Bayle: 'The more one studies man, the more one becomes aware that pride is his dominant passion.'[27] Read against this backdrop, the prominence Mandeville accords to pride is by no means original. Yet where his theory comes into its own, especially in his later work, is in historicising the accounts of pride and self-love that he inherited from the French moralists within an extensive conjectural narrative charting the development of society.[28]

In historicising questions of human sociability, Mandeville can be read as foreshadowing Scottish Enlightenment philosophers, such as Hume and Smith.[29] Even if they offer more sophisticated accounts of the development of

---

Causes of Prodigies and Miracles, as related by Historians (London, 1727), 31; John Hervey, *Some Remarks on the Minute Philosopher. In a Letter from a Country Clergyman to his Friend in London* (London, 1732), 45.

24. François de la Rochefoucauld, *Collected Maxims and Other Reflections*, trans. E. H. and A. M. Blackmore, and Francine Giguère (Oxford: Oxford University Press, 2007), 3. The epigraph was added to the 1674 edition of the *Maxims*. See also Kaye, 'Introduction', cv.

25. Pierre Bayle, *Various Thoughts on the Occasion of a Comet* [1682], trans. Robert C. Bartlett (New York: State University of New York, 2000), §164. On Mandeville's debt to and engagement with Bayle, see especially E. D. James, 'Faith, Sincerity and Morality: Mandeville and Bayle', in *Mandeville Studies: New Explorations in the Art and Thought of Dr. Bernard Mandeville (1670–1733)*, ed. Irwin Primer (The Hague: Martinus Nijhoff, 1975), 43–65; Maria Emanuela Scribano, *Natura umana e società competitiva: studio su Mandeville* (Milan: Feltrinelli, 1980), 21–46; John Robertson, *The Case for the Enlightenment: Scotland and Naples 1680–1760* (Cambridge: Cambridge University Press, 2005), 261–80; Mauro Simonazzi, 'Atheism, Religion and Society in Mandeville's Thought', in *Mandeville's Tropology of Paradoxes*, 221–42.

26. Jacques Esprit, *The Falsehood of Moral Virtue: A Moral Essay* [1678] (London, 1691), 195.

27. Bayle, *Various Thoughts*, §131.

28. See Dickey, 'Pride, Hypocrisy and Civility'.

29. See Hundert, *Enlightenment's Fable, passim*; Jack, 'Men Become Sociable'.

social norms and institutions than Mandeville, theirs are not generally classified as pride-centred theories. Hume and Smith are more often considered
exponents of 'commercial sociability'; that is, a theory based on 'the utilitarian
bonds created by commercial reciprocity.'[30] The core idea here is that, at least
in largescale societies, the appeal to self-interest and mutual utility that we
typically associate with market transactions is central to explaining human
coordination, with pride 'relegated to the margins.'[31] The extent to which
Hume and Smith depart from Mandeville on questions of sociability is a
matter of some debate,[32] but for the purposes of this book I treat them as critics of his position, in so far as they offer reasons to think that he both overstates the explanatory importance of pride and is too quick to condemn as
vicious forms of esteem-seeking that are better understood as morally neutral
and compatible with virtuous conduct. To the degree that my qualified defence of Mandeville is persuasive, it may lend some support to the view that
Hume and Smith are more Mandevillean than they first appear—if that is the
case, then I take it to count in Mandeville's favour.

When evaluating Mandeville's moral psychology, I often turn to Hume and
Smith for objections, yet neither was as starkly opposed to Mandeville as some
other eighteenth-century philosophers. Mandeville came to regard his own

30. Hont, *Politics in Commercial Society*, 6–7. See also idem., *Jealousy of Trade: International
Competition and the Nation-State in Historical Perspective* (Cambridge, MA and London: Belknap
Press of Harvard University Press, 2005), 45–51, where Hont suggests that Smith's understanding of commercial sociability can be traced back to Samuel Pufendorf, while also associating
the position with neo-Augustinian French moralists, such as Pierre Nicole, and indeed with
Mandeville himself. Although the pursuit of utility is important for Mandeville, it is not as
central to explaining human sociability as pride, so I would resist the claim that Mandeville
should be classified (first and foremost) as a theorist of commercial sociability.

31. Sagar, *Opinion of Mankind*, 17–18, and *passim* on Hume and Smith as theorists of commercial sociability.

32. The most comprehensive study of Mandeville's influence on Hume is now Mikko To-
lonen, *Mandeville and Hume: Anatomists of Civil Society* (Oxford: Voltaire Foundation, 2013).
For studies that stress the similarities between Mandeville and Smith, see Thomas A. Horne,
'Envy and Commercial Society: Mandeville and Smith on "Private Vices, Public Benefits"',
Political Theory 9, no. 4 (1981), especially 562–65; Bert Kerkhof, 'A Fatal Attraction? Smith's
"Theory of Moral Sentiments" and Mandeville's "Fable"', *History of Political Thought* 16, no. 2
(1995): 219–33; Daniel Luban, 'Adam Smith on Vanity, Domination, and History', *Modern Intel-
lectual History* 9, no. 2 (2012), especially 285–88; Robin Douglass, 'Morality and Sociability in
Commercial Society: Smith, Rousseau—and Mandeville', *The Review of Politics* 79, no. 4 (2017),
especially 614–17.

theory as the antithesis to that of Anthony Ashley Cooper, Third Earl of Shaftesbury, and Francis Hutcheson, in turn, defended a position close to Shaftesbury's against Mandeville and others who reduced all human action to various manifestations of self-love.[33] Against self-love theorists, Shaftesbury and Hutcheson both stressed the importance of our intrinsically sociable or benevolent affections. The central controversy in the sociability debate, according to Hutcheson, is whether 'all our benevolence toward the mass of mankind . . . has its origin in each man's want, weakness, and indigence', or whether we are 'disposed to benevolence by nature, and not because we expect a favour in return or calculate the advantage our benevolence will obtain for us'.[34] This way of framing the debate does not capture its full complexity, but it does identify one of the key points of dispute between Mandeville, on the one hand, and Shaftesbury and Hutcheson, on the other.

A final philosopher to mention at this stage is Rousseau, not least because he has been credited with inaugurating recognition theory. Frederick Neuhouser asserts that 'Rousseau is the first thinker in the history of philosophy to place the striving for recognition from others at the very core of human nature', and that 'nineteenth- and twentieth-century philosophies of recognition are essentially a series of footnotes to Rousseau.'[35] Rousseau undoubtedly thought that much human conflict and misery could be explained in terms of the dynamics of *amour-propre*. Some scholars have further argued that his political vision in the *Social Contract* involves harnessing an egalitarian version of *amour-propre*, although I have my doubts.[36] Elsewhere Rousseau suggests

33. For present purposes, I elide the many important differences between Shaftesbury and Hutcheson (much as I did between Hume and Smith in the previous paragraph). For an excellent overview of the main contours of the sociability debates in Britain, which is more attentive to these differences, see Christian Maurer, 'Self-Interest and Sociability', in *The Oxford Handbook of British Philosophy in the Eighteenth Century*, ed. James A. Harris (Oxford: Oxford University Press, 2013), 291–314.

34. Francis Hutcheson, 'On the Natural Sociability of Mankind' [1730], in *Logic, Metaphysics and the Natural Sociability of Mankind*, ed. James Moore and Michael Silverthorne (Indianapolis: Liberty Fund, 2006), 202.

35. Neuhouser, 'Desire for Recognition', 21. For a more circumspect assessment, which regards Rousseau as leaving a double-edged legacy for recognition theory, see Alex Honneth, 'The Depths of Recognition: The Legacy of Jean-Jacques Rousseau', in *Engaging with Rousseau: Reaction and Interpretation from the Eighteenth Century to the Present*, ed. Avi Lifschitz (Cambridge: Cambridge University Press, 2016), 189–206.

36. See Robin Douglass, 'What's Wrong with Inequality? Some Rousseauian Perspectives', *European Journal of Political Theory* 14, no. 3 (2015), especially 371–74.

that the passion can be scaled up into a form of patriotism (*amour de la patrie*), often turning to the republics of antiquity for inspiration. This could be classified as a pride-centred theory of sociability of sorts, but it departs sharply from Mandeville's when it comes to the question of how our desire for social esteem can be satisfied in a well-ordered political society. In many respects, Rousseau agreed with Mandeville's analysis of how pride and other vices operated in the European societies of their day, yet Rousseau did not view this as at all beneficial and instead set out an alternative political vision for societies that remained uncorrupted by luxury and inequality.[37]

These remarks are intended merely to outline some of the broad contours of debates on pride and sociability in European philosophy at the time. A case could be made for comparing Mandeville's theory to those of other thinkers too: there has recently been some excellent work on the desire for esteem in the philosophies of Samuel Pufendorf and John Locke,[38] for example, or we could turn to Montesquieu's ideas on honour.[39] Nonetheless, this discussion

37. I defend this interpretation of Rousseau in Robin Douglass, *Rousseau and Hobbes: Nature, Free Will, and the Passions* (Oxford: Oxford University Press, 2015), see 85–87 for the comparison with Mandeville, 160–67 on transforming *amour-propre* into patriotism, and 198–202 for the scope of Rousseau's political vision. More generally on the relationship between Mandeville and Rousseau, see Malcolm Jack, 'One State of Nature: Mandeville and Rousseau', *Journal of the History of Ideas* 39, no. 1 (1978): 119–24; Hundert, *Enlightenment's Fable*, 105–15; idem., 'Mandeville, Rousseau and the Political Economy of Fantasy', in *Luxury in the Eighteenth-Century: Debates, Desires and Delectable Goods*, ed. Maxine Berg and Elizabeth Elgar (Basingstoke: Palgrave, 2002), 28–40; Pierre Force, *Self-Interest before Adam Smith: A Genealogy of Economic Science* (Cambridge: Cambridge University Press, 2003), especially 34–42; Simon Kow, 'Rousseau's Mandevillean Conception of Desire and Modern Society', in *Rousseau and Desire*, ed. Mark Blackell, John Duncan, and Simon Kow (Toronto: University of Toronto Press, 2009), 62–81; Mauro Simonazzi, 'Bernard Mandeville e Jean-Jacques Rousseau', in *La filosofia politica di Rousseau*, ed. Giulio M. Chiode and Roberto Gatti (Milan: Franco Angeli, 2012), 231–37.

38. Most succinctly, see Heikki Haara and Tim Stuart-Buttle, 'Beyond Justice: Pufendorf and Locke on the Desire for Esteem', *Political Theory* 74, no. 5 (2019): 699–723; and, for more details on each, see respectively Haara, *Pufendorf's Theory of Sociability: Passions, Habits and Social Order* (Cham: Springer, 2018), especially 99–136; Stuart-Buttle, '"A Burthen too heavy for humane Sufferance": Locke on Reputation', *History of Political Thought* 38, no. 4 (2017): 644–80. See also David Wootton, *Power, Pleasure, and Profit: Insatiable Appetites from Machiavelli to Madison* (Cambridge, MA and London: The Belknap Press of Harvard University Press, 2018), 112–13, who argues that Locke's later psychology and account of human motivation was 'well on the way to being Mandevillian.'

39. For comparison of Montesquieu's and Mandeville's accounts of honour, see Alexander Welsh, *What is Honor? A Question of Moral Imperatives* (New Haven and London: Yale University

hopefully conveys some sense of the distinctiveness of Mandeville's theory by situating it within the relevant philosophical debates of the period, which sets us up for the more detailed examination and evaluation it will receive in subsequent chapters.

Satire and philosophy

This book takes Mandeville's philosophical credentials seriously. To some this will seem unobjectionable, but there is a strand of scholarship that has long remained resistant.[40] David Runciman, for instance, observes that Mandeville 'was not a political philosopher, but a polemicist and satirist of genius. It is dangerous to take what he has to say too literally, or expect too much overall coherence from it.'[41] This nicely captures two interrelated concerns, which recur in much of the scholarship on the question. First, that Mandeville's satirical writing style counts against reading his work philosophically.[42] Second,

---

Press, 2008), 88–96; Antong Liu, 'The Tragedy of Honor in Early Modern Political Thought: Hobbes, Mandeville, Montesquieu, and Rousseau', *History of European Ideas* 47, no. 8 (2021), especially 1248–55.

40. E.g. L. A. Selby-Bigge, 'Introduction' [1897], to his *British Moralists, being Selections from Writers Principally of the Eighteenth Century* (Indianapolis: Bobbs Merrill, 1964), xxxiii–xxxviii; Norman Wilde, 'Mandeville's Place in English Thought', *Mind* 7 (1898), 223; A. K. Rogers, 'The Ethics of Mandeville', *International Journal of Ethics* 36, no. 1 (1925), 5; Thomas R. Edwards, Jr., 'Mandeville's Moral Prose', *ELH* 31, no. 2 (1964), 203; Phillip Harth, 'The Satiric Purpose of the *Fable of the Bees*', *Eighteenth-Century Studies* 2, no. 4 (1969), 325; Hector Monro, *The Ambivalence of Bernard Mandeville* (Oxford: Clarendon Press, 1975), 247–48; Joaquim Braga, 'Simulation and Dissimulation. Mandeville's Satiric View of Commercial Society', in *Mandeville's Tropology of Paradoxes*, 243–44. The argument comes in stronger and more moderate forms. For example, Monro pushes back against Wilde's dismissive suggestion that Mandeville is a mere 'philosophical free lance', while nonetheless cautioning against expecting a consistent moral philosophy from Mandeville.

41. David Runciman, *Political Hypocrisy: The Mask of Power, from Hobbes to Orwell and Beyond* (Princeton and Oxford: Princeton University Press, 2008), 72; see also 168: 'Mandeville was not a philosopher'.

42. Some scholars have doubted whether Mandeville's writing style should even be classified as satire. For the argument that the *Fable* is better understood as paradox than satire, see Philip Pinkus, 'Mandeville's Paradox', in *Mandeville Studies*, 193–211; and for the argument that it is irony and not satire, see Louis Schneider, *Paradox and Society: The Work of Bernard Mandeville* (New Brunswick and Oxford: Transaction Books, 1987), 221–22; Simonazzi, *Le favole della filosofia*, 92–96. For criticism of these (false) dichotomies, see Béatrice Guion, 'The Fable of the Bees: *proles sine matre*', in *Mandeville's Tropology of Paradoxes*, 95–96. For present purposes, it is

and by implication, that we should not expect the levels of coherence and consistency from Mandeville that we do of most philosophers.

Consider first the alleged tension between satire and philosophy. Even if it is thought that someone cannot write philosophically and satirically at the same time, Mandeville donned many hats, with some of his writings having a stronger claim to satire and others to philosophy.[43] The second volume of the *Fable*, for example, is more clearly a philosophical work than the *Grumbling Hive* verse, which Mandeville himself presents as 'a Story told in Dogrel'.[44] There are valid questions that might be asked about the relative importance of Mandeville's satirical and philosophical goals,[45] and how the two interact, but the answers are likely to differ depending on the precise texts and even passages under consideration. We can address these questions, however, without succumbing to the false dichotomy of classifying Mandeville as *either* a philosopher *or* a satirist.

One response to the point about satire, then, is that Mandeville had both satirical and philosophical goals.[46] Indeed, we should not assume that there is any inherent tension between the two. Suppose, in very general terms, that where a philosophical goal aims to uncover the truth of the matter, a satirical goal aims to ridicule another party through an appeal to humour, irony, or other such devices. If the party in question deserves ridicule because of the falsehoods they expound, then the two goals may prove complementary. Mandeville's philosophical goals sometimes serve his satirical ones. As is well known, much of his satirical ire was directed at the hypocrisy of those who enjoyed the worldly benefits of living in a flourishing state while constantly

---

less important whether Mandeville should be classified as, say, a satirist or ironist, and more important whether any of these labels preclude taking him seriously as a philosopher. That said, satire is the term that Mandeville repeatedly uses; see *Pamphleteers: A Satyr*; *Female Tatler*, no. 94: 193; *Treatise*, 155; *Fable* I, 6; *Fable* II, 20, 43, 59, 105.

43. On this point, see also J. C. Maxwell, 'Ethics and Politics in Mandeville', *Philosophy* 26 (1951), 242; Hundert, *Enlightenment's Fable*, 50; Timothy Dykstal, *The Luxury of Skepticism: Politics, Philosophy and Dialogue in the English Public Sphere, 1660–1740* (Charlottesville: University Press of Virginia, 2001), 117.

44. *Fable* I, 5.

45. Scholars emphasising the importance of satire sometimes take aim at Kaye for neglecting Mandeville's satirical goals in favour of his philosophical ones; see especially Harth, 'Satiric Purpose', 323–25; Jacob Viner, *Essays on the Intellectual History of Economics*, ed. Douglas A. Irwin (Princeton: Princeton University Press, 1991), 314.

46. See, for example, John Robertson, *The Enlightenment: A Very Short Introduction* (Oxford: Oxford University Press, 2015), 55.

decrying the vices that underpin material prosperity.[47] A clear-headed analysis of how human nature and society actually function was precisely what was needed, Mandeville thought, to see through the moralising bluster of so many of his contemporaries.[48] This argument runs the other way too and there is a rich history of satire being adopted for philosophical purposes. Mandeville's approach resembles Francis Bacon's discussion of 'serious satire', the aim of which is to search into the depths of human depravity and corruption to unmask 'what men do in fact, and not what they ought to do'.[49] For Mandeville, satire could be deployed to help uncover the dark recesses of human nature, or to 'penetrate into the Heart of Man',[50] precisely because we are otherwise inclined to look for the most pleasing explanation of our conduct, rather than the most accurate one. This is why there is generally 'less Truth in Panegyricks than there is in Satyrs.' If we do not find what we read unsettling or disagreeable then 'we are most apt to mistake outward Appearances for Realities, and judge of Things more favourably than they deserve.'[51] A satirical approach can unnerve us and thereby encourage the introspection and self-examination required to see through the illusions we hold of both ourselves and others, which should lead to a more accurate appraisal of human nature.

Consider next the concern about coherence. Even if we acknowledge that Mandeville had philosophical and satirical goals, the objection could still be pressed that he did not write a systematic treatise in the style of, say, Hobbes,

47. *Fable* I, 6–7.

48. On this point, see also Malcolm Jack, *The Social and Political Thought of Bernard Mandeville* (New York and London: Garland, 1987), 130–31.

49. Francis Bacon, *The Advancement of Learning* [1605], ed. Joseph Devy (New York: P. F. Collier and Son, 1901), Book 7, Chap. 2, 320–21. Mandeville adopts a similar contrast, berating those writers who 'are always teaching Men what they should be, and hardly ever trouble their Heads with telling them what they really are', *Fable* I, 39. On Mandeville's debt to Bacon's 'serious satire', see Dario Castiglione, 'Mandeville Moralized', *Annali Della Fondazione Luigi Einaudi* 17 (1983), especially 244–45. Building upon Castiglione's research, see, at greater length, Phillip Hilton, *Bitter Honey: Recuperating the Medical and Scientific Context of Bernard Mandeville* (Bern: Peter Lang, 2010), 87–92, 177–93. Hilton situates Mandeville's satire within a tradition running from the ancient Cynics to early modern thinkers including Michel de Montaigne and Bacon.

50. *Fable* II, 43. In the passage in question, Cleomenes professes to hate satire and instead attributes this insight to various forms of panegyric. That he really holds the contrary view is clear from the fact that he is pretending to prefer Shaftesbury's system to the *Fable of the Bees*.

51. *Fable* II, 59. This is presumably why Horatio (Mandeville's interlocutor) 'hated Satyr', in contrast to the 'great Delight' he takes in reading Shaftesbury's 'polite manner of Writing', *Fable* II, 20.

Spinoza, or Kant.[52] Yet there are plenty of other thinkers who did not set their ideas out in an especially systematic manner and are nonetheless taken seriously as philosophers. If Rousseau's *Discourse on the Origin and Foundations of Inequality among Men* should be taken seriously as a philosophical work, then so too should much of what Mandeville wrote.[53] As long as someone is operating with a reasonably coherent theoretical framework then interrogating the conceptual relationship between their ideas may prove to be a worthwhile enterprise.[54] Mandeville's theory of sociability comfortably passes this threshold. By closely analysing the concepts that he worked with and the logic of his arguments, we can identify puzzles and tensions that repay further investigation and lead to a deeper understanding of his thought. Taking such an approach usually involves, amongst other things, applying the principle of charitable interpretation: we should search for the strongest and/or most coherent interpretation of a thinker's position from the available evidence. This can be even more important in the case of someone like Mandeville, who did not always set out his ideas in the most systematic manner, than it is with thinkers who wrote philosophical treatises. If Mandeville really was a systematic thinker but not a systematic writer, then the challenge (and fun) of piecing together a relatively coherent theory is all the greater.

The principle of charitable interpretation sometimes runs up against the injunction, more often stressed by historians, not to assume coherence, especially between different works produced over many years.[55] Balancing the two is a matter of careful judgement, but the injunction is especially salient in Mandeville's case given that the *Fable* has a very complicated publishing history.[56]

---

52. For an example of the contrast with Spinoza being used to downplay Mandeville's philosophical credentials, see Douglas J. Den Uyl, 'Passion, State, and Progress: Spinoza and Mandeville on the Nature of Human Association', *Journal of the History of Philosophy* 25, no. 3 (1987), 395.

53. For a self-consciously 'philosophical' analysis of Rousseau's *Discourse*, see Frederick Neuhouser, *Rousseau's Critique of Inequality: Reconstructing the Second Discourse* (Cambridge: Cambridge University Press, 2014). My choice of example is not without precedent. Reviewing the *Discourse on Inequality*, Adam Smith ('Letter to the *Edinburgh Review*', 250) famously remarked that 'Whoever reads this last work with attention, will observe, that the second volume of the Fable of the Bees has given occasion to the system of Mr. Rousseau'.

54. I thank Johan Olsthoorn for pressing me to clarify and helping me to articulate this point.

55. On the 'mythology of coherence', see, most famously, Quentin Skinner, 'Meaning and Understanding in the History of Ideas', *History and Theory* 8, no. 1 (1969), especially 16–22.

56. See, at greatest length, Tolonen, *Mandeville and Hume*, 103–46. Kaye's 'Description of the Editions' also remains helpful; see *Fable* II, 386–400.

In brief, the *Grumbling Hive* verse first appeared in 1705 and was subsequently incorporated into the first edition of the *Fable* in 1714, accompanied by an essay entitled 'An Enquiry Into the Origin of Moral Virtue' and a series of 'Remarks' elaborating some of the key ideas from the verse. Mandeville published a considerably enlarged edition of the *Fable* in 1723,[57] expanding the original 'Remarks' and adding two new (and much longer) essays: 'An Essay on Charity, and Charity-Schools' and 'A Search into the Nature of Society'. Towards the end of 1728 (the frontispiece reads 1729) he published a new volume entitled *The Fable of the Bees. Part II*, which comprises six lengthy dialogues, mostly between the character of Cleomenes, who defends the original *Fable*, and his interlocutor Horatio, who is initially sceptical of Mandeville's ideas. These dialogues are resumed in *An Enquiry into the Origin of Honour, and the Usefulness of Christianity in War* (1732), which Mandeville presents as a sequel to *Fable II*.

Earlier I said that I will approach *The Fable of the Bees* in the way that many scholars have long studied great works of moral and political philosophy. In light of this publishing history, however, it could be objected that the *Fable* is simply unlike many other such works. Yet all texts come with their own interpretative challenges. Hobbes, for example, published a Latin version of *Leviathan* in 1668, seventeen years after the English one, and the original *Leviathan* (1651) developed out of his earlier *Elements of Law* (1640) and *De Cive* (1642, revised 1647). How we interpret the relationship between these formulations of Hobbes's political philosophy matters both for making sense of his thought in general and for understanding *Leviathan* in particular.[58] There are plenty of scholarly debates about the extent to which Hobbes, Spinoza, or Kant changed their views between different works, as well as whether even their most systematic treatises achieved the internal coherence to which they aspired. It would be difficult to argue—and foolish to assume—that there is a perfectly consistent system underpinning Mandeville's thought, which barely changes across his various works, but this difficulty arises in respect to all philosophers, to varying degrees. As I hope to show, attending closely to the ways in which Mandeville revises his position between the different editions of the *Fable* can in fact improve our understanding of his theory of sociability, since it leaves

57. Following the charges levelled at the 1723 edition by the Middlesex Grand Jury, Mandeville published 'A Vindication of the Book' in the *London Journal*, which was then appended to the 1724 and subsequent editions of the *Fable*.

58. On these and other challenges, see Deborah Baumgold, 'The Difficulties of Hobbes Interpretation', *Political Theory* 36, no. 6 (2008): 827–55.

us better placed to distinguish the moving parts from the framing commitments of his argument.[59]

'Private Vices, Publick Benefits'
and the origins of sociability

The *Fable*, in its various iterations, is a complex and multi-layered text, which spans several literary genres and touches on an eclectic array of topics. Anyone writing on Mandeville faces a difficult choice: they can either try to convey some sense of the full range and richness of his work or they can focus on unravelling a certain strand of his thought to see where it leads. I have opted for the latter approach, fully aware that there are many other paths that could be taken to find a way through either the *Fable* itself or Mandeville's wider corpus.[60] In approaching the *Fable*, I find it helpful to distinguish between what I shall call Mandeville's 'private vices, public benefits' and 'origins of sociability' theses—the latter being my principal focus.[61] The most straightforward gloss of the 'private vices, public benefits' thesis is that most, if not all, of the benefits associated with living in a large and flourishing society are based on human vices, which is not, of course, to say that all vices are beneficial.[62]

59. This formulation is borrowed from a point originally made about Hobbes, in Robin Douglass and Johan Olsthoorn, 'Introduction', to *Hobbes's* On the Citizen: *A Critical Guide*, 5–6.

60. The two most wide-ranging Anglophone studies of Mandeville's work are Richard I. Cook, *Bernard Mandeville* (New York: Twayne, 1974), and Monro, *Ambivalence*. In terms of Mandeville's broader philosophical goals, important connections have recently been drawn between his medical work and the *Fable*, on which see Hilton, *Bitter Honey*; Harold J. Cook, 'Treating of Bodies Medical and Political: Dr. Mandeville's Materialism', *Erasmus Journal for Philosophy and Economics* 9, no. 1 (2016): 1–31; Simonazzi, *Le favole della filosofia*, 97–151; idem., 'Bernard Mandeville on Hypochondria and Self-liking', *Erasmus Journal for Philosophy and Economics* 9, no. 1 (2016): 62–81; Brandon P. Turner, 'Mandeville against Luxury', *Political Theory* 44, no. 1 (2016): 26–52; Sylvie Kleiman-Lafon, 'Introduction' to her edition of the *Treatise*, especially 7–11.

61. A similar distinction runs through Tolonen's *Mandeville and Hume*, although I disagree with his claim at 134 that 'Mandeville wanted to distance himself' from the private vices, public benefits thesis in *Fable II*. Passages where Mandeville (at least implicitly) defends the thesis, include *Fable* II, 48–50, 106–107, 127, 319–21.

62. Mandeville's critics often attributed the latter view to him. See, for example, Dennis, *Vice and Luxury*, 4–5, 13; Bluet, *Enquiry*, 83, 93, 103, 136–37; [Anon.], *The True Meaning of the Fable of the Bees: In a Letter, &c.* (London, 1726), 5 and *passim*; Alexander Innes, 'A Prefatory Introduction', to [Archibald Campbell] *Aretē-logia, Or, An Enquiry Into the Original of Moral Virtue*

This is typically cashed out in terms of economic considerations, with the pursuit of certain vices, such as vanity, stimulating demand for luxury goods and fuelling economic prosperity. The 'origins of sociability' thesis, by contrast, operates at the level of social psychology and seeks to explain how we learn to conceal our self-centred desires and act in ways that elicit social approval.[63] I remain agnostic as to whether Mandeville himself regarded these as two separate theses; the distinction serves as an interpretative heuristic and should not be mistaken for a claim about authorial intention. We can start to see why it is a helpful heuristic by sketching out the trajectory of each thesis in the development of Mandeville's thought.

Mandeville's earliest statement of the 'private vices, public benefits' thesis occurs in the *Grumbling Hive* verse of 1705. Without using the precise phrase, he memorably writes of the flourishing beehive—his allegory for contemporary English society—that 'every Part was full of Vice,/ Yet the Whole Mass a Paradise . . . The worst of all the Multitude/ Did something for the Common Good.'[64] Once the grumbling bees are granted their wish of rooting out the vices from the beehive, their numbers plummet and trade diminishes. Mandeville's examples are mainly drawn from the economic sphere. The bees all work to support one another's 'Lust and Vanity'; vices underpin the trades of lawyers, physicians, and priests; luxury and pride keep the poor employed, while envy and vanity spur industry.[65] The overall benefits are similarly construed in economic terms: industry raises the conveniences of life 'To such a Height, the very Poor/ Liv'd better than the Rich before'.[66] The verse focuses on showing that this economic activity, based on our vices, is necessary to sustain a large and prosperous state. Mandeville neither raises the question of

---

(Westminster, 1728), viii; Hervey, *Remarks*, 47; William Warburton, *The Divine Legation of Moses Demonstrated*, vol. 1 (London, 1738), Book I, §6; John Brown, *Essays on the Characteristics* (London, 1751), 146–47; Laurence Nihell, *Rational Self-Love; or, a Philosophical and Moral Essay on the Natural Principles of Happiness and Virtue* (London, 1773), 156.

63. Similarly, see Harth, 'Satiric Purpose', 331, who distinguishes between Mandeville's economic and psychological approaches. See also Daniel Luban, 'Bernard Mandeville as Moralist and Materialist', *History of European Ideas* 41, no. 7 (2015): 831–57, who argues that there are unresolved tensions throughout the *Fable* between the problem of unintended consequences and Mandeville's social theory.

64. *Fable* I, 24.

65. *Fable* I, 18, 20–21, 25, respectively.

66. *Fable* I, 26.

sociability nor gives examples of the underlying psychological qualities that lead humans to associate with one another.[67]

Mandeville's first explicit discussion of sociability appears four years later in a contribution to the *Female Tatler* from November 1709, which takes the form of a diary entry recounting a conversation between Arsinoe, Lucinda, and an Oxford gentleman. Arsinoe observes that there 'is no Animal that is naturally so little inclined to be Sociable as Man' and that we would be incapable of living together peacefully were it not for government and laws.[68] Lucinda challenges this bleak assessment by insisting that our faculty of reason raises us above the beasts and our generosity leads us to pursue the benefit of others,[69] but she is subsequently answered by the Oxford gentleman, who defends Arsinoe's position by explaining that the notion that '*Man is a Sociable Creature* . . . is very true, but generally misunderstood'. It does not mean that we possess any 'innate Virtue' or love one another's company more than other animals do—for that would be false—but, rather, that (amongst other things) the multiplicity of our desires, tastes, and opinions, along with our self-interested and discontent nature, mean that we 'are of all Animals the only Species, of which even the greatest Numbers may be made Subservient to one another, and by Skilful Management compose a lasting Society.'[70] This exchange leads into a brief recapitulation of the 'private vices, public benefits' thesis, which Mandeville then defends in his next contribution to the *Female Tatler*, published a few days later, without returning to the question of sociability.[71] He does not explicitly bridge the two theses but from these entries it is not too difficult to see how they are related. If we were naturally inclined to be sociable then public benefits would not need to be based on private vices, for we would pursue the wellbeing of others out of a genuine desire to benefit them, rather than from self-interested or vicious motives. Conversely, if sociability involves

67. See also Maurice M. Goldsmith, 'Introduction', to his edition of *Female Tatler*, 24–25.

68. *Female Tatler*, no. 62: 96–97. On the importance of this entry to Mandeville's theory of sociability, see also Andrea Branchi, *Pride, Manners, and Morals: Bernard Mandeville's Anatomy of Honour* (Leiden and Boston: Brill, 2022), 58–60.

69. *Female Tatler*, no. 62: 98. Lucinda invokes 'the Ingenious Mr. *Bickerstaff's Opinion*' here, which quells any doubts about which side of the debate the entry defends. Isaac Bickerstaff was Richard Steele's penname in *The Tatler*, to which *The Female Tatler* responded. On this background, see Goldsmith, *Private Vices, Public Benefits*, 37–41; idem., 'Introduction', 33–41.

70. *Female Tatler*, no. 62: 99.

71. *Female Tatler*, no. 64: 104–107.

harnessing our self-interested passions and desires then it could be regarded as one of the public benefits to which private vices give rise.[72]

The contrast between the two theses is more apparent when we turn to the 1714 edition of the *Fable*, especially if we juxtapose the republished *Grumbling Hive* verse with Mandeville's new essay, 'An Enquiry Into the Origin of Moral Virtue'. The two texts are separated only by a short 'Introduction', where Mandeville suggests that the 'Enquiry' will complement the subject of the earlier verse,[73] although precisely how it does so remains somewhat unclear. The *Grumbling Hive* answers the question of how economic flourishing is attained in places like England at the turn of the eighteenth century. The question Mandeville addresses in the 'Enquiry', however, is quite distinct: how do humans first come to develop notions of virtue and vice? In answering this question, he explains how those who originally established society cultivated certain psychological propensities—pride, shame, and our desire for praise and flattery—without appealing to the economic considerations so prominent in the *Grumbling Hive*. Deeper tensions between the two theses can also be detected. At the very beginning of the 'Enquiry', for example, Mandeville claims that the 'Lawgivers and other wise Men' who established society must have made 'the People they were to govern, believe, that is was more beneficial for every Body to conquer than indulge his Appetites, and much better to mind the Publick than what seem'd his private Interest.'[74] Readers familiar with the 'private vices, public benefits' thesis will be surprised to find Mandeville now telling us that social order is dependent upon people overcoming their natural appetites and concerning themselves with the public good, rather than pursuing their private interest.[75] Whether this tension can be overcome is a matter of some debate;[76] the salient point, for present purposes, is simply that the

---

72. See Shelley Burtt, *Virtue Transformed: Political Argument in England, 1688–1740* (Cambridge: Cambridge University Press, 1992), 141.

73. *Fable* I, 40.

74. *Fable* I, 42.

75. For the most famous criticism along these lines, see David Hume, 'Of Refinement in the Arts' [1752], in his *Essays: Moral, Political, and Literary*, ed. Eugene F. Miller (Indianapolis: Liberty Fund, 1985), 279–80. See also Bluet, *Enquiry*, 23–24.

76. I do not take a firm stand on this debate in what follows, although I discuss one place where the tension surfaces in Chapter 3, 'Should hypocrisy be unmasked?'. For more general defences of Mandeville against Hume's criticism, see Monro, *Ambivalence*, 189–90, 203–209, 222; Jennifer A. Herdt, *Putting On Virtue: The Legacy of the Splendid Vices* (Chicago and London: The University of Chicago Press, 2008), 271–72.

'private vices, public benefits' and 'origins of sociability' theses sometimes pull Mandeville's thought in different directions.

In so far as the 'private vices, public benefits' thesis appeals principally to economic considerations, its main tenets appear to be in place by 1714.[77] When Mandeville finally clarifies the meaning of his infamous subtitle, in 1723, it is broadly consistent with earlier statements of the thesis: 'that Private Vices by the dextrous Management of a skilful Politician may be turned into Publick Benefits.'[78] The 'origins of sociability' thesis, by contrast, undergoes far more significant developments from the 1723 edition of the *Fable* onwards, precisely because Mandeville turns his attention to refuting Shaftesbury. This is most apparent in 'A Search into the Nature of Society', which constitutes a scathing attack on Shaftesbury and contests his ideas of sociability and the origin of society, with some of the expanded 'Remarks' also reflecting this engagement. The opposition to Shaftesbury then structures the dialogues that comprise *Fable II* and *Origin of Honour*, with Cleomenes defending the *Fable* against Horatio, who starts out as an adherent of Shaftesbury's philosophy. In these later works, Mandeville often extends, defends, or revises his theory of sociability from the suggestive remarks in the *Female Tatler* and its first full articulation in the 'Enquiry' of 1714.

In terms of Mandeville's intellectual biography, then, the 'private vices, public benefits' thesis is developed mainly in the early stages of his writing career, whereas he continues to refine the 'origins of sociability' thesis throughout the 1720s. When, in 1723, he writes that political societies could be raised and maintained only with the 'assistance of what we call Evil both Natural and Moral',[79] we could read this as an instantiation of the broader 'private vices, public benefits' thesis: moral (but not natural) evil is the private vice and political society

77. See, however, Ben Dew, '"Damn'd to Sythes and Spades": Labour and Wealth Creation in the Writings of Bernard Mandeville', *Intellectual History Review* 23, no. 2 (2013): 187–205, who shows that Mandeville's economic thought takes a more mercantilist turn from the 1723 edition of the *Fable*, as he became increasingly concerned with questions of production and the organisation of labour, whereas his earlier writings focused more on consumption.

78. *Fable* I, 369, also 411–12; see also *Letter to Dion*, 36–37. Mandeville emphasises the role of politicians in redirecting vices towards public benefits from his earliest works; see, for example, *Female Tatler*, no. 64: 105–106; *Fable* I, 6–7. For the criticism of ambiguity, however, see Francis Hutcheson, *Reflections upon Laughter and Remarks upon The Fable of the Bees* (Glasgow, 1750), 41–42, who outlines five different propositions that 'private vices, public benefits' could signify.

79. *Fable* I, 325, also 369.

the public benefit.[80] Whatever his own views on how the two theses intersect, the interpretative heuristic I have proposed encourages us to see beyond the popular caricature of Mandeville as a forerunner of laissez-faire or capitalist economic doctrine. If today the 'private vices, public benefits' thesis conjures up an image of *homo economicus* guided by self-interest and instrumental rationality, then, by focusing on the 'origins of sociability' thesis, we can instead come to appreciate Mandeville as a theorist of social norms (*homo sociologicus*) who was acutely aware that human action is largely shaped by our desire for the recognition of others (*homo comparativus*).[81]

A brief roadmap

The remainder of this book is divided into five chapters, running over two parts, and a conclusion. As far as possible, I have endeavoured to write each chapter so that it can be read by itself, for the benefit of readers who prefer to dip in and out, although I of course hope that when read cumulatively the book is more than the sum of its parts. The first part, 'Moral Psychology', focuses on Mandeville's general account of human nature and its implications for questions of sociability. Chapter 1 provides a detailed analysis of Mandeville's understanding of pride and its relationship with other passions. I argue that we can accept much of what he says about the importance of pride in explaining human sociability while remaining sceptical of his attempt to reduce all human actions to some form of self-love. This should be the most accessible chapter of the book for those relatively new to Mandeville's thought, so I would recommend starting with this even if you pick and choose from the remaining chapters (or read no further). Chapter 2 asks the question: what are the moral implications if we suppose that Mandeville's analysis of human nature is largely accurate? This chapter, more than most, is oriented around some important debates within Mandeville scholarship, precisely because my own

80. Mandeville typically refrains from using the language of private vices and public benefits to make this point about sociability, although see *Letter to Dion*, 19–21, where his discussion of the necessity of vice (in the economic sphere) leads into the conclusion that we cannot conceive 'how any Society could subsist upon Earth, exempt from all Evil, both natural and moral.'

81. On the comparison between *homo economicus* and *homo sociologicus*, see Jon Elster, *The Cement of Society: A Study of Social Order* (Cambridge: Cambridge University Press, 1989), 97; on that between *homo economicus* and *homo comparativus*, see Gloria Origgi, *Reputation: What It Is and Why It Matters*, trans. Stephen Holmes and Noga Arikha (Princeton and Oxford: Princeton University Press, 2018), especially 147–70.

views on the moral status of pride—along with questions about Mandeville's sincerity and relationship with the Augustinian tradition—depart from many leading scholars.

Chapters 1 and 2 have a common format. The first half of each chapter, very roughly, defends my interpretation of Mandeville, and the second half then evaluates his position by addressing objections from other eighteenth-century philosophers, especially Hume and Smith. In doing so, my aim is not to tell a story about intellectual influence or reception history, but, rather, to treat these philosophers as interlocutors addressing similar questions to, and often raising direct criticisms of, Mandeville. A further feature of these chapters is that I draw freely from across the different editions of the *Fable* (and sometimes other works) to explain Mandeville's moral psychology, with the aim of showing that his account of human nature is broadly consistent throughout.

Chapter 3 takes a slightly different approach, as it foregrounds Mandeville's attack on Shaftesbury in 'A Search into the Nature of Society' from the enlarged 1723 edition of the *Fable*. Taking this essay as my point of departure, I look backwards to the 1714 edition and forwards to *Fable II* to address some of the puzzles and tensions in the relationship between Mandeville's ideas of sociability, hypocrisy, and virtue. One of the points I seek to impress is that if we are interested in the intellectual progression of Mandeville's ideas, then we should examine the changes between the 1714 and 1723 editions of the (first volume of the) *Fable* and not solely those between the first and second volumes.[82] The chapter should also serve as the single-most detailed study to date of Mandeville's engagement with Shaftesbury, as it emerges out of the 'Search'.

The second part of the book, 'Historical Narratives', analyses Mandeville's various explanations of how a range of interrelated moral and social phenomena first arose, including our ideas of honour, politeness, and virtue, as well as the origin of society itself. This involves studying some of Mandeville's later writings in greater depth: Chapter 4 focuses mainly on the conjectural history of *Fable II* and Chapter 5 on *Origin of Honour*. In each case, I show how Mandeville revisits and expands his origin stories from the first volume of the *Fable*, often, it appears, in response to criticisms that his work encountered during

---

82. Cf. J. Martin Stafford, 'General Introduction', to his edition of *Private Vices, Publick Benefits?*, xvi–xviii; Robertson, *Case for the Enlightenment*, 266–77; Simonazzi, *Le favole della filosofia*, *passim*; idem., 'Common Law, Mandeville and the Scottish Enlightenment: At the Origin of the Evolutionary Theory of Historical Development', *Storia del pensiero politico* 7, no. 1 (2018): 107–26; Tolonen, *Mandeville and Hume*, especially 41–102.

the 1720s, especially from William Law and George Bluet. Chapter 4 pays particular attention to the desire of dominion (a consequence of pride) and argues that it is the most important passion in Mandeville's explanation of the origin of society, while also drawing out the implications of his conjectural history for understanding political authority. Chapter 5 then turns to *Origin of Honour* and examines his account of the development of a distinctively modern sense of honour (another offshoot of pride) in recent European history. In exploring how ideas of honour, religion, and war intersect, the chapter sheds light on aspects of Mandeville's analysis of human nature and sociability that have passed under the radar of most studies.

In the Conclusion, I revisit the relationship between the 'private vices, public benefits' and 'origins of sociability' theses, highlighting one area where the pride-based considerations to which Mandeville so often appeals are surprisingly absent: his analysis of the labour supply in the economy. The book then closes with some reflections on whether we should find Mandeville's pride-centred theory of sociability compelling. Drawing together arguments from earlier chapters, I suggest that his moral psychology, in particular, holds up well not only against the criticisms that it encountered in the eighteenth century but also when considered in the light of more recent findings from social psychology.

PART I

Moral Psychology

1

Pride and Human Nature

IN THE ORIGINAL *Grumbling Hive* verse, Mandeville writes of luxury employing 'a Million of the Poor,/ And odious Pride a Million more'.[1] When he comes to explain this passage in 'Remark M', dedicated to pride, he declares of the passion that we 'are possess'd of no other Quality so beneficial to Society, and so necessary to render it wealthy and flourishing'.[2] 'Remark M' focuses principally on the role of pride in underpinning all economic activity, with Mandeville arguing that 'for the Support of Trade there can be nothing equivalent to Pride'.[3] Pride is key to explaining why we demand luxury goods and he often presents luxury and pride together as indispensable components of economic prosperity, without which all trade and industry would decline.[4] Yet pride is also at the heart of Mandeville's account of human sociability and his explanation of why humans conform to moral norms. This dimension of pride is central to 'An Enquiry Into the Origin of Moral Virtue', where Mandeville memorably concludes 'that the Moral Virtues are the Political Offspring which Flattery begot upon Pride',[5] and it is further developed in some of the 'Remarks' (especially C and R) and the later 'Dialogues', where he dissects the good manners of polite society to reveal 'that the Basis of all this Machinery is Pride.'[6]

We may, then, distinguish between two general roles that pride plays in Mandeville's work, the first relating to the economic focus of his 'private vices,

1. *Fable* I, 25.
2. *Fable* I, 124.
3. *Fable* I, 126.
4. E.g. *Fable* I, 25, 34, 36, 85, 121, 125, 248, 347; see also *Female Tatler*, no. 52: 81; no. 64: 107; *Free Thoughts*, 330.
5. *Fable* I, 51.
6. *Fable* II, 146.

public benefits' thesis and the second to his 'origins of sociability' thesis—the latter being the main theme of this book.[7] The first aim of this chapter is simply to elucidate the place of pride in Mandeville's analysis of human nature, which then sets the scene for an evaluation of the moral status of pride in the next chapter. Both chapters focus on the psychological roots of sociability, and only in the later stages of the book do I examine the role of pride in Mandeville's historical account of the origin of society. This approach mirrors Mandeville's, as it is only in his later works that his historical story is fleshed out in any detail. Even in *Fable II*, when justifying his conjectural-historical approach, Mandeville explains that he never reasons 'but from the plain Observations which every body may make on Man, the *Phænomena* that appear in the lesser World.'[8] Nonetheless, it helps to keep in mind that although Mandeville was committed to a core account of human nature, he was also well aware that this underdetermines human action in any specific social context. He thus maintains that pride is innate in all humans,[9] while also recognising that it plays out in a range of ways in different people, times, and places.[10]

The second aim of this chapter is to defend Mandeville's analysis of pride from some of the criticisms raised against it. Mandeville's more general account of human nature proved notorious in his own day, as he came to be associated with Thomas Hobbes in reviving—and allegedly even celebrating—what we now call psychological egoism; that is, the view that all our actions are, at bottom, self-interested.[11] While criticisms of Mandeville's egoism

7. For a similar distinction between pride's 'purely egotistic' manifestations and those that lead us to conform to social norms, see Dickey, 'Pride, Hypocrisy and Civility', 401.

8. *Fable* II, 128.

9. E.g. *Fable* I, 44, 275; *Fable* II, 92, 205, 266. More generally, see *Treatise*, 19; *Free Thoughts*, 156. In 'Remark R', Mandeville contrasts 'Man in his Savage State' with man 'as a Member of a Society and a taught Animal', claiming that 'his Pride has room to play' only in the latter, *Fable* I, 205–206, also 366. Tolonen (*Mandeville and Hume*, 46–47) draws on this evidence in support of his claim that in the first volume of the *Fable*, unlike the second, pride is not 'one of the original appetites' of human nature. Mandeville maintains that pride becomes more prominent as society and civilisation develop throughout both volumes, yet even in the first he describes pride as 'inseparable from [man's] very Essence', *Fable* I, 44. The most charitable interpretation is that Mandeville consistently holds both that pride is innate and that it becomes more prominent with increased socialisation.

10. E.g. *Fable* I, 121–27, 130, 205–206, 211; *Fable* II, 75–76, 112, 121–24, 138–39, 152.

11. E.g. Brown, *Essays*, 170; Adam Smith, *The Theory of Moral Sentiments* [1759], ed. D. D. Raphael and A. L. Macfie (Indianapolis: Liberty Fund, 1982), VII.iii.1.1; Nihell, *Rational Self-Love*, xvi; John Hawkins, *Life of Samuel Johnson, LL.D.* (London, 1787), 574; Leslie Stephen, *Essays*

sometimes blur into criticisms of his account of pride, I hope to show that his main claims about pride can be accepted even if we are sceptical of the way he explains seemingly other-regarding actions in terms of self-interested motives. In his later works, Mandeville places less emphasis on defending psychological egoism and more on justifying the prominence he accords to pride in explaining so much of our behaviour,[12] which suggests that the latter should be taken as the more significant strand in his analysis of human nature.

The place of pride in Mandeville's psychology

In 'Remark M', Mandeville defines pride as 'that Natural Faculty by which every Mortal that has any Understanding over-values, and imagines better Things of himself than any impartial Judge, thoroughly acquainted with all his Qualities and Circumstances, could allow him.'[13] Pride is not only concerned with thinking highly of ourselves; crucially, it further involves overvaluing ourselves in comparison to any impartial assessment of our worth. Perhaps in some cases we are justified in holding a high opinion of ourselves, but these would not count as pride on this definition. Although the definition relates solely to how we view ourselves, much of Mandeville's discussion focuses on reputation and social standing. In 'Remark N', for example, he equates pride with 'the Concern for [our] Reputation', and he later affirms that there 'is no Man that has any Pride, but he has some Value for his Reputation.'[14] The care we have for our reputation, however, ultimately derives from 'the vast Esteem we have for our selves.'[15]

We can join the dots between Mandeville's definition of pride and the emphasis he places on reputation by recognising that our sense of self-esteem is rarely, if ever, independent of our perception of how other people regard us. Receiving praise tends to inflate the view we hold of ourselves. Even if we do not witness the praise directly, we sometimes still take pride in reflecting upon

---

on *Freethinking and Plainspeaking* (London: Longmans, Green, and Co., 1873), 232, 245. See also Maurer, *Self-love, Egoism and the Selfish Hypothesis*, 58–85, who argues that labelling Mandeville as an egoist overlooks many of the most interesting features of his position.

12. Cf. Tolonen, *Mandeville and Hume*, 41–102, who defends the stronger thesis, from which I dissent, that Mandeville's later position constitutes a repudiation of his earlier one.

13. *Fable* I, 124.

14. *Fable* I, 146; *Fable* II, 333.

15. *Fable* I, 67.

the applause that we expect others do, or will, give us.[16] We are greedy for 'the Esteem of others, and the Raptures we enjoy in the Thoughts of being liked, and perhaps admired,' go a long way to determining our conduct.[17] Conversely, it is very difficult to sustain a high opinion of oneself if no one else ever reinforces it. Mandeville makes this point most explicitly in *Fable II*, where he explains that we are troubled by the realisation that we overvalue ourselves and thus seek social approval to ease our anxiety and confirm our estimations of our own worth.[18] 'The true Object of Pride', on Mandeville's account, 'is the Opinion of others',[19] and his reflections on pride closely approximate what might now be called a psychological theory of recognition, in so far as our sense of identity and self-worth are dependent upon the opinions and feedback of others.[20]

Pride, then, involves overvaluing ourselves and leads us to perform actions out of a desire for social approval. There is also a comparative element built into the passion, since the high opinion we hold of ourselves is relative to our judgements of other people's qualities. We feel pride in believing that we are better than others—or at least as good as them—and this is compounded by the social dimension of pride, where our estimation of the approval we receive is relative to the approval we observe others receiving. Indeed, for social approval to reinforce our *over*valuation of ourselves, it is important that we appear to be better than we really are. The reason why so many people wear fine clothes when going out in public, Mandeville suggests, is less because doing so immediately makes them feel better about themselves, and more due to 'the

16. *Fable* I, 55, 78.

17. *Fable* I, 68.

18. *Fable* II, 130. See also Simonazzi, 'Mandeville on Hypochondria and Self-liking', 72–78, who suggests that if our desire for esteem is not satisfied then this could cause the symptoms of hypochondria that Mandeville diagnoses at length in his *Treatise*.

19. *Fable* II, 64. Eighteenth-century discussions of pride often equivocated between the desire to think highly of oneself and the desire for the esteem and applause of others; see Arthur O. Lovejoy, '"Pride" in Eighteenth-Century Thought', in his *Essays in the History of Ideas* (Baltimore: John Hopkins University Press, 1948), 62; idem. *Reflections on Human Nature, passim*, and 178–79 in relation to Mandeville; Dickey, 'Pride, Hypocrisy and Civility', 399–401. While Mandeville draws on both ideas, he views the desire for the esteem and applause of others as derived from the desire to think highly of oneself.

20. This formulation is adapted from Mattias Iser, 'Recognition', *Stanford Encyclopedia of Philosophy*, ed. Edward N. Zalta (2019): https://plato.stanford.edu/archives/sum2019/entries/recognition/ (accessed May 27, 2022).

Pleasure of being esteem'd by a vast Majority, not as what they are, but what they appear to be'.[21] Today, theorists sometimes distinguish between respect and esteem as two different branches of social recognition. Both involve comparing ourselves to other people, but our desire for respect can be satisfied through being recognised as an equal in society—i.e. by being granted equal rights or standing—whereas our desire for esteem is fully satisfied only if we are recognised as superior to others in some way. Where respect focuses more on our shared personhood or humanity, esteem is bestowed for qualities that mark us out as distinctive.[22] If we apply this distinction to Mandeville then we could say that his analysis of pride is far more concerned with esteem than with respect. There is a long tradition in Western thought that regards pride as directly opposed to equality, from the Christian and especially Augustinian opposition between pride and equality under God,[23] down to Hobbes's observation that pride is the failure to acknowledge others as our equals.[24] Even if Mandeville does not draw the contrast so starkly, the emphasis he places on overvaluing ourselves means that our pride will rarely be satisfied through being regarded merely as an equal.[25]

21. *Fable* I, 128.

22. See especially Cillian McBride, *Recognition* (Cambridge: Polity Press, 2013), 43–46 and *passim*. McBride builds upon Alex Honneth's seminal work, which sets out a tripartite classification of different forms of recognition: love, rights, and esteem, although the last two are most important in large-scale social interactions; see Axel Honneth, *The Struggle for Recognition: The Moral Grammar of Social Conflicts* [1992], trans. Joel Anderson (Cambridge: Polity Press, 1995), 1 and *passim*. The point could alternatively be couched in terms of 'recognition' and 'appraisal' respect, which tracks the distinction I use between respect and esteem; see Stephen L. Darwall, 'Two Kinds of Respect', *Ethics* 88, no. 1 (1977): 36–49. For an account that decouples the desire for esteem from recognition more broadly, see Geoffrey Brennan and Philip Pettit, *The Economy of Esteem: An Essay on Civil and Political Society* (Oxford: Oxford University Press, 2004), especially 20, 185–89.

23. For Augustine, 'pride is a perverted imitation of God', which seeks to impose its own dominion in place of 'a fellowship of equality under God'; see St. Augustine, *The City of God against the Pagans*, ed. and trans. R. W. Dyson (Cambridge: Cambridge University Press, 1998), xix.12.

24. This is the ninth law of nature—'*against Pride*'—in the *Leviathan* version of his theory. See Thomas Hobbes, *Leviathan: The English and Latin Texts*, ed. Noel Malcolm (Oxford: Clarendon Press, 2012), Chap. 15, 234.

25. An exception could be cases where our pride is satisfied by being considered an equal in contexts when we are not really so, as this would still involve overvaluing ourselves.

Pride, fear, and self-preservation

To fully appreciate the importance of pride for Mandeville's theory of sociability, we must examine how it interacts with other passions. Sometimes it is
difficult to identify precisely where pride ends and another passion begins, in
part because Mandeville acknowledges that any given passion can be a 'Compound of many others',[26] and also because he uses terms like pride, vanity, and
vain-glory somewhat interchangeably. Nevertheless, pride clearly complements
some passions and counteracts others, and these interactions are best understood in relation to his underlying account of self-love (and later self-liking)
in motivating human behaviour. Mandeville maintains that the appetites and
passions of all animals tend directly or indirectly to the preservation and happiness of either themselves or their species.[27] In the case of humans, however,
self-love—rather than love of the species—dominates. At the beginning of the
'Enquiry', Mandeville describes man as 'an extraordinary selfish and headstrong' animal,[28] and as late as 1723 he affirms that 'all Passions center in Self-
love'.[29] On this view, specific passions such as pride, shame, and fear can be
regarded as 'different Branches' of self-love,[30] even if they point in various and
sometimes conflicting directions.

Mandeville argues that pride was given 'to Man for Self-preservation', since
it 'doubles our Happiness in Prosperity, and buoys us up against the Frowns
of adverse Fortune.' Thinking highly of oneself is a pleasurable experience, and
when we reflect on our accomplishments or persevere in the face of hardship
then this enhances our sense of self-esteem and makes us happier.[31] Although

26. *Fable* I, 140; see also 84 on the difficulty of tracing 'every Motive of those Actions that
are the Result of a mixture of Passions.' For a helpful analysis broken down in terms of original
and compound passions, see Paulette Carrive, *Bernard Mandeville: Passions, vices, vertus* (Paris:
Vrin, 1980), especially 46–49.

27. *Fable* I, 200; *Fable* II, 91.

28. *Fable* I, 41–42; see also *Free Thoughts*, 146. Notice that even in his later works, after having
introduced the concept of self-liking, Mandeville still echoes these sentiments and maintains
that 'Man is so Selfish a Creature . . . that he never loves nor esteems any Thing so well as he
does his own Individual', *Origin of Honour*, 39. The index to *Fable II* also contains an entry for
'*Selfishness* (the) of human Nature, visible in the Ten Commandments'; see *Fable* II, 373, also
272–73.

29. *Fable* I, 75, also 343–44.

30. *Fable* I, 135.

31. *Fable* II, 135–36. Mandeville is discussing self-liking in the passage in question, but the
point extends to pride.

the 'Instinct of high Value' that everyone has for themselves can be 'a very useful passion', it also proves to be 'the Cause of endless Mischiefs.'[32] In some cases, pride directly imperils our preservation by generating conflict between individuals, which is why Mandeville claims that we 'have not a more dangerous Enemy than our own inborn Pride.'[33] Outward displays of the passion are liable to instigate conflict and breed animosity, for pride is 'odious to all the World.'[34] We dislike people who sing their own praises, especially when they sing too loudly. Cicero was undoubtedly 'a Prodigious Man' of great achievements, but the fact that he was also such 'a fulsome as well as noisy Trumpeter . . . of his own Praises' shows that his vanity outshone his 'good Sense and Knowledge of the World.'[35] Contemplating our own high value may be a source of wellbeing, but we do not look so kindly upon the pride of other people.

Pride can also jeopardise our preservation by working against passions that are otherwise conducive to peace. This is the case with fear, which is raised in all animals whenever our preservation is endangered and leads us to flee rather than taking aggressive action against the perceived threat.[36] When fear and pride are opposed, the latter invariably prevails. Our concern with sustaining a high reputation may trump self-preservation, as Mandeville illustrates when discussing duelling, one of his favourite and most telling examples.[37] In such cases, pride is not directly conducive to self-preservation at all, since it compels us to fight (sometimes to the death) when our fear would otherwise lead us to avoid conflict. It might thus seem, as Hobbes had famously argued, that peaceful society can be sustained only if our fear tames our pride, rather than vice versa.[38] At one point Mandeville acknowledges that the 'only useful Passion then that Man is posses'd of toward the Peace and Quiet of Society, is his Fear, and the more you work upon it the more orderly and governable he'll be.'[39]

32. *Fable* II, 91.

33. *Fable* II, 296.

34. *Fable* I, 124; see also *Fable* I, 79–80; *Fable* II, 122, 126, 138–39.

35. *Fable* I, 335. See also *Female Tatler*, no. 58: 89, which discusses people of 'exalted Genius . . . [who] are exempt from those common Rules and little Niceties of Decency and good Breeding, and conscious of their own worth, not ashamed to speak it.' Mandeville alludes to Cicero and Richard Steele as examples, suggesting that his aim here is to ridicule the pride of those who consider themselves exempt.

36. *Fable* I, 200–202.

37. *Fable* I, 334; *Fable* II, 88–96.

38. Hobbes, *On the Citizen*, i.2.

39. *Fable* I, 206.

Even in cases where pride does not directly support self-preservation, however, it can do so indirectly. To see why, it helps to clarify that the previous quotation is taken from Mandeville's explanation of how fear can be used to counteract anger (and not pride). Indeed, he claims that anger is the passion 'most contrary' to fear, which is generated by hunger or lust and leads to conflict.[40] Although pride sometimes combats fear, it can also moderate other passions, such as anger, which themselves engender violence and discord.[41]

The role of pride in counteracting our otherwise unsociable and even violent desires is most memorably conveyed in Mandeville's 'Enquiry'. As humans are naturally selfish and cunning, those who first established society must have made 'the People they were to govern, believe, that it was more beneficial for every Body to conquer than indulge his Appetites, and much better to mind the Publick than what seem'd his private Interest.' Overcoming our natural appetites does not come easily to us, so we must have originally been rewarded with praise and flattery for 'the trouble of Self-denial'. Lawgivers appealed to our sense of pride and shame by praising those who practise self-denial as 'lofty high-spirited Creatures', while depicting those who indulge their passions as 'abject, low-minded People'. We seek to emulate the former and take pains to distance ourselves from the latter.[42] In resisting our natural appetites for the good of society, then, we are rewarded with the praise and flattery that accompanies a good reputation, even if what carries most of us 'to the utmost Pitch of Self-denial' is nothing but 'the most effectual Means that human Pride could be flatter'd with.'[43]

What is more, and as paradoxical as it may initially sound, pride can also moderate its own excesses, in the sense that we feel proud when secretly concealing the outward display of our pride from others. We want to appear virtuous, not proud, and we thus endeavour to hide any semblance of pride from our actions. Nonetheless, it is still pride that motivates us, and Mandeville even takes this to be the passion's most sophisticated manifestation. 'The Man

40. *Fable* I, 202–206.

41. Mandeville's analysis of pride is thus an example of the countervailing passions theory; see Dickey, 'Pride, Hypocrisy and Civility', 413–15; and, more generally, Albert O. Hirschman, *The Passions and the Interests: Political Arguments for Capitalism before Its Triumph* (Princeton: Princeton University Press, 1977), especially 20–31.

42. *Fable* I, 41–45.

43. *Fable* I, 51.

of Sense and Education never exults more in his Pride than when he hides it with the greatest Dexterity'.[44] This dimension of pride is central to Mandeville's account of how the sociable and moral norms of his day function, as he sums up in *Fable II*: 'all good Manners consist in flattering the Pride of others, and concealing our Own.'[45] To be sure, social norms around flattery vary in different times and places. 'To praise a Man to his Face was very common among the Ancients', Mandeville observes, whereas in 'more polish'd' times the art of flattery has become 'less bare-faced, and the Design of it upon Man's Pride is better disguis'd than it was formerly.'[46] Such disguises only work, of course, as long as most of us—unlike Mandeville—do not go around exposing the pride secretly motivating one another's acts, which is why 'common Civility' does not allow us to suspect other people's 'Actions to be the Result of Pride' even when 'it looks very like it.'[47]

Self-love and self-liking

Mandeville refines his analysis of our self-centred passions in his later work by introducing a distinction between self-love and self-liking. Nobody disputes that self-love was given to us for self-preservation, he claims, but 'as no Creature can love what it dislikes' then it is crucial that we also 'have a real liking' for ourselves which is superior to any liking we have for anyone else. Aware that we value ourselves so highly, self-liking gives rise to a sense of diffidence or apprehension, which 'makes us so fond of the Approbation, Liking and Assent of others, because they strengthen and confirm us in the good Opinion we have of ourselves.' Self-liking is thus distinguished from self-love by its focus on self-esteem, which leads us to seek out the approval of others.[48] To simplify a little, while self-love is more concerned with our sustenance, self-liking extends further and leads to us becoming preoccupied with our

44. *Fable* I, 79; see also *Fable* I, 132; *Fable* II, 17, 78–79, 122, 125, 141.

45. *Fable* II, 108.

46. *Fable* II, 152.

47. *Fable* I, 133. In this respect, research on the attribution bias may point to 'a happy fault' of our social psychology, as we are prone to attribute other people's behaviour to stable dispositional qualities rather than to a desire for esteem. For discussion, see Brennan and Pettit, *Economy of Esteem*, 74–75.

48. *Fable* II, 129–31.

reputation.[49] This account of self-liking resembles much of Mandeville's earlier analysis of pride, and he now claims that self-liking, rather than self-love, is the cause of pride.[50] One reason why self-liking should be considered the cause of pride (and not identical to pride) is that it causes other passions too, such as shame. Mandeville stresses that self-liking is, first and foremost, the high esteem we have for ourselves, which then leads us to desire the approval of others to reinforce our own sense of self-worth. In this respect, self-liking remains an intrinsically self-regarding passion and is concerned with the opinion of others only by implication.[51]

The distinction between self-love and self-liking has received considerable scholarly attention, in part because it resembles that which Jean-Jacques Rousseau would later and more famously draw between *amour de soi-même* and *amour-propre*.[52] Although the distinction helps to clarify Mandeville's moral psychology, it is important not to overstate the extent to which it separates his later and earlier writings.[53] Indeed, as early as 1710, in his anonymous contribution to the *Female Tatler*, Mandeville writes that

> Mankind is a strange Compound made up of Qualities, that contradict each other, we are all Lovers of Self-Preservation, and would naturally avoid whatever we think troublesome or hurtful, and yet we are great Admirers of Praise and desire to be thought well of by others; but as this is innate to

49. *Fable* II, 133–34.

50. *Fable* II, 131.

51. This point comes out especially prominently in the parallel discussion in *Origin of Honour*, 3–4, also 41–42. See also Gomes, 'Desire and Struggle for Recognition', 48–53.

52. Jean-Jacques Rousseau, *Discourse on the Origin and Foundations of Inequality among Men* [1755], in *The Collected Writings of Rousseau*, vol. 3, ed. Christopher Kelly and Roger D. Masters (Hanover, NH: University Press of New England, 1992), 91. I discuss some of the antecedents to Rousseau's distinction (many of which would have also been familiar to Mandeville), in Douglass, *Rousseau and Hobbes*, 152–60. For discussion of the relationship between Mandeville and Rousseau on this point, see Jack, 'One State of Nature', 121–22; Helena Rosenblatt, *Rousseau and Geneva: From the First Discourse to the Social Contract, 1749–1762* (Cambridge: Cambridge University Press, 1997), 81–82; Force, *Self-Interest before Smith*, 65; Robertson, *Case for the Enlightenment*, 392–93; Jerrold Seigel, *The Idea of the Self: Thought and Experience in Western Europe since the Seventeenth Century* (Cambridge: Cambridge University Press, 2005), 116; Kow, 'Rousseau's Mandevillean Conception of Desire', 69–70; Christopher Brooke, *Philosophic Pride: Stoicism and Political Thought from Lipsius to Rousseau* (Princeton and Oxford: Princeton University Press, 2012), 182–84; McLendon, *Psychology of Inequality*, 95–97.

53. Cf. Tolonen, *Mandeville and Hume, passim*.

all, so it follows that no body can be much pleased with the Actions of others, as long as he can perceive nothing in them but a Tendency toward their own Preservation, and consequently he that would be praised, must at least seemingly recede from that first Principle, so as to make others believe that his own benefit is not the only thing he aims at.[54]

While the psychology here is not as complex as in Mandeville's later works, this passage succinctly explains why our desires for preservation and praise often pull apart: to obtain the praise of others, we must give the impression that we act for their benefit, not our own. More generally, Mandeville reflects on how our desire for praise can lead us to do things that risk our preservation throughout his writings, even though the precise terminological distinction between self-love and self-liking is formulated only in his later work.

In an editorial note to *Fable II*, F. B. Kaye speculated that Mandeville might have introduced the distinction between self-love and self-liking in response to Joseph Butler's criticisms of psychological egoism, published in 1726, and many scholars have pursued this suggestion.[55] Butler raises a range of criticisms, some of which I return to below. The most important point for present purposes is his denial that the 'desire of esteem from others' should be regarded as a form of self-love. He instead describes it as one of our 'public affections or passions', which 'naturally lead us to regulate our behaviour in such a manner as will be of service to our fellow-creatures.'[56] Whether or not Mandeville introduced self-liking with Butler in his sights, the contrast between their positions is instructive. Mandeville does, of course, grant that our desire for social esteem leads us to regulate our behaviour in precisely the way Butler suggests, but, from Mandeville's perspective, to think that this makes it a social

54. *Female Tatler*, no. 80: 152. See also Markku Peltonen, *The Duel in Early Modern England: Civility, Politeness and Honour* (Cambridge: Cambridge University Press, 2003), 287–88; Branchi, *Pride, Manners, and Morals*, 66–67, 125–26.

55. See Kaye's note to *Fable II*, 129–30; John Colman, 'Bernard Mandeville and the Reality of Virtue', *Philosophy* 47 (1972), 135; Jack, *Social and Political Thought*, 102–106; Hundert, *Enlightenment's Fable*, 126–39; Jennifer Welchman, 'Who Rebutted Bernard Mandeville?' *History of Philosophy Quarterly* 24, no. 1 (2007), 62–63; Tolonen, *Mandeville and Hume*, 59–65; Kapust, *Flattery*, 143–45; Branchi, *Pride, Manners, and Morals*, 126–27. Following Kaye, many of these discussions focus predominantly on Sermon 11, but if Mandeville did introduce self-liking in response to Butler—on which I remain agnostic—the passage from Sermon 1 discussed here is a more plausible target.

56. Joseph Butler, *Fifteen Sermons Preached on the Rolls Chapel and Other Writings on Ethics*, ed. David McNaughton (Oxford: Oxford University Press, 2017), Sermon 1, para. 7 (hereafter i.7).

passion is to conflate its effects (or 'end') with its origin,[57] and to overlook that the only reason why we desire the approval of others is to enhance our sense of self-worth. Self-love may not be the best term to capture this, but the new term that Mandeville coins, self-liking, gives little ground to Butler and should not be taken as evidence of him backtracking from his earlier position by trying 'to discourage debate about whether humans are selfish or other-regarding by nature.'[58] To the contrary, Mandeville doubles down on his insistence that our desire for social esteem is ultimately self-centred, while acknowledging that we are moved by two very different and sometimes conflicting self-regarding passions—self-love and self-liking—the latter of which is central to explaining why we adopt the *appearance* of acting from other-regarding considerations.

Pride and shame

So far, I have mainly focused on how pride counteracts other passions to promote sociability. Yet pride also works in tandem with some passions, most notably shame. The close interaction between pride and shame is a prominent theme throughout Mandeville's analysis of sociability and the polite manners of his day.[59] In 'Remark C', he defines shame as '*a sorrowful Reflexion on our own Unworthiness, proceeding from an Apprehension that others either do, or might, if they knew all, deservedly despise us.*'[60] Much like pride, then, shame is concerned with how others have (reason to) regard us,[61] and Mandeville soon explains the relationship between the two:

57. Here Butler's note to *Fifteen Sermons*, i.7 is revealing, where he explains that the desire of esteem is a public good 'because *the end for which it was given us* is to regulate our behaviour towards society' (emphasis added).

58. The quote is from Tolonen, *Mandeville and Hume*, 22. Tolonen also argues that Mandeville allows for natural affections in *Fable II* in a way that differentiates it from the 1714 edition, but this argument (discussed below) should be kept distinct from the reasons why Mandeville introduces self-liking.

59. *Fable I*, 45, 66–69, 145, 200, 209–10, 213, 339; *Fable II*, 78; *Origin of Honour*, 11–13. Mandeville's account is a good example of what Hannah Dawson calls 'reputation-shame' (as opposed to 'guilt-shame'), in 'Shame in Early Modern Thought: From Sin to Sociability', *History of European Ideas* 45, no. 3 (2019): 377–98.

60. *Fable I*, 64.

61. Mandeville's subsequent discussion addresses some examples where people feel shame when they appear not to be at fault or do not know the reason why the action in question is considered blameworthy. These cases notwithstanding, the '*deservedly*' in his definition suggests

The Reverse of Shame is Pride, (see *Remark M.*) yet no Body can be touch'd with the first, that never felt any thing of the latter; for that we have such an extraordinary Concern in what others think of us, can proceed from nothing but the vast Esteem we have for our selves.[62]

Where pride leads us to desire the approval of others, shame leads us to fear their disapproval; they are two sides of the same coin. Indeed, the thought of being exposed as proud is itself a source of shame—Mandeville lists lust, pride, and selfishness as the 'Passions we chiefly ought to hide for the Happiness and Embellishment of the Society.'[63] We all take 'extraordinary Pleasure in hearing [ourselves] prais'd', yet we know that our delight must be hidden away to ensure that we do not rouse the envy and hatred of our company. Good manners demand that we flatter the self-esteem of others, rather than indulging our own. This is why, when dining, the 'Man of Manners picks not the best but rather takes the worst out of each Dish,' leaving the choicest cuts for others so as not to suggest that he thinks more highly of himself than he does of them. This small self-sacrifice is nothing compared to the inner pride he takes in knowing that his actions are received favourably by his company, for even their silent approval 'over-pays to Self-love with Interest, the loss it sustain'd in his Complaisance to others.'[64] Those who have mastered the art of politeness know 'not only to deny the high Value they have for themselves, but likewise to pretend that they have greater Value for others, than they have for themselves.'[65]

Although all humans are moved by pride and shame, Mandeville was well aware that the objects these passions take are socially determined. The 'fear of Shame . . . varies with Modes and Customs, and may be fix'd on different Objects, according to the different Lessons we have receiv'd.'[66] Consider the case of young girls in the polite society of Mandeville's day who have enough social acumen to feel ashamed of displaying their legs in company without having the slightest idea of why this is considered blameworthy. The different standards of modesty for men and women, Mandeville argues, owe a great deal to

---

one way in which shame is not simply the reverse of pride, since Mandeville maintains that we sometimes feel pride when receiving praise that we know to be undeserved.

62. *Fable* I, 66–67.
63. *Fable* I, 68–69.
64. *Fable* I, 77–78.
65. *Fable* II, 145.
66. *Fable* II, 95.

education and convention, and very little to natural differences. At one point he even claims that 'the difference of Modesty between Men and Women ... is *altogether* owing to early Instruction'.[67] What are considered the appropriate objects of shame—and for whom—will vary depending on the social context, yet Mandeville maintains that displays of pride are always likely to cause offence and doubts that 'there ever was a Nation ... in which the Youth of both Sexes were not expressly taught never to be Proud or Haughty'.[68]

Bringing shame into the picture also allows for a more precise understanding of how pride and fear relate to one another. As we have seen, Mandeville claims that we sometimes risk our own preservation because we care about upholding our reputation. We can (and Mandeville does) explain this in terms of pride conquering fear,[69] but it is equally accurate to say that shame has changed the object of our fear—or added a new and more powerful object—such that the fear of whatever threatens our own physical preservation pales in comparison to the fear of social disapproval. When our reputation is on the line, if 'the fear of Shame is not violent enough to curb the fear of Death, nothing else can'.[70] Some people are even willing to commit suicide rather than having their reputation tarnished, simply because they fear shame more than death.[71]

Mandeville considerably expands 'Remark C' in the 1723 edition of the *Fable*, but the underlying relationship between pride and shame remains unchanged. One reason for extending the discussion could have been to show that concealing our natural appetites out of shame is far removed from the conquest of the passions that real virtue demands,[72] an argument which becomes especially salient once Mandeville sets his philosophy out against Shaftesbury.[73] In later works, Mandeville explains shame in terms of self-liking. As self-liking is the original cause of pride and shame, both should be regarded as 'different Affections of one and the same Passion'. Mandeville takes

---

67. *Fable* I, 71–72 (emphasis added); see also *Fable* I, 69; *Fable* II, 122–24. In other places, Mandeville allows for some natural differences between the sexes, although this is usually in the context of emphasising the greater explanatory power of socialisation and education. See, for example, his discussion of the 'Compound of natural and artificial Chastity' in forming notions of female honour in *Modest Defence*, 76.

68. *Fable* II, 66.

69. *Fable* I, 334.

70. *Fable* II, 96.

71. *Fable* I, 209–10.

72. Especially *Fable* I, 72–73, 79–80.

73. See Chapter 3, 'Virtue, self-denial, and hypocrisy'.

this opportunity to correct the apparent 'Errour' of his earlier discussion, where 'he took Pride and Shame to be two distinct Passions'.[74] Yet it is difficult not to suspect him of false humility here as he owns up to a mistake that, as far as I am aware, no one had pointed out and which has little bearing on his argument (he continues to refer to pride and shame separately as passions). In fact, this seems to be a good example of Mandeville displaying the very qualities that he so masterfully exposes elsewhere, giving the outward appearance of humbly acknowledging his earlier mistakes, without giving ground to more substantial criticisms.[75] Either way, the most important point, from his earliest discussions to his last, is how closely pride and shame work together in motivating humans to comply with civil and sociable norms out of an underlying desire for social esteem—this desire being 'the Sorcerer, that is able to divert all other Passions from their natural Objects'.[76]

Criticisms of Mandeville's psychology

Mandeville's account of human psychology found few friends and many critics. Some of the sharpest philosophical objections focused on his attempt to explain all human behaviour in terms of self-love; the position now known as psychological egoism.[77] These bear at least a structural similarity to criticisms raised by those who protested that Mandeville had considerably overstated the role of pride in his analysis of how we interact with others. I hope to show, however, that the two lines of criticism can largely be treated apart. Even if we find objections to psychological egoism compelling, the implications for Mandeville's pride-centred theory of human sociability are minimal. His analysis of pride stands or falls on grounds independent of his intervention into the self-love debate. Indeed, in his later writings, Mandeville devotes little space to elaborating his self-love thesis, whereas large parts of *Fable II* defend the emphasis

---

74. *Origin of Honour*, 12–13.

75. In the 'Preface' to the *Virgin Unmask'd*, Mandeville observes that an author will often use the preface to point 'at some of the best Things in the Book, and confess they are Faults, whilst in Profound Silence he passes by those Things which he knows to be really such.'

76. *Fable* II, 96.

77. For a helpful overview of different forms of egoism, see Robert Shaver, 'Egoism', *Stanford Encyclopedia of Philosophy*, ed. Edward N. Zalta (2019): https://plato.stanford.edu/archives/spr2019/entries/egoism/ (accessed May 27, 2022). For discussion of the different meanings of self-love and egoism in relation to eighteenth-century British debates, see Maurer, *Self-love, Egoism and the Selfish Hypothesis*, 8–12 and *passim*.

he places on pride. This suggests that pride, rather than self-love, is the more important focal point for understanding his account of human nature.

Objections to psychological egoism

The most penetrating criticisms of Mandeville's psychological egoism charged him with emptying out and distorting the common meaning of self-love. One of the strongest versions of this complaint occurs in the eleventh of Butler's *Fifteen Sermons*, 'Upon the Love of Our Neighbour', which is echoed in later criticisms of the selfish system by David Hume and others.[78] Mandeville is often taken to be one of Butler's targets and, as we have seen, some commentators think that Mandeville revised his theory to address Butler. Kaye, for example, suggests that Mandeville might have added self-liking in response to the following passage, where Butler first [1] sets out and then [2] challenges the self-love thesis:

[1] Every particular affection, even the love of our neighbour, is as really our own affection, as self-love ... And if, because every particular affection is a man's own, and the pleasure arising from its gratification his own pleasure, or pleasure to himself, such particular affection must be called self-love; according to this way of speaking, no creature whatever can possibly act but merely from self-love; and every action and every affection whatever is to be resolved up into this one principle. [2] But then this is not the language of mankind: or if it were, we should want words to express the difference, between the principle of an action, proceeding from cool consideration that it will be to my own advantage; and an action, suppose of revenge, or of friendship, by which a man runs upon certain ruin, to do evil or good to another. ... There is then a distinction between the cool principle of self-love, or general desire of our own happiness, as one part of our nature, and one principle of action; and the particular affections towards particular external objects, as another part of our nature, and another principle of action.'[79]

78. See David Hume, 'Of the Dignity or Meanness of Human Nature' [1741], in his *Essays: Moral, Political, and Literary*, 81, who opens the essay by stressing the need to distinguish 'what is real, and what is only verbal, in this controversy.' See also Adam Ferguson, *An Essay on the History of Civil Society* [1767], ed. Duncan Forbes (Edinburgh: Edinburgh University Press, 1966), i.1, who claims that 'this supposedly selfish philosophy' mistakes 'the obtrusion of a mere innovation in language for a discovery in science.'

79. Butler, *Fifteen Sermons*, xi.7; see also the 'Preface', para. 35. See Note 55 above for scholarship on self-liking as a reply to Butler.

Butler succinctly outlines the self-love thesis in this passage and, in doing so, provides a fair summary of Mandeville's (early) position, irrespective of whether it was formulated with him in mind. The complaint that 'this is not the language of mankind' is also apposite, as we shall see, and Butler develops it by drawing a distinction between what could be called instances of calculated self-interest (for Butler, 'self-love' in its proper signification) and our desire for specific external goods (improperly termed 'self-love').[80] From the fact that we take pleasure in satisfying desires of the latter kind, it does not follow that the intentional object of such desires is our own pleasure or happiness. If I help a friend in pain, for example, my desire is simply to relieve their distress.[81] To be sure, having helped my friend I will likely feel happy afterwards, but it would be linguistic sophistry, Butler argues, to claim that I was acting out of a desire of promoting my own happiness or pleasure all along. Hume captures the latter point nicely: 'I feel a pleasure in doing good to my friend, because I love him; but do not love him for the sake of that pleasure.'[82]

Butler proceeds to consider a similar linguistic conflation at the heart of self-love theories, observing that 'we often use the word *selfish* so as to exclude in the same manner all regard to the good of others.' This view of selfishness, however, is importantly different to the self-love thesis [1] outlined above. If we understand self-love simply as 'an affection to ourselves', then it does not 'exclude good-will or love of others, than merely by not including it, no otherwise, than it excludes love of arts or reputation, or of any thing else.'[83] The reason why the self-love thesis might initially seem troubling is because we associate self-love with selfishness, but the only plausible way of explaining all our actions as a form of self-love must appeal to a far more expansive notion of the passion. If I act from self-love when going to the cinema, then so too do I when spending time with my friends, since the passion or desire from which

80. Butler, *Fifteen Sermons*, especially xi.4–6.

81. On the influential classification set out in C. D. Broad, 'Egoism as a Theory of Human Motives', in his *Ethics and the History of Philosophy: Selected Essays* (London: Routledge and Kegan Paul, 1952), 218–31, this is an example of an 'other-regarding but self-referential' motive (because it is *my* friend) and, therefore, still a form of psychological egoism. Eighteenth-century complaints about this being a distortion of ordinary language seem valid here too, whether we call it a form of self-love or egoism.

82. Hume, 'Dignity or Meanness', 85–86. For similar criticisms, see also Francis Hutcheson, *An Inquiry into the Original of Our Ideas of Beauty and Virtue in Two Treatises* [1725], ed. Wolfgang Leidhold (Indianapolis: Liberty Fund, 2004), II.ii.9; Ferguson, *Essay*, i.1.

83. Butler, *Fifteen Sermons*, especially xi.11.

I act in each case is my own. All my passions or desires relate to myself in this sense, simply because they are *my* passions or desires.[84] But these desires do not necessarily promote my own happiness or interests to the detriment of anyone else's, which is precisely the moral failing at issue when we behave selfishly.

There are at least two respects, then, in which Butler thinks that the self-love thesis relies on distorting 'the language of mankind'. The first conflates the pleasure we take from an action with the reason why we perform it; the second misleadingly presents all affections relating to oneself as instances of self-love, or even selfishness. It should be stressed, however, that in neither case does the distinction Mandeville draws in his later works between self-love and self-liking address Butler's criticisms, for, as we have seen, that distinction principally serves to clarify how our desire for esteem differs from self-love's more direct concern with sustenance, where both remain inherently self-regarding passions.[85]

Mandeville is vulnerable to both of Butler's criticisms when it comes to matters of psychological motivation. On the first, Mandeville sometimes supports claims about the ubiquity of self-love by appealing to the pleasure we take from performing good actions. In the 'Enquiry', for example, he entertains the possibility, if only for the sake of argument, that some people, 'from no other Motive but their Love of Goodness, perform a worthy Action in Silence'. These people neither receive nor are motivated by the praise of others, yet Mandeville nonetheless detects 'no small Symptoms of Pride' in the pleasure they take in 'Contemplating on [their] own Worth' in light of their good deed.[86] Perhaps Mandeville is merely pointing out that even the best of us are not completely free of pride, but this observation does not count in favour of psychological egoism over the view that we have other-regarding motivations, for proponents of the latter are quite willing to acknowledge that we typically feel good about ourselves after having performed benevolent actions. At times,

84. On this point, see again Hume, 'Dignity or Meanness', 85.

85. For this criticism of Kaye's interpretation, see also James, 'Faith, Sincerity and Morality', 53–54. We should not be misled here by Butler's claim that 'the principles of these action are totally different, and so want different words to be distinguished by', *Fifteen Sermons*, xi.7. Although Mandeville does introduce a different word by distinguishing self-liking from self-love, this is not the distinction that Butler criticises self-love theorists for failing to acknowledge, and the distinction that Butler does have in mind is not addressed by differentiating between self-love and self-liking.

86. *Fable* I, 57.

then, Mandeville does try to explain our seemingly other-regarding acts away as instances of self-love or pride by appealing to the pleasure we take in retrospective reflection, and, in these cases, Butler's criticism is decisive. As we shall see, however, most of Mandeville's arguments for according such prevalence to pride do aim to show how it motivates the acts in question, and these cannot be refuted so easily.

Turning to the second criticism, even though Mandeville grants that some of our natural passions concern us with the wellbeing of others, he often tries to reduce these to self-love, especially in the first volume of the *Fable*. Consider his discussion of pity in the 'Enquiry', where he gives the example of saving an innocent baby from dropping into a fire. Whatever benefit the baby receives, Mandeville claims, by intervening 'we only obliged ourselves; for to see it fall, and not strove to hinder it, would have caused a Pain, which Self-preservation compell'd us to prevent.'[87] Crucially, Mandeville's claim here is not that we fear the social disapproval of allowing the baby to drop (although that could also be the case), but, rather, that we are instinctively moved by pity, which pains us to see others suffer.[88] The criticism of Mandeville on this count is compelling. We might choose to call this self-love if we are so inclined, but it is certainly not selfishness, and the more straightforward explanation is that the pain we feel when seeing others suffer is evidence that we do have other-regarding or benevolent affections of some sort. Francis Hutcheson was not alone in regarding Mandeville's position on pity and natural affection as one of his 'intricate contradictions and inconsistencies'.[89]

---

87. *Fable* I, 56; for other examples, see *Fable* I, 75, 142, 341–44.

88. For the suggestion that the anticipated pain Mandeville has in mind here is guilt, see C. Daniel Batson, *A Scientific Search for Altruism: Do We Care Only About Ourselves?* (New York: Oxford University Press, 2019), 78–79. Batson points out that Mandeville refers to a future pain ('would have caused'), but as the baby has not yet fallen then this can be more simply explained as the direct pain that would occur from seeing the baby's suffering were it to fall. As Mandeville explains at *Fable* I, 254–55, pity consists in 'a Fellow-feeling' that is raised 'when the Sufferings and Misery of other Creatures make so forcible an Impression upon us, to make us uneasy . . . often to such a Degree to occasion great Pain and Anxiety.' Given that Mandeville is discussing pity in the passage in question from the 'Enquiry', the pain that self-preservation compels us to prevent is most plausibly understood as that which we instinctively feel upon witnessing the suffering of others.

89. Hutcheson, *Reflections upon Laughter*, 73; see also idem., *Inquiry*, II.ii.8, II.v.8. More generally, see Bluet, *Enquiry*, 110; [Anon.], *True Meaning*, 71–73; Rousseau, *Discourse on Inequality*, 36–37; Smith, *Theory of Moral Sentiments*, especially I.i.1.1, I.i.2.1–2, VII.iii.1.4. Smith does not mention Mandeville in these passages, but for discussion of his conception of sympathy as

When we turn to *Fable II*, Mandeville maintains that 'Man centers every thing in himself, and neither loves nor hates, but for his own Sake.' In every choice or voluntary act, 'Men must be determin'd by the Perception they have of Happiness; and no Person can commit or set about an Action, which at that then present time seems not to be the best to him.'[90] This is a fairly straightforward statement of (a certain form of) psychological egoism, although it does not preclude the possibility that we have affections that instinctively lead us to care for others, which we experience happiness in satisfying.[91] Drawing on several passages discussing parental affection, Mikko Tolonen contends that Mandeville repudiates his earlier position on other-regarding passions in *Fable II*.[92] Yet this conclusion is too strong. Where in the first volume of the *Fable* Mandeville had argued that the natural love mothers have for their children is a passion, and all passions centre in self-love,[93] in the second volume he sometimes invokes the 'Natural Affection' of parents for their children without explicitly adding that this is merely an offspring of self-love.[94] The difference between the two volumes at most reflects a change of emphasis,

---

either influenced by or a response to Mandeville, see Horne, 'Envy and Commercial Society', 560; Kerkhof, 'A Fatal Attraction?', 233; Force, *Self-Interest before Smith*, 14–20; Nicholas Phillipson, *Adam Smith: An Enlightened Life* (London: Penguin, 2011), 149–50.

90. *Fable* II, 178.

91. This quotation clarifies that Mandeville's position is a version of psychological hedonism, due to its emphasis on happiness, and that what matters is the subjective perception of anticipated happiness, rather than its attainment. While more ambiguous, this could be consistent with Mandeville endorsing only a 'weak' and not necessarily a 'strong' version of psychological hedonism, in terms borrowed from Arash Abizadeh, *Hobbes and the Two Faces of Ethics* (Cambridge: Cambridge University Press, 2019), 146–47. The strong version holds that pleasure is the intentional object of all our desires; the weak version holds that we desire objects only if they appear pleasurable to us (i.e. pleasure is necessarily part of the desire's causal process), even if the object of the desire is not pleasure.

92. Tolonen, *Mandeville and Hume*, 29, 73–74.

93. *Fable* I, 75. On the following page Mandeville makes the even more striking claim that 'Women have no Natural Love to what they bear', but the subsequent discussion clarifies that he does think that mothers have a natural love for their children, even if it is weak, from the moment of birth; see also *Fable* I, 142. Mandeville's point in the passage is that any sentiments that the mother feels *prior to birth* are 'the result of Reason, Education, and the Thoughts of Duty.' Hutcheson criticised this passage in his *Inquiry*, II.ii.9, for discussion of which, see Patricia Sheridan, 'Parental Affection and Self-Interest: Mandeville, Hutcheson, and the Question of Natural Benevolence', *History of Philosophy Quarterly* 24, no. 4 (2007): 377–92; Tolonen, *Mandeville and Hume*, 57–59.

94. *Fable* II, 189, 199, 201, 240.

however, not a substantive revision, and even in *Fable II* Mandeville refers to self-love leading a creature to do 'every thing to make itself and young Ones secure',[95] which indicates that he does still think of parental affection as deriving from self-love.

It may be fair to say that Mandeville tones down some of his most controversial statements regarding the self-centred basis of our seemingly other-regarding affections in *Fable II*. This could have been because he felt the need to recast his theory in light of the criticisms of self-love theories advanced by Butler, Hutcheson, and others in the 1720s, yet it may also have been due to the developments in his theory of sociability over the period (these explanations are not mutually exclusive). I examine these developments in more detail in subsequent chapters, but for present purposes the conclusion to 'A Search into the Nature of Society', added to the 1723 edition of the *Fable*, helps to illustrate the key point. There Mandeville claims 'to have demonstrated that, neither the Friendly Qualities and kind Affections that are natural to Man, nor the real Virtues he is capable of acquiring by Reason and Self-Denial, are the Foundation of Society.'[96] Leaving the claim about virtue aside for the moment, this passage is of interest because the argument about sociability does not depend on psychological egoism. Mandeville's point is that even if we grant that humans have naturally other-regarding affections, these cannot be the foundations of the societies we inhabit today. If we want to understand how society functions, then, we need to look far beyond our friendly qualities and kind affections, and instead focus on the hidden workings of pride.

Pride vs. praiseworthy motives

Where philosophers like Butler focused their attention on refuting the general case for psychological egoism, other critics took Mandeville to task for reducing so much of human behaviour to pride. Even if Mandeville tempers some of his boldest claims about the ubiquity of self-love in his later works, he gives little ground when it comes to the dominance of pride in explaining so much of human behaviour. As we have seen, Mandeville's definition of pride involves

95. *Fable* II, 133.

96. *Fable* I, 369; see also *Fable* II, 183: 'this pretended Love of our Species, and natural Affection we are said to have for one another, beyond other Animals, is neither instrumental to the Erecting of Societies, nor ever trusted to in our prudent Commerce with one another, when associated, any more than if it had no Existence.'

overvaluing ourselves. But in trying to uncover the hidden depths of pride, does his argument rest on conflating cases where we think highly of ourselves as a result of having acted appropriately with cases based on a desire for un-merited approval? Richard Fiddes captures this worry effectively, charging Mandeville with equivocation:

> *Pride*, as used by him in this Place, is an equivocal Term. If we understand by it, a natural Consciousness of Worth in a Man, arising from a Sense of his having acted according to the Order and Perfection of his Nature, there is nothing criminal or irregular in such a Principle. . . . But if by *Pride* be meant an unjust or flattering Opinion, which a Man has, above what he ought to have, of his own Abilities or Actions, this we grant to be highly irregular; but assert there is no Necessity why a wise or a good Man should be subject to this Irregularity; and consequently, why Pride, except as commonly un-derstood, and as it seems to be taken by this Author, in the worst Sense, should be an inseparable Motive to human Action.[97]

Fiddes complains that whenever an action could be attributed to one of several motives, Mandeville invariably focuses on the worst and excludes the best. Of course, we are sometimes motivated by pride and vanity, but in other cases we are genuinely motivated by a 'Desire of doing good and generous Actions', which may be accompanied by 'a laudable Desire of Fame' or 'a certain Degree of external Reputation' without in any way compromising the morality of the act.[98] There are two interrelated points here: first, we have a genuine desire to do good that is (at least conceptually) independent of the desire for social approval we receive from doing so; second, if our desire for social approval is proportionate and reasonable then it neither counts as pride nor detracts from

---

97. Fiddes, *General Treatise*, xxvi–xxvii. See also Law, *Remarks*, 78, who charges Mandeville with conflating the 'vitious Irregularity' of pride with a worthy 'Desire of Greatness'; and Adam Ferguson, *Institutes of Moral Philosophy* (Edinburgh, 1769), II.iii.3, who cites Mandeville's work when explaining how the 'desire of perfection, and even the love of virtue, have been con-founded with pride . . . from inattention to propriety of language.' For a livelier version of the more general objection, see Stephen, *Essays on Freethinking*, 258–59, who argues that Mandeville's argument is 'mere juggle . . . Pride is a dyslogistic epithet given to a natural passion that may be good or bad. Call it self-respect, and the paradox vanishes.' For a more recent en-dorsement of this line of criticism, see Stafford, 'General Introduction', xv, who complains that Mandeville's conception of pride is 'unserviceable for genuine empirical enquiry: for it encom-passes everything from moderate self-respect to inordinate vanity'.

98. Fiddes, *General Treatise*, xx–xxii.

the goodness of the first motive. I focus on the first of these two points presently, returning to the second in the next chapter, after having examined the moral status of pride in greater depth.[99]

This first line of objection finds its most philosophically adept articulation in Adam Smith's distinction between the love of praise and the love of praiseworthiness.[100] Smith agrees that we all desire praise or approval, but he criticises Mandeville for failing to see that we care more about being *worthy* of praise or approval:

> Nature, accordingly, has endowed [man], not only with a desire of being approved of, but with a desire of being what ought to be approved of; or of being what he himself approves of in other men. The first desire could only have made him wish to appear to be fit for society. The second was necessary in order to render him anxious to be really fit. The first could only have prompted him to the affectation of virtue, and to the concealment of vice. The second was necessary in order to inspire him with the real love of virtue, and with the real abhorrence of vice. In every well-formed mind this second desire seems to be the strongest of the two. It is only the weakest and most superficial of mankind who can be much delighted with that praise which they themselves know to be altogether unmerited.[101]

For Smith, the love of praiseworthiness simply is the love of virtue, whereas to desire unmerited praise is nothing but 'the most contemptible vanity.' This is not to suggest that we should shun praise altogether or that our motives must be completely disinterested. There is nothing vicious about the 'love of just fame, of true glory, even for its own sake'; indeed, this is a close second best to loving praiseworthiness or virtue for its own sake (i.e. regardless of whether we receive any praise for performing good deeds).[102]

99. See Chapter 2, 'Pride vs. a well-regulated desire for esteem'.

100. Hutcheson advances a similar line of objection, arguing that if a desire for esteem (or pride) is natural then it must be based on an antecedent 'moral Sense', which leads us to identify the goodness in the qualities or actions that become objects of esteem. See Hutcheson, *Inquiry*, II.v.6; idem., *An Essay on the Nature and Conduct of the Passions and Affections, with Illustrations on the Moral Sense* [1728], ed. Aaron Garrett (Indianapolis: Liberty Fund, 2002), I.v.8.

101. Smith, *Theory of Moral Sentiments*, III.2.7. Although Mandeville is not mentioned by name in this passage, Smith's explicit criticisms in Part VII are based on the distinctions set out here; see III.2.27 for the link, and VII.ii.4.6–14 for the criticisms.

102. Smith, *Theory of Moral Sentiments*, III.2.8, VII.ii.4.8.

The key point of disagreement between Mandeville and Smith concerns whether the love of praise precedes the love of praiseworthiness, or vice versa. For Mandeville, the reason why we often perform praiseworthy actions is to ensure that we receive praise from others, which, in turn, makes us feel better about ourselves. Smith turns this argument on its head and instead maintains that 'the love of praise seems, at least in great measure, to be derived from that of praise-worthiness.' As it is difficult to judge our own conduct impartially, even the most virtuous of us desire the praise of others to confirm that our own sense of praiseworthiness is well-founded. The praise of others will confirm this, however, only if we have not deceived those in question and are confident that they are well placed to judge our conduct fairly.[103]

Mandeville never had the opportunity to respond to Smith, but it is not too difficult to construct a reply on his behalf, especially given that *Fable II* addresses (at least implicitly) the similar criticisms levelled against him during the 1720s. The first point to highlight is that Mandeville recognises something like the praise/praiseworthy distinction. As we have seen, his very definition of pride presupposes such a distinction, since pride entails overvaluing ourselves in comparison to the opinion of 'any impartial Judge, thoroughly acquainted with all [our] Qualities and Circumstances'—that is, a judge who is perfectly placed to evaluate our praiseworthiness.[104] Mandeville could agree with Smith that 'if Reason in Man was of equal weight with his Pride, he could never be pleas'd with Praises, which he is conscious he don't deserve',[105] but he thinks that, in practice, our pride is far more powerful than our reason. We observe this in children who have not yet learned to conceal their passions and thus express joy upon receiving unmerited praise and anger when they are justly blamed.[106] More generally, if you have ever accepted praise while conscious that it is undeserved, or pretended to act altruistically when you could see some benefit to yourself—as Mandeville insists that even 'the best of us' often do—then it is really the desire for praise, not praiseworthiness, that motivates you.[107] If we sometimes feel uneasy about this, as Smith claims, then

---

103. Smith, *Theory of Moral Sentiments*, especially III.2.3, III.2.24.

104. *Fable* I, 124.

105. *Fable* I, 63.

106. *Origin of Honour*, 7–8. Mandeville gives this example to show that 'all Human Creatures are born' with the passion of self-liking, but the fact that he chooses examples of unmerited praise and blame indicates the psychological primacy he accords to our desire for praise over that for praiseworthiness.

107. *Fable* II, 110.

Mandeville could respond, first, that this rarely prevents us from accepting unmerited praise, and, second, that this could be explained as much by the fear of our falsehoods being uncovered as by any inherent uneasiness about our lack of praiseworthiness. If our uneasiness is greater to the extent that we are likely to be exposed, as seems plausible, then this would lend further support to Mandeville's position.[108]

Smith does not deny that we sometimes act from a desire for unmerited praise. The problem with 'splenetic philosophers', like Mandeville, is that they 'have imputed to the love of praise, or to what they call vanity, every action which ought to be ascribed to that of praise-worthiness.'[109] Smith's objection is that Mandeville explains away all love of praiseworthiness in terms of the love of praise—Smith does *not* claim that everything Mandeville explains in terms of the love of praise is really motivated by love of praiseworthiness. This is important because Smith's paramount concern was to save the possibility of moral virtue from Mandeville by showing that we are not *always* motivated by pride, or a desire for praise, irrespective of our merit. Whether Mandeville really did place virtue beyond human reach is a matter of some debate and his position on this question varies between different works.[110] In *Fable II*, however, his priority is to argue against the *prevalence* rather than the *possibility* of acting from inherently virtuous or praiseworthy motives; the former being sufficient to support his overarching claims about human sociability. As he puts it in the 'Preface', even if there are 'many Persons of stricter Virtue and greater Sincerity in Religion, than I have here described; but that a considerable

108. I am not aware of Mandeville making this exact point, but it seems in line with the spirit of his argument and especially the importance he places on our concern with concealing the workings of pride from others. Given the more general emphasis he places on the role of custom and education, the point here is not that the uneasiness we feel is based on calculating our chances of being exposed on a case-by-case basis, but, rather, that we become accustomed to feeling uneasy in the types of cases where there is a chance of exposure.

109. Smith, *Theory of Moral Sentiments*, III.2.27, VII.ii.4.12. Smith's use of the term 'vanity' rather than 'pride' is worth noting here. He considers them 'both modifications of excessive self-estimation', yet he deems pride sincere—the 'proud man . . . in the bottom of his heart, is convinced of his own superiority'—whereas vanity is insincere and involves desiring praise while knowing that it is undeserved; see VI.iii.34–36. Mandeville gives plenty of examples of both vanity and pride, on Smith's distinction, but in *Fable II* he spends a lot more time explaining why we fail to realise that we act from excessive self-estimation, as I discuss below.

110. For further discussion, see Chapter 3, 'Social utility and "counterfeited" virtue', and, at greater length, Robin Douglass, 'Mandeville on the Origins of Virtue', *British Journal for the History of Philosophy* 28, no. 2 (2020): 276–95.

part of Mankind have a great Resemblance to this Picture I have been drawing, I appeal to every knowing and candid Reader.'[111]

With this focus in mind, Mandeville could grant, at least for the sake of argument, that it is possible to act from a genuine love of praiseworthiness. In these rare cases, any desire for praise would be derived from the love of praiseworthiness. The important question nonetheless remains: *how much* of human behaviour is ultimately rooted in the love of praiseworthiness, rather than the love of praise? Notice that Smith does not overstate his own case here.[112] Although he claims that in 'every well-formed mind' the desire for praiseworthiness is stronger than the desire for praise,[113] he also worries about the corruption of our moral sentiments, not least that the 'great mob of mankind' worship wealth and greatness—notwithstanding the attendant 'vices and follies of the powerful'—more than wisdom and virtue.[114] In other words, many of us praise and admire qualities that are not themselves praiseworthy. Similarly, while Mandeville's critics in the 1720s insisted on the possibility of acting from genuinely virtuous motives, they nevertheless acknowledged that 'Man is cast in such a Mould, as easily to yield to the Impressions of Vanity; and that Pride is very often the secret Motive, to which his best Actions . . . are owing.'[115] This concedes the precise point that Mandeville was most concerned to defend in *Fable II*, nowhere more so than in the 'Second Dialogue'.

The aim of the 'Second Dialogue' is to show that 'there are no good Offices or Duties . . . nor any instances of Benevolence, Humanity, or other Social Virtue . . . but a Man of good Sense and Knowledge may learn to practice from no better Principle than Vain-glory'.[116] Mandeville's spokesperson, Cleomenes, proceeds to paint the portrait of a 'fine Gentleman', whose outward actions seem to exemplify all the social virtues. Cleomenes asks whether the gentleman's actions would be any different were he secretly motivated by 'an excessive Thirst after Praise, and an immoderate Desire of general Applause from

---

111. *Fable II*, 15.

112. For the argument that Smith's analysis of how society operates relies on more Mandevillean assumptions than he ever acknowledged, see Horne, 'Envy and Commercial Society', 562–65; Kerkhof, 'A Fatal Attraction?', *passim*; Luban, 'Vanity, Domination, and History', especially 285–88; Douglass, 'Morality and Sociability in Commercial Society', especially 614–17.

113. Smith, *Theory of Moral Sentiments*, III.2.7.

114. Smith, *Theory of Moral Sentiments*, I.iii.3.2; VII.ii.1.21.

115. Fiddes, *General Treatise*, xix, also lxxx–lxxxi.

116. *Fable II*, 65.

the most knowing Judges',[117] to which Horatio, the interlocutor, eventually admits the difficulty of deciding between these rival motivations. Yet this difficulty could leave us merely agnostic about whether the gentleman is truly virtuous. To show that it is more plausible to attribute the gentleman's actions to pride rather than virtue, we must examine cases where the two would result in different actions. Cleomenes suggests that 'decisive Tryals may be made' to this end by considering the example of duelling.[118] Horatio is forced to conclude that any fine gentleman would defend his honour in a duel, rather than being despised and ridiculed by his peers, even though by accepting the duel he dares 'to violate all human and divine Laws'.[119] Duelling should not be regarded as praiseworthy conduct at all, even if, in practice, those who duel to defend their honour do receive praise. When our reputation and social standing are at stake, then, social norms dictate that we must preserve our honour, even if this means breaking the law and imperilling both our own and someone's else life. We might be willing to risk our life to preserve our honour, but we seldom risk our honour to preserve our virtue.

Having considered the case of duelling, Horatio expresses one of the objections raised by Mandeville's critics in the 1720s: why insist on calling this pride? Sure, our desire for honour is not completely disinterested, but 'the Love of Praise and even of Glory are commendable Qualities, that are beneficial to the Publick.' Cleomenes allows that such passions are sometimes beneficial, while adding that, when excessive, they often prove detrimental to society. His main point, however, is that love of glory and honour are not independent passions to pride. 'Honour is the undoubted Offspring of Pride', but it is not the only form that pride takes. Honour is cultivated through 'a refin'd Education', yet those who have learned to conform to social norms and manners 'are no more destitute of Pride' than the shameless.[120] The fact that a fine gentleman will go to such lengths to defend his honour and reputation shows that he is as much driven by pride as those who are less skilled in hiding the passion. The fact that he is willing to kill someone else to defend his reputation shows both that honour is not always a commendable quality and that it is closely bound up with an inflated sense of self-worth.

117. *Fable* II, 74.
118. *Fable* II, 81.
119. *Fable* II, 87–88.
120. *Fable* II, 89–92.

As we have seen, Mandeville's argumentative strategy is to maintain that while all seemingly praiseworthy (or virtuous) motives can be plausibly explained in terms of pride, there are some cases, such as duels, where people of the highest standing will perform actions out of pride that should be (but, in practice, are not) regarded as deeply immoral. When our pride is satisfied by doing things that are clearly not praiseworthy or virtuous, our pride wins out. So, Mandeville asks, why suppose that in cases where the desires for praise (or pride) and praiseworthiness (or virtue) pull in the same direction, the latter is doing any motivational work? Parsimony of explanation, at least, suggests that it is not. It is, of course, extremely difficult to discern someone's true motives.[121] The power of Mandeville's argument is to plant the seeds of doubt in those of us who think too highly of ourselves. To this end, he further explains why we struggle to recognise the pride that lies behind so many of our actions.

Although we regularly act from pride, Mandeville argues that we often 'become ignorant, or at least insensible of the hidden Spring, that gives Life and Motion to all [our] Actions.'[122] This is partly due to the role of education and custom in shaping how we behave. We learn to conceal certain passions for fear of public censure when we are young, and we become so habituated to doing this that later in life we are no longer aware of the original passions. Yet Mandeville offers further reasons why 'a Man of so much Sense, Knowledge and Penetration, one that understands himself so entirely well, should be ignorant of his own Heart, and the Motives he acts from.' We are unlikely to detect the depths of our own pride even if we try to examine our conduct closely, precisely because we have such a strong interest in concealing such disconcerting revelations from ourselves.[123] In this respect, pride is unlike the

121. In the 'Second Dialogue', Mandeville thus presents his aim in the modest terms of showing 'the Possibility' that a gentleman could perform the finest actions 'from no other Views, and with no other Helps' that pride and shame, *Fable* II, 77. Elsewhere, however, he claims that 'when we act slowly, and what is called deliberately, the Motives of every Volition must be obvious to all them that have the Courage, as well as Capacity, to search into them', *Free Thoughts*, 62.

122. *Fable* II, 79. This might seem to imply that Mandeville thinks that *all* our actions are ultimately rooted in pride, but, read in full, it is more plausible to read the passage as referring only to actions performed in accordance with 'the strictest Rules of good Breeding', where pride and shame do always play a role.

123. Cf. Smith's remarks on self-deception at *Theory of Moral Sentiments*, III.4.6: 'this fatal weakness of mankind, is the source of half the disorders of human life. If we saw ourselves in the light in which others see us, or in which they would see us if they knew all, a reformation would generally be unavoidable. We could not otherwise endure the sight.' See also Butler, *Fifteen Sermons*, x.2, who claims that self-love biases evaluations of our own conduct to the degree 'that many men seem perfect strangers to their own characters'.

other passions we learn to conceal, where doing so confirms our own high opinion of ourselves as civil or even virtuous. If I feel envious at someone else's achievement, but can still pass off a seemingly genuine compliment, then my civility flatters my pride and I feel a little better, even though I remain aware of my original envy. The same does not apply, however, if I search a little deeper and discover that my compliment was based solely on seeking the approval of others, as it now turns out that the civility previously flattering my pride was ill-motivated all along. Our pride is never satisfied by viewing ourselves as proud; to the contrary, the more we recognise our own pride the worse we feel about ourselves. 'I can't endure to see so much of my own Nakedness', Horatio protests, as he finally grants the extent to which all good manners are based on pride.[124] If pride is the 'hidden Spring' behind so many of our actions then we can look to its nature to understand why we so rarely recognise it in ourselves. We have pride-based reasons for deceiving ourselves about the prominence of pride, in other words, for 'boldly searching into ones own Bosom, must be the most shocking Employment, that a Man can give his Mind to, whose greatest pleasure consists in secretly admiring himself.'[125] It is lucky for all concerned, then, that we have learned to conceal the hidden depths of the passion from ourselves as much as from others.[126]

Conclusion

This chapter has analysed the place of pride in Mandeville's account of human nature and defended its explanatory power against some prominent lines of criticism. While Mandeville is more generally remembered as a psychological egoist, or a theorist of self-love, I hope to have shown that, when it comes to questions of human sociability, we should focus on pride as the preeminent passion in his analysis of human nature. One reason for this is that, in his later works, Mandeville's position on self-love is somewhat more complicated.

124. *Fable* II, 108; see also *Fable* II, 301–304.

125. *Fable* II, 79–80.

126. There is an interesting parallel here between Mandeville's argument and more recent work in evolutionary biology on the benefits of self-deception. See, for example, Robert Trivers, *Natural Selection and Social Theory: Selected Papers of Robert Trivers* (New York: Oxford University Press, 2002), 255–93, and especially the suggestion at 285 that self-deception can lead to intrinsic benefits associated with having a high self-perception of oneself. With a closer focus on the importance of self-deception for moral hypocrisy, and for a defence of what I regard as a broadly Mandevillean position, see also C. Daniel Batson, *What's Wrong with Morality: A Social-Psychological Perspective* (Oxford: Oxford University Press, 2016), 93–121.

To be sure, the introduction of self-liking in those works also complicates his position on pride, and it might be objected that we should really focus on self-liking, not pride, as the most important passion in Mandeville's analysis. Given how closely the two are related, however, any such disagreement would be more a matter of emphasis than of substance. As Mandeville introduces the term self-liking only in his later works, I think that pride remains the more helpful focal point. Even in *Fable II*, Mandeville uses the term pride more often than self-liking.[127] In saying this, however, I do not mean to suggest that we should focus on pride exclusively, and earlier in the chapter, for example, I considered how pride complements shame, both of which are caused by self-liking, on Mandeville's later account.

Another reason for focusing on pride is to show that much of Mandeville's moral psychology remains plausible even if we find criticisms of psychological egoism compelling. This is partly because he does not think that *all* our behaviour is reducible to pride. To show that Mandeville is wrong about pride, then, it is not enough to point to some cases where other motivations are more prominent; instead, the challenge is to show that pride does not explain nearly as much of human behaviour as Mandeville maintains. For present purposes, I have remained agnostic as to whether he thinks it is *ever* possible to perform actions from genuinely virtuous or praiseworthy motives, without any tincture of pride. Even if we grant that something like Smith's distinction between the love of praise and the love of praiseworthiness shows that genuine virtue is within human reach, more would need to be said to establish that the latter motive—and not pride—underlies most of our social intercourse.

The aim of this chapter has been to elucidate and evaluate the place of pride in Mandeville's psychology, not to assess its moral connotations. As should have become increasingly apparent, however, psychological analysis and moral appraisal can be kept apart only up to a point, for the main reason why many of Mandeville's contemporaries found his ideas on self-love and pride so objectionable is precisely because of the implications for evaluating our conduct, especially in so far as they challenge the prevalence, or even possibility, of genuinely benevolent or disinterested behaviour. If reading Mandeville today remains a somewhat disquieting experience—as I think it does, or at least should—then this is largely down to the moral undertones of his analysis, to which I turn next.

---

127. See Mandeville's index to *Fable* II, 371–72 (for pride), 373 (for self-liking).

2

The Morality of Pride

MOST PEOPLE DO NOT TAKE kindly to being told that their seemingly sociable, civil, or virtuous behaviour is ultimately rooted in pride. Even for those of us not inclined to regard the passion as necessarily vicious, the suggestion that when we do good things for other people we are secretly motivated by a concern for our own standing and reputation remains discomforting. Mandeville does not claim that pride is behind everything we do. But he does argue that it is the dominant passion in explaining human sociability. Does it follow, then, that all human society is morally compromised? He often suggests as much. In *Fable II*, for example, he refers to how 'a most beautiful Super-structure may be rais'd upon a rotten and despicable Foundation.'[1] Notice here that to judge society as morally compromised based on its foundations is not to deny that it is an impressive and hugely beneficial achievement in other respects. This is, I think, Mandeville's own view, but there are at least two reasons to be doubtful. First, even if we grant that his earlier works depict human nature and society as vice-ridden, it has been argued that his later works—*Fable II* and *An Enquiry into the Origin of Honour*—offer a morally neutral or purely descriptive explanation of the origin of society.[2] Second, questions have often been raised about Mandeville's sincerity, especially when it comes to his moral views. Many scholars have concluded that Mandeville did not himself endorse the moral worldview that regarded pride as vicious, or sinful, and instead sought to overturn it by exposing it to ridicule.[3]

1. *Fable* II, 64. For similar statements to this effect, see *Fable* I, 6; *Fable* II, 74.

2. This claim is often made in relation to the introduction of the distinction between self-love and self-liking. See, most prominently, Hundert, *Enlightenment's Fable*, 54–55, 60–61; Tolonen, *Mandeville and Hume*, 24–29, 86; both of which I discuss further below.

3. For the view that Mandeville did not see *anything* morally unsettling in the society of his day, see e.g. Viner, *Essays*, 318: 'Mandeville had no objection on ethical or religious grounds to

The first aim of this chapter is to defend the interpretative position that Mandeville did have serious misgivings about pride—that is, he genuinely considered it a vice—which entails that human sociability, in turn, should be seen as a morally compromised achievement. This involves taking a stand in debates about the changes between the two volumes of the *Fable*, the Augustinian background to Mandeville's thought, and questions of sincerity. In each case, these debates present objections to what I take to be the most straightforward interpretation of his thought, and, in each case, I find the objections wanting. In addressing them, however, I hope to shed light on precisely why Mandeville considers pride a vice and, at least by implication, say something about the more general character of his moral philosophy.[4]

The second aim of the chapter is to offer a qualified defence of Mandeville's evaluation of the moral status of pride. I defend Mandeville against the objection that pride should not be considered vicious, or that what he calls pride is better understood as a morally neutral desire for esteem. This discussion complements that from the previous chapter, with an important shift of emphasis. Where the previous chapter focused principally on objections to the explanatory power that Mandeville accords to pride, the criticisms examined in this chapter grant this, at least for the sake of argument, but seek to overturn its morally troubling implications. While there is something to this line of criticism, I argue that, overall, there remain reasons to find Mandeville's analysis of our pride-centred nature deeply unsettling.

---

the then-existing economic structure of society'; Hundert, *Enlightenment's Fable*, 20: Mandeville viewed 'modern conditions of affluence . . . with unambiguous delight.' For the more general argument that Mandeville sought to ridicule and/or overturn austere (Augustinian/Calvinist) moral standards, see e.g. Harth, 'Satiric Purpose', 333–40; Colman, 'Reality of Virtue', 128; Dario Castiglione, 'Considering Things Minutely: Reflections on Mandeville and the Eighteenth-Century Science of Man', *History of Political Thought* 7, no. 3 (1986), 483; Russell Nieli, 'Commercial Society and Christian Virtue: The Mandeville-Law Dispute', *The Review of Politics* 51, no. 4 (1989): 581–610; Viner, *Essays*, 178–82; Maurice M. Goldsmith, 'Mandeville's Pernicious System', in *Mandeville and Augustan Ideas: New Essays*, ed. Charles W. A. Prior (University of Victoria: ELS Editions, 2000), 79–81; Jimena Hurtado Prieto, 'Bernard Mandeville's Heir: Adam Smith or Jean Jacques Rousseau on the Possibility of Economic Analysis', *The European Journal of the History of Economic Thought* 11, no. 1 (2004), 13–14; Herdt, *Putting On Virtue*, 268–69, 275, 280.

4. The most systematic study of Mandeville's moral philosophy remains Monro, *Ambivalence*, 178–248. For important work on the naturalistic basis of Mandeville's ethics, upon which I build here, see Malcolm Jack, 'Religion and Ethics in Mandeville', in *Mandeville Studies*, 34–42; idem., *Social and Political Thought*, 89–113.

The vice of pride

Mandeville consistently describes pride as a vice, both within the *Fable* and beyond. In the 'Moral' of the original *Grumbling Hive* verse, pride is listed (along with fraud and luxury) as one of the '*great Vices*' without which societies cannot flourish.[5] In 1711, he opens the 'Preface' to his *Treatise of the Hypochondriack and Hysterick Passions* by invoking the longstanding Christian and especially Augustinian view that pride is the cause of Original Sin:

> When the crafty Tempter of Mankind mediating their Ruine, attack'd our first Sire in his Pride, he shew'd himself profoundly skill'd in Humane Nature; from which the Vice I named is so inseparable that it is impossible the latter should be ever entirely destroy'd, as long as the first remains.[6]

Much of the *Treatise* exposes how detrimental the pride of physicians (and patients) is to the practice of medicine, largely because physicians are too proud to recognise the limits of their own understanding and end up inventing speculative medical systems that are not based on careful observation. Pride is the vice that most blights medicine and, unlike with many other trades, it rarely results in public benefits.[7] Indeed, the *Treatise* is probably the one text where Mandeville focuses predominantly on documenting the negative consequences of the passion.

There is little evidence of Mandeville toning down his claims about pride as his thought matured. In the 1720s, for example, we find him describing 'Covetousness and Pride' as the 'Vices against which the Gospel so justly cautions us, [and which] contain the Seeds of almost all the Iniquities and Disorders that are committed'.[8] Pride is one of several passions that 'are evil in themselves, so it is impossible that the End to be obtain'd by them should be commendable.'[9] As late as 1732, he affirms that 'Luxury and Pride will always be reigning Sins in all civiliz'd Nations'.[10] The notion that pride is vicious, then, remains prominent throughout Mandeville's writings. This is not particularly surprising if we

5. *Fable* I, 36.

6. *Treatise*, 19.

7. For discussion of how the *Treatise* relates to Mandeville's 'private vices, public benefits' paradox, see Hilton, *Bitter Honey*, 2, 147, 158–62.

8. *Free Thoughts*, 20.

9. *Tyburn*, 31.

10. *Origin of Honour*, 205.

return to the definition of pride from 'Remark M' of the *Fable*, which emphasises overvaluing ourselves in comparison to any impartial judgement.[11] Even those who maintain that there is nothing intrinsically objectionable about thinking highly of ourselves, or desiring the esteem of others, may still grant that overvaluing ourselves can be vicious. Joseph Butler is a good example: while he argues that self-love and the desire for social esteem are often conducive to virtue, he nonetheless holds that 'vice in general consists in having an unreasonable and too great regard to ourselves, in comparison to others.'[12] What Butler terms 'vice in general' closely resembles Mandeville's definition of pride.

Definitional complexities

Mandeville's insistence that pride is vicious is complicated by his own definition of vice. In 'An Enquiry Into the Origin of Moral Virtue', he speculates as to how humans would have first come to distinguish between vice and virtue, defining the former thus:

> they agreed with the rest, to call every thing, which, without Regard to the Publick, Man should commit to gratify any of his Appetites, VICE; if in that Action there cou'd be observed the least prospect, that it might be injurious to any of the Society, or ever render himself less serviceable to others.[13]

Two points are worth highlighting. The first is that we commit a vice only by gratifying our appetites or passions in a certain way. There is nothing wrong with experiencing pride, anger, envy, or any other passion, as long as we do not act from it.[14] Mandeville reiterates this point in the 'Preface' to *Fable II*: 'It is not in feeling the Passions, or in being affected with the Frailties of Nature, that Vice consists; but in indulging and obeying the Call of them, contrary to the Dictates of Reason.'[15] For ease of expression, I usually follow Mandeville

---

11. *Fable I*, 124.

12. Butler, *Fifteen Sermons*, x.6.

13. *Fable I*, 48.

14. In some cases, gratifying an appetite might involve inaction rather than action, but nothing important turns on this qualification and I set it aside in the following discussion.

15. *Fable II*, 7, also 269–71. See also *Origin of Honour*, 196, where Mandeville explains that he gives the name 'Wicked . . . to those, *who indulge their Passions as they come uppermost, without Regard to the Good or Hurt, which the Gratification of their Appetites may do to the Society.*'

in referring to pride as a vice. Strictly speaking, however, this should be taken as shorthand for the vice of *acting* from pride.

The second point is that we do not commit a vice merely by gratifying a passion like pride, but only by doing so without regard to the public in a way that could be harmful to others.[16] Does this mean that all acts originating in pride should be classified as vicious? As we saw in the previous chapter, pride is one of the passions behind our desire for social esteem. In pursuing social esteem, we typically *do* show regard for the public by acting in ways that others deem appropriate. Moreover, we can perform actions that we believe are socially beneficial—and are right to so believe—out of pride, in which case acting from pride might not be injurious to others at all. In these cases, our self-regarding motives give rise to instrumental reasons for pursuing other-regarding or public-spirited goals. Mandeville maintains that 'it is impossible to judge of a Man's Performance' without being thoroughly 'acquainted with the Principle and Motive' behind it,[17] but his definition of vice does not specify that actions performed from self-regarding motives, such as pride, are necessarily vicious.

In formulating this definition of vice, was Mandeville trying to carve out conceptual space for the possibility that acting from pride is not always vicious? He does not explore this possibility in the 'Enquiry', although he does seek to show that when we perform beneficial acts out of a desire for social approval then, in practice, most people will regard our actions as virtuous, rather than vicious. Crucially, however, this appraisal depends upon there being a gap between how others perceive our actions and the underlying yet imperceptible motives from which we act. This gap is central to Mandeville's overarching argument that what we take to be moral virtues originate in pride, shame, and flattery. To be sure, he never claims that all human conduct must

16. These qualifications were conspicuously overlooked by some of his critics. See, for example, Bluet, *Enquiry*, 30, who summarises Mandeville's position as 'they agreed to call all natural Actions VICES'. Later in the century, Samuel Johnson reportedly criticised Mandeville for defining 'neither vices nor benefits. He reckons among vices everything that give pleasure.' See James Boswell, *Life of Johnson* [1791], ed. R. W. Chapman (Oxford: Oxford University Press, 2008), 948. Less egregiously, see also Hutcheson, *Reflections upon Laughter*, 73–74. Overly reductive glosses of Mandeville's definition of vice are still found in scholarship today. For a recent example, see Erin Frykholm, 'Hume, Mandeville, Butler, and "that Vulgar Dispute"', *Archiv für Geschichte der Philosophie* 101, no. 2 (2019), 287: 'vice is anything done out of self-interested motivation'.

17. *Fable* I, 56, also 87, 260–61; *Fable* II, 120; *Virgin Unmask'd*, 73, 152; *Female Tatler*, no. 100: 213; *Free Thoughts*, 18–20.

be classified as either vicious or virtuous,[18] so we should not conclude that actions performed from pride must be vicious simply because they are not virtuous.[19] Like all passions, pride can lead to both good and evil.[20] Unlike some passions, however, pride is excessive by its nature, since it involves *over-valuing* ourselves. Given that others will often take offence when we flaunt our pride, there is always 'the least prospect' that displays of the passion 'might be injurious', thus satisfying Mandeville's definition of vice. Yet even if *displays* of pride should be classified as vicious, it is less clear how we should evaluate cases where we perform socially beneficial acts out of pride while at the same time concealing that pride from public view.

The morality of self-liking

In *Fable II*, Mandeville introduces the concept of self-liking and explains that it is the cause of pride.[21] Some scholars see this as marking a considerable break in the evaluative character of his analysis, with his later works distinguished by a morally neutral or purely descriptive mode of explanation. According to Edward Hundert, self-liking allows Mandeville to 'employ the moralized vocabulary he had inherited [from seventeenth-century French moralists] in a non-normative, descriptive fashion.' In his later writings, Hundert continues, Mandeville explains 'sociability in a language shorn of moralized concepts.'[22] More recently and at greater length, Mikko Tolonen argues

18. Cf. Kaye, 'Introduction', xlviii; Viner, *Essays*, 178–80. For helpful corrections on this point, see Sterling P. Lamprecht, 'The Fable of the Bees', *The Journal of Philosophy* 23 (1926), 573; Maxwell, 'Ethics and Politics in Mandeville', 245; Harth, 'Satiric Purpose', 326–27.

19. Actions performed from pride do not appear to satisfy the 'Conquest of his own Passions, out of a Rational Ambition of being good' criterion of virtue, *Fable I*, 48. I address some of the complexities regarding Mandeville's definition of virtue in Chapter 3, 'Social utility and "counterfeited" virtue', and at greater length in Douglass, 'Mandeville on the Origins of Virtue', especially 279–81. For present purposes, my explanation of the moral status of pride does not depend upon how we understand Mandeville's conception of virtue, precisely because he is not committed to the position that everything that is not virtuous is vicious.

20. This is one of Mandeville's main reasons for denying that we have naturally virtuous sentiments, as is especially clear from his discussion of pity, the passion which 'bears the greatest resemblance to Virtue', *Fable I*, 56, also 260–61.

21. *Fable II*, 131; see also *Origin of Honour*, 3–4, and Chapter 1, 'Self-love and self-liking', for more details.

22. Hundert, *Enlightenment's Fable*, 54–55, also 60–61. See also Luban, 'Mandeville as Moralist and Materialist', 841, who claims that the introduction of self-liking allowed Mandeville 'to

that *Fable II* 'changes the premises of the discussion from normative moral theory to social theory, leaving both Hobbism and French Augustinianism behind.' On this view, the distinction between self-love and self-liking enables Mandeville to conduct a 'morally neutral analysis of the relationship between human nature and civil society.'[23] The strongest rebuttal of these claims involves showing that, even if we grant that self-liking is morally neutral—that is, neither vicious nor virtuous in itself—Mandeville's more general analysis of human nature and society is still presented in morally laden terms. Before coming to this, however, it is worth first interrogating the specific point about self-liking, given the importance the concept has come to assume in Mandeville scholarship.

Cleomenes, voicing Mandeville's position, first introduces the distinction between self-love and self-liking in the 'Third Dialogue' of *Fable II*, in the context of explaining the origin of politeness and good manners. After hearing how self-liking operates, Horatio, the interlocutor, wonders how the passion could ever have been given to us for our preservation, instead proposing 'that it is hurtful to Men, because it must make them odious to one another; and I cannot see what Benefit they can receive from it, either in a savage or a civiliz'd State'. Without denying that there is something odious about self-liking, Cleomenes reminds Horatio of 'the many Virtues' that 'may be counterfeited to gain Applause ... by the sole Help and Instigation of his Pride.'[24] This formulation echoes the distinction between 'counterfeited' and 'real' virtue from the 1723 edition of the *Fable*—the point being that actions originating in pride, which on the later account are ultimately rooted in self-liking, can lead only to 'counterfeited' and not 'real' virtue.[25] It helps to keep Mandeville's broader argumentative goals in mind when assessing the moral connotations of

---

develop a naturalistic, ethically neutral way of discussing the theologically-laden concept of pride'; and Simonazzi, 'Reconnaissance, *Self-liking* et contrôle social', 143–44, who suggests that Mandeville introduced the term self-liking to distance his position from the Augustinian and Jansenist association between self-love and Original Sin.

23. Tolonen, *Mandeville and Hume*, 24–29. See also Jack, 'Men Become Sociable', 5, who follows Tolonen in claiming that Mandeville presents the distinction between pride and self-love 'in a new and morally-neutral tone' in *Fable II*.

24. *Fable* II, 134.

25. *Fable* I, 230. Mandeville draws the distinction between 'counterfeited' and 'real' virtue in the enlarged 1723 edition of the first volume of the *Fable*, where he targets Shaftesbury for the first time. For further discussion, see Chapter 3, 'Social utility and "counterfeited" virtue'. Rather that viewing the discussion of self-liking in *Fable II* as marking a break with the first volume,

self-liking. The main aim of the 'Third Dialogue' is to show that politeness has nothing to do with real virtue, and the concept of self-liking helps Mandeville to develop a more nuanced account of why politeness and good manners are not virtuous.[26] Even if we grant that self-liking is morally neutral, then, it still plays a crucial role in Mandeville's attempt to explain much of our sociable and civil behaviour in non-virtuous terms.

Horatio perseveres with his objection. Self-liking may well be advantageous for 'Man in the Society', who has been educated and socialised in a certain way, but what advantage accrues to 'him as a single Creature?' This challenge proves more difficult for Cleomenes to answer. In doing so, he acknowledges that self-liking leads to both good and bad consequences: it 'lays open to us the Precariousness of sublunary Happiness, and the wretched Condition of Mortals.' In this respect, however, it is no different to other natural phenomena, for there are no unqualified goods in the world. Cleomenes further recognises that self-liking is generally held 'in Disgrace, and every body disowns the Passion', yet he insists that it 'continually furnishes us with that Relish we have for Life, even when it is not worth having.' Without self-liking, we could not take any happiness in our own well-being and, so long as this liking for ourselves lasts, we will never commit suicide.[27]

If our preservation and even happiness would be impossible without self-liking, should we regard it as morally neutral? Tolonen argues that we should, invoking Mandeville's remark that all 'Passions and Instincts in general were given to Animals for some wise End', so 'why should we be ashamed of having them?'[28] The first point to note, in response, is that Mandeville had argued that all passions are given to us for preservation in the 1714 edition of the *Fable* too,[29] so the passage in question does not mark any significant revision

---

then, it makes more sense to see it as continuous with the concerns of the 1723 edition in a way that separates both from the 1714 edition.

26. Cf. Colman, 'Reality of Virtue', 135–36, who argues that acts motivated by self-liking might be considered virtuous, unlike acts motivated by pride. Mandeville never claims that acts motivated by self-liking could be virtuous and Colman's argument overlooks the fact that Mandeville introduces the concept to help distance his analysis from those who confuse polite manners for genuine virtue. On this point, see also Scribano, *Natura umana e società competitiva*, 148.

27. *Fable* II, 134–36. For helpful discussion of this dimension of self-liking, see Gomes, 'Desire and Struggle for Recognition', especially 39–44.

28. *Fable* II, 91; Tolonen, *Mandeville and Hume*, 86.

29. See *Fable* I, 200.

to Mandeville's account. Nevertheless, there remains a sense in which we can describe all passions—not just self-love and self-liking, but equally pride, envy, lust, etcetera—as morally neutral. As we have seen, Mandeville's definition of vice involves indulging our passions, not merely experiencing them, even if his language is not always so precise. Again, this does not reflect any shift in Mandeville's position. The claim that we should not feel ashamed of having passions, but only of letting them become 'detrimental or offensive to any Part of the Society', is perfectly consistent with the definition of vice in the 'Enquiry',[30] irrespective of the passion in question.

In *Fable II*, then, there is little evidence that the introduction of self-liking changes the moral character of Mandeville's analysis.[31] To the contrary, we sometimes find him discussing the passion in very similar terms to his earlier analysis of pride, such as when he describes self-liking as 'a most stubborn and an unconquerable Passion, which in its Nature seems to be destructive of Sociableness and Society, and never fails, in untaught Men, to render them insufferable to one another.'[32] The strongest evidence that self-liking is morally neutral does not appear in *Fable II* at all, but rather in *Origin of Honour*:

> When this Self-liking is excessive, and so openly shewn as to give Offence to others, I know very well it is counted a Vice and call'd Pride: But when it is kept out of Sight, or is so well disguis'd as not to appear in its own Colours, it has no Name, tho' Men act from that and no other Principle.[33]

As long as our self-liking 'is moderate and well regulated, excites in us the Love of Praise, and a Desire to be applauded and thought well of by others, and stirs us up to good Actions', then, Mandeville implies, it is not vicious; it becomes vicious only when 'it is excessive, or ill turn'd, whatever it excites in our Selves, gives Offence to others, renders us odious, and is call'd Pride.'[34] Once we distinguish a 'moderate and well regulated' self-liking from pride as its 'excessive' offshoot, then there appears to be nothing vicious about the high value we have for ourselves, which leads us to desire the praise of others and fear

---

30. The quotation is from *Fable* II, 91; for the definition see *Fable* I, 48.

31. On this point, see also Scribano, *Natura umana e società competitiva*, 155–56; Maurer, *Self-love, Egoism and the Selfish Hypothesis*, 60–64.

32. *Fable* II, 175.

33. *Origin of Honour*, 3. The discussion of self-liking in *Origin of Honour* is the main evidence adduced by Hundert, *Enlightenment's Fable*, 54–55.

34. *Origin of Honour*, 6–7.

their disapproval. To the degree that Mandeville indicates the point at which self-liking turns into the vice of pride, his emphasis falls on acting in ways that may cause offence to others. Pride remains a vice in *Origin of Honour*, then, but not everything we do out of a desire for social approval should necessarily be attributed to pride or classified as vicious.

In clarifying the relationship between self-liking and pride, Mandeville's analysis addresses the possibility we encountered in the previous section: that there is nothing necessarily vicious about performing beneficial acts even though we desire social approval. On the account from *Origin of Honour*, these acts could be rooted in self-liking *but not pride*—that is, our sense of self-worth motivating the acts could be moderate and well-regulated, rather than excessive. Nonetheless, it remains the case that we must disguise our self-liking and ensure that it does not appear in its true colours. This indicates that there is still something about the high esteem we have for ourselves that cannot be displayed without causing offence. To be moderate and well-regulated, our self-liking must be successfully concealed so that it cannot be mistaken for a display of pride. In practice, of course, we only ever *count* something as a vice when it is detected, and throughout his writings Mandeville provides plenty of examples of how we disguise or hide away our pride—in much the same terms as he now writes of self-liking—so that others do not discover our true motives. Much like pride, then, self-liking is not a passion that should be displayed openly.

Suppose we grant that Mandeville clearly distinguishes between self-liking as a morally neutral and descriptive term, and pride as a vice.[35] What follows? Hundert and Tolonen argue that in *Fable II* and *Origin of Honour*, Mandeville explains society and sociability in morally neutral terms. If they were right then we would expect Mandeville's analysis to be conducted principally in terms of self-liking, eschewing all references to pride. But this is not what we find. Mandeville's index to *Fable II* confirms that he uses pride far more frequently than self-liking,[36] and pride likewise remains central to the argument

35. As should be apparent, my own view is that this in fact grants too much. It is far from evident that when Mandeville uses the term self-liking (without further specification or qualification) he is necessarily referring to its moderate and well-regulated form, rather than its excessive form, and I see no reason why this should be the guiding assumption when reading his later works.

36. *Fable* II, 371–72 (for pride), 373 (for self-liking). An anonymous reviewer suggested that Mandeville uses pride more frequently only *before* introducing the concept of self-liking in the 'Third Dialogue' of *Fable II*. This is not the case. Mandeville refers to self-liking regularly when

of *Origin of Honour*. Mandeville maintains, for example, that establishing power or authority requires 'Flattering the Pride of All', that honour is a 'Human Contrivance, rais'd on the Basis of Human Pride', and that the 'higher you can raise a Man's Pride, the more refin'd you may render his Notions of Honour.'[37] He sometimes makes similar claims in terms of self-liking—and occasionally refers to 'Self-liking or Pride' together[38]—but the fact that he still chooses to use the term pride indicates that the vice is key to understanding the way polite manners and honour codes work in civil society. Although Mandeville allows that we can act from a moderate and well-regulated self-liking in *Origin of Honour*, he never so much as intimates that this explains more of our behaviour than pride. The prevalence of pride throughout Mandeville's later works instead signals that he had no intention of backtracking from the morally compromised vision of human nature and society laid out in the earlier editions of the *Fable*.

The problem of sincerity

There is abundant textual evidence of Mandeville *claiming* that pride is a vice. Should we doubt the sincerity of those claims? One reason for doing so goes something like this: pride was widely considered a vice at the time, but this was due to a moral and theological worldview that Mandeville did not hold and probably aimed to overturn. When he claims that pride is a vice, Mandeville is best read as merely acknowledging—perhaps also subverting, but certainly not endorsing—the place that it occupied in the moral vocabulary of his contemporaries. Consider, in this light, David Hume's remark:

> There may, perhaps, be some, who being accustom'd to the style of the schools and pulpit, and having never consider'd human nature in any other light, than that in which *they* place it, may be here surpriz'd to hear me talk of virtue as exciting pride, which they look upon as a vice . . . But not to

---

introducing and explaining the concept at *Fable* II, 129–38, but, on my count, he uses the term only five more times in the remainder of the book. By contrast, even after having introduced the concept of self-liking (i.e. after *Fable* II, 138), Mandeville mentions pride on at least twenty-five subsequent occasions. He uses self-liking and pride a similar number of times in *Origin of Honour*, with many of the remarks on self-liking clustered around the passages discussed in this section.

37. *Origin of Honour*, 46, 64, 86.
38. *Origin of Honour*, 54–55.

dispute about words, I observe, that by *pride* I understand that agreeable impression, which arises in the mind, when the view either of our virtue, beauty, riches or power makes us satisfy'd with ourselves. And that by *humility* I mean the opposite impression. 'Tis evident the former impression is not always vicious, nor the latter virtuous.[39]

Hume's definition of pride is not the same as Mandeville's. Of present interest, however, is the suggestion that pride is often deemed vicious due to the influence of the schools and the pulpit, which is starkly at odds with the naturalistic and observational basis of Hume's own analysis. Although Hume does not mention Mandeville in this context, other eighteenth-century commentators drew explicit connections. According to Robert Sandeman, for example, Mandeville's 'account of human nature, though writ in such a manner as to be read by many who have no taste for theological tracts, is really no other than what is to be found in a thousand sermons, of first repute for orthodoxy.'[40] Mandeville's insistence that virtue requires self-denial attracted similar criticism. Francis Hutcheson dismissed Mandeville's views as having probably been inspired by 'an old fanatic sermon' from his youth, while Adam Smith associated them with 'some popular ascetic doctrines which had been current before his time'.[41]

These remarks do not question Mandeville's sincerity, but by drawing connections with an outdated and unreflectively endorsed theological worldview, Hutcheson and Smith implied that serious philosophers need not take Mandeville's substantive moral claims too seriously. There is another way or running the argument, however, which *does* cast doubt on Mandeville's sincerity. If Mandeville is best understood as a naturalistic philosopher who based his analysis on observation and experience,[42] yet his moral pronouncements rely on theological premises of some sort, then perhaps he was trying to show

---

39. Hume, *Treatise,* 2.1.7.8.

40. Robert Sandeman, *Letters on Theron and Aspasio. Addressed to the Author,* vol. 1 (Edinburgh, 1757), 273. In the nineteenth century, James Mill likewise remarked that Mandeville's central propositions about human nature were established 'on the authority of religion, and the gravest Divines.' They were, Mill laments, 'part of the theological morality of Mandeville's time, not altogether renounced in our own time'. See James Mill, *A Fragment on Mackintosh* (London, 1835), 60–62.

41. See Hutcheson, *Reflections upon Laughter,* 81; Smith, *Theory of Moral Sentiments,* VII. ii.4.12.

42. For present purposes, I use 'naturalistic' merely to differentiate claims based on an observational or empirical analysis of human nature from those that instead appeal to revealed knowledge (i.e. scripture). This proves helpful for assessing the Augustinian influence on

how absurd the moral views of his day looked from a clearheaded philosophical perspective.[43] One way to cash out the insincerity objection is to draw attention to Mandeville's reworking of Augustinian moral psychology.

An Augustinian view of pride?

Mandeville's analysis of our pride-centred nature appears indebted to French neo-Augustinian moralists of the seventeenth century, for whom the dominance of pride and self-love characterised our sinful—that is, *fallen*—state.[44] But to what extent did Mandeville really endorse the moral worldview that classified pride as a vice, which, for Augustinians, relied on the doctrine of Original Sin? While some scholars hold that we must attend to Mandeville's 'starkly Augustinian view of humanity' to make sense of his philosophy,[45] others see his 'mock Augustinian stance' as no more than a satirical pose, which does not convey his true moral convictions.[46] We should tread very carefully before labelling someone as Augustinian, mock or otherwise, and be clear about the precise relationship we are seeking to uncover.[47] The crucial question presently,

---

Mandeville's thought and should not be confused with the various meanings of 'naturalism' in contemporary philosophy.

43. This argument is typically invoked in relation to Mandeville's (rigoristic) definition of virtue, but it can also be applied to his more general moral outlook. See Note 3 above for details of scholarship that adopts this general perspective.

44. For studies situating Mandeville's thought in this context, see especially Kaye, 'Introduction', lxxix–lxxxiv; Lovejoy, *Reflections on Human Nature*, 153–79; Horne, *Social Thought*, 19–31; Dickey, 'Pride, Hypocrisy and Civility'; Hundert, *Enlightenment's Fable*, 30–38; Lafond, *L'homme et son image*, 441–58; Parrish, *Paradoxes of Political Ethics*, 185–231; McLendon, *Psychology of Inequality*, 84–92.

45. Paul Sagar, 'Sociability, Luxury and Sympathy: The Case of Archibald Campbell', *History of European Ideas* 39, no. 6 (2013), 793–94. See also Crisp, *Sacrifice Regained*, 60–73, who argues that Mandeville's philosophy 'rests on what he saw as a firm Christian foundation' (61); more specifically, a version of 'Jansenist theism' that recognises external standards of morality 'grounded in divine command' (72). Alternatively, for the view that Mandeville should be read as a sincere Christian humanist in the tradition of Richard Hooker, see Elias J. Chiasson, 'Bernard Mandeville: A Reappraisal', *Philological Quarterly* 49, no. 4 (1970): 489–519.

46. Hundert, *Enlightenment's Fable*, 144. See also Colman, 'Reality of Virtue', 128. Cf. Maurer, *Self-love, Egoism and the Selfish Hypothesis*, 59, 72–73, 81 (and the accompanying endnotes), for a position closer to the one that I defend here.

47. See Michael Moriarty, *Disguised Vices: Theories of Virtue in Early Modern French Thought* (Oxford: Oxford University Press, 2011), 368–80, whose discussion of whether La Rochefoucauld should be considered Augustinian is exemplary in this respect.

which discussions of the Augustinian influence sometimes elide, is whether Mandeville's moral evaluation of pride depends upon certain theological assumptions that are in tension with his otherwise naturalistic explanation of human nature and society.

On the Augustinian account, Original Sin is understood in terms of a perverted or evil will, and this evil will begins with pride, which 'occurs when a man is too well pleased with himself' and fails to display the humility demanded by the obedience and love we owe to God.[48] The latter point is crucial: an Augustinian analysis of pride presents the vice in stark contradistinction to love of God. Mandeville adopts similar language throughout the opening chapter of his *Free Thoughts*, 'Of Religion', insisting that there 'is a vast Difference between not committing an Immorality from a Principle of Pride and Prudence, and the avoiding of Sin for the Love of GOD.'[49] As far as I am aware, though, there is only one occasion across the different editions of the *Fable* where Mandeville comes anywhere close to opposing pride to love of God. 'It is owing to the Principle of Pride', Cleomenes claims, 'that Men imagine the whole Universe to be principally made for their use ... and have pitiful and most unworthy Notions of God and his Works.'[50] Even in this passage, Mandeville does not mention the love we owe but fail to show God; his point, instead, is that the natural evils which befall humans, such as being attacked by wild animals, are not evidence against the world being governed by providence.[51] In the case of the *Fable*, then, Mandeville does not explain what is wrong with pride in terms of the love, honour, or obedience that we fail to show to God.

Although Mandeville says little about the opposition between pride and love of God, he does maintain that his analysis pertains only to our fallen condition. The prominence of this point was elevated in the second of the two editions of the *Fable* that appeared in 1714. The second was a page-for-page reprint of the first, but the title page contained a longer title advertising the inclusion of 'Several Discourses, to demonstrate, That Human Frailties, *during the degeneracy of* MANKIND, may be turn'd to the Advantage of CIVIL SOCIETY, and

48. For the original, see Augustine, *City of God*, xiv.13. On Augustinian ideas of Original Sin in seventeenth-century French thought, see Michael Moriarty, *Fallen Nature, Fallen Selves: Early Modern French Thought II* (Oxford: Oxford University Press, 2006), especially 109–56.

49. *Free Thoughts*, 19, and more generally 1, 18–20.

50. *Fable* II, 243.

51. This broader argument is summarised at *Fable* II, 260–63.

made to supply the Place of *Moral Virtues*.'[52] Mandeville reiterates the point about the degeneracy of mankind when explaining that when he refers to 'Men' in the 'Enquiry', he means 'neither *Jews* nor *Christians*; but meer Man, in the State of Nature and Ignorance of the true Deity'.[53] 'Devout Christians', he later adds, 'being regenerated, and preternaturally assisted by the Divine Grace, cannot be said to be in Nature.'[54] These qualifications closely parallel François de La Rochefoucauld's 'Preface' to the 1666 edition of his *Réflexions ou sentences et maxims morales*, which was included in the 1694 English translation.[55] La Rochefoucauld explains that he 'only considers Mankind in the present Deplorable State of Nature, as 'tis over-run with Ignorance and corrupted by Sin', and thus what he says 'does not in the least concern those Happy but few favourites whom Heaven is pleased to preserve from them by a particular Grace.'[56] For both La Rochefoucauld and Mandeville, one reason for qualifying their accounts in this manner was simply to evade certain lines of objection; most notably, in the 'Enquiry', that our ideas of virtue and vice are derived from revealed religion.[57]

52. See Kaye's 'Description of the Editions', at *Fable* II, 392.

53. *Fable* I, 40, 50; see also *Fable* I, 229, 346–48.

54. *Fable* I, 166. For the claim that Christians cannot conquer their passions and attain virtue 'whilst they are unassisted with the Divine Grace', see *Free Thoughts*, 24; also *Origin of Honour*, 56, 99–100. On the demandingness of Christian virtue more generally, see *Free Thoughts*, 1, 18–24, 33, 93, 199; *Fable* II, 18–19, 314; *Letter to Dion*, especially 22–25. While Mandeville associates the conquest of the passions required for virtue with Christianity, the account of the origin of virtue he gives in the 'Enquiry' aims to show how we could have formed notions of virtue without any knowledge of God. Mandeville occasionally suggests that the self-denial demanded by Christianity is even stricter than the 'Conquest over untaught Nature' required for 'real Virtue' (*Fable* II, 127), although at other times he writes of 'a Christian Self-denial, and the Practice of real Virtue' (*Origin of Honour*, 78) as if they are one and the same.

55. Kaye notes this at *Fable* I, 40. For discussion, see Hundert, *Enlightenment's Fable*, 32–33; and, for a position that I follow closely here, see Guion, 'The Fable of the Bees: *proles sine matre?*', 97–98. Kaye's editorial notes indicate many places where Mandeville's ideas more generally echo La Rochefoucauld's.

56. François de la Rochefoucauld, *Moral Maxims and Reflections* (London 1694), 'The Preface to the Reader'.

57. Mandeville was nevertheless still criticised by many of his contemporaries on this point. See George Bluet, *Enquiry*, 108, for example, who took the apology as evidence that Mandeville 'knows his Opinions are not true, if the Jewish, the Christian Religion, or the Being of a God itself be true'. Others claimed that the apology misses the mark because notions of good and evil are innate, their origins predate Judaism and Christianity, and are known by natural (not revealed) religion. See Fiddes, *General Treatise*, xxviii–xxx; Law, *Remarks*, 8–10; Dennis, *Vice*

While Mandeville sometimes refers to our fallen condition, it does not follow that his moral assessment of human nature relies upon certain theological assumptions.[58] One need not endorse any such assumptions to find much of the Augustinian depiction of human selfishness, pride, and weakness both psychologically compelling and morally troubling. Recall, in this context, the 'Preface' to Mandeville's *Treatise*: in appealing to Adam's pride, 'the crafty Tempter of Mankind ... shew'd himself *profoundly skill'd in Humane Nature.*'[59] The story of the fall captures something important about the human condition, even if it is only a story. To illustrate the point further, consider a parallel case. Thomas Hobbes's account of human nature and conflict was adopted by some neo-Augustinian moralists because he was taken to have offered a penetrating analysis of our (fallen) condition, even though his religious views were deemed highly suspect.[60] Conversely, the Augustinian analysis of our pride-centred nature could appeal to someone like Mandeville, irrespective of his theological commitments (or lack thereof).[61] When Mandeville claims that 'we shall find that Human Nature since the Fall of *Adam* has always been the same',[62] the important point concerns the account of human nature we are left with, not belief in a prelapsarian state of innocence from which we fell.

We can find the Augustinian picture of human nature persuasive, then, without accepting any theological assumptions. The same is largely true of Augustinian criticisms of Stoic pride, echoes of which are also present in Mandeville. For Augustine, anyone who neither recognises the dominion of God nor understands that His rewards are not of this world is guilty of pride, and,

---

and Luxury, 37–45; John Thorold, *A Short Examination of The Notions Advanc'd In a (late) Book, intituled, The Fable of the Bees, or Private Vices, Publick Benefits* (London, 1726), 6–7.

58. Cf. Colman, 'Reality of Virtue', 128.

59. *Treatise*, 19 (emphasis added).

60. Most notably, see Pierre Nicole, 'Of Charity, and Self-Love', in his *Moral Essays, Contain'd in several Treatises on many Important Duties*, vol. 3 (London, 1696), especially §4. For discussion of Nicole's Hobbism, see E. D. James, *Pierre Nicole, Jansenist and Humanist: A Study of his Thought* (The Hague: Martinus Nijhoff, 1972), especially 155–59; Charles-Olivier Stiker-Métral, *Narcisse contrarié: l'amour propre dans le discours moral en France (1650–1715)* (Paris: Champion, 2007), 202–205; Douglass, *Rousseau and Hobbes*, 24–26, 186–89.

61. On this point, see also Force, *Self-Interest before Smith*, 63. More generally, see Joost W. Hengstmengel, 'Augustinian Motifs in Mandeville's Theory of Society', *Journal of Markets and Morality* 19, no. 2 (2016): 317–38.

62. *Fable* I, 229.

on this count, Augustine reserved especial scorn for the Stoics, who 'in their stupid pride, believe that the Final Good is to be found in this life, and that they can achieve happiness by their own efforts.'[63] The Stoics denied human dependence upon God and mistakenly thought that (in our present condition) we can master our passions and live without sin.[64] Where the failure to acknowledge our dependence upon God makes sense only within a theological worldview, the more general complaint that the Stoics overestimated our capacity to control our passions and achieve true happiness can be supported by a naturalistic analysis of human nature. 'Remark O' of the *Fable* is a case in point.

Mandeville claims that the Stoics associated happiness with 'the calm Serenity of a contented Mind' that has 'subdued every sensual Appetite', and that many of them 'own'd themselves arriv'd to the height of Self-denial and . . . rais'd above common Mortals'. These precepts, however, have been 'exploded' as beyond 'all human Force and Possibility', thereby revealing that 'the Virtues they boasted of could be nothing but haughty Pretence, full of Arrogance and Hypocrisy'.[65] On the rare occasions when people really do renounce all luxury and voluntarily embrace poverty, their secret motive is to win the adoration of the vulgar; such was the case of Diogenes the Cynic, who sacrificed 'all his

---

63. Augustine, *City of God*, xix.4.

64. For a concise overview of Augustine's criticisms, see Brooke, *Philosophic Pride*, 7–10, and 76–100 on seventeenth-century French Augustinians. More comprehensively on the latter, see Moriarty, *Disguised Vices*, with 61–78 focusing on the original criticisms in Augustine.

65. *Fable* I, 150–51. Mandeville proceeds to say that 'the generality of Wise Men that have liv'd ever since to this Day, agree with the Stoicks in the most material Points', which has recently led Roger Crisp (*Sacrifice Regained*, 70) to conclude that Mandeville himself agrees with the 'Wise Men' and subscribes to a Stoic view of happiness; i.e. that 'no one is happy unless he is virtuous . . . and only the virtuous can enjoy 'real' pleasures'. In the following paragraph, however, Mandeville explains that he calls 'those Pleasures real that are directly opposite to those which I own the wise Men of all Ages have extoll'd as the most valuable'. Crisp is aware of this passage but thinks that Mandeville 'is best understood to be claiming that the pleasures of virtue are the only valuable pleasures', which I take to be the precise opposite of his point here. For similar criticism of the Stoic notion of happiness, see *Female Tatler*, no. 109: 232–33, and also the dedication to *A Modest Defence*, 48, where Mandeville observes that even 'the very *Stoicks*, who prided themselves in the Conquest of all their other Passions, were forc'd to submit to' their sexual desires. More generally on Mandeville's anti-Stoic orientation in these passages of the *Fable*, see Brooke, *Philosophic Pride*, 155–57.

Passions to his Pride in acting this Part'.[66] This fault is not unique to the Stoics (or Cynics), and much of Mandeville's critical ire was directed at the clergy of his own day, who, like the Stoics, presented themselves as paragons of a virtue they never actually practised. Mandeville even suggests that the reason why many people believe in certain forms of human distinction—including the immortality of the soul—is to flatter their pride.[67] The same is true of some of the most celebrated philosophers throughout history, who have considerably overstated the role of reason or benevolence in determining so much of our behaviour. Only 'Pride could ever make Men of the vast Wit, Sense and Penetration, that some of them have shew'd, so ridiculously forget themselves as to brag of what (if they had rightly examined it) they must have found inconsistent with Humane Nature.'[68]

The fault common to the Stoics, most clergy, and many others, then, on Mandeville's account, is that they think far too highly of their own abilities and qualities. For Augustinians, to imagine that we could attain the levels of wisdom and virtue to which the Stoics laid claim is to overestimate our capacities and to fail to acknowledge our dependence upon God. For Mandeville, it is equally to overestimate our capacities—whence the vice of pride—irrespective of our dependence upon God. We need not invoke God or divine grace to hold an overly idealised account of human excellence or moral goodness, which we then falsely present ourselves as approximating. We are guilty of pride whenever we fail to appreciate the sway of the passions in determining our behaviour or pretend that we are moved by more public-spirited motives than is truly the case. This may well be an Augustinian insight, but it is quite compatible with a naturalistic worldview: one does not need to posit the fall to hold that we are governed by self-regarding passions, yet simultaneously deceived about the true extent to which we are unknown to ourselves. There is much to find plausible in Augustinian moral psychology—including its *moral* connotations—even for those sceptical of Augustinian theology.

66. *Fable* I, 157.

67. *Fable* I, 230; see also *Treatise*, 59–60. For an impassioned rejoinder to Mandeville's comment about the immortality of the soul, see William Law, *Remarks*, 73, who observed (in what he took to be a *reductio ad absurdum*) that Mandeville's argument could equally be applied to 'the *Belief* of the *Being* and Providence of God', for these 'are the most pleasing *Truths*, and more extol and elevate Mans Nature and Condition than any thing else'. For helpful discussion of Mandeville's shifting views on whether we possess an immaterial soul, see Simonazzi, *Le favole della filosofia*, 119–28.

68. *Female Tatler*, no. 109: 233.

A satire upon morality?

Even if we can find the Augustinian picture of human nature and pride compelling without signing up to the theology, was Mandeville really troubled by our moral failings in anything like the way that the Augustinian moralists were? His 'tone of detached amusement' suggests not, some have argued, for he seems 'more ready to laugh at man than lament his tragic fallen nature.'[69] Stated in more general terms, the objection to my interpretation of the *Fable* remains that it

> does not read like a book that maintains morality and religion. Mandeville would apparently have us believe that he is sermonising against sin or satirising vice. Neither sermons not satires revel, as does the *Fable*, in the beneficial consequences of these evils or describe with such evident relish various examples of beneficial evil. . . . The tone of the book is not that of a denunciation of wrong-doing. It is hard to believe that Mandeville's professions are not ironic.[70]

Mandeville enjoyed revealing how vice-ridden the world appears from a certain moral outlook, so this objection goes, but the pleasure he evidently took in doing so counts against reading him as sincerely endorsing that outlook. To conclude that Mandeville saw anything morally troubling in the vices he exposed is apparently to miss the 'obvious funmaking gusto' of his argument.[71]

Mandeville addresses the insincerity objection many times, remarking as early as the 'Preface' to the *Fable* that several readers had 'either wilfully or ignorantly' mistaken the original *Grumbling Hive* verse for 'a Satyr upon Virtue and Morality' that aimed 'for the Encouragement of Vice.'[72] In *A Letter to Dion*, the final defence of his work, Mandeville even claims that those who doubt his sincerity would have said the same of St Paul or Jesus Christ, for such critics cannot bear to entertain the thought that the pursuit of wealth and worldly

---

69. The first quotation is from Herdt, *Putting on Virtue*, 269; the second from Colman, 'Reality of Virtue', 128.

70. Goldsmith, 'Mandeville's Pernicious System', 79. For a striking contrast, see Edwards, 'Mandeville's Moral Prose', 203, who claims that Mandeville's style 'presents real difficulties, but they should not prevent us from seeing that a major motive in his writing is plain moral indignation.'

71. Viner, *Essays*, 179; see also Cook, *Bernard Mandeville*, 89.

72. *Fable* I, 4.

glory is starkly opposed to the demands of morality and Christianity.[73] Needless to say, these remarks do little to assuage those who press the charge of insincerity, for it simply begs the question to invoke an author's own (sometimes hyperbolic) claims to sincerity in response. Nonetheless, there are at least three reasons why the insincerity objection should be resisted in this case.

The first is that the insincerity objection over-generalises in its claims about Mandeville's style. To be sure, Mandeville often adopts a light-hearted and even comical tone—'an open good-humour'd Manner',[74] as he calls it— especially when pointing to the unexpected benefits that accrue to society when private vices are turned to good use. But at other times he does not. Consider, for example, Mandeville's depiction of the 'Avarice or Pride' of the most eminent lawyers and physicians of his day, who are willing to let the innocent be convicted, or the ill perish, 'if they dislike their Fee'.[75] Or consider his account of the evils that lie behind the prosperity brought about by international trade and navigation, where, in documenting the lives lost and hardships endured by those transporting goods at sea, Mandeville invites us to picture the 'Tyrant so inhuman and void of Shame, that . . . should exert such terrible Services from his Innocent Slaves' merely to satisfy his desire for luxury garments.[76] It is difficult to detect any sarcasm or irony in such passages, which are full of disdain for those Mandeville attacks. More generally, while his tone is certainly not the high-minded preaching of theologians or moral reformers, this is unsurprising given that he strongly opposes such preaching and does not advocate moral reform. Mandeville reserves a very critical tone for his adversaries: the clergy, moral reformers, or the 'haughty Moralists, who cannot endure to hear the Dignity of their Species arraign'd'.[77] He has little time for *their* pride or hypocrisy, which he does not regard as at all beneficial. Reading the *Fable* should instead lead those 'who continually find fault with others . . . to look at home, and examining their own Consciences, be made asham'd of always railing at what they are more or less guilty of themselves'.[78]

The second problem with the insincerity objection is that it infers too much from Mandeville's style. There is no reason why a humorous and light-hearted

---

73. *Letter to Dion*, 31.
74. *Letter to Dion*, 25.
75. *Free Thoughts*, 147.
76. *Fable* I, 357–58.
77. *Fable* I, 126.
78. *Fable* I, 8, also 409.

tone cannot go hand-in-hand with finding the society you are analysing deeply flawed, especially if your aim—as often appears to be the case with Mandeville—is to reconcile your readers to the complex and compromised reality of the world we occupy. In the *Free Thoughts*, he writes that 'our State Hypochondriacks are daily buzzing in our Ears', and much as Mandeville the medical practitioner sought to cure his patients of their melancholy, so too Mandeville the 'State Physician' sought to cure his readers of their 'Discontent and Grumblings' with the current state of society.[79] The main problem with the 'State Hypochondriacks', or 'haughty Moralists', is not that they are mistaken about society's moral shortcomings, but, instead, that they fail to realise that these are the necessary price for living in a flourishing and wealthy state, and that the only alternative would involve economic ruin.[80] In this context, it is worth considering Phillip Hilton's speculative yet intriguing suggestion that Mandeville might have himself suffered from hypochondria or borderline depression.

79. *Free Thoughts*, 187. Mandeville repeatedly refers to how much the English grumble—most memorably by titling his 1705 verse *The Grumbling Hive*—and, in all cases, he argues that their grumblings are misplaced. See also, for example, *Pamphleteers*, 6; *Fable* I, 6–8, 24, 36; *Mischiefs*, 38; *Free Thoughts*, 8, 201. More generally, see J.A.W. Gunn, '"State Hypochondriacks" Dispraised: Mandeville versus the Active Citizen', in *Mandeville and Augustan Ideas*, 16–34; Turner, 'Mandeville against Luxury'. Elsewhere, Mandeville writes more generally of 'the Inconstancy and Discontentedness of Humane Nature, which always makes us repine and grumble at our present Condition' (*Virgin Unmask'd*, 33), and describes one of his characters 'as very severe against all *Grumbletonians*' (*Female Tatler*, no. 77: 142)—a description that could aptly be extended to Mandeville himself.

80. See especially *Female Tatler*, nos. 107, 109: 226–35; *Fable* I, 12–13, 183–85, 229, 325, 346, 355; *Fable* II, 106–107; *Letter to Dion*, 18–19, 31–34. What, then, are we to make of Mandeville's insistence that 'If I have shewn the way to worldly Greatness, I have always without Hesitation preferr'd the Road that leads to Virtue' (*Fable* I, 231, also 407; *Letter to Dion*, 31)? One way to reconcile these statements is to argue that Mandeville is insincere when he claims to prefer the road to virtue, or that people would be happiest in 'a small peaceable Society' (*Fable* I, 12–13). While viewing Mandeville as insincere on this point is plausible, I think his position is more complex. As moral ideals, Mandeville need not deny the appeal of small and virtuous societies—were this a realistic option, it may well be preferable. But Mandeville does not see this as a realistic option, at least for economically advanced societies. In this sense, the stark choice that Mandeville presents between the roads to worldly greatness and to virtue admits of only one answer. Nonetheless, presenting the choice in this way is not necessarily insincere and helps to convey the moral degeneracy of the road we have long followed. For related discussion of the complexity of Mandeville's views on the question of the simple life vs. worldly glory, see Thomas Stumpf, 'Mandeville, Asceticism, and the Spare Diet of the Golden Age', in *Mandeville and Augustan Ideas*, 97–116.

In the *Treatise*, by far the most autobiographical of his works, Mandeville claims that 'the beloved theme of all *Hypochondriaci* is Satyr, which I know is worth nothing, unless it bites.'[81] Satire is, of course, a beloved theme of Mandeville's own work, and it is possible that his writings reflect 'his own nature as a hypochondriac, seeking relief from the mental pain of the disease by way of humour at the expense of others'.[82] Whether or not Hilton's speculations are accurate, they at least show that there are a range of plausible explanations for why Mandeville chose to adopt a humorous or satirical tone. Indeed, the idea of writing a 'Satyr against Mankind'—and not a satire against morality—makes perfect sense for someone who views human nature and society as morally compromised to the core.[83]

A final reason to contest the insincerity objection is that Mandeville's explanation of why certain forms of conduct are regarded as vicious is eminently plausible, which we would not expect if his real aim was to overturn prevailing notions of virtue and vice. It will be the burden of the next section to defend the claim about plausibility in more detail, but, for the moment, it helps to return to the opening passage from 'Remark M', dedicated to pride. Even if pride is necessary to render society 'wealthy and flourishing', it is nevertheless

> most generally detested. What is very peculiar to this Faculty of ours, is, that those who are the fullest of it, are the least willing to connive at it in others; whereas the Heinousness of other Vices is the most extenuated by those who are guilty of 'em themselves. The Chaste Man hates Fornication, and Drunkenness is most abhorr'd by the Temperate; but none are so much offended at their Neighbour's Pride, as the proudest of all; and if any one can pardon it, it is the most Humble: From which I think we may justly

---

81. *Treatise*, 155. See also *Fable* II, 112, where Mandeville claims that while pride leads the 'stirring active Man' to love fashionable trends, it renders those of the opposite disposition 'sullen, and perhaps morose; and if he has Wit prone to Satyr, tho' he be otherwise a good natur'd Man.'

82. Hilton, *Bitter Honey*, 74–80, with the quotation at 79.

83. See John Wilmot, Earl of Rochester, *A Satyr Against Mankind* [1679], in *The Poems and Lucina's Rape*, ed. Keith Walker and Nicholas Fisher (Chichester: Wiley-Blackwell, 2010), 88–97. The *Satyr Against Mankind* exposes the pride of those who have exalted notions of human reason and excellence, and Mandeville paraphrases 'my Lord *Rochester*' approvingly at *Fable* I, 219–20. See also George Bluet, *Enquiry*, 'Preface', who observes that the 'most tolerable Part' of Mandeville's work 'is a *borrowed* Satyr upon the *Follies* and *Vices* of Mankind', although Bluet suggests that it was borrowed from Esprit and La Rochefoucauld, without mentioning Rochester.

infer, that it being odious to all the World, is a certain Sign that all the World is troubled with it. This all Men of Sense are ready to confess, and no body denies but that he has Pride in general. But, if you come to Particulars, you'll meet with few that will own any Action you can name of theirs to have proceeded from that Principle.[84]

Mandeville's observations here concern our moral appraisal of pride. The main point is simply that we do think of pride as a vice. This is supported by reflecting on our own conduct. Even if we acknowledge that we are not altogether free from pride—since denying this would be a self-defeating expression of the utmost pride—we remain unwilling to admit that our actions stem from pride on any given occasion. We often take pains to hide the passion away from others, for there are few things that cause us more shame than having our pride discovered.[85] Our strong aversion to pride is likewise corroborated by reflecting on how we judge other people's pride. We typically find the unadulterated expression of the high value that others hold for themselves morally repugnant or distasteful. The 'Pride of others is displeasing to us in every Shape',[86] which is why we have contrived artful ways of concealing the passion so that it goes undetected. Without such dissimulation, everyone would 'be offended at the barefac'd Pride of their Neighbours'.[87] We can even offer pride-based reasons for why we find other people's pride offensive. Pride leads us to care deeply about our relative standing amongst our peers. When others express an overvalued sense of their own worth then this will often convey, at least by implication, a higher relative standing between them and us than our own pride is willing to countenance. By contrast, one reason why polite manners are so effective is that they can transform a zero-sum game of pursuing social standing into cases where we take pride from flattering the pride of others. In complimenting you, I flatter your pride with my praise and flatter my own pride through my display of civility.[88]

Nothing in Mandeville's discussion counts against regarding pride as a vice. As we have seen, on the definition from the 'Enquiry', acting from pride should be classified as vicious if there is some prospect that doing so will be injurious to society. The main reason why such acts are likely to be injurious, however,

84. *Fable* I, 124.
85. See especially *Fable* I, 79–80; *Fable* II, 122.
86. *Fable* II, 126.
87. *Fable* II, 138.
88. See Chapter 1, 'Pride and shame', for further discussion.

is because we are so strongly averse to other people's pride, and thus displays of the passion will often cause offence, or even lead to conflict. Although Mandeville attributes the 'Distinction between *Virtue* and *Vice*' to 'the Contrivance of Politicians',[89] the content of virtue and vice supervenes on our natural appetites and aversions. It is not solely down to the arbitrary whim of politicians.[90] We must adopt certain ideas of virtue and vice to live peacefully together in large societies, regulating our behaviour accordingly.[91] If pride is 'odious to all the World', as Mandeville insists, then outward displays of this passion will always be liable to cause harm and should, therefore, be classified as vicious.

Mandeville rarely refers back to the definitions from the 'Enquiry' when discussing vices in the remainder of the *Fable*, instead preferring to reflect on the moral judgements that people do, as a matter of fact, make about passions like pride. Although he spends little time dwelling on the question "why regard pride as a vice?", he never even comes close to suggesting that we are wrong to do so. He does not attribute this view, for example, to a faulty understanding of human nature, or, like Hume, to the perverse influence of the schools and pulpit. For Mandeville, instead, our moral appraisal of pride derives from our innate aversion to displays of the passion; an aversion which becomes apparent through a close study of human nature. In other words, if we are committed to a naturalistic analysis of human nature and morality, then we should take our aversion to pride very seriously.

Is pride really that bad?

The main aim of this chapter, thus far, has been to defend the interpretative claim that Mandeville really does take the prevalence of pride as evidence of our morally compromised nature. I now turn to consider the plausibility of his

89. *Fable* I, 50.

90. Mandeville later defends the 'Enquiry' on this point, claiming that it aimed merely to explain how we could have originally come to recognise moral truths and describe certain forms of conduct as virtuous or vicious, for although 'the Truth of its Excellency is Eternal, the Words *Moral Virtue* themselves are not so, any more than Speech or Man himself' (*Origin of Honour*, ii). He draws a parallel with mathematical truths, which are eternal and unchanging, even though 'Knowledge of them never was acquir'd without great Labour and Depth of Thought' (*Origin of Honour*, viii). This argument may have been developed with William Law's (*Remarks*, 19–22) criticisms in mind, which compared moral truths to mathematical ones in denouncing the 'Enquiry'; see also Innes, 'Prefatory Introduction', xxix–xxxi.

91. On this point, see also Monro, *Ambivalence*, 231; Scribano, *Natura umana e società competitiva*, 157–61.

view. In light of the foregoing analysis, the first question to ask is whether, if we are committed to a naturalistic analysis of human nature, we should share Mandeville's misgivings about pride.

We can return to David Hume for a dissenting voice, for, as we saw earlier, he describes pride as an 'agreeable impression' of the mind and insists that it is not always vicious.[92] Against Mandeville's broadly Augustinian understanding of pride, Hume can be read as rehabilitating a more Aristotelian or pagan ethic that views pride more positively.[93] Yet the differences between the two are not as stark as they first appear.[94] In part, this is because they do 'dispute about words'. They do not define pride in the same way and Hume acknowledges that an 'excessive pride or over-weaning conceit of ourselves is always esteem'd vicious, and is universally hated'.[95] As pride is always excessive on Mandeville's definition, the divergence between the two on this point may seem slight. What is more, Hume observes that, as we are all proud to some degree, we find other people's displays of pride displeasing. It is for this reason that 'pride is universally blam'd and condemn'd by all mankind; as having a natural tendency to cause uneasiness in others by means of comparison.'[96] To ensure that pride does not cause offence, the rules of 'good-breeding and decency' require that we should avoid any outward expression of the passion. Even 'if we harbour pride in our breasts, we must carry a fair outside and have the appearance of modesty and mutual deference in all our conduct and behaviour.'[97] These points all resemble Mandeville's position.

---

92. Hume, *Treatise*, 2.1.7.8.

93. See Herdt, *Putting on Virtue*, 306–21; Lorenzo Greco, 'On Pride', *HUMANA.MENTE Journal of Philosophical Studies* 12, no. 35 (2019): 101–23. Similarly, with a closer focus on Cicero's influence on Hume, see Stuart-Buttle, *Moral Theology to Moral Philosophy*, 192–95.

94. The present discussion is concerned only with their moral evaluations of pride and nothing I say here should be taken to deny other important differences between the two (e.g. on sympathy or humanity). For the view that Hume's view of pride is indebted to Mandeville, see Schneider, *Paradox and Society*, 55, 113; and, more generally, Tolonen, *Mandeville and Hume*, especially 212–27. For discussion of Hume's account of pride as a critical response to Hobbes and Mandeville, see Jacqueline Taylor, *Reflecting Subjects: Passion, Sympathy, and Society in Hume's Philosophy* (Oxford: Oxford University Press, 2015), 130–53. For a balanced discussion of the ways in which Hume both follows and departs from Mandeville on pride, see Maurer, *Self-love, Egoism and the Selfish Hypothesis*, 181–86.

95. Hume, *Treatise*, 3.3.2.2.

96. Hume, *Treatise*, 3.3.2.7.

97. Hume, *Treatise*, 3.3.2.10; see also idem., *An Enquiry concerning the Principles of Morals* [1751], ed. Tom L. Beauchamp (Oxford: Oxford University Press, 1998), especially 8.9–11.

Mandeville and Hume clearly agree up to a point: we do have some innate aversion to witnessing displays of pride, and we must therefore learn to conceal the passion when conversing with others. Hume, however, accentuates the positive side of pride to a far greater degree than Mandeville, claiming that there is nothing 'more laudable, than to have a value for ourselves, where we really have qualities that are valuable.' Although we should not display our pride around others, it is important that we take a sense of pride in our lives, since this 'makes us sensible of our own merit, and gives us confidence and assurance in all our projects and enterprizes.'[98] Humility is only for outward display, whereas pride should motivate us within. The merit of pride, for Hume then, is derived both from 'its utility and its agreeableness to ourselves'.[99] Yet even Hume's positive assessment is qualified. Consider his claim that the 'world naturally esteems a well-regulated pride, which secretly animates our conduct, without breaking out into such indecent expressions of vanity, as may offend the vanity of others.'[100] This is all quite Mandevillean, as the universal esteem paid to a well-regulated pride depends upon it *secretly* animating our conduct. In other words, we esteem pride only when it does not appear in its true colours. But this implies that pride's true colours are disagreeable, which is precisely Mandeville's point.

There are, then, two main differences between Mandeville's and Hume's moral evaluations of pride. The first is less concerned with their accounts of the passion itself and more with their wider moral philosophies. They broadly agree that pride is both agreeable to ourselves and, when regulated, socially beneficial, but Mandeville does not consider either of these considerations sufficient for denying its status as a vice. This could lead us to conclude that Mandeville's account is too one-sided. From Hume's perspective, Mandeville is right to identify our innate aversion to pride, but he fails to give due account to its positive side.[101] To this criticism, Mandeville could reply that

98. Hume, *Treatise*, 3.3.2.18.

99. Hume, *Treatise*, 3.3.2.14.

100. Hume, *Treatise*, 3.3.2.13; see also 3.3.2.11 (emphasis added): 'a genuine and hearty pride, or self-esteem, *if well conceal'd* and well founded, is essential to the character of a man of honour, and that there is no quality of the mind, which is more indispensably requisite to procure the esteem and approbation of mankind.'

101. The idea that pride has two very different sides, or facets, is prominent in recent psychological research, some of which distinguishes between 'authentic' and 'hubristic' pride. The former is associated more with sociable qualities and prestige; the latter with unsociable qualities and dominance. For a helpful overview, see Jessica L. Tracy, Azim F. Shariff, and Joey T.

the positive side of pride is not what he calls pride at all, thereby reducing the dispute to semantics—this being the second main disagreement between the two. Indeed, if we recall the distinction that Mandeville draws between self-liking and pride in *Origin of Honour*, then Hume's analysis of the positive side of pride is arguably closer to Mandeville's notion of a moderate and well-regulated self-liking than it is to pride.[102] Much like Mandeville's account of self-liking, Hume recognises that we still need to conceal the outward display of our pride, even when it is based on a fair appraisal of our worth. As I argued earlier, however, Mandeville continues to explain a great deal of human behaviour as resulting from pride in his later works, so another way of casting the disagreement between Hume and Mandeville concerns how and when to differentiate between a well-regulated desire for esteem and (excessive) pride.

Pride vs. a well-regulated desire for esteem

Few of Mandeville's eighteenth-century critics went as far as Hume in trying to overturn the longstanding association between pride and vice,[103] but others still charged Mandeville with conflating pride with a well-regulated desire for esteem. For Archibald Campbell, for example, our desire for social esteem is central to explaining human sociability, yet Mandeville entangled himself in 'a strange Jumble of Ideas' by calling this pride, which is 'only to affix a very bad Name to a very good Principle, and from thence to deduce very false

---

Cheng, 'A Naturalist's View of Pride', *Emotion Review* 2, no. 2 (2010): 163–77. The authentic and hubristic facets of pride do not map exactly onto the positive and negative sides discussed here, but they at least help to illustrate the complexity of the passion.

102. In this context, see also Hume, *Enquiry concerning Morals*, Appendix 4, §3: 'the *sentiment* of conscious worth, the self-satisfaction proceeding from a review of a man's own conduct and character . . . has no proper name in our language.' This echoes Mandeville's discussion of a moderate and well-disguised self-liking, which 'has no Name, tho' Men act from that and no other Principle.' *Origin of Honour*, 3, also 7; see also Tolonen, *Mandeville and Hume*, 243–44. In a note to the passage from the Appendix, Hume adds that the 'term, *pride*, is commonly taken in a bad sense; but this sentiment seems indifferent, and may be either good or bad, according as it is well or ill founded, and according to the other circumstances which accompany it.' Hume associates this with the 'great confusion' arising from the use of *amour-propre* by La Rochefoucauld and other French moralists.

103. This is arguably still the dominant association today. For the exception that proves the rule (because its title presupposes that pride needs justifying), see Kristján Kristjánsson, *Justifying Emotions: Pride and Jealousy* (London and New York: Routledge, 2002), especially 104–35.

Consequences.'[104] John Brown likewise complained that 'the Desire of being esteemed by others, [Mandeville] stigmatizes with the Name of *Pride*',[105] and George Bluet invoked biblical evidence to show that our desire for esteem is necessary for us to 'fill any Station of Life with Advantage to the rest of Mankind'.[106] According to Adam Smith, perhaps most famously, 'the desire of acquiring esteem by what is really estimable' is certainly meritorious, and closely approximates loving virtue for its own sake.[107] These critics all maintain that there is nothing wrong with being motivated by the desire for social esteem in the first place, as long as we genuinely merit it. For Campbell again, so far from being vicious, 'the Desire for *Esteem*' should be taken, 'in the general and main Conduct of Life, to be the *great Motive to Virtue*.'[108]

This line of criticism is not always easy to differentiate from the objection that I addressed in the previous chapter, according to which Mandeville conflates pride with praiseworthy or disinterested motives.[109] Nonetheless, there is a clear analytical distinction between the two, even if they are sometimes run together in practice. In one case, we are not motivated by the desire for social esteem at all, even if we take pleasure in receiving esteem subsequently. In the other case, we are motivated by a desire for social esteem, but this need not be vicious and can even be virtuous. The importance of the latter case, considered here, is that it grants the explanatory power of our desire for esteem, yet questions whether Mandeville attributes too much of our conduct to an excessive form of this desire—pride—as opposed to a moderate

104. Archibald Campbell, *An Enquiry Into the Original of Moral Virtue* (Edinburgh, 1733), 89.

105. Brown, *Essays*, 158.

106. Bluet, *Enquiry*, 73–74.

107. Smith, *Theory of Moral Sentiments*, VII.ii.4.8.

108. Campbell, *Enquiry*, 324, also 448. Campbell defends the view that all actions are motivated by self-love, but seeks to show that this is compatible with believing in natural sociability and does not undermine religion or morality—these being the pernicious implications widely associated with the self-love theories of Hobbes, Spinoza, and Mandeville. For helpful discussion of Campbell's criticisms of Mandeville, see Christian Maurer, 'Archibald Campbell's Views of Self-Cultivation and Self-Denial in Context', *Journal of Scottish Philosophy* 10, no. 1 (2012): 13–27; idem., 'What Can an Egoist say to an Egoist? On Archibald Campbell's Criticisms of Bernard Mandeville', *Journal of Scottish Philosophy* 12, no. 1 (2014): 1–18; idem., *Self-love, Egoism and the Selfish Hypothesis*, 141–70; Sagar, 'Sociability, Luxury and Sympathy'; Tim Stuart-Buttle, 'Recognition, Sociability and Intolerance: A Study of Archibald Campbell (1691–1756)', *Global Intellectual History* 5, no. 2 (2020): 231–46.

109. See Chapter 1, 'Pride vs. praiseworthy motives' (where Smith's objections are considered in greater detail).

and well-regulated form. This dispute largely turns on the question of how to judge whether our desire for esteem should be classified as excessive or well-regulated, which is an evaluative question as much as it is an explanatory one.

The idea that we act only from pride, and not from a well-regulated desire for esteem, might seem like a hangover from the Augustinian background discussed earlier in the chapter. For the most austere Augustinian moralists, a well-regulated desire for esteem is all but impossible given our fallen state.[110] If we are guilty of pride whenever we fail to acknowledge our own wretchedness in the face of God's greatness, as Blaise Pascal insists,[111] then it is difficult to see how a well-regulated desire for esteem could ever be possible. There is little to be proud of once we recognise the extent of our sinfulness. Nevertheless, and as I argued when discussing criticisms of Stoic pride, the claim that we regularly overvalue ourselves remains plausible without invoking comparisons with God or assumptions about our fallen nature. Mandeville's analysis is especially incisive when it comes to the stories we like to tell about the place of reason or rationality in determining our behaviour. Such stories are central to his explanation of the origin of our ideas of moral virtue, where wise politicians and lawgivers 'extoll'd the Excellency of our Nature above other Animals' by bestowing 'a thousand Encomiums on the Rationality of our Souls'.[112] Whenever we embrace these encomiums and believe that reason governs our conduct, Mandeville argues, we are merely deceiving ourselves and flattering our pride. Our reason is deployed in service of our passions 'and Self-love pleads to all human Creatures for their different Views, still furnishing every individual with Arguments to justify their Inclinations.'[113]

Mandeville's position on the motivational weakness of reason finds support from psychological research indicating that a great deal of moral reasoning is about offering post hoc rationalisations for our behaviour and judgements,

---

110. On this point, see also Maurer, *Self-love, Egoism and the Selfish Hypothesis*, 10: 'Augustinian theology has a strong tendency to dispute that there are, in the deplorable reality of the postlapsarian state, any *legitimate* grounds for self-esteem'.

111. Blaise Pascal, *Pensées and Other Writings* [1670], trans. Honor Levi, ed. Anthony Levi (Oxford: Oxford University Press, 1995), no. 225: 'Knowing God without knowing our own wretchedness leads to pride.'

112. *Fable* I, 43. On the importance Mandeville attached to regarding ourselves as superior to other animals, see John J. Callanan, 'Mandeville on Pride and Animal Nature', in *Mandeville's Tropology of Paradoxes*, 132–35.

113. *Fable* I, 333.

rather than about determining them in the first place.[114] More generally, there is now a wealth of evidence from social psychology on self-serving biases, which characteristically involve taking responsibility for our positive qualities and successes, while blaming others or external factors for our negative traits and failures.[115] Everyone has their own anecdotes. Academics will be familiar with the never-ending ingenuity of their peers to explain why their latest paper was rejected for reasons that had nothing to do with its quality, whereas very few acknowledge the converse degree of good fortune involved when their work is accepted for publication. Students will have similar stories to tell about the marks they receive. When we succeed, we deserve it. When we fail, it is bad luck, or, worse still, someone else's fault.

Mandeville is thus on strong psychological ground in arguing that we regularly overvalue our own capacities and achievements. Does it follow that, in such cases, our desire for esteem is excessive, as opposed to being well-regulated? As we have seen, Mandeville does allow for a moderate and well-regulated form of self-liking, which need not manifest itself in the vice of pride. Yet as soon as our actions convey the high opinion we hold of ourselves then we move into the terrain of pride, with self-liking rendered excessive whenever it is not successfully concealed.[116] To recall, Mandeville detects pride

114. Most famously, see Jonathan Haidt, 'The Emotional Dog and Its Rational Tail: A Social Intuitionist Approach to Moral Judgment', *Psychological Review* 108, no. 4 (2001): 814–34. For an overview of critical responses to Haidt on this point, see John C. Gibbs, *Moral Development and Reality: Beyond the Theories of Kohlberg, Hoffman, and Haidt*, 3rd ed. (New York: Oxford University Press, 2014), especially 33–35. As early as 1922, Arthur Lovejoy wrote to F. B. Kaye that Mandeville's 'chief significance' lay 'in the history of what would nowadays be called social psychology. In insisting upon the sub-rational determination of most (if not all) of our motives, and in regarding the reasons which men give for their acts as largely a "rationalizing" explanation, necessitated by self-esteem, of these subconscious motivations, he, of course, anticipated a very recent fashion in psychology.' Kaye quotes this letter at *Fable* II, 452.

115. For a helpful starting point, see David G. Myers and Jean M. Twenge, *Exploring Social Psychology*, 8th ed. (New York: McGraw Hill Education, 2018), 31–39. For a survey of the social psychology research on how we use self-enhancement and self-promotion strategies to maintain a positive self-conception, which includes evidence that such strategies are found across different cultures (even if the specific form they take is culturally variable), see Mark D. Alicke and Constantine Sedikides, 'Self-enhancement and Self-protection: What they are and what they do', *European Review of Social Psychology* 20, no. 1 (2009): 1–48. On the evolutionary benefits of our 'myside bias', see Hugo Mercer and Dan Sperber, *The Enigma of Reason* (Cambridge, MA: Harvard University Press, 2017), 218–21 and *passim*. Mercer and Sperber argue that one of the two evolutionary functions of reason is to allow us to justify ourselves to others.

116. *Origin of Honour*, 3, 6–7.

when we overvalue and imagine better things of ourselves 'than any impartial Judge, thoroughly acquainted with all [our] Qualities and Circumstances, could allow'.[117] Even if one grants that we regularly overvalue ourselves, would an impartial judge disapprove of all cases where we desire social esteem to reinforce our own sense of self-worth? Smith, for example, suggests that an impartial spectator would tolerate some degree of pride, for it is usually better to be a little too proud than a little too humble.[118] If we are all disposed to overvalue ourselves, albeit to varying degrees, then perhaps our desire for esteem should be deemed excessive only when it exceeds social norms. Someone would then be guilty of excessive pride when they overvalue themselves or seek unmerited approval *to a greater degree* than would be expected given the circumstances. By contrast, a well-regulated desire for esteem, understood this way, would involve a relative judgement based on comparison with the prevailing social norms, rather than an all-things-considered appraisal of our conduct.[119] This is more or less Hume's position.[120] Social norms will vary in different times and places, and even between groups within society, as Hume acknowledges,[121] but in all cases our desire for esteem should be judged either excessive or well-regulated in relation to the social norms in question.

Does this way of thinking through what makes a desire for social esteem excessive remove the moral sting from Mandeville's analysis? To some degree, perhaps, especially when we reflect on the everyday judgements we make of others and they make of us. No sensible person doubts that humans are deeply flawed creatures, but we tend not to dwell on this too much when interacting with other people. Society would be insufferable if we constantly reminded one another of our self-serving biases and overvaluations of our conduct. Mandeville, of course, saw this very clearly. In so far as his psychological analysis is broadly accurate, though, I think there remains something morally

117. *Fable* I, 124.

118. Smith, *Theory of Moral Sentiments*, VI.iii.53.

119. For a similar point, see Smith, *Theory of Moral Sentiments*, VI.iii.23, who distinguishes between two standards of evaluation: first, 'the idea of exact propriety and perfection', and, second, 'the degree of approximation to this idea which is commonly attained in the world, and which the greater part of our friends and companions, of our rivals and competitors, may have actually arrived at.' Smith claims that we judge ourselves based on both standards to varying degrees in different cases.

120. On the comparative approach outlined here, see Hume, 'Dignity or Meanness', 82–84.

121. See Hume, *Treatise*, 3.3.2.11, for the claim that we must regulate pride in conformity with 'our rank and station in the world, whether it be fix'd by our birth, fortune, employments, talents or reputation.'

unsettling about the extent to which we are motivated by a desire for esteem, even if this is divulged only upon closer inspection of our conduct. The most troubling insight is simply that we do feel impelled to conceal our desire for social esteem, for we are conscious of how others would judge us were it to appear in its true colours.

Consider an example. Suppose that I regularly do voluntary work in the local community, even though this involves giving up other things that I enjoy. Having reflected on the consequences of undertaking this work, I genuinely believe (and am right to believe) that it benefits the community. So far, so good. My sole motivation for undertaking the work, however, is that I desire that other members of my community think highly of me. Does discovering this affect the way my voluntary work should be evaluated? On the one hand, we would probably be reluctant to describe my conduct as vicious; after all, I do not flaunt my pride in an offensive manner and have instead channelled it towards socially beneficial ends. Desiring some praise for doing so hardly seems unreasonable. On the other hand, discovering my true motivation may devalue or detract from the moral character of my conduct to some degree. Indeed, this is the reason why I would never disclose my true motivation. If I desire that members of my community think highly of me then I will want them to believe that I act from public-spirited or other-regarding motives. In this example, I am confident that an impartial judge, thoroughly acquainted with my motives, would disapprove of my desire for esteem. I have concealed my true motivation precisely because I am aware that, were my peers to realise the extent to which it explains my conduct, they would judge me unfavourably. Compared to their expectations, then, my desire for esteem is excessive, even if they never discover this.[122]

One objection to this example is that its plausibility rests on stipulating the desire for social esteem as my *sole* motivation. What about cases that involve mixed or multiple motives? Suppose that I am motivated by the desire for social esteem *and* by intrinsically other-regarding considerations.[123] I care for the community for its own sake, that is, as well as mine. Where multiple motives are at play, the presence of the desire for esteem might not devalue our evaluation of someone else's conduct.[124] If this is the case, it could simply be

---

122. Note that Mandeville sometimes classifies our overvaluation of ourselves as excessive even when 'the Excess of it never appears outwardly', *Fable* II, 91.

123. This objection loosely follows Hume, 'Dignity or Meanness', 86.

124. Although see Brennan and Pettit, *Economy of Esteem*, 36–39, who argue that, even in cases of mixed motivation, we have a reason to disesteem someone's behaviour to the degree

because, in practice, it is very difficult to tease complementary motives apart and determine which has greater sway.[125] We tend to give others the benefit of the doubt, much as civility requires.[126] More importantly, however, it could also suggest that our judgement in the original example is explained more by the *absence* of other (e.g. public-spirited) motives than by the *presence* of the desire for social esteem.

Even if Mandeville does not address this last point directly,[127] integrating it with his account helps to highlight precisely what is at stake. If we find Mandeville's analysis of human nature and sociability unsettling, then it is probably not because he shows us that even our most virtuous deeds are accompanied by a well-regulated desire for social esteem. As his critics rightly point out, there is nothing especially disconcerting about that insight. This may still involve overvaluing ourselves to some degree, but an impartial judge is unlikely to deem this excessive and condemn it as pride. The truly disquieting implications of Mandeville's analysis of pride stem from the far stronger claim, which assigns psychological primacy or dominance to our desire for esteem, and in doing so goes well beyond what any social norms or impartial judges could allow.

Conclusion

In *Origin of Honour*, Mandeville draws a contrast between the 'Moralists', who endeavour 'to rout Vice, and clear the Heart of all hurtful Appetites and Inclinations', much as if they were molecatchers ridding the country of vermin, and the 'Naturalist', who prefers to 'dissect Moles, try Experiments upon them, and enquire into the Nature of their Handicraft'.[128] Mandeville is the naturalist

---

that we think they are acting in a virtuous way only to solicit our approval. Brennan's and Pettit's main point, however, is that this does not render the desire for esteem self-defeating, as Jon Elster had suggested in *Sour Grapes: Studies in the Subversion of Rationality* (Cambridge: Cambridge University Press, 1983), 66–71.

125. See *Fable* I, 84.

126. See *Fable* I, 133.

127. At one point in the 'Third Dialogue', Horatio objects that someone might 'have had several Motives' determining their action. Cleomenes responds by denying that the person in question did, in fact, act from any public-spirited motives, but he grants, at least by implication, that we should change our evaluation of the person's conduct were we to discover that public-spirited and pride-based motives had both been at play; see *Fable* II, 120–21.

128. *Origin of Honour*, 5.

throughout, seeking to expose how human societies really function, rather than trying to bring about some sort of moral reformation. He is not a moralist in this sense, for his analysis is rarely prescriptive, and when it is his prescriptions are not based on purifying our morals. As a naturalist, however, Mandeville has plenty to say about morals. This is quite appropriate: a naturalistic analysis of human sociability should be concerned with understanding how moral norms function in society, since these play a large role in determining our behaviour.

Mandeville maintains that pride is a vice. I have argued that we can make sense of this position from a naturalistic perspective, which is to say that a close study of human nature reveals that the aversion we feel towards the display of this passion is well-grounded. In claiming that it is well-grounded, I mean simply that it is based on plausible observations about our moral sentiments and judgements. To be sure, Mandeville does not define vice in terms of pre-existing moral sentiments, but, in some cases at least, our natural appetites and aversions do factor into working out what actions 'might be injurious to any of the Society, or ever render [ourselves] less serviceable to others.'[129] The injury of pride is largely based on its propensity to antagonise people and, as we have seen, it is precisely when our desire for high esteem 'is excessive, and so openly shewn as to give Offence to others' that it 'is counted a Vice and call'd Pride.'[130] For this reason, amongst others, I see no grounds for concluding that Mandeville was trying to overturn the prevailing understanding of pride by exposing it to ridicule, for he simply does not show it to be ridiculous. Nor do I think that his assessment of pride depends on accepting any theological assumptions about the vices that characterise our fallen nature. Mandeville does claim that his analysis applies only to our fallen state, yet this is compatible with a naturalistic approach in the sense that the story of the fall presents a compelling picture of the human condition. Naturalists should focus their attention on our present state, irrespective of whether they believe there was ever a prelapsarian state of innocence.

The upshot of both this and the previous chapter is that there are good reasons to find Mandeville's moral psychology of pride unsettling. If displays of pride are typically met with disapprobation and are liable to provoke

129. *Fable* I, 48.
130. *Origin of Honour*, 3.

offence or discord, then it makes sense to describe the passion as a vice, or at least to recognise that the moral character of our conduct is in some way compromised due to its roots in pride. Pride is not a passion that we can bear to see in its true colours—either in ourselves or in others—which is why a pride-centred theory of sociability, as we shall see more in the next chapter, relies on us hiding the passion away and learning to become hypocrites.

3

Sociability, Hypocrisy, and Virtue

IN 'A Search into the Nature of Society', added to the 1723 edition of *The Fable of the Bees*, Mandeville declares that 'it is impossible we could be sociable Creatures without Hypocrisy.'[1] He associates hypocrisy with dissimulation: hiding away the sentiments and motives from which we act, while putting on an outward appearance we do not feel within.[2] Although the etymological roots of hypocrisy are theatrical, by Mandeville's day its connotations were decidedly moral and religious.[3] Hypocrisy is exemplified by feigning religious sincerity or hiding our vices behind a mask of virtue. As François de la Rochefoucauld memorably remarked, 'Hypocrisy is a form of homage that vice pays to virtue.'[4] This understanding of hypocrisy, which permeates Mandeville's work, is closely related to the moral psychology of pride explored in the previous two

---

1. *Fable* I, 349.

2. For explicit statements to this effect, see *Fable* I, 281; *Free Thoughts*, 31; *Origin of Honour*, 202.

3. As is still the case, according to the *Oxford English Dictionary* definition: 'The assuming of a false appearance of virtue or goodness, with dissimulation of real character or inclinations, esp. in respect of religious life or beliefs; hence in general sense, dissimulation, pretence, sham.' This definition is the starting point for Judith N. Shklar's seminal discussion of hypocrisy in *Ordinary Vices* (Cambridge, MA and London: The Belknap Press of Harvard University Press, 1984), 45–86, with the definition at 47. On the ecclesiological context in explaining the rise of concerns about, and charges of, hypocrisy in post-Reformation England, see James Simpson, *Permanent Revolution: The Reformation and the Illiberal Roots of Liberalism* (Cambridge, MA and London: The Belknap Press of Harvard University Press, 2019), 111–56. For a more general sketch of how the idea of hypocrisy has developed from its origin in Greek theatre to the present day, see Béla Szabados and Eldon Soifer, *Hypocrisy: Ethical Investigations* (Peterborough, ON: Broadview Press, 2004), 19–35.

4. La Rochefoucauld, *Collected Maxims*, no. 218.

chapters. One reason why passions such as pride and shame are so important is that they lead us to conceal our self-centred motives and present ourselves as genuinely civil or even virtuous creatures.[5] In the previous chapter I argued that Mandeville sees human nature as morally compromised to the core, and this becomes all the more apparent once we appreciate the extent of hypocrisy he detects underlying our moral and sociable practices.

While it is well-known that one of Mandeville's main goals was to expose the hypocrisy of his adversaries,[6] the role of hypocrisy in his theory of sociability has received little sustained attention.[7] It is a topic that merits greater analysis, not least because there is something a touch puzzling about the way Mandeville presents the relationship between hypocrisy, sociability, and virtue, which comes into view when we consider his protestations against Anthony Ashley Cooper, Third Earl of Shaftesbury—the prime target of the 'Search'. Mandeville criticises Shaftesbury's notions of virtue as 'a vast Inlet to Hypocrisy', but, as far as I am aware, no one has noticed that his various arguments in support of this criticism pull in different directions. On the one hand, Mandeville claims that Shaftesbury's notions, if made habitual, foster self-deception and lead us to counterfeit love of society and public regard.[8] On the other hand, Mandeville claims that Shaftesbury's understanding of virtue is less

5. See especially *Fable* I, 134–35, 145–46, 153, 279; *Letter to Dion*, 20.

6. See, for example, Castiglione, 'Considering Things Minutely', 467, who claims that a 'central feature of Mandeville's literary production appears to be the aim of unmasking social hypocrisy'; or, more recently, Luban, 'Mandeville as Moralist and Materialist', 848, who writes that hypocrisy was the 'fundamental theme' of Mandeville's social criticism, and that 'it is difficult to come up with a thinker who was more exhaustive in investigating and exposing hypocrisy'.

7. The most notable exception is David Runciman's chapter on Mandeville in *Political Hypocrisy*, 45–73, also 209–12. While my analysis overlaps with Runciman's in places, his is more focused on how to judge the hypocrisy of politicians, and less on the question of sociability. More recently, see also Branchi, *Pride, Manners, and Morals*, 103–10; Sandy Berkovski, 'Mandeville on Self-liking, Morality, and Hypocrisy', *Intellectual History Review* 32, no. 1 (2022): 157–78 (Branchi and Berkovski both engage with an earlier version of parts of this chapter, first published online in 2020 and now as Robin Douglass, 'Bernard Mandeville on the Use and Abuse of Hypocrisy', *Political Studies* 70, no. 2 (2022): 465–82). On the role of hypocrisy in 'An Essay on Charity, and Charity-Schools', see Jenny Davidson, *Hypocrisy and the Politics of Politeness: Manners and Morals from Locke to Austen* (Cambridge: Cambridge University Press, 2004), 31–40. For discussion of how Mandeville both drew upon and reworked ideas of hypocrisy from seventeenth-century French moralists, see Dickey, 'Pride, Hypocrisy and Civility'.

8. *Fable* I, 33; *Fable* II, 109.

advantageous to society than the contrary view that virtue requires self-denial.[9] Both claims could be true, of course, but given that hypocrisy and counterfeited (rather than genuine or 'real') virtue are central to Mandeville's own explanation of sociability, and that he appeals to considerations of social utility to explain the origin of virtue, we may suspect that Mandeville's criticisms of Shaftesbury do not quite add up.

The main aim of this chapter is to elucidate how Mandeville's position on hypocrisy relates to his views on sociability and the nature of virtue. These are the two most important points of contention with Shaftesbury, and a more general goal is thus to make sense of Mandeville's opposition to Shaftesbury, as it emerges out of the 'Search'.[10] The 'Search' is roughly an essay of two halves: in the first, Mandeville criticises Shaftesbury's ideas directly; in the second, he lays out his rival account of sociability in more detail.[11] My approach here is similar: the earlier parts of this chapter reconstruct Mandeville's criticisms, with his own ideas of hypocrisy, sociability, and virtue coming into sharper relief as the chapter progresses. Where in previous chapters I set out Mandeville's ideas in detail before considering criticisms of his position, this chapter takes a slightly different approach by placing Shaftesbury and Mandeville in dialogue from the outset and addressing objections as and when they arise.

Enter Shaftesbury

Towards the beginning of the 'Search', Mandeville declares that an attentive reader who compares the *Fable* with Shaftesbury's *Characteristicks of Men, Manners, Opinions, Times* 'will soon perceive that two Systems cannot be more opposite than his Lordship's and mine.'[12] The *Characteristicks* was first published in 1711,[13] but there is no evidence that it was on Mandeville's radar when

9. *Origin of Honour*, x.

10. While I focus on criticisms first articulated in the 'Search', I draw on parts of Mandeville's later works where he develops these further.

11. Mandeville does not explicitly present the 'Search' in this way, but something like the transition I am suggesting is implied at *Fable* I, 344.

12. *Fable* I, 324; also *Fable* II, 356.

13. Many of the treatises included in the *Characteristicks* had appeared previously; most notably, for present purposes, *An Inquiry Concerning Virtue, or Merit* (1699), *Sensus Communis: An Essay on the Freedom of Wit and Humour* (1709), *The Moralists, A Philosophical Rhapsody* (1709), and *Soliloquy: or, Advice to an Author* (1710). All references to Shaftesbury are given to

completing the 1714 edition of the *Fable*. The earliest sign of engagement is in the *Free Thoughts* (1720), where Mandeville lifts some of his references to other sources from the *Characteristicks*, typically without any acknowledgement, although he does at one point allude to Shaftesbury as 'one of the most Polite Authors of the Age'.[14] Whatever his view of Shaftesbury in the *Free Thoughts*, Mandeville turns unequivocally against him in the 1723 edition of the *Fable*. This encounter marks what is arguably the most significant development in Mandeville's philosophical trajectory, with his most important subsequent works taking the form of a dialogue between Cleomenes, who defends the *Fable*, and Horatio, 'a great Stickler for the Social System' of Shaftesbury.[15]

The 1714 and 1723 editions of the *Fable* are, in some respects, very different works.[16] The later edition is nearly twice as long and the two new essays—the 'Search', and 'An Essay on Charity, and Charity-Schools'—are each far lengthier than any of the individual essays or 'Remarks' from 1714.[17] If nothing else,

---

Characteristicks of Men, Manners, Opinions, Times, ed. Douglas Den Uyl in 3 vols. (Indianapolis: Liberty Fund, 2001).

14. *Free Thoughts*, 139. On the passages Mandeville lifted from Shaftesbury, see Irwin Primer, 'Mandeville and Shaftesbury: Some Facts and Problems', in *Mandeville Studies*, 126–141. Primer argues that Mandeville's view of Shaftesbury was wholly positive in the *Free Thoughts*, which makes the turn against him in 1723 even more puzzling; an interpretation also endorsed by Hundert, *Enlightenment's Fable*, 122. Cf. Stuart-Buttle, *Moral Theology to Moral Philosophy*, 141n, who suggests that Mandeville's comment that 'Religion, and whatever is sacred, can never become the proper Objects of Ridicule' (*Free Thoughts*, 200), should be read as a veiled attack on Shaftesbury, to which it could be added that to describe someone as a polite author is a rather backhanded compliment on Mandeville's view of politeness.

15. *Fable* II, 20.

16. See also Ben Dew, 'Spurs to Industry in Bernard Mandeville's *Fable of the Bees*', *British Journal for Eighteenth-Century Studies* 28, no. 2 (2005): 151–65, who argues that Mandeville's view on the labouring poor changes dramatically between the 1714 and 1723 editions, in response to the South Sea crisis. While Dew's focus is very different to mine in this chapter, his article is both exemplary and rare in its attention to the changes between the two editions. Branchi's recent book also dedicates a chapter to the expanded *Fable* and *Modest Defence*, claiming that they 'represent a new phase in Mandeville's thought'; see Branchi, *Pride, Manners, and Morals*, 98.

17. With calculations based on page numbers from the 1723 edition (so as not to be distorted by Kaye's editorial notes), 'An Enquiry Into the Origin of Moral Virtue' runs to 18 pages and 'Remark R'—the longest from the 1714 edition, where it was originally 'Remark Q'—to 32 pages. The 'Essay on Charity', by contrast, is 86 pages, and the 'Search' is 58 pages. The 1723 edition also includes two new 'Remarks' (N and T), and considerably expands two others (C and Y, the latter of which had originally been Remark V). See Kaye's 'Description of the Editions' at *Fable* II, 392–93, for a helpful overview.

this indicates that, by 1723, Mandeville considered the topics he was addressing to be worthy of more sustained analysis. From a philosophical perspective, the 1723 edition is a considerably richer text than the earlier one (*Fable II* would prove richer still), which can largely be explained by Mandeville's confrontation with his newfound antagonist. The *Fable* (in all its editions) is a wide-ranging work, and we should be wary of reducing its aims to any one context or target alone. Nonetheless, much of the original *Grumbling Hive* verse (1705) and the 1714 edition of the *Fable* can profitably be understood in the context of Mandeville's opposition to the Societies for the Reformation of Manners and his polemics with Joseph Addison and Richard Steele, which were also played out in the pages of the *Female Tatler*.[18] In addition, some scholars have followed István Hont in reading Mandeville's early work in an anti-Fénelonian context; that is, as countering the arguments against luxury set down by François Fénelon in his highly influential *Les aventures de Télémaque* (1699).[19] In so far as this context proves illuminating, however, it is more because Fénelon's ideas were in the air, so to speak, for Mandeville never responded explicitly to *Télémaque* (and he was usually happy to name his targets). When Mandeville turned his attention to the *Characteristicks*, then, we see him engaging directly with a work of philosophical depth and influence for the first time.

It is easy to see why Shaftesbury served as Mandeville's ideal sparring partner.[20] Shaftesbury never read the *Fable*, but many of his criticisms of Hobbes, Locke, and other modern philosophers could straightforwardly be extended

18. For helpful studies situating Mandeville's ideas against this background, see W. A. Speck, 'Mandeville and the Eutopia Seated in the Brain', in *Mandeville Studies*, 66–79; Horne, *Social Thought*, 1–18; Goldsmith, *Private Vices, Public Benefits*, 21–27, 35–46; idem., 'Introduction', 11–74.

19. István Hont, 'The Early Enlightenment Debate on Commerce and Luxury', in *The Cambridge History of Eighteenth-Century Political Thought*, ed. Mark Goldie and Robert Wokler (Cambridge: Cambridge University Press, 2006), 387–95; Runciman, *Political Hypocrisy*, 50; Brooke, *Philosophic Pride*, 153–55; Tolonen, *Mandeville and Hume*, 41n; Rudi Verburg, 'Bernard Mandeville's Vision of the Social Utility of Pride and Greed', *The European Journal of the History of Economic Thought* 22, no. 4 (2015), 666–67; Stuart-Buttle, *Moral Theology to Moral Philosophy*, 120–21.

20. An additional consideration is that Mandeville may have been worried about Shaftesbury's rising influence at the time. On this point, placing Mandeville's criticisms within the wider context of Shaftesbury's eighteenth-century reception history, see Isabel Rivers, *Reason, Grace, and Sentiment: A Study of the Language of Religion and Ethics in England 1660–1780, Volume 2: Shaftesbury to Hume* (Cambridge: Cambridge University Press, 2000), especially 173–79.

to Mandeville.[21] Shaftesbury dismissed the 'Play of Words' of those who attempt to reduce all human behaviour to self-love,[22] for example, and remained unpersuaded by others who emphasise 'the Corruption of Man's Heart' to expose 'the Falshood of *human Virtue*' as a pale imitation of the moral austerity supposedly demanded by Christianity.[23] Had *An Inquiry Concerning Virtue* post-dated the *Fable*, we would suspect Shaftesbury of having Mandeville in his immediate sights when insisting that nothing 'cou'd more strongly imply an unjust Ordinance, a Blot and Imperfection in the general Constitution of Things, than to suppose Virtue the natural Ill, and Vice the natural Good of any Creature'.[24] Shaftesbury would have considered Mandeville's notorious 'private vices, public benefits' paradox as tantamount to atheism, for if vice is more prosperous than virtue 'then is all Order in reality inverted, and supreme Wisdom lost'.[25] Shaftesbury instead regarded virtue as the 'Prop and Ornament of human Affairs; which upholds Communitys, maintains Union . . . [and] by which Countrys, as well as private Familys, flourish and are happy . . . And, thus, VIRTUE is *the Good,* and VICE *the Ill* of every-one'.[26]

For present purposes, I am not overly concerned with whether Mandeville's presentation of Shaftesbury's philosophy is fair or accurate. My aim, rather, is to illuminate the aspects of the *Characteristicks* to which Mandeville responded, thereby allowing us to better understand the development of his ideas. Mandeville was hardly a charitable reader of Shaftesbury, but his

21. For passages clearly set out against Hobbes, some of which are discussed more below, see Shaftesbury, *Sensus Communis,* in *Characteristicks,* vol. 1, ii.1 (56–59), iii.3 (75n); *Moralists,* in *Characteristicks,* vol. 2, ii.4 (175–81). Although Shaftesbury does not mention his former teacher explicitly in the *Characteristicks,* much of his philosophy was set out against Locke, on which see Rivers, *Reason, Grace, and Sentiment,* 89–92, 126–29; Daniel Carey, *Locke, Shaftesbury, and Hutcheson: Contesting Diversity in the Enlightenment and Beyond* (Cambridge: Cambridge University Press, 2005), 98–149; Stuart-Buttle, *Moral Theology to Moral Philosophy,* 89–117.

22. Shaftesbury, *Sensus Communis,* iii.3 (72–76). On this criticism of Mandeville, see Chapter 1, 'Objections to psychological egoism'.

23. Shaftesbury, *Moralists,* ii.2 (144–45). This is presumably an allusion to Jacques Esprit's *La fausseté des vertus humaines* (1678), which was translated into English as *The Falsehood of Moral Virtue* (1691). For criticisms of Mandeville that point to the influence of Esprit, see Fiddes, *General Treatise,* lxxvi, xc–xciv; Bluet, *Enquiry,* 'Preface' and 98; Law, *Remarks,* 53–54.

24. Shaftesbury, *Inquiry,* in *Characteristicks,* vol. 2, I.iii.3 (41), also II.i.1 (47).

25. Shaftesbury, *Moralists,* ii.4 (165).

26. Shaftesbury, *Inquiry,* 'Conclusion' (100). See also Shaftesbury's insistence that '*Virtue and Interest* may be found at last to agree', *Inquiry,* I.ii.1 (9).

portrayal is not without textual warrant, even if it is somewhat one-sided.[27] Three main points of disagreement can be distilled from the 'Search': the first concerns their rival explanations of the origin of society, the second whether virtue requires self-denial, and the third their opinions on 'the Certainty of the *Pulchrum & Honestum*'.[28] The nature and bearing of Mandeville's criticisms will become clearer if we briefly attend to Shaftesbury's own views on each of these closely related matters.

Shaftesbury on sociability, virtue, and beauty

In *Sensus Communis*, Shaftesbury criticises the notion that civil government and society should be understood as 'a kind of Invention, and Creature of Art'. Our '*Sense of Fellowship*' is just as natural as hunger, thirst, or sexual attraction, and this inclination is so strong that we need look no further to explain the origin of society. Shaftesbury challenges the Hobbesian argument that our naturally self-interested passions lead to a state of war, instead maintaining that war and discord arise only when our natural '*social Love, and common Affection*'—which he equates with '*Sociableness*'—are abused and misdirected to form a 'Spirit of *Faction*'.[29] Shaftesbury develops his criticisms of Hobbes further in *The Moralists*, by denying that there is any meaningful distinction between the state of nature and that of society. Even Hobbes would grant that humans naturally form families, but once 'we allow *this* social Part to Man', where should we stop? Households would have grown into tribes and tribes into nations, with the later states ultimately deriving from our 'natural Affection and the Care and Nurture of [our] Offspring'.[30] Shaftesbury's argument here quickly scales up the natural affection we observe in families and friendships to the level of society, a move he makes elsewhere too. In *An Inquiry Concerning Virtue*, for instance, he not only takes the observation that humans

27. See also Stuart-Buttle, *Moral Theology to Moral Philosophy*, 122: 'Mandeville's interpretation of Shaftesbury may have been uncharitable . . . but it was not manifestly unjust.' Cf. Hollander, *History of Utilitarian Ethics*, 48, who complains that Mandeville merely 'set up a straw man to attack'.

28. See also the summary in *Letter to Dion*, 47. While Mandeville does not mention the question of self-denial there, he presents this as one of the most important differences between himself and Shaftesbury at *Fable* II, 12, 108–27.

29. Shaftesbury, *Sensus Communis*, iii.2 (69–72).

30. Shaftesbury, *Moralists*, ii.4 (175–79). On this dimension of Shaftesbury's critique of Hobbes, see Sagar, *Opinion of Mankind*, 81–86.

cannot bear solitude as evidence of man having 'a degree of social Affection as inclines him to seek the Familiarity and Fellowship of his Fellows', but, further, insists that this is the very same *natural Affection by which he is prompted to the Good and Interest of his Species, and Community*.[31] Shaftesbury is aware that this natural affection can be corrupted in certain cases, yet all forms of society—from families to largescale political states and even the species—are ultimately founded upon it.

Shaftesbury's account of virtue is closely related to his position on sociability, for virtue involves using our reason to 'secure a right application of the Affections' and, in particular, to ensure that nothing destroys 'that natural Affection by which the Species or Society is upheld'.[32] The nature of virtue consists *'in a certain just Disposition, or proportionable Affection of a rational Creature towards the moral Objects of Right and Wrong'*, which means that we must be motivated by the appropriate affection for our conduct to count as virtuous. While this requires reflecting upon what is appropriate before acting, in doing so we are guided by our 'Sense of Right and Wrong', or 'natural *moral Sense*', which is 'as natural to us as *natural Affection* itself', and which determines our actions unless it is opposed by self-interested motives or stronger passions.[33] On a conceptual level, then, there is no reason why virtue necessarily entails self-denial, since if we follow our natural moral sense without having to overcome any other affections then our conduct will satisfy the requirements of virtue. Shaftesbury realises that virtue is rarely so easy and claims that the greatest virtue does involve resisting our angry, fearful, or amorous passions. Performing good deeds by mastering our 'ill Passions or Affections . . . is the greatest *Proof* imaginable, that a strong Principle of Virtue lies at the bottom'. Nevertheless, he also holds that we 'may be indeed more *cheaply virtuous*' in cases where there are no such passions or affections to overcome, thereby allowing for different degrees of virtue. Even the worst villains are not completely devoid of goodness and virtue.[34]

Although Shaftesbury maintains that we all have a natural moral sense, he also argues that the virtues are only perfected 'among the People of a liberal Education.'[35] The *Characteristicks* aims to contribute to such an education,

31. Shaftesbury, *Inquiry*, II.ii.1 (78–79).
32. Shaftesbury, *Inquiry*, I.ii.3 (20).
33. Shaftesbury, *Inquiry*, I.iii.1–3 (23–30).
34. Shaftesbury, *Inquiry*, I.ii.4 (21–23).
35. Shaftesbury, *Soliloquy*, in *Characteristicks*, vol. 1, i.3 (118–19).

with Shaftesbury seeking to revive a mode of polite philosophising perfected amongst the ancients and exemplified by the dialogue format, which he deems more conducive to virtue than the formal and dry reasoning practised by many of his contemporaries.[36] In doing so, he sometimes associates virtue closely with the arts, politeness, and good breeding.[37] The 'Knowledg and Practice of the social *Virtues* . . . are essential to the Character of a deserving Artist', and anyone 'who aspires to the Character of a Man of Breeding and Politeness' must develop '*a right* TASTE' not just in arts and science, but in 'Life and Manners' too.[38] This interconnection between aesthetics and morals permeates the *Characteristicks*. Beauty and the good are '*one and the same*',[39] and Shaftesbury goes so far as to claim that 'the main Scope and principal End' of the work is to demonstrate 'the Reality of a Beauty and Charm, in *moral* as well as *natural* Subjects', the truth of which is 'so firmly establish'd in Nature it-self, and so widely display'd thro' the intelligent World'.[40]

In *Sensus Communis*, Shaftesbury voices a sceptical objection to this position by having a gentleman of good understanding question whether there really is a 'common sense' upon which everyone agrees. Not only has there long been intractable disagreement on questions of religion and politics, the gentleman observes, but when it comes to morals, the 'difference, if possible, was still wider', with some 'of our most admir'd modern Philosophers' having argued 'that *Virtue* and *Vice* had, after all, no other *Law* or *Measure*, than *mere Fashion*

36. Shaftesbury, *Soliloquy*, i.3 (124–25); *Moralists*, i.1 (106–109); *Miscellaneous Reflections on the Said Treatises, and Other Critical Subjects*, in *Characteristicks*, vol. 3, iii.1 (95–96); more generally, see also *Sensus Communis*, i.2, i.5–6 (42, 47–50). For further discussion, see Lawrence E. Klein, *Shaftesbury and the Culture of Politeness: Moral Discourse and Cultural Politics in Early Eighteenth-Century England* (Cambridge: Cambridge University Press, 1994), especially 102–19; Michael Prince, *Philosophical Dialogue in the British Enlightenment: Theology, Aesthetics, and the Novel* (Cambridge: Cambridge University Press, 1994), especially 47–73; Rivers, *Reason, Grace, and Sentiment*, especially 108–13.

37. Nonetheless, Shaftesbury is often very critical of the politeness of his contemporaries (on which see Stuart-Buttle, *Moral Theology to Moral Philosophy*, 95), a side to his thought completely overlooked by Mandeville.

38. Shaftesbury, *Soliloquy*, iii.3 (205–206). See also *Miscellaneous Reflections*, iii.1 (99): 'To *philosophize*, in a just Signification, is but to carry *Good-breeding* a step higher'; and ii.2 (100), where he claims that his aim has been 'to recommend MORALS on the same foot, with what in a lower sense is call'd *Manners;* and to advance PHILOSOPHY . . . on the very Foundation of what is call'd *agreeable* and *polite*.'

39. Shaftesbury, *Moralists*, iii.2 (223).

40. Shaftesbury, *Miscellaneous Reflections*, v.3 (185).

and *Vogue*.'[41] Shaftesbury had little time for such views, later decrying 'our modern Moralists' as raising their philosophy 'from the Dregs of an illiterate mean kind'. Much as the harmony, symmetry, and proportion of music are founded in nature, so too '*Virtue* has the same fix'd Standard. The same *Numbers, Harmony*, and Proportion will have place in MORALS; and are discoverable in the *Characters* and *Affections* of Mankind'.[42] Summarising his stance on beauty in the *Miscellaneous Reflections*, Shaftesbury declares (in the third person) that 'This is the HONESTUM, the PULCHRUM, τò καλόv, on which our Author lays the stress of VIRTUE'.[43]

A digression on the 'Pulchrum & Honestum'

The foregoing remarks provide a highly selective overview of some of the key arguments of the *Characteristicks*, but, by accentuating the points on which Shaftesbury and Mandeville disagree, I hope to have presented the former's ideas in a way that will help to make sense of the latter's criticisms. Of the three main points of disagreement, by far the most important are the questions of, first, whether virtue requires self-denial and, second, how to explain the origin of society. These questions are central to Mandeville's philosophy (both within and beyond the 'Search') and will provide the focus for much of this chapter. Before addressing them, however, it is worth saying something about 'the hunting after this *Pulchrum & Honestum*', as Mandeville calls it, not least because his remarks on this were roundly attacked by his contemporaries.[44]

Amongst Shaftesbury's most serious errors, Mandeville alleges, is having looked 'upon Virtue and Vice as permanent Realities that must be ever the same in all Countries and all Ages'.[45] In developing his case, Mandeville sets forth similar considerations to those adduced by Shaftesbury's interlocutor in *Sensus Communis*. The majority of Mandeville's discussion concerns questions of beauty, and while he grants that we might be able to identify a fixed standard

41. Shaftesbury, *Sensus Communis*, i.4 (50–51).

42. Shaftesbury, *Soliloquy*, iii.3 (218).

43. Shaftesbury, *Miscellaneous Reflections* iii.2 (111n), also ii.1 (22n).

44. *Fable* I, 331, also 343. For criticism, see Robert Burrow, *Civil Society and Government vindicated from the Charge of being Founded on, and Preserv'd by, Dishonest Arts* (London, 1723), 12–13n; Fiddes, *General Treatise*, xxxi–lvi; Law, *Remarks*, 2–3, 55–65; Bluet, *Enquiry*, 22–23, 29–31, 100–104; [Anon.], *True Meaning*, 6 and *passim*; Thorold, *Short Examination*, 39–40; Brown, *Essays*, 137–45.

45. *Fable* I, 324.

for evaluating works of art—namely, how successfully they imitate nature—in 'Works of Nature' themselves, standards of beauty vary more dramatically 'according to the different Tastes and Nations and Ages.'[46] It is only towards the end of his discussion that Mandeville turns to argue that in 'Morals there is no greater Certainty', a claim which he supports with examples of polygamy, inter-family marriages, the consumption of alcohol, and disputes about the best religion.[47]

Mandeville's critics were unmoved by these considerations. From the fact that different cultures and religions disagree on some matters, they pointed out, it does not follow that there are no universal moral standards. Mandeville failed to address any hard cases, they complained, where there might be more reason to expect conformity across different times and places.[48] Mandeville's critics read him as endorsing the position now more often referred to as moral or cultural relativism; that is, roughly speaking, that moral norms are relative to different groups of people or social contexts, and that there are no fixed or universal standards. But if that is Mandeville's position then it is open to the charge of inconsistency, for, on the one hand, he argues that virtue and vice are not permanent realities, yet, on the other, he accuses Shaftesbury of having misunderstood the nature of virtue, which *always* involves self-denial.[49] Mandeville does not make similar arguments for moral relativism elsewhere, so it is tempting simply to regard his argument here as an outlier, perhaps the consequence of carrying his opposition to Shaftesbury too far.[50]

There is, however, a more charitable spin on Mandeville's arguments, which comes into view once we recall how intimately connected questions of morals, beauty, and taste are for Shaftesbury.[51] The salient question, as Mandeville presents it, is 'whether there be a real Worth and Excellency in things, a pre-eminence of one above another; which every body will always agree to that

46. *Fable* I, 325–30.

47. *Fable* I, 330–31.

48. See, for example, Fiddes, *General Treatise*, xl, liv; Brown, *Essays*, 144–45. For helpful discussion of Brown's criticisms of Mandeville in relation to wider debates about polygamy, see Colin Heydt, *Moral Philosophy in Eighteenth-Century Britain: God, Self, and Other* (Cambridge: Cambridge University Press, 2018), 215–16.

49. *Fable* I, 323.

50. See Maxwell, 'Ethics and Politics in Mandeville', 245, who further suggests that Mandeville's argument is supposed to be a *reductio ad absurdum* of Shaftesbury's position.

51. See also Monro, *Ambivalence*, 179–85, who pushes back convincingly against Maxwell's interpretation.

well understands them; or that there are few things, if any, that have the same Esteem paid them, and which the same Judgment is pass'd in all Countries and Ages.'[52] Notice that Mandeville remains agnostic about whether there are, in fact, *any* things which are always judged the same. His argument is instead set out against the stronger claim that there are fixed standards that allow us to judge the intrinsic beauty and worth of a wide range of tastes and customs across different times and places. It is this opinion—perhaps an exaggeration of Shaftesbury's position, but not an entirely unfair one—that Mandeville ridicules. When it comes to matters of taste and custom, he insists, there are no standards of intrinsic worth and beauty fixed in nature, or at least none upon which everyone agrees, even with a little understanding and good sense. Mandeville's examples of disagreement in morals reinforce this point, since they are all cases that many people at the time would have regarded as a matter of strict morality, but which he thinks are better explained as based on custom alone.

If this is not especially compelling as an argument for moral or cultural relativism, then that is probably because it was never intended as such. Mandeville is attacking what he takes to be Shaftesbury's naïve view that there are fixed standards in matters of taste and custom, against which we can evaluate whether any given practice or custom is virtuous or vicious. Mandeville could consistently deny this while also holding that virtue requires self-denial, for the latter claim does not appeal to any such standards and is instead based on the observation that we are inherently selfish creatures, naturally disinclined to place the good of others before our own. Precisely what is taken to be socially beneficial might vary depending on the cultural context, but its pursuit will always require resisting our self-centred passions to some degree.[53]

Virtue, self-denial, and hypocrisy

After memorably concluding that 'the hunting after this *Pulchrum & Honestum* is not much better than a Wild-Goose-Chace', Mandeville turns to consider the 'greatest Fault' with Shaftesbury's position: 'The imaginary Notions that Men may be Virtuous without Self-denial are a vast Inlet to Hypocrisy, which being once made habitual, we must not only deceive others, but become altogether unknown to ourselves'. Why does Mandeville consider these notions a

52. *Fable* I, 325.
53. See also *Origin of Honour*, ix.

vast inlet to hypocrisy? In the 'Search', he seems less concerned with Shaftes-bury's ideas and more with exploding Shaftesbury's pretensions to speak with any authority on virtue. The 'Author of the Characteristicks' was 'brought up in Ease and Affluence', and while he might write well of the social virtues in print, or discuss them eloquently in polite company, 'you shall never catch him fighting for his Country' or engaging in public service. Virtue requires action, but Shaftesbury's 'Quiet Indolent Nature' led him to withdraw from civic life, mistakenly believing 'himself Virtuous, because his Passions lie dormant.' Shaftesbury might have a nice turn of phrase, but his analysis of virtue is really a self-serving justification for his own conduct and inaction. The 'calm Virtues recommended in the Charactersticks, are good for nothing but to breed Drones', and will never make someone fit 'for Labour or Assiduity, or stir him up to great Atchievements and perilous Undertakings.'[54] Mandeville's index to the *Fable* captures the point succinctly: '*Shaftesbury* (Lord) . . . Refuted by his own Character'.[55]

Mandeville presents his attack on Shaftesbury as showing how, by internal-ising mistaken notions of virtue, we can become altogether unknown to our-selves. In the context of the 'Search', the 'Inlet to Hypocrisy' remark appears as little more than a passing shot at Shaftesbury. Mandeville proceeds to restate his argument, first advanced in 'Remark R', that pride is the most effective passion for subduing fear of death and making us courageous.[56] He invokes the example of duelling, before turning to historical illustrations and suggesting that Cicero would have achieved nothing were it not for his excessive vanity, while Cato's heroism stemmed from 'the implacable Hatred and superlative Envy he bore to' Caesar. Suicide was merely the least terrible option that Cato's pride could

---

54. *Fable* I, 331–33. As a reviewer perceptively pointed out to me, Mandeville is not merely offering an *ad hominem* attack of Shaftesbury here. Mandeville's own understanding of how we acquire moral norms helps to explain why other philosophers, such as Shaftesbury, are inclined to offer alternative yet erroneous explanations of sociability and virtue. Those who present humans in a more positive light do so to flatter both their own and their audience's pride, even if they are not fully aware that this is what they are doing. Mandeville thereby undercuts the standing of rival positions, not just by arguing against them directly but also by exposing the hidden motivations that lead others to endorse them. For related and insightful discussion of Mandeville's depiction of Shaftesbury's hypocrisy, see Ross Carroll, *Uncivil Mirth: Ridicule in Enlightenment Britain* (Princeton and Oxford: Princeton University Press, 2021), 71–74.

55. *Fable* I, 378.

56. Mandeville may have had Shaftesbury's remarks on '*true* Courage' in *Sensus Communis*, iii.3 (74–75) in his sights here.

countance.[57] These examples are typical Mandeville: exposing what are often taken as exemplary cases of virtue as secretly rooted in self-regarding passions, such as pride. Neither Cicero nor Cato were motivated by any 'Social Love' or genuinely public-spirited concerns; instead, their excessive desire for esteem and praise overcame their naturally more timorous passions and 'Love of Ease and Idleness', with which we are all born.[58] Mandeville's main point against Shaftesbury here is that virtue does not come easily to us. Yet he neither spells out how these examples relate to the accusation that Shaftesbury's views on self-denial are a vast inlet to hypocrisy, nor returns to this point in the subsequent discussion.

Why 'a vast Inlet to Hypocrisy'?

The 'Search' was not Mandeville's last word on the matter, however, and he revisits the argument that the 'System that Virtue requires no Self-denial is . . . a vast Inlet to Hypocrisy' at greater length in *Fable II*. The problem with Shaftesbury's position, Mandeville now explains, is that

> It will on all Accounts furnish Men with a more obvious Handle, and a greater Opportunity of counterfeiting the Love of Society and Regard to the Publick, than ever they could have receiv'd from the contrary Doctrine, *viz*. That there is no Merit but in the Conquest of the Passions, nor any Virtue without apparent Self-denial.[59]

To defend this claim, Mandeville compares the fortunes of two men from 'the middling People', who are both 'tolerably well educated' and 'set out with the same Stock of Virtues and Vices'. The only difference is that one is indolent—like Shaftesbury, albeit from a lower social class—and the other active. The indolent man will likely remain poor and despairs at the difficulty of raising his condition, but if he has any sense then he will explain his lack of industry away as evidence of his modesty and frugality, endeavouring 'to colour over his Frailty with the Appearance of Virtue'. This allows him to indulge his inclinations 'with little Offence or Disturbance to his Neighbour', thereby acquiring 'many amiable Qualities, that shall have all the Appearances of Social Virtues, whilst nothing extraordinary befalls him.' The case is very different for the

---

57. *Fable* I, 333–36.
58. *Fable* I, 333.
59. *Fable* II, 109.

active man, however, who seeks to improve his condition by ingratiating himself with patrons and benefactors. He flatters them in return for favours yet cares only for his own interest. While 'his Complaisance may be engaging . . . the Heart is untouch'd'. The dissimulation this demands leaves him restless and, in following 'the Dictates of his Nature', the active man encounters many obstacles and temptations to 'deviate from the Rules of strict Virtue', which hardly ever trouble the indolent man. If virtue requires a victory over the passions, as Mandeville maintains, then neither are truly virtuous, for they both follow the dictates of their own nature: one prefers an easy life, the other pursues wealth. If we believe that people can be virtuous without self-denial, however, then we are more likely to mistake the unobtrusive life of the indolent man for virtue. Of the view that virtue requires self-denial, Mandeville thus concludes, 'Hypocrites have less Latitude than in the contrary System.'[60]

The indolent man and active man are both hypocrites, for they each offer moralising glosses on their actions (or lack thereof) to present themselves as being more virtuous than is really the case. They are both aware that this is what they are doing, and their hypocrisy is therefore a straightforward case of hiding away their true motives to put on a virtuous façade. By denying that virtue requires self-denial, Shaftesbury's system devalues virtue and even the indolent man can pass for virtuous. In this respect, Shaftesbury's notions of virtue make it too easy to counterfeit love of society and public regard. On Mandeville's more demanding conception, it is (unsurprisingly) easier to identify cases that fall short of the requirements of virtue.[61] Yet this does not fully explain Mandeville's original criticisms of Shaftesbury. More needs to be said to show why the view that virtue does not require self-denial, if made habitual, would lead to us becoming 'altogether unknown to ourselves'. In other words, how does Shaftesbury's view foster self-deception?

Mandeville does not address this question directly, but the most straightforward answer is that, by lowering the bar for virtue, we come to mistake our

---

60. *Fable* II, 111–19.

61. Some commentators have questioned the sincerity of Mandeville's insistence that virtue requires self-denial, instead suggesting that he aimed to satirise and thereby overturn the prevailing understanding of his day. See Harth, 'Satiric Purpose', 333–40; Nieli, 'Commercial Society and Christian Virtue', 594–95; Viner, *Essays*, 178–182. I think this misunderstands the nature of Mandeville's satire, but, more decisively, much of his opposition to Shaftesbury turns on the question of whether virtue requires self-denial, which makes little sense unless his claims about self-denial are taken seriously. On this point, see also Rogers, 'Ethics of Mandeville', 8; Maurer, *Self-love, Egoism and the Selfish Hypothesis*, 70–75.

own imperfections and weaknesses for positive qualities or virtues. The indolent man, in Mandeville's example, can pass for frugal and modest while merely following his natural inclinations. If the indolent man believes that virtue requires self-denial then he is more likely to realise his own shortcomings, even if he manages to deceive other people, whereas if he internalises the view that we can be virtuous without self-denial then he may come to deceive himself too, failing to recognise his lack of industry and ambition as serious shortcomings. In this respect, Shaftesbury's ideas are little more than 'a high Compliment to Human-kind',[62] serving principally to flatter our pride, which, as we have seen in earlier chapters, encourages us to overvalue ourselves and present the most favourable spin on our self-serving conduct.

On Mandeville's interpretation, Shaftesbury's stance on virtue leads us to mistake good breeding and polite manners for virtue. From 1723 onwards, Mandeville thus insists that what passes for good manners in polite society has 'nothing to do with Virtue or Religion'.[63] In developing this argument in *Fable II*—in a passage leading into the 'Inlet to Hypocrisy' charge—Horatio asks whether 'by the help of a careful Education this Victory [over untaught Nature] is obtain'd, when we are young, may we not be virtuous afterwards voluntarily and with Pleasure?'[64] Cleomenes answers in the affirmative: *if* education leads us to conquer our passions then we can become habituated to virtue without subsequently experiencing this conquest. Yet he denies the conditional, instead maintaining that from infancy we are taught only to conceal our passions and never to conquer them.[65] On Shaftesbury's account,

---

62. *Fable* I, 324.

63. *Fable* I, 79; *Fable* II, 138, 146, 281.

64. A similar objection had been raised by William Law (*Remarks*, 33), criticising Mandeville for explaining away virtue in terms of custom and education. Law claims that actions are virtuous if they are in accordance with duty, irrespective of any self-denial involved, and that 'he who thro' long habits of Goodness, has made the Practice of Virtue to have less of Self-denial in it, is the most virtuous Man.' Mandeville's response is twofold: first, and *contra* Law, such actions would only be virtuous due to the original self-denial involved; second, in practice we are rarely habituated in such a way. Mandeville later gives a little more ground on the second point, allowing 'that Men may contract a Habit of Virtue, so as to practice it, without being sensible of Self-denial . . . But then it is manifest, that this Habit is the work of Art, Education and Custom; and it never was acquired, where the Conquest over the Passions had not been already made'; see *Origin of Honour*, x–xi.

65. *Fable* II, 109. Mandeville first draws the distinction between conquering and concealing the passions in the 1723 additions to 'Remark C' and invokes it frequently thereafter; see *Fable* I, 68–69, 72, 77, 145–46, 235, 261; *Fable* II, 17, 66, 78–79, 100–101, 108–109, 111, 121–22, 125, 330–31.

education is about cultivating and perfecting our naturally sociable affections, such that those of us who have received a well-rounded liberal education will become the most virtuous of all. It is easy to see why someone like Shaftesbury might like this to be true, but, from Mandeville's perspective, it overlooks the extent to which education and socialisation teach us only to mask (and not to overcome) our otherwise unsociable and self-centred passions.

A striking illustration of this point occurs in one of the 1723 additions to the *Fable*, where Mandeville contrasts the behaviour of a 'brutish fellow' and a 'fashionable Gentleman', each seeking to satisfy their lust. The brutish fellow instantly declares his sexual desire for a lady and is immediately shunned from all civil company. The fashionable gentleman, by contrast, starts by courting the favour of the lady's father, before flattering and eventually winning her hand in marriage, after which she 'suffers him to do what he pleases, and the upshot is, that he obtains what he wanted without having ever ask'd for it.' The 'fine Gentleman', Mandeville maintains, 'need not practice any greater Self-Denial than the Savage'. The savage or brutish fellow, in fact, is the more sincere and honest of the two, but the fine gentleman is far more skilled at navigating the demands of polite society to satisfy his sexual desire.[66] Most well-educated gentlemen, of course, would resist the suggestion that they are no more virtuous than savages, which is precisely why they find Shaftesbury's notions of virtue so comforting.

In exposing those notions as 'a vast Inlet to Hypocrisy', Mandeville suggests that what starts out as hypocrisy—deceiving others about our moral character—may eventually lead to self-deception. If Shaftesbury's views are made habitual and we become *completely* unknown to ourselves, then we may even question whether this still counts as hypocrisy. That is, at least, if hypocrisy requires some awareness of the deception inherent in our own conduct,[67] the presence of which we have pride-based reasons to conceal even from

---

A similar distinction is found in *Free Thoughts*, 20, where Mandeville claims that when we do good things out of a concern for our reputation, this 'is not conquering the Passions, but bartering one for another.'

66. *Fable* I, 72–73. Mandeville's point here is that neither the fine gentleman nor the brutish fellow overcomes their sexual desire. Strictly speaking, the former does practice a little more self-denial by denying the attempt to immediately satisfy his lust.

67. For the more general argument that 'a hypocrite *must* be self-conscious to a certain degree', see, for example, Christine McKinnon, 'Hypocrisy, with a Note on Integrity', *American Philosophical Quarterly* 28, no. 4 (1991), 323.

ourselves.[68] Mandeville equivocates a little on this point. In the *Free Thoughts* he claims that 'it is unjust to call People Hypocrites, when they set out with no ill design, and by their fair Appearance deceive themselves more ten to one, than they can do others of any tollerable Experience.'[69] In the 1723 additions to the *Fable*, however, he writes of that 'strong Habit of Hypocrisy, by the Help of which, we have learned from our Cradle *to hide even from our selves* the vast Extent of Self-Love, and all its different Branches.'[70] We need not read too much into these different formulations presently, for in most cases self-deception is not an all-or-nothing matter, so we could at least see hypocrisy engendering self-deception up to the point where we become completely unaware of ourselves as being anything other than the façade we display in public.[71] Even if we are not cognisant of all the hidden motives behind our actions— and the more successfully we are socialised, the deeper they are buried—most of us nonetheless remain aware that our public persona *is* a persona and typically understand some of the ways in which we present ourselves and our motives in an overly favourable light. Mandeville probably thought this true of Shaftesbury, although he was not too concerned with specifying the precise balance of self-deception and conscious hypocrisy that best captured his adversary's characteristics.

Social utility and 'counterfeited' virtue

Suppose Mandeville is right to claim that his conception of virtue gives less latitude for hypocrisy than Shaftesbury's. We may still ask: why does this matter? If that seems like an odd question, at first glance, then it helps to keep in mind that in 1714, in 'An Enquiry Into the Origin of Moral Virtue', Mandeville had explained the origin of our moral notions in terms of their social function. The distinction between vice and virtue was 'broach'd by skilful Politicians, to

---

68. *Fable* II, 79–80. See Chapter 1, 'Pride vs. praiseworthy motives' for further discussion of this point.

69. *Free Thoughts*, 31.

70. *Fable* I, 135 (emphasis added). On this passage, see also Luban, 'Mandeville as Moralist and Materialist', 848–50, who discusses cases of 'refined hypocrisy' where we are not necessarily conscious of the gap between our actual and professed motives.

71. For the stronger view that it is difficult to identify hypocrites precisely because hypocrisy usually involves or engenders self-deception, see Daniel Statman, 'Hypocrisy and Self-deception', *Philosophical Psychology* 10, no. 1 (1997): 57–75. Statman argues convincingly (on grounds that resemble Mandeville's) against those who see hypocrisy and self-deception as opposites.

render Men useful to each other as well as tractable', so that they could be governed 'with the greater Ease and Security.'[72] To be clear, the point here is not that Mandeville conceptualises virtue *as* some form of social utility (i.e. whatever promotes social utility is called virtuous),[73] but, rather, that the reason why humans would have originally come to distinguish between virtue and vice is because it proved socially advantageous to do so.[74] From the perspective of the 'Enquiry', then, it would make sense to ask whether Shaftesbury's or Mandeville's way of understanding virtue would have originally proved more conducive to rendering humans peaceful and sociable creatures.

Mandeville does not address this question explicitly in either the 'Search' or *Fable II*, but in the 'Preface' to *An Enquiry into the Origin of Honour* he does appeal to social utility on this very point: 'The Opinion, that there can be no Virtue without Self-denial, is more advantageous to Society than the contrary Doctrine, which is a vast Inlet to Hypocrisy, as I have shewn at large.'[75] Although this statement purports to recap his earlier arguments, the stress that Mandeville places here on 'more advantageous to Society' had not been so pronounced in his previous explanations of why Shaftesbury's notions are a vast inlet to hypocrisy. This change of emphasis raises a further question: even if Shaftesbury's notions of virtue give people 'a greater Opportunity of counterfeiting the Love of Society and Regard to the Publick',[76] why does this count against them if we are evaluating rival conceptions in terms of their social utility?

One reason to press this question is because Mandeville's own explanation of sociability accords a central role to hypocrisy and a counterfeited love of society. As early as 1709, he had described a character in the *Female Tatler* as 'a

---

72. *Fable* I, 47.

73. Mandeville's definition of virtue in the 'Enquiry' (at *Fable* I, 48–49, discussed further below) does refer to endeavouring 'the Benefit of others', but the emphasis he places on self-denial and, more ambiguously, acting from 'a Rational Ambition of being good', indicate that producing a socially beneficial outcome is neither necessary nor sufficient for any given act to count as virtuous, for the simple reason that virtue is judged by motives, not consequences.

74. For more detailed analysis of Mandeville's functionalist explanation of social and moral norms, see Eugene Heath, 'Mandeville's Bewitching Engine of Praise', *History of Philosophy Quarterly* 15, no. 2 (1998), especially 218–20. More generally on Mandeville as a precursor of functionalism, see Louis Schneider, 'Mandeville as a Forerunner of Modern Sociology', *Journal of the History of Behavioral Science* 6, no. 3 (1970), especially 225–27.

75. *Origin of Honour*, x.

76. *Fable* II, 109.

Hypocrite, all her Virtue is but Counterfeited',[77] and in the 1723 additions to the *Fable* he draws a clear distinction between 'real' and 'counterfeited' virtue—a distinction absent from the 1714 edition and which he probably added to help sharpen his attack on those, such as Shaftesbury, who mistake good manners for virtue. One of the main aims of the *Fable*, Mandeville now tells us, is to reveal 'the difference between such Actions as proceed from a Victory over the Passions, and those that are only the result of a Conquest which one Passion obtains over another; that is, between Real, and Counterfeited Virtue.'[78]

This distinction is slightly different to that which Mandeville draws between concealing and conquering our passions.[79] A concealed passion can still determine our actions, even if it is hidden from sight, whereas a passion is conquered only if it ceases to motivate us. Mandeville sometimes writes of conquering the passions (in the plural) in general terms,[80] which seems to be what he means by contrasting the victory over the passions necessary for 'real' virtue with cases of 'counterfeited' virtue where one passion conquers another. He never spells out precisely what a victory over the passions would entail, but it cannot merely be a matter of one passion overcoming another. If not another passion, then what part of us does achieve the victory required for real virtue?[81] If we are governed by our passions, as Mandeville maintains,[82] then it is unclear that the victory over the passions required for 'real' virtue is within our natural reach.[83] He seems willing to endorse this implication in

77. *Female Tatler*, no. 76: 138.

78. *Fable* I, 230. See also the 'Vindication of the Book' at *Fable* I, 405, where Mandeville claims that the *Fable* offers 'a strict Test of Virtue, an infallible Touchstone to distinguish the real from the counterfeited.' For other discussions of counterfeited virtue, see *Fable* I, 254; *Fable* II, 100–101, 112, 119–20, 134, 216.

79. A difference I overlooked in Douglass, 'Mandeville on the Origins of Virtue', 283–84.

80. *Fable* I, 48–49, 51, 72, 74, 151, 162; *Fable* II, 109; *Origin of Honour*, x–xi.

81. In the 'Enquiry', Mandeville contrasts the use of our 'Rational Faculties' to yielding 'without Resistance to every gross desire', before suggesting that we can oppose our 'most violent Inclinations' with 'the Help of Reason', which might shed some light on the famous claim that virtue requires conquering our passions 'out of a Rational Ambition of being good'; see *Fable* I, 43–44, 48–49, 250. However, it is difficultly to see how, on Mandeville's psychology, there could be a rational ambition that did not originate in passion. As he writes in 1732, even those who 'strictly follow the Dictates of Reason, are . . . compell'd so to do by some Passion or other', *Origin of Honour*, 31.

82. *Fable* I, 39, 140; *Fable* II, 139; *Origin of Honour*, 6, 31.

83. The qualifier 'natural' is important because the attainment of virtue might be possible only for 'Devout Christians, who . . . being regenerated, and preternaturally assisted by the

1723, defending himself against those who will 'quote my Lord *Shaftesbury* against me, and tell me . . . that it is an Affront to Virtue to make it inaccessible'.[84] Whether or not real virtue is impossible or just exceedingly rare, as Mandeville later claims,[85] much of the 1723 edition of the *Fable* seeks to reveal the extent to which we rely on counterfeited virtue to make society function.

With the distinction between counterfeited and real virtue at hand,[86] it is evident that the examples of Cicero and Cato discussed earlier are cases of counterfeited virtue, since they acted from vanity and envy. Similarly, it now becomes apparent that when, in 1714, Mandeville had claimed 'that the Moral Virtues are the Political Offspring which Flattery begot upon Pride',[87] he was telling a story about how we come to practise counterfeited virtue, not real virtue.[88] Yet how does this distinction relate to Mandeville's criticisms of Shaftesbury's understanding of virtue? One utility-based criticism is found both in his attack on Shaftesbury in the 'Search' and at the end of his discussion of indolence in *Fable II*. Much as Shaftesbury will never be found fighting for his country, so too the 'indolent Man . . . will never serve his Friend, or his Country, at the Expence of his Quiet.' Amongst the indolent, then, the view that you can be virtuous without self-denial is likely to breed passivity, even if,

---

Divine Grace, cannot be said to be in Nature', *Fable* I, 166. While Mandeville is not discussing virtue in this passage, we find the claim that Christians can attain virtue and conquer their passions only with the assistance of divine grace in other works; see *Free Thoughts*, 24; *Origin of Honour*, 56.

84. *Fable* I, 233.

85. *Fable* II, 15, 50, 56, 336. Some of Mandeville's critics in the 1720s objected that he had erroneously concluded that we are never virtuous from the (uncontroversial) fact that there are many cases where we do not act virtuously. See Law, *Remarks*, 48–49; Fiddes, *General Treatise*, lxxx–lxxxi.

86. The observation that Mandeville's theory rests on at least two different conceptions of virtue is now discussed at greatest length in Maurer, *Self-love, Egoism and the Selfish Hypothesis*, especially 70–80. While I agree with Maurer's overarching argument, I find the distinction between 'real' and 'counterfeited' virtue a more helpful focal point than the one he draws between the 'social virtues (plural)' and 'moral virtue (singular)'. The distinction between 'real' and 'counterfeited' virtue also maps onto that between 'total self-denial' and 'partial self-denial' drawn by Colman, 'Reality of Virtue', 131–32. Colman is right to argue that only partial self-denial is possible on Mandeville's account, but the additions to the 1723 edition clarify that, *contra* Colman, this is insufficient for real virtue.

87. *Fable* I, 51.

88. Perhaps unsurprisingly, Mandeville's various invocations of the term virtue led critics to charge him with inconsistency. See Burrow, *Civil Society vindicated*, 21–22n; Law, *Remarks*, 90–91; Campbell, *Enquiry*, 527; Hutcheson, *Reflections upon Laughter*, 74–76.

in other respects, indolence is conducive to peaceful coexistence.[89] Although the indolent man counterfeits the virtues of modesty and frugality, his main failing is that he does not go out of his way to serve or help others. This failing, however, is one that could be remedied by counterfeiting other virtues, as is the case with the active man in the same example, or with Cicero and Cato. To put the point polemically, counterfeited virtue could be sufficient to address the consequentialist worries that Mandeville raises against Shaftesbury's account of virtue, for what is really at stake is whether counterfeited virtue breeds action or passivity.

As this stage, it may help to take stock of Mandeville's reasons for holding that Shaftesbury's notions of virtue are a vast inlet to hypocrisy. Mandeville claims that the idea that there can be no virtue without self-denial is more socially beneficial than the contrary view. While he does offer utility-based reasons for thinking that virtue must require *some* self-denial, these considerations do not support the precise way he conceptualises the self-denial required for real (as opposed to counterfeited) virtue; that is, as involving a victory over the passions, rather than one passion subduing another.[90] Given that Mandeville insists that good manners and politeness are not virtuous because they involve concealing our passions, rather than overcoming them, we might think that he owes us more of an explanation as to why we should conceptualise real virtue in such demanding terms. Later in the chapter I shall suggest that Mandeville's theory contains the resources for constructing such an explanation, even if he did not piece it all together himself. Yet Mandeville's most prominent argument against Shaftesbury does not turn on the social utility of conceptualising virtue in different ways at all, but rather aims to show that the idea that we can be virtuous without self-denial, once made habitual, will lead to us becoming altogether unknown to ourselves. This line of criticism does not entail that there is anything socially disadvantageous about Shaftesbury's understanding of virtue, for, as Mandeville was well aware, hypocrisy and dissimulation have many social benefits.

89. *Fable* II, 119.

90. While Mandeville draws this distinction sharply in the 1723 edition of the *Fable*, in *Fable II* some of his remarks are more equivocal, such as when he claims that virtue requires '*some* Conquest or other, *some* Victory great or small over untaught Nature', or that there cannot be 'any Virtue without *apparent* Self-denial', *Fable* II, 109 (emphasis added). I discuss these ambiguities at greater length, and the differences between the various editions, in Douglass, 'Mandeville on the Origins of Virtue', especially 288–89.

Sociability and hypocrisy

If Shaftesbury's greatest error concerns the question of how to understand virtue, it is worth keeping in mind that this is not the principal question that the 'Search' addresses. That question, rather, is in what sense humans are 'made for Society'. Where Shaftesbury holds that our social love and generous affections lead us to seek the welfare of others, Mandeville denies that 'the good and aimable Qualities of Man . . . make him beyond other Animals a sociable Creature', and instead seeks to show the impossibility of raising and maintaining 'any Multitudes into a Populous, Rich and Flourishing Nation . . . without the assistance of what we call Evil both Natural and Moral.'[91]

Mandeville declares that he is himself 'a great Lover or Company', but the type of person with whom he prefers to converse is a creature of 'Artful Instruction'; that is, someone whose education has left them 'thoroughly imbued with the notions of Honour and Shame.'[92] It is only through socialisation, in other words, that we learn to become good company. Mandeville proceeds to offer two further reasons why, *contra* Shaftesbury, our love of company and aversion to solitude are not evidence of natural sociability or innate goodness. First, the desire for company should not be regarded as 'a Mark of some Intrinsick Worth in Man', since it is as common to the weakest minds and the lowest ranks of society as it is to the highest; indeed, it is 'Men of Sense and of Knowledge' who most value solitude, precisely because it affords an opportunity for peaceful reflection. Second, our love of company is ultimately based on self-love. We pursue friendships and civilities for as long as they are reciprocal and never lose sight of our own interest and advantage.[93] If we often pretend otherwise then this serves only to illustrate the hypocrisy undergirding sociability.

The use and abuse of hypocrisy

When Mandeville turns 'to investigate into the nature of Society' for himself, his main thesis is that 'the Sociableness of Man' arises from nothing but the 'multiplicity of his Desires, and the continual Opposition he meets with in his

---

91. *Fable* I, 324–25, also 344, 369. The 'Search' thus revisits and develops the argument that Mandeville had announced in the opening pages of the 'Preface' to the *Fable* in 1714; see *Fable* I, 3–4.

92. *Fable* I, 337.

93. *Fable* I, 340–43.

Endeavours to gratify them.'[94] Those who instead base sociability on 'the generous Notions concerning the natural Goodness of Man' offer a misleading picture of the human condition in its current state.[95] If there ever was a time when the necessities of life were abundant and our desires could be satisfied without hardship then it has long passed, and there is no reason why anyone would have ever contrived to design large societies in such a 'State of Innocence' or 'Golden Age'. The political societies we now inhabit instead originate from the problems generated by our fallen condition, in which all our actions 'have no other Centre' than our own interest and pleasure. Where Shaftesbury had argued that the natural affections which bind families could be scaled up to the level of political society, Mandeville claims that 'in the Wild State of Nature' parental authority would have soon dissolved into war, as descendants quarrelled for pre-eminence. The earliest forms of government that subsequently emerged would have been based on averting conflict, rather than on any naturally sociable qualities driving us to live together on a large scale.[96]

Once we see human nature and the origin of society in this light, Mandeville argues, it is evident that we could never have become 'sociable Creatures without Hypocrisy.' If our natural affections are not the basis of human sociability, then sincerity and openness will rarely lead to successful social interaction. More often than not, we are required to conceal our natural inclinations and innermost motives rather than expressing them outwardly. As we are naturally driven to please ourselves and pursue our own advantage, 'all Civil Commerce would be lost, if by Art and prudent Dissimulation, we had not learn'd to stifle' our self-centred ideas. If 'all we think was to be laid open to others in the same manner as it is to our selves, it is impossible that endued with Speech we could be sufferable to one another.'[97]

The reason why hypocrisy is so important, then, is that, first, we care principally for ourselves, and, second, we are naturally averse to other people displaying their own self-centredness when we interact with them. Both points are crucial: if we were indifferent to others' displays of self-love then there would be no need for dissimulation, even if we are all self-interested. Yet this is not the case and successful social interaction requires hiding our self-love away and giving the appearance of acting from other-regarding considerations.

94. *Fable* I, 344.
95. *Fable* I, 343.
96. *Fable* I, 346–48.
97. *Fable* I, 349.

This is why in 'all Civil Societies Men are taught insensibly to be Hypocrites from their Cradle', a point which Mandeville illustrates with a characteristically grim example. The sexton who tends the church graveyard 'would be stoned should he wish openly for the Death of the Parishioners, tho' every body knew that he had nothing else to live upon.'[98] While some people's livelihoods depend on the misfortunes or even fatalities of others, the point applies equally to more mundane cases. As Adam Smith famously remarked, in market exchanges we typically address ourselves to the self-love of those with whom we trade 'and never talk to them of our own necessities but of their advantages.'[99] From Mandeville's perspective, however, there is something deeply hypocritical about such interactions, for what we really care about is our own necessities and not their advantages. The shop assistant offering help cares more for your custom than your wellbeing but knows that the key to their profit involves pretending otherwise. The same is true of polite manners in general, which invariably involve humouring others and exaggerating our interest in their affairs. To claim that we could never become sociable creatures without hypocrisy is not to say that all social interaction is hypocritical. Mandeville's key point, rather, is that our social norms depend upon us learning to be hypocrites much of the time, which does not entail the stronger conclusion that everything we do is hypocritical.

Although sociability requires hypocrisy, we should not conclude that hypocrisy is always beneficial. As with most things, Mandeville argues that hypocrisy can be turned to good or ill use, a point he develops in *Origin of Honour* by distinguishing between 'Malicious' and 'Fashionable' hypocrites. Malicious hypocrites 'take Pains to appear Pious and Devout, in order to be Villains' by deceiving others who take them to be sincere. Fashionable hypocrites, by contrast, attend church and 'counterfeit Devotion . . . without any Design upon others . . . from no other Principle than an Aversion to Singularity, and a Desire of being in the Fashion.' While malicious hypocrites are 'the

---

98. *Fable* I, 349. Cf. Berkovski, 'Self-liking, Morality, and Hypocrisy', 173, who suggests that 'the inward–outward discrepancy' between our motives and our actions 'is not a sufficient mark of hypocrisy', proposing instead that hypocrisy 'involves manipulation of others to your own advantage'. If not openly avowing the fact that you benefit from the misfortunes of others (as in the case of the sexton) counts as *manipulating* people, then I could agree with Berkovski, although manipulation strikes me as too strong a term for examples such as this.

99. Adam Smith, *An Inquiry into the Nature and Causes of the Wealth of Nations* [1776], ed. R. H. Campbell and A. S. Skinner (Indianapolis: Liberty Fund, 1981), I.ii.2.

worst of Men', fashionable hypocrites 'are rather beneficial to Society, and can only be injurious to themselves.' This distinction is not unique to cases of religious practices and belief, with Mandeville's discussion of hypocrisy returning to one of his favourite themes and concluding that all 'good Manners and Politeness must come under the same Denomination.'[100] Hypocrisy may prove beneficial in so far as it leads people to conform to social norms.[101] It starts to become malicious when people feign sincerity in order to wield power over others through the pretence of moral purity. Even though fashionable hypocrisy is generally beneficial and malicious hypocrisy generally harmful, the key distinction between the two is one of motivation (not outcome): fashionable hypocrites deceive out of a desire for social approval without intending to harm anyone else, whereas malicious hypocrites act from more nefarious motives.[102]

Mandeville's distinction between these two types of hypocrisy occurs towards the end of a long discussion of Oliver Cromwell, the archetypal hypocrite of the period, and the use of Christianity in motivating his army during the English Civil War. Both Cromwell and the clergy supporting him satisfy the criteria of malicious hypocrites, for they were well aware of their own moral shortcomings—or, in Cromwell's case, lack of sincere belief altogether—but presented their cause as unequivocally righteous to spur enthusiasm amongst

100. *Origin of Honour*, 201–202.

101. This, of course, depends on the social norms themselves being beneficial. Mandeville was well aware that social norms can be oppressive, as is perhaps displayed most clearly in the *Virgin Unmask'd*, the main aim of which, he states in the 'Preface', is to expose 'whatever is dreadful in Marriage'—marriage being, amongst other things, an extremely powerful social norm. Here and elsewhere, Mandeville repeatedly describes (married) women as having been enslaved by men; see, for example, *Virgin Unmask'd*, 30, 86, 127; *Female Tatler*, no. 68: 119, no. 88: 171; no. 96: 202.

102. Cf. Runciman, *Political Hypocrisy*, 57, who claims that the distinction is drawn 'in terms not just of motive but of self-awareness . . . [because] the fashionable hypocrite acts without design.' Mandeville, however, is clear that the malicious hypocrite and the fashionable hypocrite both know they are being hypocritical. The point about acting 'without design *upon others*' (emphasis added) concerns the motivation of the fashionable hypocrite. For an alternative interpretation of the distinction, set out against both Runciman's and my own interpretations, see Berkovski, 'Self-liking, Morality, and Hypocrisy', 165–74. Berkovski argues that malicious and fashionable hypocrisy are continuous and, in contrast to my view, sees 'malicious hypocrisy as a central and paradigmatic kind of hypocrisy' (174). One advantage of my interpretation is that it explains, rather than blurs, Mandeville's distinction between the two forms of hypocrisy.

the troops.[103] The dangers of malicious hypocrisy, however, come across most strongly in Mandeville's discussion of the clergy elsewhere:

> the more Men Pretend to Virtue and Religion, the less fit they are to judge others. The reason is plain: Hypocrites are under greater temptation to be cruel, than other Sinners; because they are always in hopes that we shall (what many are Fools enough to do) judge of the Holiness and Purity of their own Hearts from the hatred and strong aversion they express against Vice, which must make them unmercifully severe against the least Frailties of others.[104]

Mandeville's concern here is with malicious hypocrites, who like to portray themselves as exemplars of virtue with the authority to castigate the shortcomings of others and demand a moral reformation. These prove to be the most intolerant of people, seeking to punish others for the slightest of faults and thereby shelter their own vices under a façade of moral austerity. What is more, malicious hypocrites tend to see everyone else's hypocrisy as an evil that needs to be rooted out of society, failing to recognise that fashionable hypocrisy is indispensable for sociability and prosperity. The problem with such people is not that they are wrong to identify the sinful or vicious nature of the laypeople, but that they deceitfully present themselves as exempt from such vices so that they can exercise authority over others. In exposing their hypocrisy, Mandeville seeks to bring malicious hypocrites down to (or perhaps even below) the level of the rest of us. Beware the morally righteous, he warns, for theirs is the hypocrisy that breeds intolerance and civil discord.

Hypocrisy and the origin of virtue

If many of the clergy are prime examples of malicious hypocrites, then what about Shaftesbury? Perhaps Mandeville saw some malicious hypocrisy in the hope that the *Characteristicks* could educate its readers to become more virtuous. Nonetheless, the type of hypocrisy he claims Shaftesbury's ideas encourage, and which much of the *Fable* seeks to unmask, is the fashionable hypocrisy central to polite society. Against Shaftesbury and his followers, Mandeville

---

103. *Origin of Honour*, especially 163–94, also 217–18. Cf. Runciman, *Political Hypocrisy*, 58–64, who argues that Cromwell was both a malicious *and* a fashionable hypocrite. Runciman's discussion of Cromwell is otherwise very insightful and my disagreement on this point turns mainly on how he understands the distinction between malicious and fashionable hypocrites.

104. *Free Thoughts*, 159–60.

insists that 'real' virtue, unlike the 'counterfeited' virtue involved in good manners, requires a victory over the passions. As we have seen, however, Mandeville does not fully explain why we should conceptualise real virtue in such demanding terms, leaving him open to the charge that his definition is arbitrary or based on outdated religious or ascetic views.[105] Another way of approaching this problem is to ask whether Mandeville's explanation of human sociability and his understanding of virtue—both of which are developed against Shaftesbury—can be rendered coherent. If Mandeville explains the origin of virtue in terms of its social utility, and the practice of counterfeited virtue is socially beneficial, then, we may ask, why should counterfeited virtue be regarded *as counterfeit* at all?

Although Mandeville does not address this question directly, we can reconstruct a plausible answer on his behalf. To do so, it helps to read him backwards, in a sense, with the caveat that what emerges will inevitably be a somewhat speculative interpretation of how different aspects of his argument can be pieced together. Mandeville's most important statement of the origin of virtue was set out in the 'Enquiry' of 1714, even though he only distinguished explicitly between 'real' and 'counterfeited' virtue from 1723 onwards. Earlier I suggested that if we read the later distinction back into the 'Enquiry' then it becomes apparent that Mandeville is telling a story about how we come to practise counterfeited virtue, not real virtue. The story is even more complicated, however, because while he explains how we come to *practise* counterfeited virtue, he seeks to show how we come to acquire the *idea* of real virtue. The distance between the two is crucial for making sense of Mandeville's position: counterfeited virtue can be judged counterfeit only if it falls short of some widely endorsed idea of real virtue.

In the 'Enquiry', Mandeville regards ideas or virtue and vice as central to explaining how humans could 'ever be made sociable'.[106] He famously claims that everyone would have come to agree 'to give the name of VIRTUE to every Performance, by which Man, contrary to the impulse of Nature, should endeavour the Benefits of others, or the Conquest of his own Passions out of a Rational Ambition of being good.'[107] This definition is not without its ambiguities and there are a few points worth noting. First, virtue necessarily

105. For criticisms of Mandeville's understanding of virtue along these lines, see Law, *Remarks*, 30–38; Campbell, *Enquiry*, 525–30; Hutcheson, *Reflections upon Laughter*, 81; Smith, *Theory of Moral Sentiments*, VII.ii.4.12.

106. *Fable* I, 41.

107. *Fable* I, 48–49.

requires some self-denial ('contrary to the impulse of Nature'), whether or not this entails a more demanding conquest of the passions. Second, if we read the 'or' in the definition as a disjunctive then it follows that conquering the passions is not a necessary condition for virtue. Third, it is unclear precisely what counts as 'a Rational Ambition of being good', and whether this qualifies both 'endeavour the Benefits of others' *and* 'the Conquest of his own Passions', or just the latter.[108] Without attempting to resolve these ambiguities presently, it is worth highlighting that, by 1723, Mandeville strongly implies that he had offered a definition of 'real' virtue in the 'Enquiry'. In explaining why acts motivated by pity fall short of virtue, he now claims that 'it is not sufficient barely to conquer a Passion, unless it likewise be done from a laudable Principle, and consequently how necessary that Clause was in the Definition of Virtue, that our Endeavours were to proceed from *a rational Ambition of being Good*.'[109] This clarifies that there can be no virtue without a rational ambition of being good and that the laudable principle in question is distinct from pity, and doubtless from pride or shame too, which Mandeville discounts from being virtuous motives on the grounds that they (as with all passions, on his account) are ultimately self-centred. The 1723 gloss of the 1714 definition thus stipulates that virtue requires a conquest of the passions motivated by a rational ambition of being good.

From a 1723 vantage point, then, the most charitable interpretation is to read the 'Enquiry' as explaining the origin of our *idea* of real virtue, even if we only ever *practise* counterfeited virtue.[110] Indeed, even without the counterfeited/real distinction at hand, we can still identify a clear gap in the 'Enquiry' between the idea and practice of virtue. To see this, notice that Mandeville does not claim that we give the name of virtue to every performance, by which, contrary to the impulse of nature, we endeavour the benefits of others out of a desire for praise and an aversion to shame (or irrespective of motive altogether). This would be a definition of what he later calls counterfeited virtue, and, while this more accurately describes our actual conduct, Mandeville maintains that we do not call this (real) virtue. To put the point another way,

108. For further discussion of some of these definitional complexities, see Colman, 'Reality of Virtue', 131–34.

109. *Fable* I, 260.

110. To avoid any confusion, my claim here is not that Mandeville intended the 'Enquiry' to be read this way in 1714, but, given the ambiguities in the 'Enquiry', this way of reading his position fits best with the 1723 articulation of his ideas.

he thinks that to live peacefully together in large societies we need to have an idea of virtue which goes beyond performing socially beneficial acts from self-centred motives, even though, in practice, such performances are widely mistaken for virtue.[111]

On Mandeville's analysis of human nature, we could go so far as to say that it is a necessary feature of our moral practices that we have an idea of virtue which exceeds what is humanly possible. This might sound like a surprising claim, not least because there is a tendency to posit a stark tension between Mandeville's empirical analysis of human nature and his rigoristic definition of virtue, following F. B. Kaye's influential discussion.[112] But Kaye sets up a false dichotomy, as becomes apparent once we bear in mind some of the key points from this and the preceding chapters. Mandeville doubts whether we ever act from genuinely other-regarding motives and, even if we do so very occasionally, these motives cannot be the basis of human sociability. If real virtue requires a victory over the passions then it is beyond human reach. Even so, we continue to hold moral standards according to which acts are not clas-sified as (really) virtuous if they are based solely on self-regarding motives. Whether or not this is true of all moral judgements, there is a certain class of actions where Mandeville's position seems eminently plausible: if we think that someone is motivated exclusively by a desire for praise or aversion to shame then this detracts from the merit we accord to their socially beneficial conduct. Recall the example from the previous chapter: you are unlikely to judge my voluntary work virtuous upon discovering that my only motive for undertaking it is a desire for social esteem. We are naturally averse to the self-love and pride of others, and do not regard someone's conduct as virtuous if we suspect these to be their principal motives. In practice, however, we do not

---

111. See also Berkovski, 'Self-liking, Morality, and Hypocrisy', 164, who asks why the lawgiv-ers in the 'Enquiry' had to define virtue in such demanding terms and could not 'be satisfied with apparent virtue; that is, with an utilitarian standard of benefiting society, never mind the motives?'. I think the most straightforward answer is that our moral evaluations of other people's conduct are based on the motives we attribute to their actions, and we disapprove of others to the extent that we think they act from self-centred motives rather than public-spirited ones. The lawgivers cannot override this feature of our moral psychology and turn people into utilitarian judges who disregard motives when making moral evaluations. Berkovski seems to attribute to me an interpretation whereby people are motivated by the pursuit of virtue for its own sake (I assume this is what he means by 'motivated by their pursuit of virtue'), but, as the emphasis I place on pride throughout should make clear, this is not my position.

112. Kaye, 'Introduction', lii–lvi.

usually detect the self-love or pride secretly motivating others' displays of counterfeited virtue. Crucially, the point here is not that we recognise someone's self-centred motives and consider their conduct virtuous regardless, but, rather, that we do not attribute their conduct to these motives in the first place. Most of the time, counterfeited virtue passes for real virtue. It is only when we see it up close, carefully dissected by someone like Mandeville, that we realise it is counterfeited, and, once seen it this light, we are no longer willing to let it pass for the real thing.

If the foregoing summary is broadly accurate then we can see Mandeville offering two closely related considerations to explain why hypocrisy is ineliminable from our moral practices. First, and most simply, we have pride-based reasons for conforming to moral norms, but in so conforming we hide these motives away and present ourselves as acting from more public-spirited or other-regarding principles.[113] Second, in maintaining these moral standards, we hold others to higher expectations than is realistic and disapprove of failings in them that we too share. Hypocrisy pervades our self-presentation and our judgements of others. On Mandeville's account, then, there is a striking disparity between the demands of our ethical standards and a realistic analysis of our moral psychology. As this disparity takes place at the level of motives, our moral practices can survive so long as counterfeited virtue generally passes for real virtue. Mandeville's explanation of the origin of virtue is thus strengthened by most people operating with an overly dichotomised distinction between indulging and conquering our passions,[114] or between vice and real virtue. If we know that others will expose our actions for counterfeited virtue then our pride will no longer motivate us to perform those actions, so it helps that we are regularly deceived about the true motives behind both our own and others' conduct.[115] Indeed, were everyone to identify one another's hidden motives in day-to-day interactions then we would cease to reward counterfeited virtue with social esteem and start to find the company of others a lot more insufferable. Hypocrisy is therefore a feature, not a bug, of our moral practices.

The disparity between the demands of real virtue and our practices of counterfeited virtue is one that fits well with the theological picture of our fallen

113. Some support for Mandeville's position can be found in empirical research on moral hypocrisy. For a helpful starting point, see Batson, *What's Wrong with Morality*, 93–148.

114. See *Fable* I, 42.

115. On this point, see also Monro, *Ambivalence*, 189–90.

condition, which Mandeville sometimes invokes. Yet nothing in my analysis turns on whether, say, he genuinely believed in a prelapsarian state of innocence or the possibility of attaining real virtue through the assistance of divine grace. What is important, however, is that the 'Enquiry' eschews all knowledge of revealed religion and addresses the problem of how those unenlightened by scripture, such as the pagans, could have acquired notions of virtue and vice that approximate those found in Christianity.[116] As his discussion of the Stoics elsewhere demonstrates, Mandeville did not regard the idea that virtue requires a conquest of the passions as unique to Abrahamic religions, even if the Stoics were so blinded by pride that they mistakenly considered this within their reach.[117] There is nothing incoherent about an ethical theory that demands more than can plausibly be expected on a realistic analysis of our moral psychology. This is arguably true of some secular philosophies today, such as certain varieties of utilitarianism, or, more generally, any ethical theory that holds, for example, that individuals have far-reaching duties to alleviate widespread human (and animal) suffering, or to combat climate change.[118] If we take these demands seriously then we will inevitably fall short. One of the insights well-captured by the idea of our fallen condition is that we are simply incapable of living up to the demands of morality, and this is not necessarily a failing of how we think about morality. From this Mandevillean perspective, claims of moral righteousness are always laced with hypocrisy and those who extol their own moral qualities—virtue signalling, as we might call it today— tell us more about their pride than they do their integrity.

Should hypocrisy be unmasked?

If human sociability and moral practices rely on hypocrisy and (self-)deception, then is this a truth that should be widely disseminated? After all, sociability depends upon us not identifying the true motives of one another's actions, for to do so would be to reveal precisely that which we have so successfully learned

116. *Fable* I, 50–51. For further discussion of how Mandeville's analysis resembles Augustinian moral psychology without relying on acceptance of its theological premises, see Chapter 2, 'An Augustinian view of pride?'

117. *Fable* I, 150–51.

118. To be sure, it is easy to imagine Mandeville satirising the haughty moralism of some proponents of these views today, but, on my interpretation, the object of his ridicule would be the hypocrisy of the proponents, not the ethical position itself.

to conceal from others. In the original *Grumbling Hive* verse, Mandeville suggested that once the mask of hypocrisy is 'flung down' economic ruin would soon follow,[119] and we might expect similar consequences for our moral and sociable norms. Many of Mandeville's contemporaries thought that the *Fable* was a deeply subversive work. In most cases, critics complained that it abounds with dangerous errors, but a more incisive worry is that it divulges truths that are best left hidden. John Hervey, for example, observed that the *Fable* contains 'many great Truths', but also 'many disagreeable ones, and what are much less fit to be told, than if they were not Truths'. Would Mandeville not have done better to keep his penetrating insights to himself?

> I would have said, that his endeavouring to show, that People do Actions they have reason to be proud of, from Motives, which if nicely scrutinized, they would have reason to be ashamed of, will never contribute to the multiplying such Actions; and that if Actions, which are beneficial to Mankind and Society, often proceed from the same Principles with some that are detrimental, it would be more for the Benefit of the World, to have such Sources lie conceal'd; as the Discovery of these two Streams, flowing from the same Fountain, will take away one of the chief Inducements many People have for doing what is good; which is the Pride and Vanity of being thought to act upon better, nobler, and more laudable Principles than their Neighbours.[120]

To this objection, Mandeville could simply respond that he always remained sceptical of the public learning much from even the most 'instructive and elaborate Writings', and that he never claimed any good would come from reading the *Fable* 'besides the Reader's Diversion'.[121] It was not written for the improvement of society, but for Mandeville's own pleasure and the amusement 'of People of Knowledge and Education, when they have an idle Hour which they know not how to spend better'.[122] To expect nobler aims is

---

119. *Fable* I, 28.

120. Hervey, *Remarks*, 45–46. On this point, Hervey follows Bishop Berkeley, who had alluded to Mandeville's account of virtue when asking why, if virtue 'is a Trick of Statesman', do you 'betray and divulge that Trick or Secret of State, which wise Men have judged necessary for the good Government of the World?' See George Berkeley, *Alciphron, or the Minute Philosopher* (London, 1732), Second Dialogue, §11. For further discussion of this tension, especially in relation to the dialogues of *Fable II*, see Dykstal, *Luxury of Skepticism*, 122–25.

121. *Fable* I, 8–9.

122. *Fable* I, 404–405, also 369; *Fable* II, 5; *Letter to Dion*, 30.

rather to miss the point.[123] Although some of his contemporaries relished pointing out that Mandeville, on his own account, could not really be virtuous and must have written for selfish reasons—the *Fable* itself being 'the sophistical Offspring which Flattery begot upon Pride'[124]—this line of criticism leaves his arguments untroubled, for there is no reason to suppose that he thought himself exempt from the pride and hypocrisy he uncovered in others.[125] Unlike Shaftesbury, Mandeville is not so easily refuted by his own character.

Mandeville does, however, respond to the charge that his work is subversive. For the most part, this involves maintaining that there can be no harm in making us better known to ourselves.[126] Indeed, most people are 'so desperately in Love with Flattery' that they would be unwilling to accept the uncomfortable truths he reveals anyway; 'nothing would more clearly demonstrate the Falsity of my Notions,' Mandeville claims, 'than that the generality of the People should fall in with them'.[127] In the final defence of his work, though, responding to George Berkeley's attack, he directly addresses the question of whether it is more beneficial to accentuate the positive or negative side of human nature:

> You, Sir, think it for the Good of Society, that human Nature should be extoll'd as much as possible: I think, the real Meanness and Deformity of it to be more instructive. Your Design is, to make Men copy after the beautiful Original, and endeavour to live up to the Dignity of it: Mine is to enforce the Necessity of Education, and mortify Pride.[128]

123. In the 'Preface' to *Virgin Unmask'd*, Mandeville criticises the 'Hypocrisie and Dissimulation' of authors who preface their books by claiming to have written them with 'no other Aim than the Reader's Good, which commonly is an Abominable Lie.' However, see also the 'Preface' to *Free Thoughts*, 9–11, where Mandeville does claim that the book's defence of moderation serves the public good and defends his own character in writing it.

124. Campbell, *Enquiry*, 186–87; see also Law, *Remarks*, 5–6, 88–89; Fiddes, *General Treatise*, cx; Thorold, *Short Examination*, 43; [Anon.], *True Meaning* 108–109.

125. On this point, see Sandeman, *Letters on Theron*, 271–72. See also *Fable* II, 6–7.

126. *Fable* I, 57, 230.

127. *Fable* I, 230–31; see also *Letter to Dion*, 15.

128. *Letter to Dion*, 48; see also *Fable* II, 296. This defence sits a little uneasily with Mandeville's own explanation of the origin of virtue, where he argues that we do need to be deceived by a picture of human excellence that provides us with an ideal to emulate. Yet even when painting this picture, the lawgivers also make clear that living up to it is extremely demanding, since it is 'troublesome to resist, and very difficult wholly to subdue' our natural inclinations,

In developing this point, Mandeville returns to his argument that evil, if not the basis of civil society, is 'at least a necessary Ingredient in the Compound'. It is naïve to think that the good of society is consistent with the good of each of its members, or that affluence can be achieved without the vices flourishing.[129] Society can never be a harmoniously ordered whole, for largescale coexistence is necessarily characterised by compromises, not just between different groups and interests within society, but equally between economic prosperity and virtue.[130] It is important to recognise this, lest we demand the impossible and then decry corruption whenever society inevitably falls short. Those who extol human nature too often elide these trade-offs, however, pretending that social utility and moral purity are mutually conducive, and in such cases it is beneficial to pull 'off the Disguises of [the] artful Men' who propagate these falsehoods for self-serving reasons.[131] Mandeville does not address the worry that revealing the ubiquity of fashionable hypocrisy may undermine the practice of sociability, yet it is difficult to see how he could challenge the mistaken view of society endorsed by those who call for moral reform without drawing attention to the more general relationship between hypocrisy and sociability.

These remarks speak to a broader question concerning the very purpose of (moral) philosophy. Here again, the contrast between Shaftesbury and Mandeville is instructive. Towards the end of the *Characteristicks*, Shaftesbury claims that his aim 'has been to correct *Manners*, and regulate *Lives*',[132] and one of his main worries with selfish theories of human nature is that they would undermine the practice of virtue (irrespective of their truthfulness). On this

---

with success coming only to those who make 'a continual War with themselves', *Fable* I, 43–44.

129. *Letter to Dion*, 48–49.

130. Given that Mandeville maintains that counterfeited virtue is (a) socially beneficial and (b) leads us to perform many of the same acts as we would if our motives satisfied the criteria for real virtue, it may be objected that he overstates the purported trade-off between economic prosperity and virtue here. One response available to Mandeville is that although successful social norms depend upon the practice of counterfeited virtue, economic prosperity further requires the pursuit of certain vices. In other words, both counterfeited virtue and vices that do not involve counterfeiting virtue often prove socially beneficial. This is an occasion where the 'origins of sociability' and 'private vices, public benefits' theses each draw our attention to different sides of Mandeville's analysis.

131. *Letter to Dion*, 8, and 22–25 on the 'easy Christianity' of Mandeville's adversaries, who forget 'it is impossible to serve God and Mammon'.

132. Shaftesbury, *Miscellaneous Reflections*, iii.2 (114).

point he was followed closely by Francis Hutcheson, who listed Shaftesbury and others as examples to support his claim that 'to engage Men to publickly useful Actions, is certainly the most necessary Point in Morals.'[133] For both Shaftesbury and Hutcheson, moral philosophy should never lose sight of its practical influence and the question of whether to emphasise the best or worst aspects of human nature must take into account the social and educative consequences either way. Where Shaftesbury and Hutcheson thought that there was a practical imperative to exalt the sociable and benevolent side of human nature, Mandeville was instead content for readers to say of him (as they did of Michel de Montaigne): 'that he was pretty well vers'd in the Defects of Mankind, but unacquainted with the Excellencies of human Nature.'[134]

The disagreement here is not based solely on the comparative social benefits of presenting human nature in a positive or negative light, for what if revealing the truth about human nature does not improve morals and is not socially beneficial? From Mandeville's perspective, there is no reason to assume that truth and utility will necessarily converge, which is to say that we might have to choose, to some degree at least, between an accurate analysis of human nature and one which encourages a certain type of conduct. Faced with this choice, Mandeville opts for the truthful over the useful, and especially over the pleasing, in marked opposition to Shaftesbury's 'generous and refined' notions, which may be capable 'of Inspiring us with the most Noble Sentiments concerning the Dignity of our exalted Nature: What Pity it is they are not true.'[135]

These concerns remain important, if less stark, when we compare Mandeville to David Hume and Adam Smith. While Hume is more often remembered as an anatomist rather than a painter of human nature,[136] in the essay 'Of the

---

133. Hutcheson, *Essay*, ii.4. For discussion of this point, see also Michael B. Gill, *The British Moralists on Human Nature and the Birth of Secular Ethics* (Cambridge: Cambridge University Press, 2006), 143; Maurer, *Self-love, Egoism and the Selfish Hypothesis*, 95–97.

134. *Fable* I, 5.

135. *Fable* I, 324. See also *Fable* II, 357, where Mandeville concludes the book with an attack on Shaftesbury, observing that 'the Ideas he had form'd of the Goodness and Excellency of our Nature, were as romantick and chimerical as they are beautiful and amiable'. More generally, see Mandeville's discussion of 'the Painter' at *Fable* II, 35–37.

136. David Hume's famous distinction between the 'Anatomist' and 'Painter' of human nature was first set out in his 1739 letter to Francis Hutcheson; see *The Letters of David Hume*, ed. J.Y.T. Greig (Oxford: Clarendon Press, 1932), vol. 1, Letter 13, 32–33. See also Hume, *Treatise*, 3.3.6.6; idem., *An Enquiry concerning Human Understanding* [1748], ed. Tom L. Beauchamp

Dignity or Meanness of Human Nature' he argues that 'the sentiments of those, who are inclined to think favourably of mankind, *are more advantageous to virtue*, than the contrary principles, which give us a mean opinion of our nature.'[137] For the purposes of this essay, at least, in which Mandeville may well have been an implicit target, Hume is as much concerned with how we ought to present human nature if we want to encourage virtuous conduct as he is with uncovering the innermost principles of our actions; indeed, it is telling that he frames the debate in terms of the former question. Similarly, in classifying Mandeville's moral philosophy as 'licentious', Smith observes that it is starkly at odds with systems that make virtue consist in either propriety, prudence, or benevolence, all of which tend 'to encourage the best and most laudable habits of the human mind'. The tendency of Mandeville's system, by contrast, is 'wholly pernicious'.[138] To be sure, this is not Smith's sole or even most important objection, but here we do see him stressing the apparently noxious consequences of Mandeville's ideas, rather than (or in addition to) their falsity. Hume and Smith, while not so inclined to paint human nature in the bright brushstrokes of someone like Hutcheson, still show some practical concern for emphasising the positive aspects of our conduct that is foreign to Mandeville.

None of this is to deny that there are real and important differences between Mandeville's and his various critics' views of human nature, which should not be understated.[139] But nor should we neglect that their differences are partly explained by the fact that Mandeville was simply a lot more willing to accentuate the negative aspects of human nature than many of his contemporaries. He might have considered this socially beneficial up to a point, for there is at least something to be said for humbling the pride and exposing the hypocrisy behind the moralising bluster of his adversaries, whose calls for moral reform and admonitions against vice would, if heeded, undermine the basis of economic prosperity. Nevertheless, a concern for the social and moral consequences of his arguments does not appear to have guided Mandeville's writing

---

(Oxford: Oxford University Press, 1999), 1.8. For discussion of Mandeville and Hume in these terms, see Castiglione, 'Considering Things Minutely', 479–84; Tolonen, *Mandeville and Hume*, especially 7 and 152–55.

137. See Hume, 'Dignity or Meanness', 81 (emphasis added).

138. Smith, *Theory of Moral Sentiments*, VII.ii.4.5–6.

139. Cf. Castiglione, 'Considering Things Minutely', 485, who I think is only half right to claim that 'there was no real divergence between [Mandeville's] and Smith's view of the mechanisms that govern self-centred human actions. They seemed to disagree rather as to whether or not it was advisable to present them in a favourable light.'

to anything like the degree of Shaftesbury or Hutcheson. Mandeville was not one to let considerations of social utility get in the way of tracing 'Self-love in its darkest Recesses . . . beyond any other System of Ethicks'.[140]

Conclusion

Although Mandeville's accounts of human nature and sociability were not originally developed against Shaftesbury, by 1723 he had come to view the *Characteristicks* as the antithesis of his own position. Mandeville largely succeeded in reframing the debate as one between himself and Shaftesbury, at least if the title of Hutcheson's *Inquiry* of 1725 is anything to go by, which presents the work as a defence of the principles of Shaftesbury against the *Fable*.[141] Hutcheson was not alone in seeking to vindicate Shaftesbury against Mandeville,[142] and even when the two were attacked together—as subversive deists, for example—they were still taken to represent opposing outlooks on human nature.[143] The view that Shaftesbury and Mandeville epitomised the two poles of eighteenth-century British philosophy persisted well into the nineteenth century, with Leslie Stephen describing their theories as 'the Scylla and Charybdis between which it was a delicate matter to steer a straight course.'[144]

140. *Fable* I, 405.

141. The full title reads: *An Inquiry into the Original of Our Ideas of Beauty and Virtue; in Two Treatises. In which the Principles of the late Earl of Shaftesbury are Explain'd and Defended, against the Author of the Fable of the Bees: and the Ideas of Moral Good and Evil are establish'd, according to the Sentiments of the Antient Moralists. With an Attempt to introduce a Mathematical Calculation in Subjects of Morality.* The lengthy subtitle ('*In which*' onwards) was removed from the title page of the second (1726) and subsequent editions.

142. For example, see Fiddes, *General Treatise*, xxxi–lvi, lxxvii–lxxviii.

143. Philip Skelton, *Deism Revealed, or, the Attack on Christianity Candidly Reviewed In its real Merits*, vol. 2 (London, 1751), 268: '*Shaftesbury* labours to prove mankind, of whom he knew but little, benevolent, public-spirited, and, by nature, good. *Mandeville* takes as much pains to prove them the reverse of all this.' See also John Brown, *Thoughts on Civil Liberty, on Licentiousness, and Faction* (London, 1765), 100–101, who observes that although Shaftesbury's system was based on 'the *unaided Excellence*' and Mandeville's on 'the *incurable Depravity of human Nature*', they both '*disgraced* CHRISTIANITY.' Brown discusses Mandeville's philosophy in more detail in his *Essays on the Characteristics* (which, as its title suggests, is targeted at Shaftesbury), especially 137–58.

144. Stephen, *Essays on Freethinking*, 198–278, quoted here at 243; idem., *History of English Thought in the Eighteenth Century*, vol. 2 (London: Smith, Elder, and Co., 1876), 15–46. See also

The two most important disagreements that Mandeville identified between himself and Shaftesbury concern the nature of virtue and explanation of human sociability, yet the theme of hypocrisy proves a helpful vantage point for exploring some of the complexities of the debate. From Mandeville's perspective, Shaftesbury was (a) guilty of hypocrisy himself, (b) promulgated notions of virtue that encouraged hypocrisy and even self-deception, but (c) failed to register the importance of hypocrisy in explaining sociability. If maintaining all three charges seems somewhat puzzling then so it should, for even if they are not necessarily incompatible, they at least operate at different levels of analysis, which I have tried to tease apart throughout this chapter.

For Mandeville, human sociability requires hypocrisy because we cannot bear to see the true motives behind one another's conduct. If we were generally motivated by some social love then there would be no need to disguise this when interacting with others, but this is not the case. Our social practices and moral standards rely on channelling our self-centred passions—pride and shame, above all else—and giving them the outward appearance of other-regarding or public-spirited sentiments. Counterfeited virtue and (self-)deception are thus conducive to sociability. If Shaftesbury's notions of virtue (as Mandeville understood them) lead us to counterfeit love of society and become unknown to ourselves, then this might count against them, but this is not chiefly because they are socially disadvantageous, as Mandeville sometimes claimed. Or, if they are socially disadvantageous, it is less because they lead us to counterfeit virtue (for this would be beneficial) and more because they lower the bar for virtue so far that they do not even give us an ideal worth counterfeiting, thereby breeding passivity and indolence.

If real virtue requires a victory over the passions, as Mandeville insists in 1723, then even counterfeited virtue must involve some self-denial (with pride or shame typically subduing other passions), for otherwise it would not be a close enough approximation to pass for the real thing. Counterfeited virtue, then, involves some self-denial *and* is socially beneficial, but it still falls short of the demands of real virtue on Mandeville's account. As we are naturally averse to the self-love or pride of others, we have come to conceptualise virtue in terms that demand a conquest over these passions, whether or not this is within our reach. Fortunately, we have developed social practices where counterfeited virtue regularly passes for real virtue, and for the most part we can

Wilde, 'Mandeville's Place in English Thought'. On Stephen's role in reviving interest in Mandeville, see Schneider, *Paradox and Society*, 57.

pursue our lives without looking behind the artifices of sociability to detect the hypocrisy upon which our peaceful coexistence depends.

This chapter brings to a close the first part of the book, which has focused on the psychological origins of sociability. This has largely involved examining Mandeville's observations on how practices and norms of sociability (or civility, politeness, and morals) operate in the societies of his own day—that is, *an analysis of where we are now*. Mandeville thought that these observations revealed important general truths about human nature, but he was also acutely aware of the importance of social context and historical contingency. Our passions develop and manifest themselves in various ways in different times and places. In his later works, in particular, Mandeville became increasingly interested in *an analysis of how we arrived here*, which involves seeing honour codes or polite manners, for example, as historically specific achievements. It is to these historical narratives that I turn in the second part of the book.

PART II
Historical Narratives

4

The Desire of Dominion and
Origin of Society

MANDEVILLE ADDRESSES QUESTIONS of sociability throughout the different editions of the *Fable of the Bees*. The opening paragraph of the 'Preface' to
the 1714 edition declares that 'what renders [man] a Sociable Animal' is 'his
vilest and most hateful Qualities',[1] with 'An Enquiry Into the Origin of Moral
Virtue' then outlining the steps taken by 'Lawgivers and other wise Men, that
have laboured for the Establishment of Society'.[2] 'A Search into the Nature
of Society', added to the expanded 1723 edition, centres on the question of
which 'Qualities of Man . . . make him beyond other Animals a sociable
Creature',[3] and, as we shall see in this chapter, Mandeville sets out his most
detailed and sophisticated reflections on the origin of 'Society, and the Sociableness of Man' in *Fable II*.[4] Society and sociability (or 'Sociableness') are
terms of art for Mandeville. The former refers specifically to a body politic
where we live under civil government and the latter, in turn, to the qualities
that make us fit for such a life.[5]

Throughout these discussions of sociability Mandeville both analyses
human nature in general terms and investigates how civilised society developed

1. *Fable* I, 4.
2. *Fable* I, 42.
3. *Fable* I, 325.
4. *Fable* II, 177.
5. See *Fable* I, 347: 'I hope that the Reader knows that by Society I understand a Body Poli-
tick, in which Man either subdued by Superior Force, or by Persuasion drawn from his Savage
State, is become a Disciplin'd Creature'. For other clarifications of this focus, see *Female Tatler*,
no. 62: 99; *Fable* I, 4; *Fable* II, 183.

from a savage state.[6] This chapter and the next examine the latter dimension of Mandeville's theory of sociability; that is, his accounts of the development of social norms and institutions, which are expounded at greatest length in *Fable II* (the focus of this chapter) and *An Enquiry into the Origin of Honour* (the focus of the next). In earlier chapters I argued that Mandeville's analysis of human nature remains broadly consistent between his different works, yet far more significant changes come into view once we turn to his historical narratives. This is not to say that there is a radical break between the two volumes of the *Fable*, but the second does add several layers of historical nuance to the first.[7] This chapter is thus especially attentive to the progression of Mandeville's ideas and aims to provide the most thorough examination to date of how his historical narratives develop between the different editions of the *Fable*.

The standard way of approaching these developments is to ask whether, or to what extent, Mandeville shifts from a 'conspiratorial' to an 'evolutionary' mode of explanation.[8] This way of framing the debate is one of my targets throughout the chapter, for while it draws attention to some salient changes it

---

6. I use the terms savage and civilised (or variants thereof) throughout this chapter when discussing Mandeville's ideas, which is not to suggest that I endorse the connotations that these terms often carried at the time. For helpful entry points into the various ways that savage and civilised peoples were juxtaposed in eighteenth-century political thought and discussion of how this discourse relates to European imperialism and its critics, see, for example, Sankar Muthu, *Enlightenment Against Empire* (Princeton and Oxford: Princeton University Press, 2003), 11–71; J.G.A. Pocock, *Barbarism and Religion, Volume Four: Barbarians, Savages, and Empires* (Cambridge: Cambridge University Press, 2005), especially 157–80; Silvia Sebastiani, *The Scottish Enlightenment: Race, Gender, and the Limits of Progress*, trans. Jeremy Carden (New York: Palgrave Macmillan, 2013), especially 73–101; Robert Launay, *Savages, Romans, and Despots: Thinking about Others from Montaigne to Herder* (Chicago and London: The University of Chicago Press, 2018), especially 146–85. Mandeville occasionally contrasts European civilisation with African or American savages (e.g. *Female Tatler*, no. 62: 98; *Fable* II, 198–99), but for the most part his historical narratives proceed at a high level of abstraction modelled more closely on Epicurean stories of societal development, with strong echoes of Book Five of Lucretius's *De rerum natura*. This is well documented in Hundert, *Enlightenment's Fable*, especially 45–51, 93–96.

7. These layers are effectively brought out at places in Hundert, *Enlightenment's Fable*, 62–96, although he does not focus on charting the developments between Mandeville's different works. See also Tolonen, *Mandeville and Hume*, 41–102, who explores Mandeville's intellectual development more systematically and does argue for a radical break between the first and second volumes.

8. This characterisation of the debate follows Stafford, 'General Introduction', xvi–xviii.

overlooks many others. Most importantly, by focusing on the *mode* of explanation, the standard approach loses sight of important differences in the *object* of explanation (or explanandum). For example, Mandeville seeks to recount not only the development of society from savage families, but also the origins of our notions of moral virtue, honour, and politeness, with his later narratives accompanied by digressions on, amongst other things, the origins of natural religion and language. We should not assume that Mandeville explains all these phenomena in the same way, which immediately complicates questions about whether the mode of explanation changes between his works, as different modes of explanation may be more or less appropriate depending on the precise object of investigation. The main goal of this chapter, then, is to tell a more nuanced story about the evolution of Mandeville's thought, which both touches upon the problems raised by the standard approach while also bringing other complexities into view.

As the chapter progresses, I turn to a more detailed study of Mandeville's account of sociability and the origin of society in *Fable II*. In doing so, the second aim of this chapter is to chart how what Mandeville variously terms our 'Desire of Dominion',[9] 'domineering Spirit',[10] 'Instinct of Sovereignty',[11] or 'Desire of Superiority',[12] plays out in his historical narratives. This is key to understanding Mandeville's pride-centred theory of sociability, since the 'Desire of Dominion is a never-failing Consequence of the Pride, that is common to all Men'.[13] Although Mandeville had referred to 'the love of Dominion and that usurping Temper all Mankind are born with' in the 1723 edition of the *Fable*,[14] the importance he accords to our love of dominion and sovereignty is far greater in *Fable II* and represents one of its most significant theoretical innovations.[15] Indeed, our desire of dominion is *the* most important passion in Mandeville's later account of the origin of society, for without it 'Multitudes could never have been form'd into Societies.' The difficulty, however, is that we are all sent 'into the World with a visible Desire after Government, and no Capacity for it at all',[16] so what needs to be explained is how we could ever

9. *Fable* II, 204.

10. *Fable* II, 223, 272, 310.

11. *Fable* II, 271–75, 281, 310, 313; see also *Origin of Honour*, 43, 68–69.

12. *Fable* II, 132, 223, 267.

13. *Fable* II, 204.

14. *Fable* I, 281.

15. On this point, see also Tolonen, *Mandeville and Hume*, 95.

16. *Fable* II, 205.

have come to develop this capacity given that our desire of dominion is prone to drive us into conflict with one another. Mandeville's analysis of the origin of society, then, is largely a story about how the social dynamics of our desire of dominion play out at different stages of the civilising process.

My approach in this chapter involves tracing how Mandeville's ideas take shape between his various origin stories, both (chronologically) across the different editions of the *Fable* and within the historical narratives that span the final four dialogues of *Fable II*. In doing so, I emphasise where and how Mandeville's later origin stories either build upon or depart from his earlier ones, while drawing attention to places where *Fable II* addresses difficulties raised by some of his critics in the 1720s. In the conclusion I return to the question of whether it makes sense to classify Mandeville's narratives as 'evolutionary' and consider the implications of his account of sociability for his ideas on political authority.

Mandeville's origin stories

Mandeville recounts several stories about the origins of different phenomena across his works, the relationship between which he never fully explains. Many scholars have approached these stories by asking whether he shifts from a conspiratorial to an evolutionary explanation of the origins of society and morals. J. Martin Stafford offers a succinct statement of one pole of the debate:

> Mandeville expounded two distinct and incompatible accounts of the origin of virtue and the establishment of society. Part I of the *Fable* incorporates the *conspiratorial thesis*: namely, that 'lawgivers, moralists, philosophers and skilful politicians' conspired to foster in people the notions of honour and shame, and by flattery prevailed upon them to subdue their selfish natural appetites and act for the common good. . . . In Part II of the *Fable* it is entirely superseded by the *evolutionary thesis*: namely, that morality and political institutions evolved slowly as human wisdom and experience accrued over many ages and generations.'[17]

The notion that there is a pronounced shift from a conspiratorial to an evolutionary mode of explanation between the two volumes of the *Fable* probably remains the minority view, albeit one with some important adherents amongst

---

17. Stafford, 'General Introduction', xvi.

those who have focused on questions of sociability.[18] A more widely endorsed interpretation is that the role Mandeville assigned to wise lawgivers
and moralists should only ever have been read metaphorically, not literally.
According to F. B. Kaye, for example, Mandeville's 'description of the invention of virtue and society by lawgivers and wise men ... is a parable and not
an attempt at history.' What he 'was attempting to show by his allegory of the
growth of society and morality was the ingredients that make it up, and not
the actual process of growth.'[19] This line of interpretation has been defended
at greatest length by Maurice Goldsmith, who argues that the 'skilful politician
is a Mandevillean fictive literary device', which serves as 'a shorthand term for
indicating gradual development.'[20] On this view, there is no inconsistency
between the two volumes of the *Fable*; the second simply spells out in detail
what Mandeville had only gestured towards allegorically in the first. Even
amongst commentators who do not come down decisively on one side of this
debate, the standard view (endorsed by both sides) remains that the conspiratorial and evolutionary accounts reflect two different stories Mandeville tells
about the origin of society,[21] which, if read literally, stand in tension with one
another.[22] The debate then turns on whether the conspiratorial account
should be read literally or metaphorically.

18. See Scribano, *Natura umana e società competitiva*, 154–55; Simonazzi, *Le favole della filosofia*, 235–36, 306–308; idem., 'Common Law', 116, 126; Tolonen, *Mandeville and Hume*, 11–12;
Martin Otero Knott, 'Mandeville on Governability', *Journal of Scottish Philosophy* 12, no. 1
(2014), especially 21–24; Frank Palmeri, 'Bernard de Mandeville and the Shaping of Conjectural
History', in *Mandeville's Tropology of Paradoxes*, 19.

19. Kaye, 'Introduction', lxiv.

20. Goldsmith, *Private Vices, Public Benefits*, 61–64, with the quotation at 62. For similar
views, see, for example, Lovejoy, *Reflections on Human Nature*, 176; Irwin Primer, 'Introduction',
to his edition of Mandeville, *The Fable of the Bees* (New York: Capricorn Books, 1962), 11; Nathan Rosenberg, 'Mandeville and Laissez-Faire', *Journal of the History of Ideas* 24, no. 2 (1963),
194–95; Colman, 'Reality of Virtue', 129; Herdt, *Putting On Virtue*, 273; Eugene Heath, 'Carrying
Matters Too Far? Mandeville and the Eighteenth-Century Scots on the Evolution of Morals',
Journal of Scottish Philosophy 12, no. 1 (2014), 106–107; Kapust, *Flattery*, 141–42.

21. For a helpful overview framed this way, see Jack, 'Men Become Sociable', 7–11. For an
example indicating that this framing goes beyond the specialist Mandeville scholarship, see the
summary of Mandeville's 'two stories' about socialisation in James A. Harris, 'The Government
of the Passions', in *The Oxford Handbook of British Philosophy in the Eighteenth Century*, 280.

22. See, for example, Kaye, 'Introduction', lxv–lxvi: 'the gradualness of evolution' stressed in
Fable II 'completely contradicts the *literal* interpretation of the allegory' from the 'Enquiry'. For

Stafford's way of presenting the debate is a helpful starting point, for at least three reasons. First, it focuses on the place of skilful politicians in instigating morals and society, rather than on their role in managing economic activity in commercially advanced states.[23] The two debates are sometimes analysed together,[24] but the latter—i.e. was Mandeville a proponent of laissez-faire or government intervention?—is distinct and entirely peripheral for present purposes.[25] Second, Stafford's formulation captures the tendency of the standard approach to assume that the object of explanation is relatively stable between the two volumes of the *Fable*, such that it makes sense to talk in general terms of Mandeville having an account, or two accounts, of 'the origin of virtue and the establishment of society.' Third, Stafford articulates, more clearly than most, the two views that are supposedly opposed to one another. Mandeville never describes his account as either 'conspiratorial' or 'evolutionary', so the question we are concerned with is not what he means by these terms, but, rather, in what ways they do or do not map onto different arguments that he does articulate. Although I address some of these interpretative questions in what follows, my overarching goal is to complicate this way of construing the

---

a notable counterpoint, see Burtt, *Virtue Transformed*, 142: 'Mandeville's work provides two complementary accounts of the origin of civil society.'

23. Mandeville sometimes refers to the 'dextrous Management' of 'Good Politicians' in regulating trade through (for example) taxes and prohibitions (*Fable* I, 116), but this is distinct from the role of wise lawgivers, moralists, or politicians in the civilising process, which provides the basis for the conspiratorial thesis. When, in 1723, Mandeville explains that the infamous subtitle of the *Fable* alludes to how 'Private Vices by the dextrous Management of a skilful Politician may be turned into Publick Benefits' (*Fable* I, 369), he seems to be referring to the role of politicians in ensuring that trades based on vices generate wealth and prosperity, rather than to the conspiratorial thesis regarding the origins of virtue and society.

24. See, for example, Rosenberg, 'Mandeville and Laissez-Faire', especially 186–89, 194–95; F. A. Hayek, 'Lecture on a Master Mind: Dr. Bernard Mandeville', *Proceedings of the British Academy* 52 (1966), especially 134–36; Ronald Hamowy, *The Scottish Enlightenment and the Theory of Spontaneous Order* (Carbondale and Edwardsville: Southern Illinois University Press, 1987), 7–10. On this point, see also Dickey, 'Pride, Hypocrisy and Civility', 414–15, who criticises Hayek for not appreciating the differences between Mandeville's economic and social theories.

25. For critical summaries of (and contributions to) this debate, see Harry Landreth, 'The Economic Thought of Bernard Mandeville', *History of Political Economy* 7, no. 2 (1975): 193–208; Salim Rashid, 'Mandeville's *Fable*: Laissez-Faire or Libertinism?', *Eighteenth-Century Studies* 18, no. 3 (1985): 313–30; Renee Prendergast, 'Mandeville and the Doctrine of Laissez-faire', *Erasmus Journal for Philosophy and Economics* 9, no. 1 (2016), especially 104–12.

debate by bringing to light certain complexities in Mandeville's origin stories that the standard approach elides.

The role of human contrivance (1714–23)

The main evidence for the conspiratorial thesis is drawn from the 'Enquiry' of 1714, where Mandeville memorably charts how 'Lawgivers and other wise Men' endeavoured to establish society and 'civilize Mankind'. To summarise, very briefly, the lawgivers flattered those they hoped to govern by extolling 'the Excellency of our Nature above other Animals', before presenting the species as divided between a class of 'low-minded People', who unreflectively indulge their natural appetites, and a class 'of lofty high-Spirited Creatures', who seek to conquer their passions and promote the public welfare. This involved cultivating notions of shame and honour, appeals to which motivated people to emulate, or at least admire, anyone counted amongst the higher class, while feeling ashamed about being associated with the lower class. Mandeville concludes that this 'was (or might have been) the manner after which Savage Man was broke' and that 'the first Rudiments of Morality, broach'd by Skilful Politicians', played a pivotal role in rendering us 'tractable'. With this 'Foundation of Politicks' in place, he continues, 'it is impossible that Man should long remain uncivilized', and it is in the context of this civilising process that all would have come to agree on definitions of virtue and vice, the distinction between which was 'the Contrivance of Politicians'.[26] In the 'Enquiry', then, Mandeville claims that deliberate intervention and foresight were required to instil notions of human excellence and moral worth at certain points of the civilising process, and nowhere in the text does he suggest that the role of lawgivers and politicians should be understood metaphorically. Mandeville appears to follow Epicurean discussions of the origin of justice quite closely here,[27] which

---

26. *Fable* I, 42–50.

27. For a strikingly similar contemporary example, see John Digby, *Epicurus's Morals, Translated from the Greek by John Digby, Esq. with Comments and Reflections Taken out of several Authors* (London, 1712), 142–44. Digby's commentary refers to a class 'of Wise Men, who ow'd all their *Wisdom* to their natural Principles and Composition', and who instigated laws to civilise 'the *Primitive Men*' who otherwise 'liv'd after a Beastlike manner, without *Method* or *Order*'. For a more detailed historical story, which still appeals to the role of 'Ancient Sages and first Lawmakers' in civilising 'the rash multitude', see Walter Charleton, *Epicurus's Morals, Collected Partly out of his owne Greek Text, and Diogenes Laertius, And Partly out of the Rhapsodies of Marcus Antonius, Plutarch, Cicero, & Seneca* (London, 1656), Chap. 27, especially 158–59. On these

counts against reading his invocations of lawgivers as nothing more than 'a joke at the expense of civic humanism' and its appeals to founding legislators.[28]

The 'Enquiry' includes some observations on the origin of society,[29] yet the subject matter, as its title clearly indicates, is the origin of moral virtue. Mandeville's account swiftly takes us from 'Savage Man' to civilised society in only a few pages. The main aims of the 'Enquiry' include showing that our ideas of virtue and vice are acquired rather than innate;[30] that we could arrive at these ideas without knowledge of revealed religion;[31] and that these ideas can be upheld even though the vast majority of people, if not everyone, are motivated principally by shame and pride.[32] Given these aims, there is no reason to assume that Mandeville regarded the 'Enquiry' as exhausting everything he had to say about the origin of society. It is at least plausible that he saw himself as outlining only the broad contours of what must have been a longer and more complicated developmental story in order to support certain claims about the origin of virtue.[33] Either way, the explanatory priority of the 'Enquiry' is the origin of virtue, not the origin of society, a point which it helps to keep in mind when comparing the text to his later works.

---

influences, see Hundert, *Enlightenment's Fable*, 48–49; and, more generally, Robertson, *Case for the Enlightenment*, 269–70. While Mandeville seems to follow Epicurean narratives most closely, the idea of wise lawgivers civilising people from their otherwise bestial state would have also been familiar to his contemporaries from Cicero's account of the origin of eloquence at the beginning of *De inventione*. See Branchi, *Pride, Manners, and Morals*, 83, who highlights this connection in terms of the role of rhetorical persuasion in both Cicero's and Mandeville's accounts.

28. Cf. Maurice M. Goldsmith, 'Regulating Anew the Moral and Political Sentiments of Mankind: Bernard Mandeville and the Scottish Enlightenment', *Journal of the History of Ideas* 49, no. 4 (1988), 605.

29. This is often treated as its principal focus; see, for example, Goldsmith, *Private Vices, Public Benefits*, especially 49–64.

30. For example, the two-page 'Introduction' preceding the 'Enquiry' emphasises that the latter will explain 'how Man . . . might yet by his own Imperfections be taught to distinguish between Virtue and Vice', *Fable* I, 40.

31. *Fable* I, 50–51.

32. Mandeville at least entertains the possibility of people who act 'from no other Motive but their Love of Goodness', *Fable* I, 57.

33. Even if we endorse this (charitable) interpretation, it does not follow that Mandeville's invocations of lawgivers and politicians should be taken as a metaphor for the more complicated story. All that follows is that Mandeville did not tell us the full backstory to their appearance.

The 'Enquiry' is profitably (yet rarely) read alongside 'Remark R',[34] which is effectively an essay on honour. It is of interest presently because Mandeville sketches out another historical story, which touches on the origin of government, and because we find more evidence for the conspiratorial thesis: honour too, he claims, is 'an Invention of Moralists and Politicians'.[35] One of Mandeville's main arguments is that politicians originally cultivated honour by appealing to people's pride and shame to incite them to fight for their society, which reveals that honour is not founded upon natural courage. What we call natural courage (in all animals) is based on anger, which, in turn, derives from lust or hunger. Although anger can overcome fear, leading us to clash with one another, 'Man in his Savage State' rarely needs to fight to satisfy his lust or hunger; he is a timorous rather than an angry creature.[36] Things appear very differently, however, 'if we examine [man] as a Member of Society and a taught Animal', for then we find that pride, envy, avarice, and ambition have roused him 'from his natural Innocence and Stupidity.' In drawing this contrast between 'Man in his Savage State' and as 'a Member of Society', Mandeville suggests (without spelling out the transition in any detail) that as social interaction became more frequent our knowledge increased and our desires and wants multiplied, such that we would have often been 'cross'd in the Pursuit of them' and 'Man would in a little time become the most hurtful and noxious Creature in the World.'[37]

The opposing passions of fear and anger are central to understanding how natural courage operates and the dangers that it poses. If human conflict arises when man's anger overcomes his fear, then the 'first Care of all Governments is by severe Punishments to curb his Anger when it does hurt'. We can live peacefully together as long as our fear of punishment overcomes our anger and we start to learn that self-preservation is best served by observing the laws;

34. For a notable exception, see Bluet, *Enquiry*, 24–35, who summarises the narratives of the two texts together to expose some of the tensions between them. See also [Anon.], *True Meaning*, 85–95.

35. *Fable* I, 198.

36. This is a strikingly different presentation to the beginning of the 'Enquiry', where Mandeville had depicted man 'in the wild State of Nature' as 'an extraordinary selfish and headstrong, as well as cunning Animal', *Fable* I, 41–42. See also Bluet, *Enquiry*, 24, who mockingly observes that Mandeville appears to be committed to the view that 'Man in his savage Nature was a peaceable, quiet, timorous, extraordinary selfish, headstrong, cunning, innocent, stupid, silly, Animal.'

37. *Fable* I, 200–206.

indeed, cultivating fear in this way is sufficient for the internal 'Peace and Quiet of Society'.[38] At this stage, Mandeville is still building up to his main claims about the origin of honour, but it is worth highlighting that this account already adds an additional layer of complexity to that of the 'Enquiry', which had nothing at all to say about the fear of punishment as a motive in establishing society and civilising humans.

By appealing to fear of punishment to quell internal discord, it 'is possible by good Government to keep a Society always quiet in it self'. Nonetheless, societies that hope to extend their territories or defend themselves from foreign conquest need to mobilise people to fight. Politicians must persuade their subjects that all prohibitions on killing cease when dealing with 'Enemies to the Publick'. This might be achieved if politicians present public enemies as objects of anger, thereby appealing to their subjects' natural courage, but Mandeville gives a few reasons (which need not detain us here) why such courage is 'soon exploded' once war is underway, leaving governments with the problem of finding 'out an Equivalent for Courage that will make Men fight.' Developing his insight from the 'Enquiry' about how 'easily Men were induc'd to believe any thing that is said in their Praise', Mandeville now argues that lawgivers or politicians must have taught people that 'the generality of Men had within them a Principle of Valour distinct from Anger, or any other Passion,' a belief which many people would uphold because it flatters their pride, even though they have not experienced the principle themselves. Failures to display valour would soon become a source of shame while the performance of valorous acts would be associated with honour, and once 'the Notions of Honour and Shame are received among a Society, it is not difficult to make Men fight.'[39]

The main purpose of 'Remark R' is to show that honour is an artificial passion, which is cultivated by politicians or lawgivers within society by appealing to our pride and shame. As with the 'Enquiry', Mandeville assigns a very specific role to political contrivance in inculcating certain ideas of human excellence at important points in the civilising process,[40] and there is no textual

---

38. *Fable* I, 206–207.

39. *Fable* I, 207–10.

40. The index added to the 1723 edition of the *Fable* captures this role succinctly: '*Moralists* . . . Their Artifices to civilize Mankind', *Fable* I, 376. In 'Remark N', also added in 1723, Mandeville similarly refers to the 'Care of the Politician in civilizing the Society' through 'the happy Contrivance of playing our Passions against one another.' See *Fable* I, 145, and the index entry for '*Politicians*' at 377.

evidence from the 1714 edition of the *Fable* that counts against reading this literally.[41] More revealing, however, is that juxtaposing the 'Enquiry' and 'Remark R' discloses that Mandeville did not, in fact, lay out a single account of the origin of society in 1714, since it remains unclear the extent to which fear of punishment or praise and flattery were the key factors in drawing humans out of their savage condition and towards society. Mandeville did not attempt to reconcile the two narratives from the 'Enquiry' and 'Remark R', possibly because, to offer a charitable explanation, they have different subject matters: the first is concerned with moral virtue, the second with honour.

Where the 1714 edition of the *Fable* contains some reflections on the origin of society in the context of explaining the origins of moral virtue and honour, in 'A Search into the Nature of Society', added to the enlarged 1723 edition, Mandeville turns directly 'to investigate the nature of Society' itself.[42] As we shall see, it is this account of sociability and the origin of society—set out against Shaftesbury, his newfound antagonist—which Mandeville would defend, elaborate, and sometimes revise at far greater length in *Fable II*. The 'Search' does not add much to the evidence for the conspiratorial thesis, beyond one brief allusion to the role of 'the Politician' in civilising people through flattery, recalling the discussion of honour from 'Remark R'.[43] The most straightforward explanation for this is that Mandeville does not revisit questions about the origin of moral virtue or honour at all in the 'Search',[44]

41. Cf. Goldsmith, *Private Vices, Public Benefits*, 64, who claims that even in the 1714 edition of the *Fable*, following the earlier *Female Tatler* entries, 'Mandeville explicitly refers to the gradual process by which various social institutions, including skills and crafts, have come into being.' The passages that Goldsmith cites on the development of different skills and crafts, however, do not address the origin of moral virtue or honour. As Goldsmith points out, Mandeville does recognise that 'many Comforts of Life that are now enjoy'd' would have taken a great deal of time to develop and that, when it comes to arts like brewing and bread-making, 'to have invented them at once . . . would have required more Knowledge . . . than the greatest Philosopher has hitherto been endowed with', *Fable* I, 169–71. Crucially, however, Mandeville does not refer to wise lawgivers or skilful politicians at all *in this context*, so the evidence Goldsmith draws on, if anything, counts against reading such invocations elsewhere as allegorical. This is a good example of where a closer focus on the relevant explanandum could have helped to avoid overgeneralisation.

42. *Fable* I, 344.

43. *Fable* I, 334.

44. To be sure, Mandeville does defend and develop his argument that virtue requires self-denial (see Chapter 3, 'Virtue, self-denial, and hypocrisy'), but he does so without explaining how our ideas of virtue would have originally arisen, as he had done in the 'Enquiry'.

which is precisely the context in which he had earlier appealed to the intervention of politicians or lawgivers. His investigation into 'the nature of Society' is instead focused on showing 'that no Societies could have sprung from the Amiable Virtues and Loving Qualities of Man, but on the contrary that all of them must have had their Origin from his Wants, his Imperfections, and the variety of his Appetites'.[45]

Mandeville rejects the explanatory power of appeals to a 'Golden Age' of simplicity and abundance, where everyone could easily obtain and be 'contented with the Necessaries of Life'. Perhaps our amiable virtues and loving qualities could have flourished in such an age, but if it ever existed then 'no Reason or Probability can be alleged why Mankind ever should have rais'd themselves into such large Societies as there have been in the World'. Human sociability, as we now know it, cannot be based on whatever qualities we might associate with 'the State of Innocence', depictions of which tell us nothing instructive about how we would have come to form political states. The world that we find ourselves occupying, at least 'since the Fall of our first Parents', is an inhospitable place where the natural environment poses countless threats to our survival, whether these be severe weather conditions or insects tormenting us. In this unforgiving setting humans must constantly toil to survive, for 'every thing is Evil, which Art and Experience have not taught us to turn into a Blessing.'[46]

Although Mandeville claims to be 'diving into the very rise of' society,[47] he seems less concerned with charting the *rise* of society itself and more with showing that the background conditions from which it must have emerged were ones of scarcity and hardship, rather than abundance and ease. Societies may have 'sprung' to satisfy the necessities of life, yet Mandeville maintains that our desires, vanity, and pride must have increased before we became capable 'of being rais'd into large and vastly numerous Societies'. As in 'Remark R', however, he has relatively little to say about the latter process. The same is true when it comes to explaining how humans would have progressed from 'the Wild State of Nature' to the earliest form of government. Mandeville outlines this transition in a single paragraph. Children obey their parents out of reverence—'something between Love and Fear'—and for a couple of generations this could provide the basis for one man (Mandeville assumes paternal

45. *Fable* I, 346.
46. *Fable* I, 344–47.
47. *Fable* I, 344.

authority) 'to maintain a Superior Sway over all his own Offspring and Descendants, how numerous soever they might grow'. Quarrels over succession would subsequently arise between the sons and war ensue, but Mandeville proceeds to claim that, as man is 'a fearful Animal' that 'loves Peace and Quiet', he would soon be willing to submit to government, of which monarchy must have been the first.[48] This extremely brief sketch leaves plenty of questions unanswered—most glaringly, why would the descendants have quarrelled if they all loved peace and quiet?—and the main reason for mentioning it now is because Mandeville revisits it in far greater depth in *Fable II*, where the transition summarised in this one paragraph ends up spanning the final three dialogues. Although he would eventually return to questions about the origins of moral virtue and honour in *Origin of Honour*, in *Fable II* he was far more concerned with filling in the gaps of the earliest stages of social development, with which he never fully got to grips in the first volume.

Mandeville's historical turn

The conspiratorial thesis was central to Mandeville's earliest enquiries into the origins of moral virtue and honour. That thesis was roundly attacked in the 1720s, however, with Mandeville's critics highlighting the explanatory shortcomings of his invocations of politicians and lawgivers. According to William Law, for example, Mandeville's account of the origin of moral virtue was not only incompatible with the teachings of scripture, but equally failed on its own terms. It omitted many important details such as 'the Philosopher's Name, who first discover'd this *Flattery*', or 'how many Ages of the World had pass'd, before this Consultation of the Philosophers' took place. Mandeville owes us an account of 'what the World was doing before these Philosophers' intervened; 'whether before this, there was any Fear of God, any Belief of a Providence, any Duty to Parents, any Sense of Equity, any Notions of Faith, or any Regard to Truth.'[49] One of Law's many objections was that Mandeville provided no evidence to prove that humans ever lived in an animalistic state of nature without any notions of morality or religion. Law denied the starting point of Mandeville's

48. *Fable* I, 346–48.

49. Law, *Remarks*, 16–19. More generally on Law's criticisms of Mandeville, see Andrew Starkie, 'William Law and *The Fable of the Bees*', *Journal for Eighteenth-Century Studies* 32, no. 3 (2009): 307–19. See also Branchi, *Pride, Manners, and Morals*, 134–35, who suggests that Mandeville's focus on 'gradualism and impersonality' in *Fable II* was a way of answering Law.

'Enquiry' and thus regarded the intervention of lawgivers and politicians as an answer to a non-existent problem. A further difficultly with the chronology was more sharply captured by George Bluet. If we do accept Mandeville's starting point, then how could wise politicians or lawgivers have ever attained the knowledge required to instruct and civilise everyone else? Are we to believe that 'one of the innocent, stupid Animals' presented at the outset of the 'Enquiry' was 'at the same time a Wizard or a Conjurer'?[50] Mandeville's account is question-begging, Bluet suggests, because it fails to explain 'how the Politician (Man being yet in his State of Innocence and Stupidity) should shew so much Stratagem and Cunning.'[51]

As we have seen, the problems that occupied Mandeville in the 'Search' did not rely on politicians or lawgivers inculcating notions of human excellence and valour, and the same is true of much of *Fable II*. Nevertheless, there is evidence that Mandeville was concerned with answering or at least evading the objections raised by his critics. Most importantly, and as we shall see as this chapter progresses, much of his explanation of the steps towards society involves showing how humans gradually developed the knowledge and capacity to govern others, which, as Law and Bluet pointed out, his earlier works had conspicuously overlooked. Rather than starting with wise lawgivers and politicians, Mandeville instead seeks to show how leaders could have eventually emerged from savage families to discover 'various ways of curbing Mankind',[52] now acknowledging that it was only much later, after the invention of written laws, that lawgivers would have ever perfected their craft. It was experience, not innate genius, which allowed Solon, Lycurgus, Socrates, and Plato to formulate wise laws, for it 'is the Work of Ages to find out the true Use of the Passions, and to raise a Politician' skilled in 'the Art of Governing.'[53] This is not to deny that lawgivers played an important role in the civilising process— albeit not the same role as they played in the 'Enquiry' or 'Remark R'—but

50. Bluet, *Enquiry*, 25. See also Innes, 'Prefatory Introduction', xxvii–xviii.

51. Bluet, *Enquiry*, 28.

52. *Fable* II, 269.

53. *Fable* II, 318–19. When discussing the development of arts and crafts, Mandeville similarly claims that 'we often ascribe to the Excellency of Man's Genius, and the Depth of his Penetration, what is in Reality owing to length of Time, and the Experience of many Generations, all of them very little differing from one another in natural Parts and Sagacity', *Fable* II, 142, also 321–22. While the object of explanation is different here (Mandeville proceeds to discuss shipbuilding), he repeatedly downplays the importance of individual genius in his explanations of the civilising process.

their interventions were based on accumulated knowledge rather than super-human personal qualities.[54]

Elsewhere in *Fable II*, Mandeville openly refrains from attributing the development of social norms to political genius. The discussion of politeness in the 'Third Dialogue' proceeds without mentioning the role of politicians at all until Horatio asks: 'What Moralist or Politician was it, that could teach Men to be proud of hiding their Pride?' Mandeville's spokesman, Cleomenes, replies that the very beginnings of politeness are uncertain and should instead be assigned to 'human Sagacity in general, and the joynt Labour of many Ages'. When investigating the 'Origin of any Maxim or political Intervention', we need not trouble ourselves 'with enquiring after the Time or Country, in which it was first heard of'—those pesky details Law had requested—for we can instead look to the frailties in human nature that the maxim or invention serves to remedy, which often involves the 'Use of Conjectures' in speculating about how certain social norms or institutions developed.[55] Mandeville recalls this exchange in *Origin of Honour*, although in the latter case he does first claim that 'Moralists and Politicians' instilled notions of honour by trying to make man 'an Object of Reverence to himself.'[56] Horatio asks how we can be sure 'that this was the Work of Moralists and Politicians', to which Cleomenes responds:

> I give those Names promiscuously to All that, having studied Human Nature, have endeavour'd to civilize Men, and render them more and more tractable, either for the Ease of Governours and Magistrates, or else for the Temporal Happiness of Society in general. I think of all Inventions of this Sort, the same which told you of Politeness, that they are the joint Labour of Many. Human Wisdom is the Child of Time. It was not the Contrivance of one Man, nor could it have been the Business of a few Years[57]

While this passage can be cited in support of an allegorical reading of Mandeville's invocations of politicians, moralists, or lawgivers,[58] it is worth stressing

---

54. The exception is Moses, whose knowledge of 'the Unity of God' so greatly surpassed 'the abominable Notions of the Deity' entertained by his contemporaries that it must have been divinely inspired, *Fable* II, 218–21, also 283, 315–16.

55. *Fable* II, 128.

56. *Origin of Honour*, 39.

57. *Origin of Honour*, 40–41.

58. See, for example, Rosenberg, 'Mandeville and Laissez-Faire', 194.

that it continues to accord an important explanatory role to those who 'endeavour'd to civilize Men'. What Mandeville denies here is that one person appeared out of nowhere to civilise everyone else, instead explaining that the wisdom required to govern others would have been accumulated over time through the 'joint Labour of Many'. In so far as his appeals to 'Moralists and Politicians' should be understood metaphorically, therefore, what they represent is a longer historical process *that still involves politicians and lawgivers trying to govern and civilise others*. In this passage, at least, Mandeville does not deny an important role for human contrivance, and this reflects one strategy for answering his critics from the 1720s: rather than abandoning the conspiratorial thesis entirely, he sought to supplement it with a more nuanced and detailed backstory.[59]

There is an important shift between the two volumes of the *Fable*, which I think is best described as Mandeville's historical turn: in *Fable II* he investigates at length stages of the civilising process that occupied only a few pages or even paragraphs in the first volume. Mandeville's approach resembles what Dugald Stewart famously called '*Theoretical* or *Conjectural History*', that is, 'a species of philosophical investigation' that uses conjectures when there is no direct evidence available to show how some phenomenon or event '*may have been* produced by natural causes.'[60] We could alternatively call this a genealogical approach.[61] Although Mandeville uses conjectures for this purpose in

59. See also Burtt, *Virtue Transformed*, 142, who observes that in *Fable II* Mandeville seeks to explain 'how the politicians and civilizers on which many of his arguments rest might have themselves arisen.' For other accounts that acknowledge the important role political leaders continue to play in *Fable II*, see Hundert, *Enlightenment's Fable*, 77–78; Sagar, *Opinion of Mankind*, 47–48.

60. Dugald Stewart, 'Account of the Life and Writings of Adam Smith, L.L.D.' [1793], in Smith, *Essays on Philosophical Subjects*, 293. See also *Fable* II, 231, where Mandeville defends the merits of a conjectural approach for investigating periods prior to the invention of letters, of which there are no written records. For more general discussion, see Palmeri, 'Shaping of Conjectural History'; Joaquim Braga, 'Hypothetical Thought in Mandeville's Deconstructive Genealogy of Sociability', *I castelli di Yale* 4, no. 2 (2016): 145–59; Branchi, *Pride, Manners, and Morals*, 129–36.

61. See Charles Griswold, 'Genealogical Narrative and Self-Knowledge in Rousseau's *Discourse on the Origin and Foundations of Inequality among Men*', *History of European Ideas* 42, no. 2 (2016): 276–301. Griswold notes (278) the resemblance between genealogical narrative and conjectural history, and much of what he says about the relationship between genealogy and self-knowledge in Rousseau could be extended to Mandeville's narratives. See also Stephen H. Daniel, 'Myth and Rationality in Mandeville', *Journal of the History of Ideas* 47, no. 4 (1986), 609, who suggests that Mandeville's mythic approach constitutes 'a genealogy of morals'. For

both volumes of the *Fable*, it is only in the extended narratives of *Fable II* that he fully conveys the sense in which the phenomena under investigation are themselves historical accomplishments that must have taken a great deal of time to arise. Viewing the progression of Mandeville's thought in terms of this historical turn is more satisfactory than the notion that he simply renounces the conspiratorial thesis between the two volumes, for at least three reasons. First, Mandeville's argument in the 'Search', added to the 1723 edition of the *Fable*, does not depend on the conspiratorial thesis, so if there is a shift away from that thesis then it does not fall between the first and second volumes—whereas Mandeville's historical turn does. Second, *Fable II* still assigns an important role to leaders and lawgivers, but it is not the same role as that played by politicians and lawgivers in the 'Enquiry' and 'Remark R', where their specific intervention involved instilling notions of human excellence. Third, in *Fable II* Mandeville does not address the origins of moral virtue and honour, which is precisely the context in which he invoked politicians and lawgivers in the first volume.

The claim that Mandeville abandoned his conspiratorial mode of explanation is logically independent of the claim that he embraced a more evolutionary mode of explanation. If all that is understood by describing his theory as evolutionary is that it emphasises the long and gradual development of social institutions,[62] then what I am describing as Mandeville's historical turn could equally be called an evolutionary turn. The term evolutionary, however, often carries additional connotations, and we will be better placed to evaluate whether those connotations accurately capture Mandeville's approach in *Fable II* after having examined his historical narratives in greater depth.

Sociability and the steps towards society

Mandeville's conjectural history of society spans the final four (and especially final three) dialogues of *Fable II*. In what follows I reconstruct the most important steps and highlight how and where it builds upon or departs from his

---

comparison of Mandeville's approach with Nietzsche's genealogy of morals, see Ekbert Faas, *The Genealogy of Aesthetics* (Cambridge: Cambridge University Press, 2002), 125–29.

62. This seems to be all that Kaye ('Introduction', lxv–lxvi) has in mind, for example, when discussing Mandeville's 'precocious feeling for evolution'. More recently, see Renee Prendergast, 'Knowledge, Innovation and Emulation in the Evolutionary Thought of Bernard Mandeville', *Cambridge Journal of Economics* 38, no. 1 (2014), 89, who claims that previous evolutionary readings 'all recognised that for Mandeville, the evolution of all aspects of social life was the result of a cumulative process taking place over long time periods.'

earlier origin stories. In the 'Third Dialogue', Mandeville offers some brief reflections on how self-liking operates in 'a savage State', this being the earliest stage of his conjectural history. Nourishing himself on nuts and acorns, a solitary man would have fewer opportunities and little temptation 'of shewing this Liking of himself, than he has when civiliz'd'. Yet if a hundred such men encountered one another then, even if there was no need to fight over women or food, their self-liking 'would appear in the Desire of Superiority', which would soon 'breed Contention, and . . . War before there could be any Agreement among them; unless one of them had some one or more visible Excellencies above the rest'. In 'Remark R', to recall, Mandeville had presented humans as naturally timorous creatures driven to conflict only by lust or hunger—the two causes of anger—but here he brackets these considerations to stress that our self-liking, in the form of a desire of superiority, would nevertheless lead untaught savages to fight one another in a condition of rough equality. Self-liking is an independent cause of anger and therewith conflict; it leads 'untaught Man' to desire that others 'agree with him in the Opinion of his superior Worth, and be angry, as far as his Fear would let him, with all that should refuse it'. The desire of superiority thus derives from self-liking, or pride, and involves not only valuing ourselves above others but also seeking their affirmation to confirm this inflated self-valuation.[63]

Mandeville clarifies that his consideration of 'single Savages' is not supposed to explain the first beginnings of societies, which probably originated when 'several Families of Savages' joined together to agree upon a form of government whereby the problem of 'Superiority was tollerably well settled'. His reason for 'dwelling on the Behaviour of Savages', instead, is to uncover the seeds of politeness and good manners, which eventually developed as a sophisticated way of mitigating the problems originally generated by our desire of superiority.[64] Once we 'submit to Government, and are used to living under the Restraint of Law', we gradually learn from experience and imitation to conceal our pride and desire of superiority from others. Two points are worth emphasising here. First, Mandeville claims that we 'fall as it were into these Things spontaneously', by which he means that the adoption of social

---

63. *Fable* II, 132–33; see also 176–77 on how self-liking and anger interact. For more details on self-liking, see Chapter 1, 'Self-love and self-liking', and for helpful discussion of how self-liking relates to the instinct of sovereignty, see Gomes, 'Desire and Struggle for Recognition', 55–89.

64. *Fable* II, 132–33.

norms requires little understanding or foresight on the part of most of those involved. We come to practise good manners without being aware of the underlying reasons why we do so, much as we take a run-up before leaping a long distance without understanding the mechanics of velocity.[65] Although the 'most crafty and designing' will be the first who learn to conceal their passions, the development of politeness (unlike Mandeville's earlier accounts of moral virtue and honour) does not rely on politicians or lawgivers contriving notions of human excellence to civilise others. Second, and more importantly for present purposes, these reflections on the seeds of politeness leave the earliest stages of the civilising process unexplained, as Mandeville maintains that good manners and politeness are perfected once humans have submitted to government and laws, without yet providing any details of how the earliest governments were able to resolve the contention that our desire of superiority is liable to breed.

Towards the end of the 'Third Dialogue', Mandeville suggests that it would have taken three hundred years from a savage state to make even 'small Progress in good Manners', with another two or three centuries required to bring them to perfection. The Romans did not start from such savage beginnings, but they 'had been a Nation above six Centuries, and were almost Masters of the World, before they could be said to be a polite People.'[66] Although this point is raised by Horatio, Cleomenes does not query it and Mandeville clearly thought that it would have taken several centuries, if not longer, to develop such advanced social norms out of a savage state.[67] He also grants that notions of virtue and religion would have developed earlier than norms of politeness, with the latter only progressing alongside the rise of luxury.[68] This reveals another gap in his civilising story: at what stage between savage families and civilised societies did ideas of religion and virtue first arise? By the end of the 'Third Dialogue', then, Mandeville openly acknowledges what had arguably been the case since his earliest reflections on the origins of moral virtue and honour: to fully understand the development of society, a more detailed

---

65. *Fable* II, 139–41.

66. *Fable* II, 145–46.

67. Mandeville returns to this question in the 'Sixth Dialogue', claiming that the length of time required to draw 'a well-civiliz'd Nation from such a Savage Pair' is 'very uncertain', while insisting that nothing in his conjectural history contradicts the account of human history found in the Pentateuch, *Fable* II, 316–20.

68. *Fable* II, 146–47.

account of the initial stages of the civilising process is required. Supplying such an account would be the main burden of the remainder of *Fable II*, for which he first needed to provide a more complete picture of the savage state out of which society eventually emerged.

On 'the Sociableness of Man'

Mandeville's analysis of the savage state is largely negative in character; that is, much of his discussion involves denying the prevalence of certain qualities invoked by other philosophers to explain human sociability. As we shall see, his own account of the social dynamics of savage families comes into view only after he has stripped away many of the attributes that he regards as the consequence, rather than the cause, of increased socialisation. Mandeville examines the 'Cause of Sociableness in Man' in the second half of the 'Fourth Dialogue', situating his own position between a stylised version of Shaftesbury's and Hobbes's rival views. One holds that we have 'a natural Affection' that leads us to love our species 'beyond what other Animals have for theirs', the other that we are 'born with Hatred and Aversion, that makes us Wolves and Bears, to one another'.[69] In carving out his own position, Mandeville suggests that there are two reasons why 'Man is call'd a Sociable Creature':

> First, because it is commonly imagin'd, that he is naturally more fond, and desirous of Society, than any other Creature. Secondly, because it is manifest, that associating in Men turns to better Account, than it possibly could do in other Animals, if they were to attempt it.[70]

Mandeville defends the second reason but his criticisms of the first highlight the main points of disagreement with Hobbes and Shaftesbury. Against Shaftesbury, Mandeville flatly denies that humans possess any greater love of species than other animals, first because 'Man centers every thing in himself' and loves or hates others only 'for his own Sake', and second, because no societies have ever been raised or maintained through dependence on natural affection.[71] The disagreement with Hobbes is more subtle. Cleomenes claims that man's 'perpetual Desire of meliorating his Condition' and love of ease and

---

69. *Fable* II, 177–78. Shaftesbury presented his opposition to Hobbes in similar terms; see, for example, *Sensus Communis*, ii.1 (56).

70. *Fable* II, 180.

71. *Fable* II, 178, 182–83. These considerations recall the 'Search'; see *Fable* I, 341–47.

security are 'sufficient Motives to make him fond of Society; considering the necessitous and helpless condition of his Nature.' Horatio immediately objects that these are Hobbes's assumptions regarding our natural condition, to which Cleomenes responds that humans become increasingly 'necessitous and helpless . . . in their Nature' the more they are socialised. It is the multiplicity and unreasonableness of our desires that make us fond of society, but savages would have had few desires and thus little need of society. The 'most civiliz'd People stand most in need of Society, and consequently none less than Savages.'[72] We should study people in the least inhabited parts of the world, rather than in towns and cities, to 'find our Species come nearer the State of Nature'.[73] With Hobbes, then, Mandeville agrees that we seek society for self-centred reasons,[74] but he further argues that our fondness for society is an effect and not the cause of humans associating together.

Mandeville's point about the multiplicity of our desires is part of his wider argument that human sociability comprises a compound of different qualities gradually acquired over time.[75] These qualities include reasoning and speech, neither of which we are born capable of using. When it comes to speech, 'a dozen Generations proceeding from two Savages would not produce any tolerable Language.'[76] It nonetheless makes sense to say that we have the capacity for reasoning and speech, in a way that distinguishes humans from other animals, and, more generally, when we say that 'Man is a Sociable Creature' this can mean only that 'in our Nature we have a certain Fitness, by which great Multitudes of us co-operating, may be united and form'd into one Body'. Humans, unlike other animals, are capable of society in this sense alone. If this is what it means to describe humans as sociable creatures, however, then it follows that the 'undoubted Basis of all Societies is Government', since without government largescale coexistence would be impossible. To become 'governable'—and not merely submissive—we must come to regard subjection to government as personally advantageous, reconciling ourselves to submission

72. *Fable* II, 180–81, also 285.

73. *Fable* II, 190, also 301.

74. For the classic statement, see Hobbes, *On the Citizen*, i.2: 'All society, therefore, exists for the sake of advantage or of glory, i.e. it is a product of love of self, not of love of friends.'

75. *Fable* II, 182, 188.

76. *Fable* II, 190. Cf. Campbell, *Enquiry*, 19–21, for whom the distinctively human faculty of speech should be taken as evidence that 'we plainly seem to be form'd to the Offices of Society' and that 'Men are certainly created with an inward Turn of Mind that naturally determines us to associate together.' See also Fiddes, *General Treatise*, lxxxiv–lxxxv.

so that we are favourably disposed towards society and willing 'to exert ourselves in behalf of the Person that governs'.[77] Mandeville thus sees human sociability as the outcome, not the cause, of a well-governed society. We 'become sociable, by living together in Society'.[78]

To say that 'Man is a Sociable Creature', then, is not to make a claim about the desires or needs of humans in a state of nature. Why does Mandeville nevertheless insist that it makes sense to call humans sociable creatures, in his precise meaning of the term? One reason is that he seems to have been concerned to square his account with our knowledge 'from Revelation that Man was made for Society'.[79] In the earlier 'Enquiry', Mandeville had anticipated the objection that explaining the origin of virtue in terms of pride, shame, and flattery could be taken as 'perhaps offensive to Christianity'. The fact that these 'Frailties and Imperfections' can lead us 'into the Road of Temporal Happiness' is perfectly consistent with a providential framework and should be taken to illuminate the 'depth of the Divine Wisdom' in designing man for society.[80] Yet many of Mandeville's critics still protested that his ideas were incompatible with a proper understanding of God's design. Richard Fiddes, for example, argued that having 'designed Man for a sociable Creature', God must have endued 'Man with those Capacities, Dispositions, and Powers' most conducive to society,[81] while John Dennis charged Mandeville with denying 'the Government of the World by Providence, and perhaps the very Being of God himself.'[82] These critics could be answered on their own terms, however, once we recognise that although 'the Sociableness of Man' is the work of 'the Author of Nature, Divine Providence', God's design does not always reveal itself immediately. Humans share little with species such as bees, where it 'is visible, that Nature has design'd them for Society'. Bees are naturally disposed to work together and there is no reason to suppose that the honey and wax they produce have been improved over many generations through 'Tryals [or] Essays'.

77. *Fable* II, 183–84. On the importance of this distinction, see Otero Knott, 'Mandeville on Governability'.

78. *Fable* II, 189.

79. *Fable* II, 185.

80. *Fable* I, 57. See also *Female Tatler*, no. 62: 96, where Arsinoe, voicing Mandeville's view, remarks that it should be considered one of the 'Miracles of Providence, to have made Man the only Sociable Creature, when by their Nature none of all the rest seem'd less fit for it'.

81. Fiddes, *General Treatise*, lxxii–lxxvii. A similar argument is found in Shaftesbury, *Moralists*, ii.4, 178.

82. Dennis, *Vice and Luxury*, 50.

Nor do bees argue about the ideal constitution of their hive. Human sociability is also derived from our God-given capacities, yet a great deal of 'Art and uncommon Industry' is required to turn the raw ingredients into the final product. It appears that 'Nature had design'd Man for Society, as she has made Grapes for Wine.' As with a good wine, it is only by being carefully squeezed together under the right conditions that human sociability emerges. Many different schemes of government have been proposed to this end, which have frequently given rise to disagreements and 'fatal Quarrels', alongside some successes.[83] Most grapes do not end up as wine and fermentation takes plenty of perfecting and mistakes along the way before you can produce a vintage worth drinking.[84]

Mandeville vs. Temple on the savage family

Mandeville's analysis of 'the Sociableness of Man' uncovers a considerable gulf between the savage state and society. To understand the transition between the two, he turns to William Temple's *An Essay Upon the Original and Nature of Government* (1672), directly quoting a couple of passages towards the end of the 'Fourth Dialogue' before returning to analyse the arguments in more detail in the subsequent dialogue.[85] Mandeville had drawn on Temple's *Observations upon the United Provinces of the Netherlands* (1673) when discussing frugality and the Dutch economy in the first volume of the *Fable*,[86] but the engagement with the *Essay* is original to *Fable II*. Given that he had read Temple's *Observations* much earlier, it seems unlikely that Mandeville first

83. *Fable* II, 185–89, also 233.

84. See also Sagar, *Opinion of Mankind*, 48, who adds that fermentation requires the 'directing intelligence of a wine maker.' To extend Mandeville's analogy, the winemakers of human sociability are the leaders of bands, at the most experimental stage, and later the lawgivers, who come closer to perfecting the art.

85. Mandeville's engagement with Temple's *Essay* has received relatively little scholarly attention. For notable exceptions, see Scribano, *Natura umana e società competitiva*, 98–105; Daniele Francesconi, 'Mandeville sull'origine della società', *Il pensiero politico* 28, no. 3 (1995), especially 420–31; Otero Knott, 'Mandeville on Governability', 31–39; Sagar, *Opinion of Mankind*, 87–89.

86. *Fable* I, 189–94. For discussion and broader context, see Alexander Bick, 'Bernard Mandeville and the "Economy" of the Dutch', *Erasmus Journal for Philosophy and Economics* 1, no. 1 (2008): 87–106; Hans Blom, 'Decay and the Political Gestalt of Decline in Bernard Mandeville and his Dutch Contemporaries', *History of European Ideas* 36, no. 2 (2010): 153–66.

encountered the *Essay* only at some point after 1723, although he may well have come to see that targeting Temple could help him to sharpen the arguments (originally set out against Shaftesbury) from the 'Search', while at the same time addressing some of the objections raised by his critics in the 1720s.

Temple challenges what he takes to be the typical way of framing debates about sociability and the origin of government, in some respects foreshadowing Mandeville's own positioning vis-à-vis Hobbes and Shaftesbury. On one side, Temple observes, some philosophers maintain that we are 'sociable creatures, and naturally disposed to live in numbers and troops together'; on the other side are those who depict us as 'naturally creatures of prey, and in a state of war one upon another'. Amongst their many errors, adherents of both sides to this debate neglect the sources of natural authority amongst humans, instead appealing (implausibly) to contracts to generate authority where there was none before. If civil authority originated in a compact then it would have been the heads of families, not solitary individuals, who first came together to agree upon the terms of civil association, yet those heads of family 'have already an authority over such numbers as their families are composed of.'[87] Temple assumes that the heads of families will be fathers and argues that we cannot understand political authority until we uncover its foundations in paternal authority.

The father hunts animals and gathers food for his children until they are old enough to do so for themselves, at the same time defending the family from attacks by wild beasts. Through instruction and example, he teaches his children

> what qualities are good, and what are ill, for their health and life, or common society (which will certainly comprehend whatever is generally esteemed virtue or vice among men) cherishing and encouraging dispositions to the good; disfavouring and punishing those to the ill; and lastly, among the various accidents of life, lifting up his eyes to heaven, when the earth affords him no relief; and having recourse to a higher and a greater nature, whenever he finds the frailty of his own; we must needs conclude, that the children of this man cannot fail of being bred up with a great opinion of his wisdom, his goodness, his valour, and his piety. And, if they see constant plenty in the family, they believe well of his fortune too.[88]

87. William Temple, *An Essay upon the Original and Nature of Government*, in *The Works of Sir William Temple Bart*, vol. 1 (London, 1757), 37–39.
88. Temple, *Essay*, 40.

Children are thus brought up to recognise paternal authority, following the advice of their father and obeying his commands. Temple quickly scales his argument up, claiming that the father has a natural right and authority to be 'governor in this little State', which would extend over all his descendants, such that the father soon becomes 'the governor or King of a nation'. The 'natural and original governments of the world', on Temple's account, springs 'from a tacit deference of many to the authority of one single person', which appears to grow seamlessly out of the father's paternal authority within the family.[89]

Mandeville agrees with Temple that to understand the origin of government we must start by analysing the social dynamics of the family, but he argues that Temple moves far too quickly. As Cleomenes reads the passages from the *Essay* considered above, Horatio interjects that the father 'is no Savage, or untaught Creature; he is fit to be Justice of the Peace'. Did he 'spring out of the Earth, I wonder, or did he drop from the Sky?'[90] There is something a touch ironic about these jibes, since the role that Mandeville had previously assigned to politicians and lawgivers in explaining the origins of moral virtue and honour had (rightly) been criticised on very similar grounds by George Bluet.[91] As we saw earlier, Mandeville had skipped rapidly over the transition from savage families to the earliest form of government in the 'Search'. His problem with Temple's account, however, was not solely the speed of transition but also 'the Character of his Savage', whose 'Just Reasoning' and 'Notions of Right and Wrong' are 'unnatural to a wild Man'.[92] Much like Shaftesbury and Hobbes in their different ways, then, Temple's chief mistake was to read qualities back into the earliest families that would have emerged only through a much longer and more complex process of socialisation.

Mandeville argues that the wildest of savages would have no notions of right or wrong, justice or injustice, and would instead 'take every thing to be his own, that he could lay his Hands on.' This applies even in the family where parents treat their children as property, pursuing their dominant passions with little foresight or reflection. These passions include natural affection, which leads parents to love their children and provide them with food and other

89. Temple, *Essay*, 40–41.

90. *Fable* II, 192–93.

91. Bluet, *Enquiry*, 25.

92. *Fable* II, 199. Given Mandeville's presentation of Temple's account, it is worth noting that Temple had not actually claimed that the first fathers of families would have been savages or wild men.

necessities. Yet fathers would also display anger towards their children upon occasions of disobedience, sometimes resulting in violence, which may later be assuaged by pity as their anger cools. As a result, 'the Savage Child would learn to love and fear his Father', and these two passions, mixed together with the esteem we naturally have for everything that excels us, produce 'that Compound, which we call Reverence.'[93]

Reverence, then, is the compound passion central to understanding paternal (or parental) authority,[94] comprising a mix of fear, love, and esteem. Horatio, voicing a position close to Temple's, suggests that once we understand the natural basis of reverence then we can immediately 'see the Origin of Society'. The reverence children have for their parents will be retained in adulthood and passed onto their own children so that the original parents can soon command authority over all their descendants. Not so fast, cautions Cleomenes. One problem with this argument is that natural affection decreases as children grow up and, as adults, they may come to resent the dominion that their parents continue to exercise over them. This is one reason why, once civil societies are formed, laws or norms dictate that paternal authority should last only until children reach a certain age. A greater problem, however, is that the original savage parents would prove incapable of successfully governing several generations of their family.[95] The first 'Savage Pair' would certainly regard all their descendants as under their jurisdiction, and if there was no 'Intermixture of Foreign Blood' then they would even consider 'the whole Race to be their natural Vassals'. But there is no reason to suppose that they would have yet developed the capability to govern effectively, having never learned to curb their own passions and lacking the foresight and knowledge required to establish rules regulating everyone else's behaviour. Mandeville's key point here is that we naturally have 'a visible Desire after Government' but no capacity for it. Indeed, he claims that this desire is another 'Instance of Divine Wisdom' (conspicuously neglecting Horatio's perplexity that God would have sent us

93. *Fable* II, 199–202.

94. It is unclear the extent to which Mandeville thinks that authority inheres in the father alone or in both parents. Sometimes he refers to the father or paternal authority specifically, but he also refers to 'the Usurpation of Parents' and the jurisdiction of the 'Savage Pair', *Fable* II, 204. In this context, it is sometimes difficult to work out when Mandeville's more general use of 'man' and 'men' is supposed to be gender specific.

95. Mandeville thus refutes his earlier claim from the 'Search' that the second generation of parents in a wild state of nature would be able to govern all their 'Descendants, how numerous soever they might grow', *Fable* I, 348.

into the world without any capacity for governing). We could never become fit for society without pride, ambition, and a 'Thirst of Dominion', as these are the very passions that motivate those who seek to govern others.[96]

At this stage in the 'Fifth Dialogue', Mandeville's narrative digresses and Horatio twice implores Cleomenes to return to his explanation of the origin of society.[97] There are two points worth distilling from the foregoing analysis of the savage family, which Mandeville touches upon in his digressions. The first concerns the importance of reverence. If savage parents do not have the capacity for government then it might appear that little progress has been made in explaining the origin of society, yet Mandeville maintains that the reverence children feel for their parents does constitute 'a considerable Step.'[98] The reason for this, quite simply, is that reverence is central to understanding how all authority works and it can be observed even in the savage family. This is why Mandeville states 'that the very first Generation of the most brutish Savages, was sufficient to produce sociable Creatures', even if more was required to 'produce a Man fit to govern others'.[99] Savage children are potentially governable, but savage parents are originally incapable of governing.

The importance of reverence may explain why Mandeville's discussion strays onto the topic of natural religion at this point,[100] where he argues that our 'Tendency to Religion' is based on fear. The seeds of religion can be found in uneducated savages who would fear all natural phenomena that appear threatening (extreme weather, thunder and lightning, etcetera) and then start attributing these events to invisible causes.[101] Before long, a wild couple would start communicating their fear of invisible causes to one another—this would be one of the first things they name—and children would easily observe and adopt this fear from their parents.[102] Fear is the basis of religion in civilised society too, which is why 'the Heathens, and all that have been ignorant of the true Deity' represented their gods as passionate and revengeful rather than as

96. *Fable* II, 202–205.

97. *Fable* II, 221, 230.

98. *Fable* II, 221.

99. *Fable* II, 231.

100. As opposed to revealed religion, which alone 'deserves the Name of Religion', and which came into the world from 'God, by Miracle.' *Fable* II, 205–206.

101. *Fable* II, 207–209; see also *Origin of Honour*, 21–22.

102. *Fable* II, 213.

equitable and merciful. Religion, in short, is synonymous with fear of god.[103] Mandeville's discussion of natural religion contains a few swipes at 'the Roguery of designing Priests',[104] who capitalise on our fear of invisible causes for their own advantage. The principle of fear lies at the heart of all 'Priestcraft or Inhumanity' in the world, and many 'Lawgivers and Leaders of the People' have relied principally upon fear to subject those they wished to govern. But fear is not reverence. Reverence, to recall, consists of love, esteem, and fear, even if 'the latter alone is capable of making Men counterfeit both the former'. Whereas 'Tyrants' and 'industrious Priests' seek to create submissive subjects through fear, to make people governable, Mandeville implies, political authority (and true religion) must also be based on love and esteem.[105] The second and fifth of the Ten Commandments are a case in point, he later explains, since they both appeal to fear, love, and esteem 'to make human Creatures governable', the former by inculcating the 'utmost Veneration to Him, at whose command they were to' obey, and the latter by reinforcing the reverence children display towards their parents.[106]

The second point to distil from Mandeville's analysis of savage families, to which he returns in another digression, both accentuates his disagreement with Temple over whether savage children learn 'whatever is generally esteemed virtue or vice among men' from their fathers, and helps to answer William Law's objection that there is no reason to suppose that humans ever existed in a savage state without notions of God, equity, or duty to parents.[107] As we have seen, analysis of the savage family can explain the reverence children have for their parents and the origin of our ideas of God, but Mandeville insists that this falls short of any equitable or 'reasonable Notions of Right and Wrong'. The ideas of right and wrong we hold in society are acquired through education. All we are born with is 'a Desire of Superiority' whereby we instinctively take everything to be our own without any awareness of moral constraints. This 'domineering Spirit' can be moderated only through social

103. *Fable* II, 217–18. Cf. Law, *Remarks*, 27, who had claimed that all ages have ascribed 'Goodness, Justice and Truth' to God. Mandeville stresses that the natural origin of our ideas of God is our desire 'to know the Cause of Evil', whereas knowing the cause of goodness is far less useful and adds little to our happiness, *Fable* II, 212.

104. *Fable* II, 210.

105. *Fable* II, 214–18.

106. *Fable* II, 278–81.

107. Temple, *Essay*, 40; Law, *Remarks*, 19.

intercourse and experience.[108] Without belabouring the point, Mandeville takes a clear stand here on the important question of whether a desire of dominion and superiority is natural to humans or whether it appears only under certain social relations, especially those characterised by inequality.[109] On Mandeville's account, then, society is not the cause of—and can be a cure for—our desire of superiority.

In defending his claim that reasonable notions of right and wrong are acquired through socialisation, Mandeville addresses the objection that parents have a natural right over their young which entails a corresponding duty on the part of the children. He grants that we have considerable obligations 'to good Parents, for their Care and Education'—qualifiers which implicitly question whether such obligations apply in his depiction of the savage family—before arguing that there can be 'no Obligation for Benefits that never were intended.' To his earlier claim that savage parents follow their dominant passions when looking after their children, Mandeville now adds that parents reproduce out of instinct alone and that 'a Wild Woman' would bear several children before even guessing at the cause. Although parents may be the efficient cause of their children, the motives which lead even 'the most civiliz'd Pair' to reproduce have little to do with the preservation and care of the species and a lot more to do with satisfying their carnal desires. This is one of many cases where we impute to our 'free Agency' actions that are independent of our will and thereby take credit for the beneficial consequences 'tho' Nature does all the Work.'[110]

I claimed earlier that Mandeville does not revisit the origin of moral virtue in *Fable II*, yet this discussion of the 'Question concerning the Notions of Right and Wrong',[111] as Horatio puts it, might be taken as evidence to the contrary. Mandeville's argument that the notions of right and wrong are

---

108. *Fable* II, 223–24.

109. The latter position is now most famously associated with Rousseau, but Mandeville would have encountered it in Archibald Campbell's (*Enquiry*, 230–39) criticisms of Hobbes's idea of 'our Desire of Dominion'. Campbell argues that it is only under civil government, where property is in the hands of a few, that some people develop the 'second Nature' that Hobbes had mistaken for our original constitution. Mandeville read the *Enquiry* in its 1728 edition (see *Fable* II, 24–28), which Alexander Innes had published under his own name without acknowledgement of Campbell's authorship.

110. *Fable* II, 224–29. Mandeville's (Hobbesian) account of the will suggests that belief in free agency, much like belief in the immortality of the soul, is itself a product of human pride.

111. *Fable* II, 221.

acquired, rather than natural, certainly reinforces one of the main conclusions from his earlier 'Enquiry', but he says little here about the content of the notions of right and wrong (or virtue and vice, terms which he avoids in this context) or precisely how they would have originated. His emphasis instead falls on the negative goal of showing that reasonable notions of morality and equity are not to be found in the original savage family, where instead the desire of superiority dominates.

The first two steps

Mandeville returns to the problem of how to derive the 'Origin of Society . . . from the Savage Family' midway through the 'Fifth Dialogue', the remainder of which is concerned with outlining the first of three steps towards society. Mandeville's criticisms of Temple may seem to pose an insurmountable challenge for any such account, since it appears that savages' desire of dominion would lead them to fight one another as soon as their numbers grow, resulting in 'a perpetual State of War'. It is difficult to see how war could be avoided without anyone having yet acquired the capacity to govern others. Where this scenario does not transpire, however, it is because humans are driven to associate by a 'common Danger, which unites the greatest of Enemies'. The danger in question is that of 'wild Beasts', which must have posed a severe threat given 'the defenceless Condition, in which Men come into the World'. Mandeville supports his contention by appealing to ancient stories from various countries that are 'stuff'd with the Accounts of the Conflicts Men had with wild Beasts',[112] and the experience of more recently observed 'savage Men' that are greatly inconvenienced by wild animals.[113]

Although the first step towards society is relatively straightforward, Mandeville's defence of it involves a long discussion of the role of providence in both creating an existential threat to human survival in the first place and then in ensuring that wild beasts did not devour the entire species long before societies were formed. This discussion clarifies, amongst other things, that

---

112. *Fable* II, 230–32. The danger posed by wild animals was a crucial step in many Epicurean narratives of human development, leading men and women who had themselves been 'wide-wandering like wild beasts' to settle together in huts as families. For the classic account, see Lucretius, *On the Nature of the Universe*, trans. Ronald Melville (Oxford: Oxford University Press, 1997), Book 5, lines 925–1014; and for an early modern rendition, see Charleton, *Epicurus's Morals*, Chap. 27, 149–50.

113. *Fable* II, 261.

humans would naturally settle in temperate climates where wild creatures are not a direct threat, but that even there wolves, wild boars, and other animals would still be 'our perpetual Enemies' because they devour and spoil our means of sustenance. It is in this context that humans would have first discovered the use of fire and developed spears and other weapons for the purpose of fending off animals.[114] Without analysing Mandeville's account of providence in detail, it is worth highlighting how he tries to square it with his argument (as he had put it in the 'Search') that humans could never become sociable creatures 'without the assistance of what we call Evil both Natural and Moral.'[115] Everything we call natural evil must be part of God's design, which includes humans being killed by wild animals, along with plagues, diseases, and many other natural causes of death. These are the means by which the populations of all animals are regulated, humans included, and were we not 'so full of our Species, and the Excellency of it', we would recognise the compatibility of human death with 'the System of the Earth.'[116] It 'is ridiculous to think, that the Universe was made for our sake'. Everything we call natural evil must have been contrived for reasons that we either cannot know or fail to appreciate.[117]

On Mandeville's account, moral evil is consistent with providence too, which counts against those who invoke God's design to claim that we must have a natural affection for other members of the species comparable to that of parents for their children. Indeed, the evils that wild animals have caused humans pale in comparison 'to the cruel Usage, and the Multiplicity of mortal Injuries, which Men have receiv'd from one another.'[118] Again, wars and violence may be one of the means by which God has prevented over-population, and, either way, it is clear from 'the time that *Cain* slew *Abel*, to this Day' that God's design includes a great deal of violence and moral evil.[119] Leaving aside

114. *Fable* II, 238–42.

115. *Fable* I, 325.

116. *Fable* II, 251. See also Law, *Remarks*, 26, who, in a slightly different context, had complained that Mandeville must either yield to his criticisms or 'put the *Epicurean* upon me, and say that God may disregard us'.

117. *Fable* II, 260–64. Mandeville allows that 'if they be real Evils' then they are the consequence of Original Sin, which, he had earlier agued, was foreknown but not predestined; see *Fable* II, 236.

118. *Fable* II, 246.

119. *Fable* II, 254–56, also 309–10 (where '*Moses*' is a mistake and should read Cain). The story of Cain and Abel was often invoked in debates about human sociability. Hobbes added it

the problem of how to reconcile moral evil, predestination, and free will—'an inexplicable Mystery, I will never meddle with'[120]—Mandeville maintains that the prevalence of moral evil in the world makes it 'plain, that such a real Love of Man for his Species would have been altogether inconsistent with the present Scheme . . . All Men would have been Levellers, Government would have been unnecessary, and there could have been no great Bustle in the World.'[121] In characteristically Mandevillean fashion, then, providence is compatible with what we call both natural and moral evil, and those who insist that God must have created us with a love for our species flatter themselves by assuming that the world was designed solely for our purposes, not His.

The threat posed by wild animals may have been the first danger leading savage families to associate for common defence, but this alone would have been insufficient to generate society. 'The second Step to Society', Mandeville announces at the beginning of the 'Sixth Dialogue', 'is the Danger Men are in from one another'. This danger stems from the pride and ambition 'that all Men are born with'. As families start to associate, our domineering spirit would lead some individuals to 'strive for Superiority' over others, resulting in quarrels and conflict. Although Mandeville does not make the point explicitly, once groups of families had become increasingly adept at defending themselves from wild animals then presumably the bonds that originally drew them together would weaken and discord arise. Different families are 'of little use to one another,' Mandeville declares, 'when there is no common Enemy to oppose.' By this stage, however, some individuals would already be known for displaying qualities of 'Strength, Agility, and Courage', leading the weaker and more fearful to join with those they judge most capable of protecting them from others who also seek superiority. The danger humans pose to one another, then, would 'naturally divide Multitudes into Bands and Companies', each with their own leader, and Mandeville claims that this is the stage of societal development which has been observed in 'the unciviliz'd Nations, that are still subsisting in the World', where 'Men may live miserably many Ages.'[122]

---

to the 1688 Latin edition of *Leviathan* (Chap. 13, 195) as an example illustrating that our natural condition is one of war. Cf. Campbell, *Enquiry*, 242–44, who argued that the story does not support Hobbes's position.

120. *Fable* II, 252. See at greater length *Free Thoughts*, 63–75, where Mandeville's debt to Pierre Bayle on this question is explicit.

121. *Fable* II, 259.

122. *Fable* II, 266–67.

On this account—unlike both Temple's *Essay* and Mandeville's earlier sketch in the 'Search'—the transition from the savage family to society must pass through a stage in which humans associate together in bands, where the stronger will conquer the weaker but there is not yet any stable government.[123] Parental authority within the family, therefore, does not seamlessly translate into monarchical government, and the experience of 'unciviliz'd Nations' suggests that people could live in this intermediary stage between savage families and society for a long time without the survival of the species being imperilled.[124]

Why do humans living in bands not swiftly advance into more civilised societies? Mandeville argues that this condition would still be characterised by 'unruly Passions, and the Discords occasioned by them', which would make it very difficult to develop new inventions without other people spoiling them.[125] We would still be inclined to follow 'the unbridled Appetites' of our untaught nature and seek to judge and resolve any disputes in our own favour.[126] No one would honour contracts when it is not in their interest to do so and the fear of invisible causes that characterises (natural) religion would not be a powerful enough instrument to govern people without civil sanctions to reinforce it. To see how progress could be made towards society, we must instead look to the ambition of the band's leader, who would seek to be 'obey'd in civil Matters, by the Numbers he led'. Although communities would still be 'unsettled and precarious' at this stage, Mandeville argues that they would be sufficiently stable to last for at least 'three or four Generations', by which time leaders could come to understand human nature better and start working out how to rule more successfully. In particular, leaders would forbid violence towards other members of the community and their families, and once they invent penalties for disobedience they would soon discover that individuals should not be judges in their own cases and that the old are generally wiser than the young. The rules that allow people to live peacefully together, then, were originally devised by the leaders of bands so that they could govern others more effectively.[127] This is not the same role as that played by wise lawgivers and politicians in Mandeville's earlier origin stories, but it is nonetheless one

123. Cf. *Fable* I, 348 and Temple, *Essay*, 40–41.
124. *Fable* II, 267.
125. *Fable* II, 267.
126. *Fable* II, 270–71.
127. *Fable* II, 267–68.

that relies on a top-down process with leaders motivated by their own interest and ambition, rather than by any public-spirited concerns.

The third step and the origin of language

With the invention of 'Prohibitions and Penalties', Horatio suggests, it seems that we have surmounted all the difficulties in understanding the origin of society. Not yet, counters Cleomenes, for there remains a third and final step still to be studied; that is, 'the Invention of Letters', or written language. The administration of justice will remain deeply imperfect until a society has written laws, especially when the spoken language is not greatly advanced and the observance of contracts relies on nothing more than verbal commitments. It is this final step towards society that distinguishes civilised states from savage communities. This 'great Insight into the Nature of Man' may be summarised succinctly: 'No Multitudes can live peaceably without Government; no Government can subsist without Laws; and no Laws can be effectual long, unless they are wrote down'.[128]

Mandeville does not explain how the earliest formulations of penalties and prohibitions eventually led to the introduction of written laws, although it is reasonable to assume that the same process by which leaders started to understand how to curb the passions of their subjects would subsequently result in them discovering the benefits of codified laws. Instead, Mandeville turns his attention to defending the claim that laws are required to socialise and discipline all subjects, rather than merely to punish the relatively few 'bad Men in all Multitudes.' As anyone who is uninstructed and left alone 'will follow the Impulse of their Nature, without regard to others', we should in fact regard all people as 'bad, that are not taught to be good'. Working his way through the Ten Commandments to illustrate this point, Mandeville argues that every wise law is designed to counteract 'that Instinct of Sovereignty' or 'domineering Spirit, and Principle of Selfishness' within us, while also seeking to instil reverence for civil authority. Our desire for revenge, for example, is one of the clearest manifestations of this instinct of sovereignty, as it presupposes 'both a Right to Judicature within, and an Authority to punish', which is why all civil societies prohibit these powers from being exercised by individuals. Mandeville argues that the Ten Commandments all concern 'the Temporal Good of Society', even those (such as keeping the sabbath) which might appear to be

128. *Fable* II, 268–69.

duties to God alone. Without considering each commandment presently, Mandeville's overarching point is that laws are required to make us sociable creatures by moderating the self-centred passions that would otherwise breed conflict and imperil society.[129]

The invention of written laws allows multitudes to form into a body politic and Mandeville claims that from this stage many other features of civilised society swiftly follow. Property and personal safety can now be secured, which provides the foundation for the division of labour and greater economic productivity.[130] Rather than dwelling on these points, however, Mandeville returns to the topic of speech, which he had touched upon briefly in the 'Fourth Dialogue' when suggesting that it would take a dozen generations before savages would produce 'any tolerable Language'.[131] He now adds that speech must have been 'very barren and precarious' before the invention of letters, as we can see by investigating the 'Origin of all Languages' (that 'were not taught by Inspiration').[132] In 'the wild State of Nature' there would have been little need for a spoken language and savages could have easily expressed their desires and aversions through signs and gestures alone. Spoken language, as with many arts and sciences, would have developed only by 'slow degrees . . . and length of time'. A 'wild Pair' living together for several years would discover that they can communicate more effectively through sounds than physical gestures

129. *Fable* II, 271–83; see also the Index entry at *Fable* II, 364: '*Commandments* (the Ten) are a strong Proof of the Principle of Selfishness and Instinct of Sovereignty in human Nature'. The example of revenge occurs in Mandeville's interpretation of the Ninth Commandment at *Fable* II, 274–75.

130. *Fable* II, 283–84, also 300.

131. *Fable* II, 190.

132. Mandeville's account of the development of language has often been singled out for acclaim. See, for example, Hayek, 'Lecture on a Master Mind', 138, who describes Mandeville as 'wholly a pioneer' and 'the chief source of that rich speculation on the growth of language which we find in the second half of the eighteenth century.' See also Jack, 'Men Become Sociable', 11–12; and for specific claims about Mandeville's influence on later thinkers, see F. B. Kaye, 'Mandeville on the Origin of Language', *Modern Language Notes* 39, no. 3 (1924): 136–42; Rüdiger Schreyer, 'Condillac, Mandeville and the Origin of Language', *Historiographia Linguistica* 1, no. 2 (1978): 15–43; Hundert, *Enlightenment's Fable*, 86–115. For more general studies that helpfully situate Mandeville's ideas within wider European debates about the origin of language, see Paolo Rossi, *The Dark Abyss of Time: The History of the Earth and the History of Nations from Hooke to Vico* [1979], trans. Lyida G. Cochrane (Chicago and London: The University of Chicago Press, 1984), 195–270; Avi Lifschitz, *Language and Enlightenment: The Berlin Debates of the Eighteenth Century* (Oxford: Oxford University Press, 2012), 16–38.

when representing objects that are out of sight, with their children and subsequent generations gradually improving on these rudimentary foundations.[133]

On Mandeville's account, however, the 'Design of Speech' was not to convey our thoughts and sentiments accurately to others. The original motive behind speech, instead, is our desire to persuade others.[134] This persuasion could either take the form of seeking approval and credit for our opinions, or of making others submit to our will and doing things that we would compel them to do were they under our power. In both cases, persuasion is closely bound up with our more general desire of superiority. When a small child points and cries the name of a toy, their goal is to persuade you to do their bidding and obtain it for them; the first things children 'endeavour to express with Words are their Wants and their Will'. Amongst more educated and 'polite People', we equally see the 'natural Ambition and strong Desire Men have to triumph over, as well as persuade others' manifested in more elaborate forms of speech and gestures, which, when mastered, constitute 'a bewitching Engine to captivate mean Understandings'. The norms of polite society demand that we typically conceal the original design behind our speech, which is why it is the height of good manners to address others calmly and without elaborate body gestures. This displays our own humility while flattering our audience by appealing to their reasoned judgement rather than expecting them to be swayed by the emotive force of our speech. In courting our audience's favour through the flattery of reason, we nevertheless hope to persuade them to repay the compliment. In other cases, Mandeville suggests, even insults and heated language can be evidence of civil behaviour in so far as they provide an outlet for our anger without resorting to violence or disobeying the law.[135]

These 'polite' forms of discourse are perfected *after* the invention of letters. Mandeville's analysis implies that the use of speech helps to turn us into

133. *Fable* II, 284–88.

134. The idea that speech developed out of gestures as people started to recognise the convenience of naming things is an Epicurean insight (see, for example, Lucretius, *Nature of the Universe*, Book 5, lines 1028–55), but I do not know of anyone before Mandeville who accorded such a central role to the desire to persuade others. Adam Smith later says something similar in *The Theory of Moral Sentiments*, VII.iv.25: 'The desire of being believed, the desire of persuading, of leading and directing other people, seems to be one of the strongest of all our natural desires. It is, perhaps, the instinct upon which is founded the faculty of speech, the characteristic faculty of human nature.' For an account that stresses the differences between Smith and Mandeville on the origin of language, see Kapust, *Flattery*, 132–69.

135. *Fable* II, 289–95.

sociable creatures only as we become increasingly civilised. To be sure, speech must have developed to a tolerable level before leaders could start issuing prohibitions, and even more so before laws could be written down, but it is the prohibitions and laws themselves that ultimately do the socialising work. In civilised society, however, norms of polite speech can go one step further in providing a sophisticated outlet for tempering and concealing our desire of superiority without leading to discord and quarrels. At this point in the 'Sixth Dialogue', we have thus come full circle from Mandeville's initial venture into the behaviour of savages when explaining the origin of politeness and good manners in the 'Third Dialogue', with his account of human sociability and the steps towards society revealing the extent to which 'the good Qualities Men compliment our Nature and the whole Species with, are the Result of Art and Education.'[136] Where most members of polite society would prefer not to regard themselves as the descendants of savages, Mandeville insists that 'there is no Difference between the original Nature of a Savage, and that of a civiliz'd Man'[137]—the only thing separating the two is the process of socialisation that Mandeville has recounted in such detail. The more civilised we become, however, the less we can tolerate having our nature and 'despicable Origins' exposed, which is why 'the Flatterers of our Species keep this carefully from our View'.[138]

Addendum on whether Cleomenes and Horatio switch roles

In the 'Search', Mandeville had set his reflections on the origin of society out against those who appeal to 'a Golden Age' of abundance and ease,[139] but this did not dissuade his critics from invoking Horace, Tacitus, or Virgil as authorities when maintaining that in 'the first Ages of the World . . . Mankind liv'd together in Peace and Amity, with mutual Trust and Confidence.'[140] Mandeville returns to this point in the 'Sixth Dialogue': if human existence was miserable before the invention of written laws, Horatio asks, then why have poets celebrated the 'Golden Age, in which they pretend there was so much Peace,

---

136. *Fable* II, 306.
137. *Fable* II, 214.
138. *Fable* II, 301.
139. *Fable* I, 346.
140. See Campbell, *Enquiry*, 240–42, who cites Virgil and Tacitus for evidence; and Dennis, *Vice and Luxury*, 36, who draws on Horace.

Love, and Sincerity?' The poets wrote to please their contemporaries, Cleomenes answers, for everyone is flattered to hear their ancestors praised as virtuous and happy, but there is no reason to take 'the Fictions of Poets' for accurate accounts of human history.[141] At this point Horatio's line of questioning changes tack, objecting that it is incredulous to dismiss the poets while at the same time endorsing the Biblical origins of humanity in Adam and Eve. 'I don't insist upon the Golden Age,' Horatio protests, 'if you'll give up Paradise: A Man of Sense, and a Philosopher, should believe neither.' Cleomenes is unmoved. Humans cannot have created themselves and the idea of miraculous creation is more plausible than either Epicurus's view that 'every thing is deriv'd from the Concourse and fortuitous Jumble of Atoms', or the Spinozist doctrine that we are all parts of an eternal whole. Although miracles are beyond human comprehension, our reason assures us that the world we inhabit must have been caused by 'the Contrivance of a being infinite in Wisdom as well as Power.'[142] We must believe in something, and the history of Moses is 'the most ancient and least improbable' account of the world's beginnings. We also have evidence that Moses was divinely inspired as both his knowledge of God's unity and the understanding of human nature contained in the Ten Commandments far surpassed the wisdom of his contemporaries.[143]

Scholars are divided over whether Cleomenes here—as with his discussions of providence in earlier dialogues—really represents Mandeville's position. Some argue that when Cleomenes states his belief in the Biblical origins of humanity it should merely be taken as 'an ironical pose' to evade responsibility 'for unorthodox sentiments.' In such cases, it is through Horatio that 'Mandeville himself speaks'.[144] By 'making the detractor of the *Fable* a sceptical deist and its defender a believing Christian', Mandeville could evade criticism while casting doubt on sacred history.[145] Other commentators are unpersuaded and I side with those who deny that Mandeville switches the roles of

141. *Fable* II, 306–307.

142. *Fable* II, 308–12. Horatio had earlier conceded that there are many incomprehensible truths, or 'Objects of Faith', which surpass our understanding and to which we should submit with humility, as long as they are not contrary to reason or our sensual perception, *Fable* II, 54. This discussion follows the distinction that Mandeville had earlier drawn 'between Things that are above Reason, and surpass our Capacity, and such as are against Reason, and contradict Demonstration', in *Free Thoughts*, 58.

143. *Fable* II, 315–18.

144. Kaye's editorial note to *Fable* II, 21.

145. Goldsmith, *Private Vices, Public Benefits*, 65, also 75–76.

Cleomenes and Horatio in these exchanges.[146] Even if we cannot uncover Mandeville's personal view regarding the Biblical origins of humanity or the workings of providence with any confidence, we can nevertheless make some interpretative headway while remaining agnostic about his own beliefs.[147] Mandeville introduces Cleomenes as someone who 'believ'd the Bible to be the Word of God, without reserve, and was entirely convinced of the mysterious as well as historical Truths that are contain'd in it.'[148] Whether or not Mandeville himself shared these beliefs is far less important than recognising that he (sincerely) aimed to show that his arguments were compatible with Christianity,[149] and in this sense Cleomenes—as a Mandevillean Christian— continues to represent Mandeville's position in the exchanges with Horatio on providence and Biblical history.

Mandeville had good reason to reemphasise the consistency of his position with Christian doctrine given that the *Fable* had been denounced from the pulpit and attacked as a deeply irreligious work. William Law had mockingly declared the need to reply to Mandeville 'as if I was speaking to a Christian',[150] and Mandeville returned the challenge by making a sincere Christian his own spokesman. Indeed, there are passages in *Fable II* where Mandeville appears to have had Law's criticisms directly in his sights. Targeting the 1714 'Enquiry', for example, Law had objected 'that Scripture makes it morally impossible' to suppose that humans were ever in a state of nature devoid of moral notions, for Noah's family was fully educated 'in the Principles of Virtue and moral Wisdom'.[151]

---

146. James, 'Faith, Sincerity and Morality', 51–52; Robertson, *Case for the Enlightenment*, 274–77. Both James and Robertson point to the influence of Pierre Bayle, although James emphasises that Mandeville's religious views do not go as far as Bayle's in stressing the 'contra-rationality of Christian belief'.

147. On this point, I agree with J.A.W. Gunn, 'Mandeville and Wither: Individualism and the Workings of Providence', in *Mandeville Studies*, 117–18: 'No clear case can, of course, be made about Mandeville's personal feelings regarding a deity. It suffices to show that what he wanted to say was consistent with the notion of providence'. See also Irwin Primer, 'Mandeville on War', in *Mandeville and Augustan Ideas*, 127: 'Whether Cleomenes' reference to providence reflects any real acceptance of Christianity by Mandeville is simply unknown.'

148. *Fable* II, 17.

149. See *Fable* II, 102, where Cleomenes advises that the *Fable* should be read in precisely this sense: 'Always look upon him in this View, and you'll never find him inconsistent with himself.'

150. Law, *Remarks*, 1.

151. Law, *Remarks*, 10. Horatio raises this objection (without referring to Law) at *Fable* II, 196–97. Kaye's editorial notes to the passage identify Law as the source.

Maybe so, Mandeville replies, but the existence of savage communities in parts of the world today demonstrates that humans must have fallen into a condition resembling a state of nature at some point after Noah led his family off the arc. The Old Testament does not inform us of 'all the Revolutions, that have happen'd among Mankind' subsequently, and the starting point of Mandeville's conjectural history—the savage state—allows for the possibility that there could have been earlier periods of human history known only through revealed religion. Conjectures about human interaction in a wild state of nature, therefore, in no sense 'render the Truth of the sacred History suspected'.[152]

Mandeville maintains that the truths of scripture are nowhere contradicted and sometimes supported by his conjectural history. Sacred history is not exhaustive and leaves plenty of scope for philosophers to speculate about how the species developed in those places and periods that the Bible does not cover. In arguing thus—and, crucially, in preserving a place for revealed religion—Mandeville sought to distance himself from the accusation of deism.[153] To Law's complaints about the irreligion and obscenity of the 'lively *beaux*', who take 'Jests upon Scripture . . . as true Proofs of *Deism* and Politeness',[154] Mandeville could reply that this worry is valid but misses its target, since it was Shaftesbury—and not himself—who had written for 'the Modern Deists and all the *Beau Monde*'.[155] Again, whether or not Mandeville personally believed in the truths of Biblical history, he was clearly concerned to show that his own philosophy complemented Christian doctrine whereas Shaftesbury's undermined it.[156] The 'First Dialogue' announces that 'the *Characteristicks* have made a Jest of all reveal'd Religion, especially the Christian',[157] and throughout *Fable II* Mandeville argues that polite social norms are nothing more than a pale imitation of real virtue and Christian morality. Politeness and 'good Manners are not inconsistent with Wickedness', and people may 'seem well-bred, and at the same time have no Regard to the Laws of God, and live in Contempt of Religion'.[158] Mandeville brings the book to a close by stressing his

152. *Fable* II, 198–99. See also *Fable* II, 264, where Mandeville returns to this point as evidence that 'Mankind will always be liable to be reduced to Savages'.

153. See also *Free Thoughts*, 15–16, where Mandeville defines a deist as someone who believes in God and Providence 'but has no Faith in any thing reveal'd to us'.

154. Law, *Remarks*, 70.

155. *Fable* II, 102.

156. This point is brought out very effectively by Stuart-Buttle, *Moral Theology to Moral Philosophy*, especially 132–35.

157. *Fable* II, 47, also 52–53.

158. *Fable* II, 281, also 313–14 on how this relates to 'the growth of Deism in this Kingdom'.

opposition to Shaftesbury on this very point. In revealing 'the Corruption of our Nature' and the 'Insufficiency of Human Reason and Heathen Virtue to procure real Felicity', Mandeville presents his own work as having strengthened the case for Christianity and revelation. It is Shaftesbury, by contrast, whose attempts to reconcile 'Innocence of Manners and worldly Greatness' lend support to deism and politeness. By 'ridiculing many Passages of Holy Writ', Shaftesbury had 'endeavour'd to sap the Foundation of all reveal'd Religion, with Design of establishing Heathen Virtue on the Ruins of Christianity.'[159]

Conclusion

The main purpose of this chapter has been to chart the development of Mandeville's historical narratives between the different editions of the *Fable*, focusing especially on the role played by the desire of dominion in explaining the transition from a savage state to a civilised society. Without the desire of dominion, Mandeville argues, society would be neither necessary nor possible: unnecessary because it is the danger that our undisciplined pride and desire of dominion pose to one another that leads to the second step towards society, and impossible because without the desire of dominion leaders would never have emerged to govern others. This emphasis on the desire of dominion is unique to *Fable II* and constitutes one of its most important theoretical developments. As is widely recognised, Mandeville's approach in *Fable II* is also very different to that of the earlier editions of the *Fable*, and the differences go well beyond the adoption of the dialogue format. One aim of this chapter has been to cut through some of the debate—and confusion—amongst scholars who ask whether Mandeville shifted from a 'conspiratorial' to an 'evolutionary' mode of explanation between the two volumes of the *Fable*. By way of conclusion, I return to the question of whether his approach should be classified as evolutionary, while summarising the more general limitations of framing the debate in this way, before highlighting some of the implications of Mandeville's account of the origin of society for theorising political authority.

A theory of social evolution?

I have argued that the difference in approach between the two volumes of the *Fable* is best characterised in terms of a historical turn: in *Fable II* Mandeville explores historical stages of the civilising process at length that he had passed

159. *Fable* II, 356–57.

over extremely briefly in the first volume. This historical approach is often described as 'evolutionary', which is unobjectionable in so far as it captures the long and gradual development of the various phenomena under investigation. To classify Mandeville's explanation as evolutionary, however, often carries further connotations, such as denying, or at least downplaying, the role of 'conscious and deliberate interventionist actions on the part of particular individuals at specific points in historical time'.[160] As F. A. Hayek put it, the 'burden of [Mandeville's] argument is throughout that most institutions of society are not the result of design'.[161] Should we regard Mandeville's theory as evolutionary in this more specific sense?

One piece of evidence that counts in favour of doing so, as Hayek recognised, is Mandeville's analysis of the origin of language. No one ever set out with the goal of developing a complex language to facilitate communication, but such languages gradually emerged from their origin in our desire to persuade one another. These developments also had unintended consequences. Written laws and society became possible once language had advanced to a certain level, but the earliest linguistic innovators had no such endpoint in view. We must be a little careful here, as any human practice or institution can be understood as an unintended consequence if we adopt a sufficiently long-term perspective and trace its causes far enough back. Mandeville's account of the origin of language, however, is importantly different to the interventions of the leaders and lawgivers who try to govern others and legislate, which do not fit so well with Hayek's interpretation. To be sure, the leaders and lawgivers may have learned from those who went before them in a long-term process of trial and error,[162] yet the agents in question were actively trying to design a certain type of social order and without their efforts no social order could have emerged.[163] Mandeville seeks to deny only the superhuman genius of a Solon or a Lycurgus and not that they succeeded in drawing up laws for those they

---

160. Rosenberg, 'Mandeville and Laissez-Faire', 194.

161. Hayek, 'Lecture on a Master Mind', 137.

162. Hayek, 'Lecture on a Master Mind', 136. For criticism of Hayek's reading of Mandeville as an early theorist of cultural evolution, on the grounds that Hayek neglects the extent to which social institutions and scientific discoveries result from experimental reasoning, see Christina Petsoulas, *Hayek's Liberalism and its Origins: His Idea of Spontaneous Order and the Scottish Enlightenment* (London and New York: Routledge, 2001), 87–95.

163. For more general criticism of Hayek's theory of spontaneous order along similar lines, see Daniel Luban, 'What is Spontaneous Order?', *American Political Science Review* 114, no. 1 (2020), especially 74–79.

governed. Legal orders were not designed *ex nihilo*, but they were nevertheless the result of certain individuals trying, and eventually succeeding, to formulate rules that would allow them to govern other people more effectively.

Hayek claims that 'Mandeville for the first time developed all the classical paradigmata of the spontaneous growth of orderly social structures: of law and morals, of language, the market, and of money, and also of the growth of technological knowledge.'[164] This quote epitomises the problem of assuming that Mandeville had one explanation for a range of distinct social phenomena. Hayek's point about spontaneity is plausible, for example, when we consider Mandeville's account of how politeness and good manners developed without conscious design. Most people practise good manners with little foresight and without any understanding of how they have learned to conceal their pride in socially acceptable ways; we fall 'into these Things spontaneously', as Mandeville himself says, learning through imitation and experience.[165] Hayek's spontaneous growth interpretation is less persuasive, however, when we turn to Mandeville's analysis of the origin of society. To recall, Mandeville uses the analogy of fermentation to explain the sense in which humans are designed for society; humans eventually become sociable creatures in a process analogous to that by which grapes become wine. Yet it would be very odd to say that wine emerges spontaneously, or evolves, from grapes. Consider the second step towards society, where humans associate in 'Bands and Companies' under different leaders who are actively seeking to rule others and expand their power. If there is a process of social experimentation involved here then it is a top-down one where band leaders use coercion to secure their position—'the strongest and most valiant . . . swallow up the weakest and most fearful'—while designing prohibitions and penalties to curb the disorderly passions of those they seek to govern.[166] This process is far removed from Mandeville's account of how norms of politeness and good manners emerge once humans live in civilised society.[167]

164. Hayek, 'Lecture on a Master Mind', 129. See also Hamowy, *Scottish Enlightenment*, 9–10, who follows Hayek in arguing that Mandeville's spontaneous order theory 'runs throughout his work and is applied to a multiplicity of institutions', and that this is Mandeville's most important influence on the Scottish Enlightenment.

165. *Fable* II, 139.

166. *Fable* II, 267–68.

167. On a related note, see Heath, 'Bewitching Engine of Praise', 207, who distinguishes between two different evolutionary processes once a government is in place: 'One concerns the piecemeal efforts of "politicians" to change and improve the basic legal framework of society;

I have focused on Hayek's interpretation presently because he is one of the most famous theorists—and certainly the most famous Mandeville commentator—of an evolutionary or spontaneous order theory of social development.[168] Yet the limitations of Hayek's interpretation reflect a broader tendency amongst scholars to attribute a single mode of explanation to Mandeville's investigation of a range of distinct social phenomena. Debates about whether Mandeville shifts from a conspiratorial to an evolutionary explanation between the two volumes of the *Fable* have mostly overlooked the critical point that there is no stable explanandum across the texts in question. This has important implications when considering whether Mandeville abandoned his conspiratorial explanation of the origins of moral virtue and honour. As we have seen, the leaders of bands and (later) lawgivers do play an important role in Mandeville's civilising story in *Fable II*, but, crucially, it is not the same role as that played by wise lawgivers and politicians in either the 'Enquiry' or 'Remark R' of the original *Fable*. In the earlier texts, lawgivers flattered the pride of those they hoped to govern by appealing to notions of excellence and valour that supposedly set humans apart from other animals. Flattery plays no equivalent role in the steps towards society in *Fable II*. One reason for this—although Mandeville does not join all the dots himself—is that language was insufficiently advanced prior to the invention of letters. Flattery comes into play only within society, so it cannot be part of the explanatory process by which society emerges in the first place (as the 'Enquiry' seemed to suggest).[169] Mandeville's index to *Fable II* captures this point succinctly:

the other concerns the emergence of nonlegal norms of behavior.' This distinction is helpful, although it is worth stressing that it applies only once humans are living in society, whereas Mandeville's conjectural history in *Fable II* focuses much more on how society itself emerges.

168. My interest here is limited to what Hayek's interpretation tells us about Mandeville, but for insightful discussion of the importance of Mandeville for the development of Hayek's own thought, see Emily Skarbek, 'F. A. Hayek and the Early Foundations of Spontaneous Order', in *F. A. Hayek and the Modern Economy: Economic Organization and Activity*, ed. Sandra J. Peart and David M. Levy (New York: Palgrave Macmillan, 2013), especially 107–112. On the transmission of Mandeville's ideas to Hayek, see Mark Charles Nolan, 'Paul Sakmann's and Albert Schatz's Mandeville Studies: Their Link to Hayek's "Spontaneous Order" Theory', *Journal of the History of Economic Thought* 38, no. 4 (2016): 485–506.

169. Cf. Hundert, *Enlightenment's Fable*, 90–93, who reads the discussion of language in *Fable II* as complementing Mandeville's earlier conclusion that 'the Moral Virtues are the Political Offspring which Flattery begot upon Pride', at *Fable I*, 51. More generally on Mandeville's account of language and flattery, see Kapust, *Flattery*, 135–48, although he does not consider this complication.

'Flattery ... The Beginning of it in Society'.[170] The broader point that bears emphasising, however, and which remains largely neglected in existing scholarship,[171] is that Mandeville's analysis of the steps towards society in *Fable II* proceeds without explaining the origin of our ideas of either moral virtue or honour, the topics which had been at the heart of his earlier civilising stories. Indeed, it is unclear precisely where these origin stories would fit into the narrative arc of *Fable II* and the fact that Mandeville returns to these topics in *Origin of Honour*, as we shall see in the next chapter, suggests that he saw this as a problem which needed addressing.

A theory of political authority?

The most original feature of *Fable II* is the detailed historical narratives that Mandeville develops in support of the underlying claims he had long been making about human sociability. As we have seen, these narratives constitute a lengthy investigation into the origin of society and Mandeville was well aware that our ideas about the scope and purpose of political states are shaped, in part at least, by views on their origin. He follows William Temple in eschewing social contract explanations and advancing a more historically oriented approach to thinking about political society, which looks forward to David Hume and Adam Smith, amongst others.[172] The problem with social contract theories is not principally one of historical plausibility—that is, did any such contracts ever occur?—but, rather, that they model political authority in terms of a transfer of rights from individuals to some form of governing or sovereign body. From Mandeville's perspective, this overlooks the sources of authority found in savage families and bands, which are the building blocks of authority within society.

Although Mandeville does not theorise political authority in any detail, his conjectural history of society offers some important, albeit underdeveloped, insights on the topic. The first is the importance of reverence, which originates

170. *Fable* II, 365, also 145.

171. For a notable exception, see Simonazzi, 'Common Law', 126, who argues that the most important difference between the two volumes is 'that *Fable II* elaborates a new theory on the origin of society in which law takes over the key role occupied by ethics in *Fable I*.'

172. For a concise statement of this tradition as an alternative to contractarian thought, see Paul Sagar, 'Of Mushrooms and Method: History and the Family in Hobbes's Science of Politics', *European Journal of Political Theory* 14, no. 1 (2015), especially 110–12; and, more generally, idem., *Opinion of Mankind*, especially 67–102.

in savage families where children would fear, love, and esteem their father.[173] Reverence to authority is necessary for us to become governable rather than merely submissive creatures; it is, therefore, 'of the highest Moment to all Government, and Sociableness itself'. Even though its origin predates society, reverence is key to understanding and maintaining political authority. Good laws seek to inculcate reverence in their subjects without forgetting that children receive their first notions of authority in the family, which is why 'the Honour and Deference' children have for their parents is the foundation of 'the Principle of human Obedience' in all societies.[174] Given the importance Mandeville accords to reverence in passages such as this, it is surprising that he does not say more about it elsewhere, especially, for example, when offering some general reflections on how states maintain themselves towards the end of the 'Sixth Dialogue'. A well-ordered state is analogous to a knitting frame or clock, which, once designed, can be operated without much skill or knowledge thereafter. If the government and civil administration of a state are 'wisely contriv'd' then 'every Man of midling Capacity and Reputation may be fit for any of the highest Posts',[175] which is fortunate since 'consummate Statesmen' are so few and far between.[176] These remarks are unlikely to inspire reverence in the individual qualities of the political elite in any state, but Mandeville's view, we may at least speculate, could be that the appropriate object of reverence in a civilised society is the political and legal system itself, rather than those who hold political office at any given time. This is in marked contrast to tyrannical and arbitrary rulers' reliance on fear alone, with subjects only counterfeiting love and esteem because they are afraid of the consequences of openly expressing the hatred they feel within.[177]

Even if we can detect the source of authority within savage families, Mandeville does not think that society comes easily to humans, for we have plenty of other passions that are liable to overcome reverence. He insists that the capacity to govern others is not found in savage families; it instead develops gradually as those families unite into bands, which eventually grow into societies with written laws. Our desire to rule over others—the 'Instinct of Sovereignty'—is deep-rooted in human nature, but the desire itself will result

173. See Note 94 above on the ambiguity between paternal and parental authority.
174. *Fable* II, 280–81.
175. *Fable* II, 322–23.
176. *Fable* II, 340.
177. *Fable* II, 216–17.

in conflicts over superiority until the leaders of bands learn how to curb the unruly passions of those they seek to govern. Up until this point, a common enemy is required to keep people together, whether that enemy be wild animals or other domineering humans. If we are interested in the origin of society, then, we should have something to say about how political leaders and lawgivers come to acquire the knowledge and skills required to govern others and, as we have seen, this problem is at the heart of Mandeville's conjectural history.

That conjectural history is not without its limitations, however, and recon-struction and interpretation of Mandeville's arguments should not be mis-taken for endorsement. Compared to other eighteenth-century investigations into the history of civil society, it is striking how little Mandeville has to say about the development of agriculture and private property, or questions of economic subsistence.[178] A more general criticism is that his historical narra-tives are too conjectural to be taken seriously. As Adam Ferguson complained, with Jean-Jacques Rousseau in his sights, 'the natural historian' is 'obliged to collect facts, not to offer conjectures', and doing so reveals that humans are always found 'assembled in troops and companies'.[179] To this line of objection, Mandeville could respond that his conjectural approach is quite different to that of the natural historian, but the worry persists that, even as conjectures, the earliest stages of his narrative do not map onto any plausible stage in human history. Rather than imagining how a savage couple would interact in a wild state of nature, perhaps Mandeville should have commenced his nar-ratives at the second step towards society, with humans associating in 'Bands and Companies', especially as this is the stage which he thought corresponded with contemporary accounts of uncivilised communities.[180]

Mandeville seeks to show that many of the qualities we take as distinctively human—including our capacity to govern others—were acquired only through a long process of socialisation and education, but in doing so he overreaches and sometimes goes too far in his attempts to strip human nature bare. Viewed against more recent findings, it is clear that he considerably underestimated

---

178. See also Goldsmith, *Private Vices, Public Benefits*, 76–77; Hundert, *Enlightenment's Fable*, 187; Francesconi, 'Mandeville sull'origine della società', 431–33.

179. Ferguson, *Essay*, i.1.

180. *Fable* II, 267. Cf. *Fable* II, 231, where Mandeville acknowledges the improbability of some of his conjectures, but nevertheless claims that they help to reveal the implausibility of William Temple's rival account.

the capacity for successful human cooperation in prehistoric or stateless communities.[181] Yet one of Mandeville's most important claims about human nature does find some support from those who have marshalled anthropological and ethnological evidence to argue that there is a universal drive to dominance in human nature, along with an aversion to being dominated by others. Even egalitarian hunter-gatherer bands rely on social sanctions to discipline those who seek to dominate other members of the community and to tame the pride of those whose successes in hunting would result in a dangerously inflated sense of self-worth.[182] Mandeville, of course, did not entertain the possibility of anything like hunter-gatherer bands developing an egalitarian ethos that could effectively counteract our desire of dominion, evidence of which undermines many of his claims about a savage state. Nevertheless, he did see the desire of dominion as an inescapable feature of the human condition and thought that sociability would be impossible without norms and sanctions to regulate our pride-centred nature. On this score, at least, his view of human sociability is more plausible than his adversaries' insistence that the desire to dominate others is only a product of inegalitarian social relations, and that our natural affection, or love of species, would otherwise be sufficient to render us sociable creatures. From Mandeville's perspective, to the contrary, the desire of dominion will always be with us and thus the search for ways to ensure that it does not lead to conflict and discord must remain central to the success of any form of human association.

181. For the more general argument that a great deal of modern political theory relies on myths about stateless societies, along with evidence debunking those myths, see Karl Wilderquist and Grant S. McCall, *Prehistoric Myths in Modern Political Philosophy* (Edinburgh: Edinburgh University Press, 2017).

182. Most notably, see Christopher Boehm, *Hierarchy in the Forest: The Evolution of Egalitarian Behavior* (Cambridge MA and London: Harvard University Press, 1999), especially 40–63 for evidence from hunter-gatherer bands, and 124–48 on the universal drive to dominance. For helpful discussions that (in very different ways) draw on Boehm and bring the evidence to bear on debates within political theory, see Gerald Gaus, 'The Egalitarian Species', *Social Philosophy and Policy* 31, no. 2 (2015), especially 12–19; Wilderquist and McCall, *Prehistoric Myths*, especially 166–69.

5

Honour, Religion, and War

MANDEVILLE'S LAST MAJOR WORK, published in 1732, is entitled *An Enquiry into the Origin of Honour, and the Usefulness of Christianity in War*. Although not officially a third part or volume of the *Fable of the Bees*, there is good reason to treat it as such: it continues the dialogues between Cleomenes (Mandeville's spokesman) and Horatio (his interlocutor) from *Fable II*, while addressing similar themes to the earlier volumes.[1] As its title suggests, *Origin of Honour* revisits and extends Mandeville's explanations of how various social and moral phenomena first arose. In the previous chapter I showed that these origin stories underwent a historical turn in *Fable II*, in the sense that Mandeville explained in considerably greater depth the long and gradual development of the phenomena under investigation. Where *Fable II* mostly deals in conjectural history, however, *Origin of Honour* is more concerned with examining the specific historical circumstances that led to the principle of honour taking root in medieval Europe under the cloak of Christianity.

Mandeville maintains that the principle of honour is a 'Human Contrivance, rais'd on the Basis of Human Pride',[2] and his account of its development is one example of how his more general pride-centred theory of sociability plays out under particular historical and cultural conditions. The principle of honour is not for everyone. The 'Vulgar, Children, Savages and many others' all display symptoms of pride, but none of them are 'affected with any Sense of

---

1. See *Origin of Honour*, xi, where Mandeville refers the reader to the 'Preface' of *Fable II* for character sketches of the two interlocutors. *Origin of Honour* had a different publisher to *Fable II*, which may explain why it was not presented as a third part of the *Fable*. On the publishing history, see Tolonen, *Mandeville and Hume*, 137–39.

2. *Origin of Honour*, 64, also 86, 97–98; see also *Fable I*, 209–10, 216, 221–22; *Fable II*, 92, 124.

Honour'.[3] Honour is found most amongst soldiers and well-educated ladies who have their pride flattered and their fear of shame increased to a far greater degree than is common amongst other groups in society.[4] Where female honour consists in chastity, 'Courage and Intrepidity always were, and ever will be the grand Characteristick of a Man of Honour'.[5] *Origin of Honour* focuses predominantly on male honour,[6] for one of its central concerns is to analyse the qualities required for success in war.[7] The close association between honour and war is evident throughout Mandeville's writings. The original *Grumbling Hive* verse mentions honour in relation to the 'Soldiers, that were forc'd to fight',[8] and one of Mandeville's earliest discussions of the nature of honour centres on the question of whether a young gentleman should 'cross the Seas in quest of Honour, and . . . learn the difficult Art of War'.[9] When addressing the same topic in the 1714 edition of the *Fable*, Mandeville likewise explains how notions of honour were first raised to 'make Men fight'.[10] More generally, he often stresses that his analysis of modern society applies only to a 'warlike Nation'

3. *Fable* II, 92.

4. *Fable* II, 123; see also *Fable* I, 121.

5. *Origin of Honour*, 63.

6. For the few pages devoted to female honour, see *Origin of Honour*, 53–60. Unless otherwise specified, I follow Mandeville in using honour to refer to male honour.

7. The topic of war has rarely received focused treatment from Mandeville scholars, but for a notable exception see Primer, 'Mandeville on War'. Mandeville's ideas on honour have received a little more attention, thanks chiefly to the work of Andrea Branchi. For Branchi's most important studies (in English), see 'Vanity, Virtue and the Duel: The Scottish Response to Mandeville', *Journal of Scottish Philosophy* 12, no. 1 (2014): 71–93; 'Courage and Chastity in Commercial Society: Mandeville's Point on Male and Female Honour', in *Mandeville's Tropology of Paradoxes*, 199–211; 'Honour and the Art of Politics', *I castelli di Yale* 6, no. 2 (2018): 29–43; *Pride, Manners, and Morals*. For other helpful studies on Mandeville and honour, see Mauro Simonazzi, 'Self-liking, onore e religione nella *Ricerca sull'origine dell'onore e sull'utilità del cristianesimo in guerra* di Bernard Mandeville', *Il pensiero politico: rivista di storia delle idee politiche e sociali* 32, no. 3 (1999): 352–82; Peltonen, *Duel in Early Modern England*, 263–302; Welsh, *What is Honor?*, 89–93; Mikko Tolonen, 'The Gothic Origin of Modern Civility: Mandeville and the Scots on Courage', *The Journal of Scottish Philosophy* 12, no. 1 (2014): 51–69; Peter Olsthoorn, *Honor in Political and Moral Philosophy* (Albany, NY: SUNY Press, 2015), especially 36–42; idem., 'Bernard Mandeville on Honor, Hypocrisy, and War', *The Heythrop Journal* 60, no. 2 (2019): 205–18; Stuart-Buttle, *Moral Theology to Moral Philosophy*, 136–47; Liu, 'Tragedy of Honor', 1248–51.

8. *Fable* I, 22. This point is highlighted by Olsthoorn, 'Honor, Hypocrisy, and War', 211. See also *Pamphleteers*, 7: 'Tell m' in what place was th' *English* Honour stain'd;/ Or in whose Time the Soldiers better train'd?'

9. *Female Tatler*, no. 80: 151.

10. *Fable* I, 208, 210.

and this qualification is just as important as the emphasis he places on the society in question being large and flourishing.[11]

To understand the origin of honour, we must also attend to its relationship with religion and especially Christianity. Where the basis of natural religion is fear of an invisible cause, the principle of honour was conceived specifically to 'influence Men, who Religion had no Power over.'[12] As we shall see, religion ceased to have this hold over a certain portion of society following the advent of Christianity, and the subsequent interplay between honour and fear of an invisible cause is a central theme of *Origin of Honour*. It is also a complex one, which, to anticipate, cannot simply be reduced to a story about how honour came to replace religion in the European states of Mandeville's day.

One of my overarching aims in this chapter is to demonstrate that *Origin of Honour* deserves much greater scholarly attention than it has currently received. Its contribution goes well beyond filling in some gaps and clarifying certain ideas from Mandeville's earlier works, for it also sheds light on aspects of his thought that are barely, if at all, developed elsewhere. In what follows I do not offer an exhaustive analysis of *Origin of Honour*, but in showing how it both deepens and broadens our understanding of Mandeville's theory of sociability, I hope to convey a more general sense of the work's importance and distinctiveness. My approach is similar to that of the previous chapter, in that I trace how Mandeville's analysis of honour both builds upon and departs from his earlier discussions, focusing especially on its relationship with virtue and his account of duelling. Towards the end of the chapter, I then turn to some of the most neglected material in *Origin of Honour* and examine Mandeville's remarks on love of country and religious enthusiasm. These could be classified as collective passions, in so far as their motivational force depends upon belonging to a group that pursues a shared cause, yet, on Mandeville's account, they are still best explained in terms of our pride-centred nature.

The origins of virtue and honour, revisited

The 'First Dialogue' of *Origin of Honour* commences with Horatio asking Cleomenes why he has 'never attempted to guess at the Origin of Honour, as you have done at that of Politeness, and your Friend in his Fable of the Bees

11. *Female Tatler*, no. 52: 81; *Fable* I, 6, 245; *Tyburn*, 28–29; *Origin of Honour*, 83. In a similar vein, consider the contrast Mandeville draws between 'a small, *peaceable* Society' and 'a vast Multitude abounding in Wealth and Power, that should always be *conquering others by their Arms abroad*', *Fable* I, 13 (emphasis added).

12. *Origin of Honour*, 15.

has done at the Origin of Virtue.' Cleomenes proceeds to offer three reasons why he has 'hitherto kept it to my Self,' but none of these take issue with the question itself.[13] Yet the relationship between *Origin of Honour* and the first two volumes of the *Fable* is not as straightforward as Mandeville would have us believe, and it is worth pausing to consider the implications of presenting the development of his origin stories in this way.

First, and most strikingly, it is disingenuous of Mandeville to suggest that the *Fable* had not addressed the origin of honour, which raises the question of why he implies that *Origin of Honour* is entering uncharted territory. Revealing 'the mean Origin of Honour' was, in fact, a central theme of 'Remark R' from the first volume,[14] and Mandeville explicitly recalls that discussion later in *Origin of Honour* when stressing the incompatibility of Christianity and honour.[15] Another piece in this puzzle is that although the first two dialogues do focus on the origin of honour, the book opens with a 'Preface' that reconsiders the origin of virtue. Mandeville had not joined all the dots between his explanations of the origins of virtue and honour in the 1714 edition of the *Fable* (nor had he returned to these origin stories in *Fable II*),[16] and the 'Preface' further complicates the relationship between the two concepts. As will become apparent, Mandeville's new account of the origin of virtue has a surprising amount in common with his old account of the origin of honour, even if the way he frames the 'First Dialogue' serves to conceal these resemblances.

Second, by singling out politeness from *Fable II*—which is only one of several origin stories in that work—the exchange between Cleomenes and Horatio highlights that honour and politeness are separate phenomena, each worthy of independent investigation. Mandeville's discussion of the origin of politeness in the 'Third Dialogue' of *Fable II* followed a lengthy analysis of the man of honour in the 'Second Dialogue', and although he never

13. *Origin of Honour*, 1.

14. *Fable I*, 220. Although readers would not have known his authorship, Mandeville had also explained the basis of honour in terms of our admiration 'of Praise and desire to be thought well of by others' as early as 1710 in the *Female Tatler*, no. 80: 152–54. He subsequently referred to this as a discussion of 'the Origin of Praise', *Female Tatler*, no. 84: 160. Similarly, Chapter 4 of *Tyburn* examines honour and valour, and in the 'Preface' Mandeville claims to have 'searched into the Origin of Courage'.

15. *Origin of Honour*, 77; see also 54 and 60, where Mandeville refers to *Fable II* on the differences between male and female honour.

16. See Chapter 4, 'The role of human contrivance (1714–23)'.

claimed that the origins of honour and politeness are one and the same,[17] he did refer to 'the Rules of Politeness, and all the Laws of Honour', or 'true Notions of Honour and Politeness',[18] in a way that suggests they are very closely related. Mandeville says relatively little about the relationship between honour and politeness in *Origin of Honour*, but later in this chapter, with his analysis of honour laid out, we will be better placed to understand how and where his origin stories intersect—and, just as importantly, where they do not.

Virtue and honour

Mandeville presents the 'Preface' to *Origin of Honour* as a defence of 'An Enquiry Into the Origin of Moral Virtue'.[19] For present purposes, however, the most interesting aspect of the 'Preface' is that it departs in important respects from his 1714 account. Mandeville continues to associate the origin of virtue with 'the first Forming of all Societies', but he now stresses that the earliest virtues were those of strength and courage, which would have been invaluable in the 'Struggles for Superiority' that marked 'the Beginnings of Civil Government, and the Infancy of Nations'.[20] Although he does not draw the connection explicitly, these struggles appear to map onto the second step towards society from *Fable II*, where those who wanted to govern others 'would strive for Superiority' and fight one another, resulting in the emergence of 'Bands and Companies' with rival leaders vying for pre-eminence.[21]

Mandeville turns to the etymology of the words moral and virtue to support his case, explaining their derivation in Greek and Latin from ideas of war and fortitude. The origin of virtue is found in the qualities that were desirable during periods of conflict and, in this context, virtue was associated with the self-denial required to struggle against 'the most violent and stubborn [passion], and consequently the hardest to be conquer'd, the Fear of Death'. In times of war and civil strife, the self-denial displayed by those who were willing

---

17. The key passage here is at *Fable* II, 128, where Horatio acknowledges 'that no body knew, when or where . . . the Laws of Honour were enacted', but nonetheless asks 'when or which Way, what we call good Manners or Politeness, came into the World?'

18. *Fable* II, 12, 313.

19. *Origin of Honour*, i.

20. *Origin of Honour*, iii.

21. *Fable* II, 266–67. On this connection, see also Faas, *Genealogy of Aesthetics*, 127–28. For more details of this stage in Mandeville's conjectural history, see Chapter 4, 'The first two steps'.

to imperil their lives to defend their community became the epitome of virtue. The original meaning of virtue was simply 'Daring and Intrepidity', which is compatible with the 'Savageness, and brutish Courage' that characterised the earliest stages of society. The term virtue subsequently came to be used more capaciously. Cicero listed modesty, justice, and temperance as 'the softer and easier Virtues', as 'the Self-denial they require is more practicable and less mortifying than that of Virtue itself, as it is taken in its proper and genuine Sense'. Even as the term virtue extended beyond conquest over the fear of death, it was still reserved for the display of some 'Conquest over our selves', such that no matter how beneficial any action or quality might prove, it does not 'deserve the Name of Virtue, strictly speaking, where there is not a palpable Self-denial to be seen.'[22]

Mandeville insisted that virtue requires self-denial throughout the different editions of the *Fable*, and the etymological evidence he marshals in the 'Preface' lends further support to that position. As in the earlier 'Enquiry', he seeks to explain why it would have proved socially advantageous for humans to conceptualise virtue in terms of overcoming certain passions for the public benefit. Yet there are also important differences between the 1714 and 1732 versions of his argument. There is no suggestion in the 'Preface' that for an act to count as virtuous it must be motivated by a rational ambition of being good, or that it was only by being flattered with notions of 'the Excellency of our Nature' that we were originally induced to practise virtue.[23] If the idea of virtue first arose around the time of the second step towards society, then the arts of flattery would have been rudimentary, if they existed at all,[24] which might explain why Mandeville omits this aspect of his earlier account. The most striking revision, however, is the centrality he now accords to overcoming the fear of death and instilling the qualities required for success in war, which had received no discussion in the 'Enquiry'. On this point, in fact, the 'Preface' more closely follows 'Remark R', where Mandeville was concerned with the origin of honour, not virtue. There he argued that notions of honour were first cultivated to ensure that people will defend their community against attack and engage in conquest to expand its territory.[25] The courage or valour involved in the principle of honour is artificial, not natural, and is based on pride and shame; it

22. *Origin of Honour*, iii–vi, also ix.
23. Cf. *Fable* I, 42–52.
24. On this point, see also Chapter 4, 'A theory of social evolution?'.
25. *Fable* I, 207.

'consists *in a Superlative Horror against Shame, by* Flattery *infused into Men of exalted* Pride.'[26]

If the 'Preface' to *Origin of Honour* develops ideas from 'Remark R' at least as much as it does those from the 'Enquiry', then this raises questions about how (the origins of) honour and virtue are related—questions that are all the more pressing in so far as the two qualities are distinct.[27] Mandeville never addresses the problem in the way I have outlined it here, but at one point in the 'First Dialogue' he does have Horatio object 'that Honour is of the same Origin with Virtue'. Cleomenes replies that the invention of honour is 'of a much later date' and 'has been far more beneficial', precisely because (in the latter case) honour is less demanding than virtue. The rules of honour are 'more skilfully adapted to our inward Make' by allowing us to enjoy more pride in, and demand recognition of, our honourable qualities, whereas a 'Virtuous Man expects no Acknowledgment from others'.[28] This response is in keeping with much of what Mandeville said about the nature of virtue in the earlier volumes of the *Fable*, especially his claims that virtue must be motivated by a rational ambition of being good,[29] or that 'real' virtue—as opposed to its 'counterfeited' variety—requires a victory over the passions, rather than one passion conquering another.[30] The problem, however, is that this demanding conception of virtue is not obviously supported by the points he makes in the 'Preface'. Nothing in his new account of the origin of virtue indicates that the self-denial involved in overcoming the fear of death could not be motivated by pride or the expectation of public acclaim,[31] and he gives us no

26. *Fable* I, 210.

27. Mandeville is not always clear about how far they are distinct. In 'Remark R', for example, he first describes honour as 'a certain Principle of Virtue not related to Religion', before later stressing the difference between 'Men of real Virtue' and those of 'real Honour', *Fable* I, 198 and 222, respectively.

28. *Origin of Honour*, 42–44. The passage revisits arguments from *Fable* I, 222.

29. *Fable* I, 48–49, 260.

30. *Fable* I, 230, 405. Although Mandeville refers to a man 'of real Virtue' (43) and the 'Practice of real Virtue' (78) in *Origin of Honour*, he does not invoke the distinction between real and counterfeited virtue that he had drawn most sharply in the expanded 1723 edition of the *Fable*.

31. Compared to his earlier works, Mandeville says surprisingly little about the underlying motivations of self-denial in the 'Preface'. We know from 'Remark R' that anger and lust are also capable of overcoming fear of death, although Mandeville there explained that this natural courage cannot be relied upon in war and must be replaced by artificial courage; see *Fable* I, 208–10. Tolonen ('Gothic Origin', 56) suggests that the courage of soldiers in the ancient world 'was based on anger and hatred rather than pride and self-esteem', but Mandeville does not deny

grounds for attributing more disinterested motives to those who fight for their communities in war. The 'Preface', then, does not explain why virtue should be understood in the very demanding terms that Mandeville later argues differentiate it from honour, and it initially remains unclear why the examples he offers there should be classified as cases of (real) virtue rather than honour.[32]

Mandeville's claim that the invention of honour is of a much later date than that of virtue helps to unravel the puzzle, since his main concern in the 'First Dialogue', as we shall see, is to recount the origin of the distinctively *modern* sense of honour. The 'Enquiry' and 'Remark R' from the first volume of the *Fable*, along with the 'Preface' to *Origin of Honour*, focus on explaining phenomena that originated in the early formation of societies, whereas the modern sense of honour, Mandeville now maintains, is of Gothic origin and was not 'to be met with a Thousand Years ago in any Language'.[33] For the purposes of *Origin of Honour*, then, the distinction that really matters is between the modern sense of honour and whatever else preceded it, whether that was a different form of honour, virtue, or something else. Mandeville's contention at the beginning of the 'First Dialogue' that he had 'never attempted to guess at the Origin of Honour' is, strictly speaking, false. What is true is that he had said relatively little about the origin of *modern* honour in his earlier works, and it is the attention he gives to this that sets *Origin of Honour* apart from his other origin stories.

Modern honour

At the beginning of the 'First Dialogue', Mandeville offers three reasons to explain why he had not previously disclosed his thoughts on the origin of honour: first, the word honour is ambiguous and often used in different senses; second, it would take a long time to explain its origin clearly; and, third, there is no commonly received name for the passion upon which honour is

---

that pride and self-esteem played a part in the ancient world, even if they did not develop into the modern principle of honour.

32. See also Chapter 3, 'Hypocrisy and the origin of virtue', where I discuss a very similar problem in relation to the 'Enquiry' and suggest how Mandeville's more demanding claims about the nature of virtue could be reconciled with his explanation of the origin of virtue. My proposed reconciliation, however, rests on there being a clear gap between the idea and practice of virtue, which is not nearly as apparent in the 'Preface' to *Origin of Honour*.

33. *Origin of Honour*, 14–15.

based.[34] Mandeville proceeds to discuss the third reason at some length and in doing so he returns to his account of self-liking from the 'Third Dialogue' of *Fable II*. In particular, he clarifies that pride and shame 'are different Affections of one and the same Passion', that is, self-liking,[35] which helps to make sense of why he routinely claims that honour is based on pride and shame, while also stating that 'the Origin of Honour ... has its Foundation in Self-liking'.[36] Although this discussion provides a welcome elucidation of the concept of self-liking, it is the first of Mandeville's three reasons that sets the scene for his historical reflections on the development of modern honour.

In highlighting the ambiguities surrounding honour, Mandeville observes that the word is sometimes used as a verb and other times as a noun, and that honour is variously considered the principle of virtue, synonymous with virtue itself, or the reward of virtue.[37] In its 'literal Sense', he explains a little later, honour is a 'Technic Word in the Art of Civility', referring to the ways in which we gratify each other's self-liking. In this sense, as both a verb and a noun, honour is 'as Ancient as the oldest Language'.[38] In 1714 Mandeville defined honour as 'the good Opinion of others', which corresponds with what he now calls its literal meaning.[39] Honour, so understood, 'is a Term of Art to express our Concurrence with others, our Agreement with them in their Sentiments concerning the Esteem and Value they have for themselves.' We honour other people by complimenting them and, conversely, we shame or dishonour others by criticising them and conveying that 'we differ from them in their Sentiments concerning the Value' they have for themselves. This is a ubiquitous feature of social interaction, which we encounter as much 'among the worst of Rogues' as 'among the better Sort of People.'[40] There is, however, also a 'much more modern' and distinctive notion of honour that signifies 'a Principle of Courage, Virtue, and Fidelity, which some Men are said to act from, and to be aw'd by, as others are by Religion.' It is in relation to this understanding that we can talk about honour as 'a Principle' of courage and analyse the character of 'a Man of Honour', whose bravery in battle is matched only by his

---

34. *Origin of Honour*, 2.

35. *Origin of Honour*, 9.

36. *Origin of Honour*, 40. For further discussion of the distinction between self-love and self-liking, see Chapter 1, 'Self-love and self-liking', and Chapter 2, 'The morality of self-liking'.

37. *Origin of Honour*, 2.

38. *Origin of Honour*, 14.

39. *Fable I*, 63.

40. *Origin of Honour*, 9–10.

unwillingness to bear any personal affront.[41] Where the literal sense of honour can be used in relation to all ranks of society, the principle of honour was designed specifically 'to create artificial Courage among Military Men.' The distinction associated with honour relies on everyone believing that the principle is found 'not among Mechanicks, or any of the Vulgar, but in Persons of high Birth, Knights, and others of Heroick Spirit and exalted Nature.'[42] This sense of honour was unknown in antiquity and cannot easily be expressed in Greek or Latin; it is, instead, 'entirely Gothick, and sprung up in some of the most ignorant Ages of Christianity.'[43] The modern sense of honour, then, first developed in what we would now more usually call medieval Europe.

Mandeville's narrative in *Origin of Honour* subtly deviates from the distinction he had drawn in 'Remark R' between ancient and modern honour.[44] He had earlier claimed that where 'Men of ancient Honour' would always keep their word, prefer the public interest to their own, refrain from lying, defrauding, or wronging others, and never suffer insult, 'the Moderns seem to be more remiss' and care only about avenging insults while mostly neglecting the other rules.[45] Don Quixote was the last man of ancient honour and it was an ideal best contained to chivalric novels where 'Knights-Errant . . . did abundance of Good throughout the World, by taming Monsters, delivering the Distress'd, and killing the Oppressors'.[46] In *Origin of Honour*, however, Mandeville refrains from discussing ancient honour as a principle of action and the chivalric ideal is incorporated within his explanation of how the modern sense of honour developed.[47] Indeed, he now argues that it makes sense to talk about honour as a distinctive quality that men possess and act from only in relation

41. *Origin of Honour*, 14–15.

42. *Origin of Honour*, 60–61; see also *Fable* I, 199; *Fable* II, 92, 354.

43. *Origin of Honour*, 15.

44. See also John P. Wright, 'Hume on the Origin of "modern honour": A Study in Hume's Philosophical Development', in *Philosophy and Religion in Enlightenment Britain: New Case Studies*, ed. Ruth Savage (Oxford: Oxford University Press, 2012), 189–90. As Wright notes, Mandeville's use of the terms 'modern' and 'ancient' is flexible and does not always map onto subsequent ideas of modern and ancient periods, so we should be wary of imposing our own chronology of modernity onto what he says about modern honour.

45. *Fable* I, 199.

46. *Fable* I, 218; see also *Female Tatler*, no. 94: 197.

47. There is one reference to 'Men of Ancient Honour' at *Origin of Honour*, 90, but notably it is when Horatio recalls the point about Don Quixote from 'Remark R'.

to the modern sense of the word.[48] This helps to explain why he cast the 'Preface' as explaining the origin of virtue, not honour, for in the earliest stage of society there was no distinctive principle of honour that could be attributed to those who overcame their fear of death to serve the community. Those who performed courageous deeds were of course honoured—in the literal sense of the word as ancient as language itself—but the quality they possessed would have been called bravery or virtue, not honour.[49]

One implication of Mandeville's revised account is that a distinctively modern sense of honour applies only to men and not to women. In earlier works, he paid much more attention to the different forms that honour takes in each of the sexes, seeking to show that in both cases honour appeals to the same passions despite male honour consisting in courage and female honour in chastity. The objects of honour are socially constructed along gendered lines, but the underlying passions that give rise to honour are no different. Women have been known to display at least as much 'Intrepidity and Fortitude of the Soul' in overcoming the fear of death to defend their chastity as men have when fighting for their country.[50] Indeed, pride and shame are cultivated more amongst educated ladies than gentleman, precisely because their honour comes under threat at an earlier age as they have to ward off the advances and even bribes of lustful men.[51] In *Origin of Honour*, Mandeville claims to have little to add to his earlier remarks on female honour, but, in noting that the words honour and chastity have been used synonymously since ancient times, he implicitly acknowledges that there is no equivalent to the story that he is

48. In criticising Mandeville's account of honour and duelling in 1725, George Bluet (*Enquiry*, 84) suggested that we would do better to revert to Cicero's explanation of the relationship between virtue and honour: 'Honour is the Applause that the judicious part of the World bestows upon the Practice of Virtue'. On his 1732 account, Mandeville could agree that this is a sensible way of talking about honour in its literal sense, but that Cicero was clearly not thinking about honour as a principle of action in its distinctively modern sense.

49. *Origin of Honour*, 15.

50. *Female Tatler*, no. 90: 181–82, also no. 88: 172. Many of Mandeville's entries from January and February 1710 document the heroic and virtuous deeds of women, and several take the motto 'Nor is the weaker sex inferior in great deeds of valour', as Goldsmith notes at *Female Tatler*, 175. For further discussion of Mandeville's views on women and female virtue in the *Female Tatler*, see Maurice M. Goldsmith, '"The Treacherous Arts of Mankind": Bernard Mandeville and Female Virtue', *History of Political Thought* 7, no. 1 (1986), 107–14; Branchi, *Pride, Manners, and Morals*, especially 1–6, 51–55.

51. *Fable* II, 122–25. More generally, see also *Modest Defence*, 76–81.

telling about the distinctively modern sense of honour when it comes to women.[52]

If the principle of honour developed only in medieval Europe, then how can we explain why it was not to be found in earlier periods? Although Mandeville does not address this question directly, he gestures towards an answer in his discussion of the temporal benefits of religion and the reasons why nothing 'has ever been thought to be more obligatory or a greater Tie upon Man than Religion.'[53] Here Mandeville returns to his explanation of the origin of natural religion from *Fable II*.[54] We attribute the occurrence of events that we do not understand to the intervention of an invisible and intelligent cause, and this is especially the case with unexpected evils like earthquakes, plagues, or thunder and lightning. Our earliest idea of a deity is thus as an object of fear; we are 'more prone to believe that the invisible Cause is a bad mischievous Being, than that it is a good benign one'. The fear of an invisible cause is natural to all humans and anyone who aspires to rule society must learn to turn this fear to their own advantage. Someone who denies the existence of an invisible cause will never be followed by those they hope to govern, yet there remains plenty of scope for rulers to fill out the content that the invisible cause takes in various ways—including polytheism, animal worship, etcetera—as long as they do not contradict what people have already been taught.[55]

The main reason why 'no large Society of Men can be well govern'd without Religion',[56] then, is a negative one: denying the existence of an invisible cause would undermine the credibility of anyone seeking to rule. Political leaders must study human nature closely and humour our passions, in this case by working with our fear of an invisible cause rather than denying it.[57] Doing so also yields significant temporal benefits. The 'chief Use' of religion 'is in Promises of Allegiance and Loyalty.' Our oaths and vows are far more reliable if we believe that we will be punished by an invisible power for breaking them.[58] The more this belief influences our actions, the closer we 'keep to Justice and all Promises in Engagements.'[59] At first glance, this may strike us a surprising

52. *Origin of Honour*, 54–55.
53. *Origin of Honour*, 16.
54. *Fable* II, 207–21.
55. *Origin of Honour*, 20–22, also 27–28.
56. *Origin of Honour*, 17.
57. *Origin of Honour*, 20, 27–28, 153.
58. *Origin of Honour*, 23–24.
59. *Origin of Honour*, 33.

argument given that Mandeville also claims that fear of a future state has minimal impact in preventing wickedness and crime. The punishments inflicted by
civil laws, he instead maintains, are far better at keeping us in awe than fear of
the 'Flames of Hell, and Fire everlasting'.[60] If fear of a future state is of little use
in this case, then why does fear of an invisible cause strengthen our oaths and
promises? Mandeville does not explain the differences between these cases,
but two considerations may be relevant. The first is the imminence of the
punishment. If you expect to be rewarded or punished for your deeds by an
invisible power in the very near future then this focuses the mind in a way that
belief in divine retribution in the afterlife does not. Fear of a future state, even
amongst sincere believers, does not have the motivational power to regulate
our day-to-day behaviour.[61] The second consideration—and this is more
speculative—is that the fear of punishment inflicted by civil powers is less
effective when keeping an oath entails risking one's life. To be sure, not all
promises fall within this category, but when oaths of allegiance involve a com-
mitment to risking one's life during times of war then fear of imminent punishment from an invisible power may be more effective in keeping someone to
their word than any punishments anticipated from civil powers.

What does this discussion of the temporal benefits of religion have to do
with the origin of honour? The principle of honour, Mandeville explains, 'is
an Invention of Politicians, to keep Men close to their Promises and Engagements, when all other Ties prov'd ineffectual; and the Christian Religion was
often found insufficient for that Purpose'.[62] The implication here is clear, even
if Mandeville does not spell it out explicitly: the principle of honour was superfluous in societies where politicians harnessed the temporal benefits of
religion effectively, such as ancient Greece and Rome, and successfully appealed to fear of an invisible cause to strengthen the allegiance of the people
they governed. The precepts of the gospel, by contrast, are not so well at-
tuned to human nature. Christianity is too demanding for civil purposes: it tells
us that all good actions must be performed out of love of God and promises
rewards and punishments only in the life to come.[63] When Christ and the
Apostles taught the practice of humility and the renunciation of all worldly

60. *Origin of Honour*, 17–18.

61. *Origin of Honour*, 18–19, see also 36: 'The Care of Self-Preservation we are born with, does
not extend itself beyond this Life'.

62. *Origin of Honour*, 30.

63. *Origin of Honour*, 30–33. For this view of Christianity, see also *Free Thoughts*, 18–22.

riches and vanity, they were 'striking at the very Fundamentals of Human Nature.'[64] Those of us unassisted by divine grace have 'no Notion of another World, or future Happiness', and whatever beliefs about the afterlife we endorse have little practical influence on our conduct, which is why everyone sins in private. 'The Practice of nominal Christians', Mandeville concludes, 'is perpetually clashing with the Theory they profess.'[65] The political problem to which the principle of honour was the answer, then, arose from the temporal shortcomings of the Christianity of the gospel.

The origin of honour

One of the points Mandeville repeats throughout his various discussions of honour is that its principle directly contradicts the teachings of Christianity.[66] In *Origin of Honour*, however, he adds a historical dimension to this argument by claiming that the principle emerged only because the precepts of the gospel were of such limited temporal benefit. The principle of honour was invented, in other words, to be everything that Christianity was not. The stark opposition between the two was evident in 'the Beginning of Christianity, and whilst the Gospel was explain'd without any Regard to Worldly Views'; a time when it was thought impossible to be both a soldier and a Christian. From the second century onwards, however, 'arrant Priests' started to disapprove of the strictness of the gospel and sought to refashion Christianity to advance their earthly dominion. In spiritual matters they may have been 'the Successors of the Apostles, but in Temporals they wanted to succeed the Pagan Priests'. To this end, they repudiated the doctrine of the gospel by declaring that Christians are permitted to fight in a just war. The Christians who were subsequently willing to take up arms were, unsurprisingly, hardly paragons of virtue in other respects. 'Pride, Avarice and Revenge raged among them', along with many other vices, and the priests thus needed to find a way of humouring these vices and channelling them towards their own ends.[67]

In discussing the ambitions of these 'arrant Priests', Mandeville identifies a pivotal moment in understanding how the practice of Christianity broke with

64. *Origin of Honour*, 99.

65. *Origin of Honour*, 38.

66. *Fable* I, 221–22; *Fable* II, 83, 87–88, 97–98, 124; *Origin of Honour*, especially 45, 77, 82–83, 92.

67. *Origin of Honour*, 33–34.

the teachings of the gospel. Yet it would be several centuries before the Church of Rome succeeded in blending notions of Christianity and honour to its own advantage—Mandeville dates this development to around the turn of the first millennium, seven to eight hundred years before he was writing.[68] To further elucidate the psychological basis of honour, however, he temporarily sets this history aside and returns to the generic role of 'Moralists and Politicians' who searched 'for Something in Man himself, to keep him in Awe.'[69] The principle they discovered, that of honour, is even more effective than the 'Fear or Reverence' we have for an invisible cause, precisely because honour relates more closely to ourselves. As 'Man is so Selfish a Creature, that . . . neither loves nor esteems any Thing so well as he does his own Individual', skilful politicians would have endeavoured to see 'if Man could not be made an Object of Reverence to himself.' Reverence comprises a combination of love, esteem, and fear. While we all naturally love and esteem ourselves, the force of education is required to 'make a Man afraid of himself' by 'improving upon his Dread of Shame' so that it becomes even more powerful than the fear of death.[70] To the objection that shame should be understood as fear of other people's opinions, not fear of ourselves, Mandeville responds that the underlying fear is having a low evaluation of ourselves, and we fear the disapproval of others only in so far as it impacts that self-evaluation.[71]

We all experience shame in certain contexts. What distinguishes the principle of honour is the extent to which it raises our love, esteem, and especially fear, to the degree that a 'Man is taught in good Earnest to worship himself.' The language of worship is no exaggeration on Mandeville's part; indeed, he frequently refers to the idolatry involved in honour—we become 'Idols to our

68. *Origin of Honour*, 45.

69. On the general question of whether Mandeville's references to 'Moralists and Politicians' should be read literally or metaphorically, see Chapter 4, 'Mandeville's origin stories'. In this case, Mandeville explains that he is referring not to any single individual but to all those who, over time, have studied human nature and learned to govern people more effectively, *Origin of Honour*, 40–41. This does still seem to be a top-down process of social learning, however, especially (as we shall see) when it comes to the role of the Church of Rome in combining honour and Christianity.

70. *Origin of Honour*, 39–40.

71. *Origin of Honour*, 41–42. See also Chapter 1, 'Self-love and self-liking', where I argue in more detail that self-liking is ultimately a self-regarding passion, which means that our pride, shame, and desire for the good opinion of others should also be considered as self-centred rather than public passions.

Selves'[72]—and this helps to explain why a man of honour regards the principle to which he is bound as superior to both the laws of God and those of his country. Once we see honour in this light, it becomes clear why the one thing a man of honour cannot tolerate, above all else, is insult. We cannot stand to have the objects of reverence and worship demeaned, and this applies whether we revere a deity, our parents, or even ourselves. A man of honour must have the liberty 'to proclaim himself to be such'—thereby worshipping himself openly—and to hold anyone who doubts his honour to account. No one else can judge or excuse any insult he receives, and in this respect the principle of honour pays homage to the 'Instinct of Sovereignty' we are all born with.[73]

Mandeville's analysis of honour invites comparisons with what he says about fear of an invisible cause. Both can be turned to good use by political leaders who know how to humour our passions. Much as they should not deny the existence of an invisible cause, so too they should not question whether a man of honour really does possess a principle of courage. Where skilful politicians retain plenty of scope to mould the content of religious belief, they may likewise 'add to, or take from the Principle of Honour, what Virtue or Qualification' they see fit.[74] They can thereby 'breed Men of Honour' who will be willing to risk their lives for the society, having been inspired 'with lofty and romantick Sentiments concerning the Excellency of their Nature'. The main temporal benefit of honour, as with religion, is to strengthen oaths and allegiance by raising the stakes of failing to keep one's word. When 'a Man asserts a Thing upon his Honour', Mandeville asks, 'is it not a Kind of Swearing by himself, as others do by God?'[75] In one case we fear imminent punishment from an invisible cause; in the other we fear the shame of not living up to the principle inside ourselves that we worship. Both fears can conquer that of death, and wise politicians must learn how to harness them effectively whenever they need people to fight.

Having outlined the psychological mechanisms behind honour, Mandeville returns to its relationship with Christianity and explains how the Church of Rome managed to reconcile the two by turning 'the Simplicity of the Gospel ... into Gaudy Foppery and vile Superstition.' For all their hypocrisy and corruption, the Roman clergy nonetheless understood human nature very

72. *Origin of Honour*, 89, also 41, 64–65, 69–70.
73. *Origin of Honour*, 42–44, also 68–69.
74. *Origin of Honour*, 141.
75. *Origin of Honour*, 86–87.

well and expertly deployed that knowledge to their own advantage. They were happy to indulge the vices of many and humour the folly of others, while 'Flattering the Pride of All.' Most importantly, by establishing the military orders of knighthood, they convinced 'all Men of Valour' that soldiers could be good Christians and 'that the Height of Pride is not inconsistent with the greatest Humility.' In doing so, the clergy appealed to the principle of honour rather than the teachings of the gospel, which allowed them to raise the military forces required for their temporal dominion. The statesmen and soldiers included 'the boldest and most wicked' of men, but romantic legends of chivalrous knights led the laity to believe that those who fought in fact united 'superlative Bravery . . . with the strictest Virtue.'[76] The myth that a soldier could be a virtuous Christian served the Church of Rome well.

The principle of honour, on Mandeville's account then, developed precisely because fear of an invisible cause was not strong enough in early Christianity to bind people to their word. The worldly glory of the Church of Rome instead relied on cultivating honour codes amongst those who would otherwise pose a dangerous threat to its power. Even if the sovereign of each state should be considered 'the Fountain of Honour, yet the Sovereigns themselves had their Titles, as well as Coats of Arms, from the Popes.'[77] This is not to say, however, that fear of an invisible cause became redundant once the principle of honour took root, for this sense of honour was, by design, associated only with the military and the highest ranks of society. Fear of an invisible cause still proved very useful for governing the multitude. The Church of Rome appreciated this too, spreading lies about witchcraft, spirits, and the works of the devil to instil fear amongst the laity, without ever teaching anything 'that contradicted Vulgar Opinions.' In appealing to both honour and fear of an invisible cause to consolidate its power, 'No Set of People have so artfully play'd upon Mankind as the Church of *Rome*.'[78]

Christian virtue

Of all Mandeville's origin stories, his account of modern honour has the clearest political implications. This is unsurprising. Rather than offering a conjectural history of society at an abstract level, *Origin of Honour* sees him attending

76. *Origin of Honour*, 46–48.
77. *Origin of Honour*, 94.
78. *Origin of Honour*, 112–13, also 50–51.

closely to the power dynamics of recent European history. As the 'Second Dialogue' progresses, for example, it becomes increasingly evident that Mandeville is deeply concerned that the tyranny of the Church of Rome could resurface in Protestant Europe.[79] The main reason for this, in short, is that the Roman clergy remained unrivalled in their understanding of human nature and political wisdom. From the foregoing discussion, it would be tempting to conclude that the power of the Church of Rome involved governing the highest ranks of society through honour and the multitude through superstition, while stripping Christianity of the strict self-denial required for a truly virtuous life. This is not the full story, however, and the way the Church of Rome paid homage to Christian virtue contained important lessons for Protestant states.

Mandeville attributes the immediate success of the Reformation in Europe to 'the strict Lives and Austerity of Manners' of Luther and Calvin, yet their moral exemplarity was short-lived and their political naivety soon apparent. Once the 'Zeal of the Reformation' waned amongst both the clergy and laity, it proved very difficult to claim that what set the Reformed churches apart from Catholicism was their purity of morals. We know from the infancy of Christianity that the precepts of the gospel are too demanding for people to follow, and the Reformed churches faced a similar problem to that encountered by the successors of Christ and the Apostles.[80] The fact that the Church of Rome succeeded in turning the gospel into a tool for earthy dominion is thus all the more remarkable and repays close attention. Key to its success was a division of labour. The 'great Prelates' look after the temporal interests of the church, the 'little Bishops and ordinary Priests take Care of the Mystical Part',

---

79. For a general account of Mandeville's views on Catholicism, which surprisingly omits any discussion of *Origin of Honour*, see Charles W. A. Prior, '"Then Leave Complaints": Mandeville, Anti-Catholicism, and English Orthodoxy', in *Mandeville and Augustan Ideas*, 51–70. For the broader context of anti-Catholic thought in the period, and especially its use in countering Jacobitism, see Colin Haydon, *Anti-Catholicism in Eighteenth-Century England: A Political and Social Study, c. 1714–80* (Manchester and New York: Manchester University Press, 1993), especially 117–63; idem., 'Eighteenth-Century English Anti-Catholicism: Contexts, Continuity, and Dissimulation', in *Protestant-Catholic Conflict from the Reformation to the Twenty-first Century: The Dynamics of Religious Difference*, ed. John Wolffe (New York: Palgrave Macmillan, 2013), 46–70.

80. *Origin of Honour*, 98–100. More generally on the religious zeal behind the Reformation, which was animated by opposition to the idolatry, superstition, and extravagance of the Church of Rome, see *Free Thoughts*, 35–38.

while the religious orders lead exemplary lives that at least appear to 'comply with the harshest Precepts of Christianity'.[81] Crucially, the laity are led to believe that the austere lives of the religious orders are 'capable of averting God's Vengeance' from the sins of the multitude.[82] Even if they cannot live up to the strictures of the gospel themselves, they 'will sooner believe a Man to come from God, who leads an Austere Life himself, and preaches Abstinence and Self-denial to others ... than they will another, who takes greater Liberties himself, and whose Doctrine is less severe.' In this respect, the religious orders lend moral authority to the Church of Rome. What is more, the laity believe that they can have a share in the self-denial of the religious orders by, for example, abstaining from meat on Fridays, which is why many Catholics will follow this rule fastidiously even though they commit many other sins.[83]

Mandeville claims that the Church of Rome posed a serious threat in Britain and that for every Catholic that converts 'to the Reform'd Religion, Ten Protestants turn Papists'.[84] Part of the difficulty facing the Reformed churches stemmed from them not being as deceitful as the Church of Rome. The Protestant clergy acknowledge their own fallibility and encourage the laity to read scripture for themselves, appealing to reason far more than superstition. One consequence of doing so, however, is that the laity are more disposed to question the moral authority of the clergy, especially when they fall short of the exacting standards they preach. 'The *Roman* Pastors', by contrast, 'kept their Flocks in the Dark' and taught them 'blind Obedience'.[85] The Reformed churches also lack a common cause and disagreement between different sects provides fertile ground for the revival of Catholicism.[86] Yet the most important reason why 'the Protestant Interest lost Ground soon after it was establish'd' is that the clergy neglected the maxims that brought about the Reformation in the first place, thereby nurturing 'the Growth of Irreligion and Impiety'. To ward off the appeal of Catholicism, the Protestant clergy must recall the 'Sanctity of Manners and exemplary Lives of the Reformers', with

81. *Origin of Honour*, 103.
82. *Origin of Honour*, 105–106.
83. *Origin of Honour*, 110–12.
84. *Origin of Honour*, 124.
85. *Origin of Honour*, 118.
86. *Origin of Honour*, 122–23. See also Mandeville's more extensive discussion of schism in *Free Thoughts*, especially 112, where he argued that were it not for the intransigence of the clergy of the Reformed churches then they could have united to destroy the Church of Rome altogether.

their 'Disregard of Wealth and Worldly Enjoyments, either real of counterfeited'.[87] Rather than condemning the irreligion and libertinism of the laity, then, the clergy would do better to turn their attention closer to home and ensure that their own conduct epitomises the precepts of the gospel, at least in outwards appearance.[88]

Mandeville had exposed the pernicious influence of the clergy on post-Reformation politics at length in his earlier *Free Thoughts*. This mostly entailed showing that their moral credentials are no better than the laity and that they are as much driven by pride and ambition as everyone else. The clergy are chiefly to blame for persecution and schism in Europe, which could be remedied only if they ceased meddling in political matters and if governments refrained from delegating civil powers to the church.[89] Much of this is implicit in *Origin of Honour* too, yet one of the most striking aspects of Mandeville's later analysis is the contrasts he draws with the division of labour within the Church of Rome and the importance of the religious orders leading exemplary moral lives. This suggests that there can be temporal benefits to having religious orders who really do appear to live by the teachings of the gospel, since this lends credence to the church's claim to being the true custodian of Christian doctrine. The founders of all sects and schisms are followed because they display greater piety and more austere morals than the clergy of the established religion at the time—this is an eternal truth, Mandeville declares, 'that must flow from the Fabrick, the very Essence of Human Nature.' The established religion will therefore be less susceptible to schism to the degree that its clergy appear to lead devout lives. A national church that tolerates dissenters and seeks to promote Christian virtue by practising the self-denial it preaches could remedy the problems encountered by the Reformed churches. Mandeville thus concludes that the Protestant clergy 'will never be able long to keep up their Credit with a mix'd Multitude, if no shew is made of Self-denial',[90] even if the chances of them ever heeding this advice, on his own analysis, appear remote.

In laying bare 'the Politicks, Penetration and Worldly Wisdom of the Church of *Rome*, and the Want of them in the Reformers',[91] Mandeville offers

---

87. *Origin of Honour*, 124–25.

88. Mandeville notes that divine assistance is required to act from a truly religious motive, *Origin of Honour*, 56, 99–100.

89. *Free Thoughts*, especially 155–60.

90. *Origin of Honour*, 128–29.

91. *Origin of Honour*, 127.

a bleak assessment of the challenges facing the Protestant states of his day. Underlying this assessment, however, is a comparison between how well the different churches understood human nature, a point which has more general implications for his account of the origin of honour. Even though the principle of honour was invented to remedy the temporal deficiencies of Christianity, and even though honour is a more recent and greater achievement than virtue, it remains the case that neither virtue nor religion are rendered superfluous by the principle of honour. Mandeville's story, in other words, is not one about how honour came to replace virtue and religion in European society. Honour was only contrived to help govern a certain class of society, and the worldly wisdom of the Church of Rome involved combining this with superstitions that played upon the laity's fear of an invisible cause and displays of religious austerity that buttressed its moral authority.

The passions of war

Honour is a principle contrived to make men fight and a central theme of *Origin of Honour* is how to motivate soldiers during war. The last two dialogues of the book address this theme at length, even if Mandeville's main aim in doing so is to show that the Christianity of the gospel is of little use on the battlefield. These dialogues remain the most neglected parts of the book, yet they contain some of his most illuminating reflections on how self-centred individuals come to take pride in belonging to certain communities and in fighting for causes they deem morally righteous. As with his discussion of the Church of Rome, Mandeville's analysis of Oliver Cromwell's success in the English Civil War also serves as a case study of how political leaders can successfully manipulate the passions of their subjects, or soldiers, for their own advantage.

Before turning to the last two dialogues, however, I consider an aspect of the 'Second Dialogue' that I have not yet addressed: the practice of duelling. In *Origin of Honour*, Mandeville treats the question of how to regulate this practice with a keen eye on its consequences for a state's army. The political leaders of warlike nations face a stark dilemma. On the one hand, if there are too many duels then many brave men who could otherwise serve may needlessly be killed. On the other hand, the principle of honour that gives rise to duels makes men good soldiers, so any measures taken to prevent the practice must avoid destroying the principle itself. In discussing this dilemma in *Origin of Honour*, Mandeville returns to a topic that had long interested him and in examining it I hope to clarify the relationship between honour and politeness.

Mandeville does not mention politeness at all when analysing duelling in *Origin of Honour*, but this silence is itself striking given the emphasis he had previously placed on the importance of the practice in contributing to the polite norms of civilised European society.

Duelling, honour, and politeness

On Mandeville's account, duelling developed out of the medieval practice of single combats, where 'Persons of great Quality' would ask leave of the sovereign to resolve disputes between themselves. As the principle of honour spread more widely, the 'Fashion of Duelling' became more common and 'all Swords-men took it into their Heads, that they had the Right to decide their own Quarrels, without asking any Body's Leave.'[92] That honour naturally leads to conflict is to be expected; as we have seen, honour is a principle that was contrived to make men fight and it involves idolising oneself to the extent that one cannot bear any personal insult. By the beginning of the seventeenth century, Mandeville claims, 'the Sense of Honour was arrived at such a Degree of Nicety all over *Europe*, especially in *France*, that barely looking upon a Man was often taken for an Affront.'[93]

Mandeville examines Louis XIV's edicts against duelling in some detail to reveal how the ill effects of the practice can be mitigated. His position in *Origin of Honour*, however, is best understood in light of his earlier views on the

92. *Origin of Honour*, 51–52. This passage also refers to notions of honour being 'industriously spread among the Multitude', which counts in favour of Stuart-Buttle's (*Moral Theology to Moral Philosophy*, 143) argument that *Origin of Honour* charts the 'democratization of the principle of honour'. On balance, however, I think the use of multitude here is anomalous or misleading. Mandeville more often suggests that the principle of honour is found only amongst soldiers and the well-educated classes of society, even in more recent European history. See, for example, *Origin of Honour*, 63, where he claims that as 'Duelling was made a Fashion, the Point of Honour became . . . a common Topick of Discourse *among the best bred Men*' (emphasis added). Given that the initial appeal of the principle of honour involved distinguishing men of honour from the vulgar, it seems unlikely that the principle could be extended to most people in society, including the uneducated and vulgar, without losing much of its distinctive motivational force. In this respect, I think there remains something intrinsically anti-democratic and anti-egalitarian about Mandeville's conception of honour.

93. *Origin of Honour*, 64. In 'Remark R', Mandeville had similarly claimed that 'the Principle of Honour . . . was melted over again, and brought to a new Standard' at the beginning of the seventeenth century, without developing the historical narrative in any detail; see *Fable* I, 218.

matter and the criticisms that those views encountered.[94] In Mandeville's first extended discussion of duelling, one of the characters in the *Female Tatler* declares that the 'strict Observance of this point of Honour . . . is a necessary Evil, and a large Nation can no more be call'd Polite without it, than it can be Rich and Flourishing without Pride or Luxury'.[95] This succinctly summarises the view that Mandeville proceeded to defend in the first volume of the *Fable*. The fear of being challenged to a duel for causing offence leads people to regulate their own speech and conduct, which in turn helps to perfect 'the Politeness of Manners, the Pleasure of Conversation, and the Happiness of Company in general'.[96] Ancient Rome and Greece may have produced valiant men without recourse to anything approximating the modern duel, but they knew nothing of the levels of politeness and refined conversation observed in eighteenth-century Europe. Mandeville nevertheless maintained that the laws against duelling should be severe. When one person is killed in a duel the other should be punished by death, which would make even 'the most resolute and most powerful cautious and circumspect in their Behaviour', preventing many duels from arising in the first place.[97] In this way, the benefits of having men of honour ready to imperil their lives in defence of their reputation could be retained, while minimising the frequency of duels.

Mandeville's views were attacked during the 1720s. One response was straightforward repudiation. According to John Thorold, for example, it is ridiculous to say that 'those who are guilty of Duelling go by true Rules of Honour'. Mandeville was simply mistaken about the rules of honour and had he understood them properly then their alleged opposition to virtue and

---

94. The most thorough study of Mandeville's views on duelling is Peltonen, *Duel in Early Modern England*, especially 285–98. In what follows I cover similar ground to Peltonen, but I pay more attention to the changes between Mandeville's works. Peltonen maintains that, for Mandeville, duelling made the progress in politeness possible. As we shall see, there is plenty of evidence from Mandeville's early work to support this interpretation but relatively little from his later work, especially *Origin of Honour*, which suggests that his view may well have changed over time.

95. *Female Tatler*, no. 52: 81.

96. An argument that led one of Mandeville's critics to complain that 'you see how little he values the Lives of Men, while he is willing that they should be sacrificed to the idle chat of a Company, under the name of Politeness.' See John Disney, *A View of Ancient Laws against Immorality and Profaneness* (Cambridge, 1729), 'Introduction'.

97. *Fable* I, 219–20; see also *Female Tatler*, no. 52: 78–81.

Christianity would disappear.[98] Yet Mandeville had anticipated such objections and dismissed them for overlooking the distinctive quality of honour: 'either there is no Honour at all, or it teaches Men to resent Injuries, and accept Challenges'.[99] More to the point, disputing whether the rules of honour as practised are the 'true' rules of honour does not constitute an adequate response to the problem of duelling. After all, Mandeville agreed that duelling is starkly opposed to real virtue and the teachings of Christianity. Against those who complained that the *Fable* supported duelling by showing 'the Necessity of keeping up that Custom, to polish and brighten Society in general', Mandeville could quite accurately respond that his tone was often ironic and that 'the Politeness of Manners and Pleasure of Conversation' to which duelling contributes are 'Things he laughs at and exposes throughout his Book.'[100] In *Fable II*, it is thus Horatio, Mandeville's sparring partner, who is 'a Man of Strict Honour', whereas Cleomenes once followed the rules of honour but has since been reformed.[101] That Mandeville ridicules men of honour and duelling, however, is not to say that he recommends trying to eliminate the practice. Critics of duelling fail to see that it is the price we must pay for living in a polite society, and politicians are well advised to turn such vices to good use rather than trying to root them out altogether.[102]

A more incisive criticism is that Mandeville underestimated the scope for politicians to preserve the benefits of politeness without recourse to the evil of duelling. Advancing this line of objection in 1725, George Bluet saw no need to deny that the practice of duelling had contributed to progress in manners or that the 'fear of Shame, and the Prospect of Honour, are both very powerful

98. Thorold, *Short Examination*, 20–21. The need to exonerate honour was keenly felt by critics of duelling during the period. See, for example, John Cockburn, *The History and Examination of Duels, shewing Their Heinous Nature and the Necessity of Suppressing them* (London, 1720), 146–81, who defends at length 'the true Standard' of honour—based on virtue and right reason, rather than custom and superstition—against the 'Counterfeit Honour' that prevailed in Europe at the time. More generally on this point, see Donna T. Andrew, 'The Code of Honour and Its Critics: The Opposition to Duelling in England, 1700–1850', *Social History* 5, no. 3 (1980), especially 417–20.

99. *Fable* I, 219; see also *Fable* II, 93.

100. *Fable* II, 101–102.

101. *Fable* II, 16, also 57.

102. That Mandeville did not see any tension between ridiculing men of honour and showing how skilful politicians can turn honour to good use is, again, very clear from his contributions to the *Female Tatler*, especially no. 84: 160–63.

Motives to human Action'. Even so, Bluet protests, the notion that people could never behave politely without duelling contradicts 'both Reason and Experience.'[103] Turning to the edicts of Louis XIV to support his case, Bluet explains that they commanded the support of the French gentry and nobility, before suggesting that similar measures should be adopted in England. He attributes the success of the edicts to the severity of the punishments against duelling, the fear of which 'have kept People within the Bounds of good Manners, as effectually as the Fear of being called upon to fight did before.'[104]

For Bluet, the example of duelling illustrates a broader problem with Mandeville's 'private vices, public benefits' thesis. If the custom of duelling was 'a *political* Evil' and putting an end to it 'a *publick Benefit*', then it was the abolition of the vice—and not the vice itself—that proved beneficial. Mandeville was so preoccupied with showing how private vices lead to public benefits that he overlooked more effective remedies for many vices. In the case of duelling, fear of severe punishment could end the practice without destroying good manners. A 'strict Regard to Virtue and Morality' would be more effective still, as the 'Spirit of Virtue, as well as Religion, is mild and gentle.'[105] Even if vices sometimes produce beneficial consequences, it does not follow that those vices should be tolerated, especially when the benefits in question may be attained by other means and the vice itself stamped out.

Mandeville's discussion of duelling in *Origin of Honour* implicitly answers Bluet's criticisms. Where the attempts of earlier French kings to suppress duelling failed, Mandeville agrees that it was finally prevented during Louis XIV's reign. Voicing an opinion close to Bluet's, Horatio suggests that this was because those who participated in duels were strictly punished and never pardoned. Cleomenes acknowledges the importance of severe penalties but places greater weight on the 'Courts of Honour . . . erected throughout the Kingdom' to resolve disputes between men of honour. These courts made it

---

103. Bluet, *Enquiry*, 73.

104. Bluet, *Enquiry*, 75–81, with the quotation at 77. By the 1720s, this account of the measures taken against duelling in France was widely accepted. See, for example, Cockburn, *History*, especially 348–49 for the claim that 'Duels were at last entirely suppressed in *France*' following Louis XIV's edicts. According to Andrew ('Code of Honour', 417), Cockburn's *History* was 'the textbook and source for all subsequent writing on duelling', and it may well have been a key source for Bluet's and later Mandeville's discussion of duelling in France. Historians today are less convinced of the success of the edicts; see François Billacois, *The Duel: Its Rise and Fall in Early Modern France*, trans. Trista Selous (New Haven: Yale University Press, 1990), 175–81.

105. Bluet, *Enquiry*, 81–82.

possible to abolish the custom of duelling 'without parting with the Notions of Honour', as to weaken those notions too would 'have been certain Ruin to a warlike Nation, that once had received them'. The courts of honour were charged with resolving disputes in a way that restored the honour of the offended person. Different prison sentences were attached to various injuries, 'from the most trifling Offences to the highest Outrages', and in all cases, upon release, the offender had to declare that they had wronged the offended party and ask for forgiveness. If the original offence involved violence then the person wronged could retaliate in kind as part of the punishment. Anyone who refused to submit to these penalties would be hanged.[106]

Bluet had noted that under the French regulations 'the Offender was obliged to make a very humble submission to the Party grieved',[107] but, from Mandeville's perspective, he failed to appreciate the full significance of this point. The reason why Louis XIV's edicts proved so successful is that they humoured the pride and 'Instinct of Sovereignty' of the offended person. As in a duel, the offended party would receive personal satisfaction and even had some discretion to pardon the offender. Where for most crimes the offender would ask pardon of God or the monarch, under these 'Laws of Honour' only the person who had been wronged could pardon or 'forgive the Trespasses committed against himself'. All laws seek to remedy some frailty in human nature, in most cases by restraining the passions of those who are otherwise subject to punishment. The laws of honour, however, 'are the reverse of all others'. The mischief they are designed to address is the instinct of sovereignty of the offended (and not the offending) party, which they accomplish by indulging that passion rather than trying to curtail it. In effect, the laws acknowledge that men of honour have the right to take justice into their own hands when they suffer injury, but they implore the person who is wronged—as a favour to the monarch—to receive their satisfaction and reparation through the courts of honour, instead of taking up arms themselves.[108]

To drive his point home, Mandeville compares the laws of honour to those prohibiting theft. You may forgive someone who steals from you, but you

---

106. *Origin of Honour*, 64–67. Mandeville had earlier discussed Louis XIV's reign at length in the *Virgin Unmask'd*, especially 140–82, without mentioning the edicts against duelling. This suggests that his attention might have been drawn to their importance subsequently, most likely from sources such as Cockburn or critics like Bluet.

107. Bluet, *Enquiry*, 77.

108. *Origin of Honour*, 68–70, also 75–76.

cannot pardon their crime. The criminal is punished for wronging the public, not you personally, and were you to abet their escape then you would become liable for punishment too. In the case of the affronts regulated by the laws of honour, by contrast, 'the Injury is reckon'd to be done to him only who receiv'd it'. The public and impersonal character of other laws does not apply, and this is key to satisfying the instinct of sovereignty underlying the offended person's honour. The laws of honour 'don't pretend to mend the Heart, and lay no greater Restraint on the Spirit of Revenge, than Matrimony does on the Desire of Procreation'.[109]

How does this discussion of duelling answer Bluet's criticisms? Crucially, Mandeville allows that well-crafted legislation can end duelling, but he insists that this can be achieved only by humouring rather than seeking to destroy the vicious passions that first gave rise to the practice. The real evil behind duelling is the offended party's demand for satisfaction, and the success of Louis XIV's edicts was based on accommodating this demand. The measures taken against duelling in France, then, are an example of how politicians can turn our vices to good use, which is perfectly consistent with Mandeville's broader arguments about how vices should be managed and redirected towards beneficial ends.

Mandeville stresses that even though the edicts paid lip service to the fact that duelling contravenes the teachings of Christianity, everyone in France knew that the 'Sinfulness of it was the least Consideration.' The 'chief Motive' behind the measures was instead to prevent the state's military capacity from becoming depleted as a result of many of its bravest men dying in duels.[110] So far from supporting Christianity, the edicts were 'destructive to Religion' and contained no appeal to the reasons that 'a sincere Follower of the Apostles' should have for finding duelling abhorrent.[111] If, counterfactually, men of honour really did have a 'strict Regard to Virtue and Morality' then Mandeville could agree with Bluet that the edicts would have been unnecessary, yet Bluet would still have been mistaken to think that such a remedy could ever retain the temporal benefits associated with honour. 'Pride, Anger, and the Spirit of Revenge' are so necessary 'for the Advancement of Dominion and worldly Glory' that no warlike nation can do without them. If you remove pride, Mandeville declares, then 'you spoil the Soldier' and can no longer 'preserve in him

---

109. *Origin of Honour*, 73–74.
110. *Origin of Honour*, 72–73.
111. *Origin of Honour*, 76.

his Principe of Honour.'[112] The case of the French edicts show how politicians can harness pride, anger, and the spirit of revenge effectively, but this approach is incompatible with trying to make men of honour better Christians.

The discussion of duelling in *Origin of Honour* is also noticeable for what it omits. Mandeville does not return to his earlier argument that duelling supports politeness and it is difficult to tell whether he still endorses the close relationship between the two posited in his earlier works. Indeed, he says very little about politeness at all in *Origin of Honour*. This could be because he had already addressed the origin of politeness in *Fable II* (as he reminds us at the beginning of the 'First Dialogue'). Yet duelling plays no part in that origin story either, since politeness was a feature of many societies where the practice of duelling never developed. Mandeville did not think that politeness was a uniquely modern or European phenomenon. If we 'look back on old *Greece*, the *Roman* Empire, or the great Eastern Nations, that flourish'd before them', then 'we shall find, that Luxury and Politeness ever grew up together, and were never enjoy'd asunder.'[113] Politeness is a conversational virtue amongst equals that involves hiding our true sentiments—chiefly our sense of superiority—to avoid offending others.[114] On Mandeville's narrative, politeness is found only amongst civilised societies with a taste for luxury, but the European nations of his day were by no means the first such societies. Duelling, then, cannot be a necessary condition for politeness. Nevertheless, it could still be the case that in recent European history duelling contributed to the progression of polite manners, perhaps by taking them to a height unknown in past times.[115] Whether Mandeville still held this view in *Origin of Honour* is unclear, but if he did then it is surprising that he felt no need to mention it explicitly in what proved to be his final and most historically detailed analysis of duelling.[116]

112. *Origin of Honour*, 83.

113. *Fable* II, 147. See also *Letter to Dion*, 19, where Mandeville claims that the 'Epithets of polite and flourishing are never given to Countries, before they are arriv'd at a considerable Degree of Luxury'.

114. *Fable* II, 138–39.

115. See *Fable* II, 101–102, where Mandeville recalls his argument from 'Remark R' that duelling contributes to politeness. However, there are also passages where (for example) he discusses the development of European manners, suggesting that they are 'more polish'd' than those amongst the ancients, without even alluding to the role of duelling; see *Fable* II, 151–52.

116. Cf. Peltonen, *Duel in Early Modern England*, 293, who draws on *Origin of Honour* to support his conclusion that, for Mandeville, 'duelling was an essential part of the modern culture of honour and politeness.' The evidence Peltonen cites is a remark about the 'Height of

Although Mandeville does not say much about politeness in *Origin of Honour*, the foregoing discussion helps to clarify the relationship between honour and politeness. Politeness is a general phenomenon that we may observe as any society becomes increasingly civilised, which is why its origin story is included within the broader conjectural history of society set out in *Fable II*. The principle of honour, by contrast, is a far more specific cultural and historical phenomenon, which first developed in medieval Europe. The rise of honour predates that of politeness in recent European history, yet *Origin of Honour* neither examines the interaction between the two in any detail nor comments on how honour shaped the character of modern European politeness.

Love of country and religious enthusiasm

In the 'Third Dialogue' of *Origin of Honour*, Mandeville turns to address the second part of the book's title more directly: the usefulness of Christianity in war. The dialogue begins, however, with some brief remarks on the pride we take in belonging to certain communities. At the height of ancient Rome's glory, the city 'became a Goddess *Dea Roma*' and was worshipped throughout the empire. Her divinity consisted in her 'vast Power, which every Free man had the Privilege to imagine, he had a Share in.' Nothing other than the citizens' pride could have led them to deify a city.[117] These manifestations of pride are not consigned to antiquity and Mandeville suggests that many Europeans in his day show similar levels of deference and esteem when speaking on behalf of their native cities. If we often feel pride in belonging to the cities we inhabit, then does it follow that pride is not an entirely self-centred passion, as the objects of pride are greater than ourselves? Not on Mandeville's account. Without even entertaining this possibility, he instead concludes that those who pay respect and submission to a greater whole of which they are a part are, in fact, 'their own Worshippers, and sincerely adore themselves.'[118]

Politeness' (which I discuss more below) from the 'Fourth Dialogue'; see *Origin of Honour*, 232. However, Mandeville does not mention duelling once after the 'Second Dialogue' and I see no reason to read the passage from the 'Fourth Dialogue' back into his earlier discussion.

117. The heading for this passage in the Contents of *Origin of Honour* reads 'The Reason of the high Value Men have for Things in which they have but the least Share in', which nicely captures the sense in which this involves the overvaluation of ourselves that is characteristic of pride.

118. *Origin of Honour*, 131–33.

Mandeville's explanation of this point is frustratingly brief. He raises similar considerations in the *Free Thoughts*, arguing that as the common people rarely achieve great things themselves, they are 'fond of every thing that belongs to the Publick, which is Praise-worthy.' We all count ourselves 'a Sharer' in our country's glories, such as victory in war, even if we played no part in the battle. We all take pleasure in saying 'our Army, our Fleet, our Government, our Funds', as if the possessions and accomplishments of the society to which we belong are our own.[119] In *Origin of Honour*, Mandeville likewise observes that 'Self is never forgot' in love of country.[120] There is nothing impersonal or disinterested about these passions; we love our country or city for our own sake, not for anyone else's.

These passages shed light on a relatively undeveloped and unappreciated aspect of Mandeville's account of human nature. In most cases, he focuses on exposing the hidden depths of pride motivating our behaviour as individuals. To be sure, pride is an intersubjective passion. Our self-esteem is shaped by the views that other people hold of us, and those views are in turn based on social norms and expectations. For the most part, though, Mandeville examines cases where we feel pride or shame in our individual conduct. The foregoing discussion of duelling is a case in point. Yet we clearly do also take pride and shame in the actions of the social groups to which we belong, even when we have not contributed to the actions in question. Mandeville says little about these manifestations of pride throughout most of his work, but in *Origin of Honour* we find some of his most suggestive remarks. Although it remains unclear precisely how the opening few pages of the 'Third Dialogue' are supposed to relate to its main subject matter,[121] one speculative connection concerns the emphasis Mandeville places on religious zeal and enthusiasm, for, like love of country, these are what we might call collective passions, which rely on people being motivated by a shared cause and having their sense of self-worth enhanced by belonging to a certain group. Whether or not Mandeville expected readers to draw any parallels between his reflections on love of country and religious enthusiasm, they are both passions that, under the

---

119. *Free Thoughts*, 77–78.

120. *Origin of Honour*, 136.

121. Horatio abruptly announces that he wants to talk about a different subject at *Origin of Honour*, 133.

right circumstances, could complement honour in strengthening soldiers' allegiance in war.[122]

Much of the 'Third Dialogue' sets out to correct the 'common Notion ... that the best Christians make the best Soldiers.'[123] Mandeville's argument, in brief, is that even if the best soldiers are found amongst Christians, those soldiers are certainly not the best Christians. Nothing in the gospel can ever justify or promote war and in any given conflict neither party can plausibly claim to have the true precepts of Christianity on their side.[124] When preachers do appeal to the word of God in defence of their cause, they invariably turn to the Old Testament, 'which is an inexhaustible Fund of Declamation on almost every Subject and every Occasion.'[125] You will never hear anyone appeal to the Christian virtues of humility and weakness during the heat of battle.[126] None of this is to deny that many soldiers are *sincere* Christians. Mandeville insists that 'there are no *Atheists* among the Common People.'[127] You can be a sincere Christian as long as you believe that the scripture is the word of God and fear being punished for your sins in the afterlife, even if, in practice, you fail to perform many good deeds. Being a sincere Christian is one thing, being a *good* Christian quite another.[128] This is key to Mandeville's analysis. Although the Christianity of the gospel is of no use during war, religion can play a considerable role in motivating soldiers to fight, as long as they sincerely believe they are doing God's work.

The main reason why religious wars are so cruel and bloody, Mandeville argues, is because both sides are supremely confident in the justice of their cause. 'Difference in the least Things is capable of raising Anger', and few

---

122. On love of country, see also *Origin of Honour*, 177, where, after noting that the 'Love of one's Country is natural', Mandeville points out that it motivates bad men as much as good men, and those who fight against the king as much as those who fight for him. As with the principle of honour and religious enthusiasm, Mandeville seeks to show that soldiers can be motivated by a sincere love of country without being good Christians.

123. *Origin of Honour*, 133. For a helpful survey of some of the sources that endorsed this common view, and which may have been in Mandeville's sights, see Primer, 'Mandeville on War', 132–33.

124. *Origin of Honour*, 156–57, 170–71.

125. *Origin of Honour*, 158, also 169–70.

126. *Origin of Honour*, 161.

127. *Origin of Honour*, 189.

128. *Origin of Honour*, 195–96.

beliefs are held so fervently as that in the truth of the religion someone professes.[129] Soldiers who believe that they are fighting for God's cause will be inspired with courage and it is thus 'an everlasting Maxim in Politicks, that whenever Religion can be brought into the Quarrel, it ought never to be neglected'.
Whatever differences of belief there are between the contending parties should
be magnified, 'for Nothing is more comfortable to Men, than the Thought that
their Enemies are likewise the Enemies of God.'[130] Religious belief, to recall, is
based on fear of an invisible cause, and soldiers who are confident of receiving
assistance from this invisible cause can be roused 'into an Enthusiasm, that
shall dissipate their Fears [of death], and make them despise the greatest
Dangers.'[131]

Mandeville notes that Greek and Roman histories recount many occasions
when religious superstition was skilfully managed to stir up courage in war.
His main focus, though, is more recent examples: Cromwell's army in the English Civil War and the Huguenot forces in the French Wars of Religion. In both
cases, 'skilful Divines' played a key role in making 'Zealots and Enthusiasts' of
the troops, who firmly believed they were doing God's work and would 'sing
Psalms one Hour, and demolish an Hospital the next'.[132] Both Cromwell's
army and the Huguenots saw themselves as fighting against the irreligion and
idolatry of their adversaries, which is why it made sense for those leading the
forces to demand acts of devotion and austerity of manners. The clearest illustration of this, which Mandeville considers at length in the 'Fourth Dialogue', is the days of fasting and humiliation that Cromwell made his troops
observe. At first glance, such severe self-denial might seem counterproductive,
as it would mortify the pride and lower the spirits of the soldiers.[133] Yet the
self-denial in question sounded a lot stricter than it proved to be in practice,[134]
and the main effect was instead to reinforce the soldiers' (false) belief that they
were good Christians who could expect God to favour them in battle.[135] In
war, it is important to accentuate the points of difference with your enemies.
If the enemies have been characterised in terms of their loose morals and

129. *Origin of Honour*, 138–39.
130. *Origin of Honour*, 159–60.
131. *Origin of Honour*, 172, and more generally 153–54.
132. *Origin of Honour*, 143–46.
133. *Origin of Honour*, 204–205.
134. *Origin of Honour*, 209–10.
135. *Origin of Honour*, 220–21.

irreligion, then acts of devotion will help to assure soldiers of the righteousness of their cause. It takes very little for soldiers to be persuaded that they
have God and justice on their side, as we all enjoy being flattered and are 'easy
Casuists in our own Concerns'.[136]

The religious zeal and enthusiasm witnessed in Cromwell's army was a
political contrivance. Mandeville argues that the acts of devotion proved
beneficial even though Cromwell was an atheist, the clergy were mostly hypocrites, and many of the soldiers lived wicked lives.[137] This wickedness was
no great obstacle to rousing enthusiasm amongst them, however, precisely
because wickedness does not preclude sincerity of belief. Most soldiers are
superstitious and there are always plenty among them who are prone to enthusiasm.[138] Cromwell knew to keep religion subservient to his political
ends.[139] His true motives were personal glory and 'immortal Fame', yet he
understood the role that a façade of moral austerity and religious zeal could
play in advancing his political ambitions, and, with these in mind, he 'could
counterfeit Enthusiasm and seem to be a Saint'.[140]

In discussing the examples of Cromwell and the Huguenots, Mandeville
maintains that their armies did not comprise good Christians despite their acts
of devotion and outward show of religion. Instead, what we see—much like
in his earlier analysis of the Church of Rome—is skilful politicians and clergy
twisting the gospel to their own worldly ends. In stirring up enthusiasm
amongst his troops, Cromwell displayed a masterful understanding of human
nature. Although Mandeville does not dwell on the psychological basis of enthusiasm, it clearly presupposes fear of an invisible cause and plays upon the
multitude's susceptibility to superstition. It also appeals to pride, for what
could inflate someone's sense of self-worth more than believing that their
cause has divine sanction? Yet the pride in question is not based on someone's
individual deeds but, instead, derives from the esteem in which their cause or
group is held. Enthusiasm is thus a collective passion, in the sense that it holds
sway only over someone who believes that their companions are also motivated by a religious zeal that commands God's favour. What is more, someone's doubts about their own claims to being a good Christian may even be

136. *Origin of Honour*, 198–99, also 148–51.
137. *Origin of Honour*, 166, 171–201.
138. *Origin of Honour*, 144.
139. *Origin of Honour*, 212.
140. *Origin of Honour*, 230–31, also 164, 183, 218.

quelled by the conviction that most of their fellow troops really are motivated by a religious zeal, which is one reason why 'Enthusiasm among a Multitude is as catching as Yawning'.[141]

Mandeville's focus on enthusiasm and religious zeal should not be taken to detract from the importance of honour.[142] Cromwell drew on both religion and honour to motivate his army, never allowing any religious doctrines to be taught that would undermine the principle of honour.[143] The 'Observance of the Point of Honour and Hatred to their Enemies are inseparable' from the soldier's calling,[144] and enthusiasm served mainly to strengthen the latter by assuring soldiers that their enemies are also subject to God's wrath. Much like the Church of Rome, Cromwell's political genius resided in understanding how to mobilise different passions to one and the same end.

Towards the end of the 'Fourth Dialogue', Mandeville observes that Cromwell's success depended on consulting 'the Humour of the Age' and that the measures he took to incite enthusiasm are no longer appropriate. Displays of piety made sense when religious purity was one of the main causes of war, but that time has now passed. 'What in *Oliver*'s Day was intended by a Mark of Religion and Shew of Sanctity, is now aim'd at by the Height of Politeness, and a perpetual Attachment to the Principle of modern Honour.' A 'Spirit of Gentility' has developed within the military in the past forty to fifty years, with much greater stress now placed on soldiers appearing neat and clean than had previously been the case, to the extent that gratifying 'their Vanity is made Part of the Discipline'.[145] We should be careful not to read too much into this passage.[146] Where his analysis of religious enthusiasm in the English and

141. *Origin of Honour*, 201.

142. Cf. Primer, 'Mandeville on War', 131, who contrasts the 'political Christianity' of Cromwell's army with the account of modern honour discussed in the first two dialogues of *Origin of Honour*.

143. *Origin of Honour*, 182, also 160.

144. *Origin of Honour*, 143.

145. *Origin of Honour*, 231–33. See also *Fable* I, 132, where Mandeville writes of the 'puny young Striplings' fighting gallantly against France, 'tenderly Educated, nice in their Dress, and curious in their Diet'. Mandeville's more general point is that there is no reason to worry about a taste for luxury weakening the army.

146. Cf. Branchi, *Pride, Manners, and Morals*, 147–48, who cites this passage in support of his claim that, for Mandeville, modern 'honour has gradually replaced religion on the battlefield.' More generally, see Runciman, *Political Hypocrisy*, 62, who draws on this passage to support his claim that 'Mandeville's central point, indeed his primary polemical purpose in writing about Cromwell in the *Enquiry*, is to insist that times have changed.'

French wars of the seventeenth century spans much of the final two dialogues of the book, his comments on what has changed since then takes up only a couple of pages. Indeed, this is pretty much all Mandeville says about the development of politeness in *Origin of Honour*. He soon reminds us that there 'are no great Numbers of Men without Superstition' and that it would be 'as impossible to get an Army of all *Atheists*, as it would be to have an Army of good Christians.'[147] Earlier in *Origin of Honour*, to recall, Mandeville had argued that no large society can be well governed without religion and that religion should be brought into war whenever possible—this is 'an *everlasting* Maxim in Politicks'.[148] The comment about what has changed since Cromwell's day, then, should not be taken to deny the importance of religion in general. Fear of an invisible cause is one of our natural passions and anyone who hopes to govern a society or command an army cannot afford to neglect it. Mandeville's point, instead, is merely that acts of devotion are no longer required to make men brave, for they proved beneficial only when religious sanctity was one of the major points of dispute between the warring parties.

Conclusion

Origin of Honour remains one of Mandeville's least studied works. In this chapter I hope to have shown that it merits closer investigation, since it both sheds new light on problems that he had been grappling with since the earlier volumes of the *Fable* and draws attention to aspects of his thought that might otherwise go unappreciated. In terms of his historical narratives, *Origin of Honour* revisits and considerably complicates the relationship between the origins of virtue, honour, and politeness. I have suggested that we can map Mandeville's revised account of the origin of virtue onto the second step towards society from the conjectural history of *Fable II*, but the emergence of the principle of honour lies beyond the scope of that narrative, precisely because of its cultural and historical specificity: Mandeville now argues that the principle of honour was a Gothic invention that first developed in medieval Europe.

It is important to keep this point in mind when considering the relationship between politeness and honour. Politeness is sometimes taken to be a central

147. *Origin of Honour*, 235.
148. *Origin of Honour*, 159–60 (emphasis added).

theme of *Origin of Honour*.[149] If anything, however, it is striking how little Mandeville has to say about politeness there, and its absence is especially conspicuous in his analysis of the edicts against duelling in France, given that he had argued that duelling supports polite manners in some of his earlier works. When Mandeville examines developments unique to recent European history in *Origin of Honour*, he rarely mentions politeness. In *Fable II*, conversely, he provides a conjectural explanation of the origin of politeness that is not specific to any given time or place. Polite manners may be found in any civilised society where luxury flourishes,[150] yet the principle of honour arose only in Christian Europe.[151]

Due to its historical specificity, the development of modern honour requires a different type of explanation to the phenomena explored in Mandeville's other origin stories—recognising this is key to understanding what sets *Origin of Honour* apart from his earlier works. Compared to the two volumes of the *Fable*, *Origin of Honour* contains a lot more discussion of European history and it is especially attentive to sixteenth- and seventeenth-century religious politics (in this respect, it shares more with the *Free Thoughts*). This leads Mandeville to extend his analysis of human nature to topics that he discusses little elsewhere, such as religious enthusiasm, and to consider more real-world examples of how wise politicians cultivated and humoured their subjects' various passions to maintain their power. As we have seen, the political wisdom of figures like Cromwell, or the Roman clergy, involved combining notions of honour, fear of an invisible cause, and sometimes even Christian virtue to govern successfully.

War and religion are themes that loom large in *Origin of Honour*. This point bears emphasising given that Mandeville is more often remembered as 'the

---

149. Most recently, for the claim that in *Origin of Honour* 'Mandeville identifies the age of politeness as the last stage in the "history of pride"', see Branchi, *Pride, Manners, and Morals*, 21, also 137, 148.

150. *Fable II*, 146–47.

151. In this respect, Mandeville's position is very different to those who today seek to theorise a more general conception of honour based on a wider range of cultural and historical examples. See, for example, Kwame Anthony Appiah, *The Honor Code: How Moral Revolutions Happen* (New York and London: W. W Norton, 2010), who draws parallels between how changing norms of honour contributed to the abolition of duelling in Europe, the transatlantic slave trade, and Chinese foot-binding. Mandeville's challenge to this approach is to suggest that there is something unique about the conception of honour that developed in medieval Europe and lay behind duelling, which wider comparisons risk overlooking.

first thoroughgoing defender of commercial modernity'.[152] Throughout many of his works, Mandeville does analyse the workings of what is sometimes called commercial modernity, or modern commercial society.[153] But this is not the side of Mandeville's thought on display in *Origin of Honour*. If, very schematically, we think about commercial modernity in terms of the rise of luxury, refinement in the arts and manners, and increased domestic and foreign trade, then *Origin of Honour* has barely anything to say about these topics. On the one hand, this suggests that we would do well to pay more attention to *Origin of Honour* in its own right, and not read it simply as an appendix to the earlier volumes of the *Fable*. On the other hand, however, taking the historical narratives of Mandeville's late works together should lead us to think carefully about the terms we use to categorise his thought. The conjectural history of society in *Fable II* is not supposed to apply uniquely to the experiences of modern European states (which is why it does not cover the origin of honour), and when he does turn to more recent European history, in *Origin of Honour*, he chooses to focus a lot more on war and religion than on the features we now associate with commercial modernity. Despite what we might expect, then, Mandeville's historical narratives are not concerned with explaining the emergence of commercial society in modern Europe.

152. Hundert, *Enlightenment's Fable*, 249.

153. The term 'commercial society', more generally associated with Adam Smith and other Scottish Enlightenment thinkers, is frequently read back onto Mandeville's work. Hundert uses the term regularly throughout *Enlightenment's Fable*, for instance, and it often appears in titles of studies of Mandeville's thought. See, for example, Horne, 'Envy and Commercial Society'; Nieli, 'Commercial Society and Christian Virtue'; Dario Castiglione, 'Excess Frugality and the Spirit of Capitalism: Readings of Mandeville on Commercial Society', in *Culture in History: Production, Consumption and Values in Historical Perspective*, ed. Joseph Melling and Jonathan Barry (Exeter: University of Exeter, 1992), 155–79; Kyle Scott, 'Mandeville's Paradox as Satire: The Moral Consequences of Being a Good Citizen in a Commercial Society', *Politics and Policy* 37, no. 2 (2009): 369–94; Douglass, 'Morality and Sociability in Commercial Society'; Branchi, 'Courage and Chastity in Commercial Society'. The use of the term has recently been subjected to closer scrutiny. In relation to Smith, see Paul Sagar, *Adam Smith Reconsidered: History, Liberty, and the Foundations of Modern Politics* (Princeton and Oxford: Princeton University Press, 2022), especially 45–53, and, more generally, see Robin Douglass, 'Theorising Commercial Society: Rousseau, Smith and Hont', *European Journal of Political Theory* 17, no. 4 (2018): 501–11; Paul Cheney, 'István Hont, the Cosmopolitan Theory of Commercial Globalization, and Twenty-First-Century Capitalism', *Modern Intellectual History* 19, no. 3 (2022): 883–911.

Conclusion

IN HIS FINAL DEFENCE of *The Fable of the Bees*, Mandeville observed that the 'Book contained several Essays on Politicks; the greatest Part of it was a Philosophical Disquisition into the Force of the Passions, and the Nature of Society, and that they were silly People, who made any other Construction of it'.[1] Mandeville was prone to overstating his case when defending his work, and I have no intention of dismissing other approaches to reading the *Fable*. Yet this quotation nicely captures what I regard as the most rewarding way of studying the text.

In the first place, we should take Mandeville's philosophical credentials seriously, especially when it comes to his analysis of the force of the passions and the nature of society—the key components of his theory of sociability. What about the several essays on politics? Questions of human sociability underpin all politics, for Mandeville. 'An Enquiry Into the Origin of Moral Virtue' and 'A Search into the Nature of Society' are essays on the foundation of politics, in this respect, as are many of the dialogues from *Fable II* and *An Enquiry into the Origin of Honour*. 'All sound Politicks, and the whole Art of governing,' Mandeville declares, 'are entirely built upon the Knowledge of human Nature.'[2] This knowledge involves combining general truths about the various passions that motivate us with an awareness of how those passions can be expected to play out under particular social and historical circumstances. Mandeville's accounts of the political wisdom of the Church of Rome and Oliver Cromwell can be read as case studies illustrating this broader point: their achievements were based on their profound understanding of both human nature in general and the exigencies of their time and place.

1. *Letter to Dion,* 54–55.
2. *Fable* II, 320–21.

In another respect, however, I have not examined Mandeville's political thought in any detail, largely passing over his interventions into eighteenth-century party politics and proposals for social reform.[3] This is partly a consequence of taking a more philosophical than historical approach, and partly because Mandeville's theory of sociability rarely generates specific answers to particular social or political problems.[4] What it does offer, instead, is a more general perspective from which such problems should be viewed. In 'The Moral' to the original *Grumbling Hive* verse, Mandeville ridicules the idea that a large and flourishing society could prosper without vice as 'a vain/ EUTOPIA seated in the Brain', and his more general approach to politics is perhaps best characterised as anti-utopian. We should be deeply sceptical of political projects that depend upon rooting out moral corruption or expect that people will dispassionately do the right thing without being handsomely repaid in the currency of social esteem. A 'well-order'd Society' may be a fine achievement, but we should not forget that 'so beautiful a Machine is rais'd from the most contemptible Branches.'[5] One of the main aims of the *Fable* was to reconcile its readers to this morally compromised vision of society. This is not to say that Mandeville was opposed to all attempts to improve society; his point, instead, was simply that reform should be seen through the lens of choosing the lesser evil, rather than pursuing some vision of moral perfection.[6]

3. For notable studies covering these aspects of Mandeville's political thought, see Monro, *Ambivalence*, 75–103; H. T. Dickinson, 'The Politics of Bernard Mandeville', in *Mandeville Studies* 80–97; J.A.W. Gunn, *Beyond Liberty and Property: The Process of Self-Recognition in Eighteenth-Century Political Thought* (Kingston: McGill-Queen's University Press, 1983), 96–119; Goldsmith, *Private Vices, Public Benefits*, 78–119; Annie Mitchell, 'Character of an Independent Whig—"Cato" and Bernard Mandeville', *History of European Ideas* 29, no. 3 (2003): 291–311; Simonazzi, *Le favole della filosofia*, 241–73.

4. Consider here, for example, that despite Mandeville's stark opposition to Shaftesbury on questions of sociability, the two shared a broadly Whig outlook on many political issues, with Mandeville happy to acknowledge 'the many admirable Things that [Shaftesbury] has said against Priestcraft, and on the Side of Liberty and Human Happiness', *Letter to Dion*, 48.

5. *Fable* I, 6.

6. On this point, see especially *Modest Defence*, 89–90; *Letter to Dion*, 42–45. Mandeville's attitude towards reform is complicated by the debate concerning whether he intended his most ambitious and controversial proposal—for the state to run and regulate public brothels—to be taken at all seriously. For contrasting views, see Richard I. Cook, '"The Great Leviathan of Leachery": Mandeville's *Modest Defence of Publick Stews* (1724)', in *Mandeville Studies*, especially 25–26; Irwin Primer, 'Introduction', to his edition of the *Modest Defence*, 1–25; Laura J. Rosenthal, *Infamous Commerce: Prostitution in Eighteenth-Century British Literature and Culture* (Ithaca

This anti-utopian perspective follows from holding 'that what we call Evil in this World, Moral as well as Natural, is the grand Principle that makes us sociable Creatures'.[7] I have focused on one evil more than any other by classifying Mandeville's theory of sociability as *pride-centred*. In this concluding chapter, I first discuss the explanatory limitations of this focus by examining one case where pride-based considerations are notably absent from Mandeville's analysis, before drawing the book to a close with some brief reflections on whether we should find his theory of sociability compelling.

Pride in the economic sphere

Throughout this book I have focused more on Mandeville's 'origins of sociability' thesis than on his notorious 'private vices, public benefits' one. The distinction between the two theses serves as an interpretative heuristic, and we could alternatively see his pride-centred theory of sociability as one of the many ways in which private vices lead to public benefits. After all, sociability is itself a public benefit that arises from redirecting private vices, such as pride and hypocrisy, towards positive ends. Mandeville does not join the dots in this way himself, but we could do so on his behalf to show how his investigations into the nature of society follow from the infamous subtitle of the original *Fable*.[8]

My main reason for distinguishing the two theses is that the 'private vices, public benefits' one is typically associated with the economic sphere, even though Mandeville never circumscribed its scope in this way (as is clear from his analysis of duelling, for instance). One consequence of focusing on his 'origins of sociability' thesis, instead, is that we come to see him more as a theorist of moral and social norms and less as a theorist of markets. But does this way of presenting matters risk setting up a false dichotomy? Mandeville was adamant, for example, that norms of politeness emerge only in societies that have reached a certain level of economic development, with a flourishing market for luxury goods.[9] For the most part, however, he does not explore

---

and London: Cornell University Press, 2006), 42–69; Simonazzi, *Le favole della filosofia*, 247–56; Emily C. Nacol, 'The Beehive and the Stew: Prostitution and the Politics of Risk in Bernard Mandeville's Political Thought', *Polity* 47, no. 1 (2015), especially 73–82.

7. *Fable* I, 369.

8. See Burtt, *Virtue Transformed*, 141, who treats Mandeville's theory of sociability as one instantiation of the broader 'private vices, public benefits' thesis.

9. *Fable* I, 184–85; *Fable* II, 147; *Letter to Dion*, 19. On the interaction between the politeness of court society and the luxury generated through commerce, see Peltonen, *Duel in Early*

the interplay between social norms and economic development as much as we might expect. As we have seen, this is especially notable in the historical narratives of *Fable II* and *Origin of Honour*, where economic considerations are not particularly prominent in either Mandeville's conjectural history of society or his account of how the principle of modern honour developed in more recent European history.

Foregrounding questions of sociability helps us to see beyond the familiar view of Mandeville as an early theorist (or even champion) of the emerging capitalist economy. Yet in resisting a common caricature of any thinker, there is always the danger of overreaching and going too far in the other direction. It could be objected that I have downplayed the importance of material gain and the pursuit of wealth in ways that, were they given due weight, would complicate or even undermine the importance of pride in Mandeville's theory of sociability.[10] A partial response is to recall that pride plays a significant role in both the 'origins of sociability' and 'private vices, public benefits' theses. In 'Remark M', dedicated to pride, Mandeville claims that the passion is one of 'the great Promoters of Trade' as it stimulates demand for luxury goods. We purchase fine clothes to impress other people and when they subsequently pay us a compliment, or attribute a desirable social status to us, then our pride is flattered and we view ourselves more highly.[11] But this response takes us only so far. Although pride is central to Mandeville's account of consumption and economic demand, the passion does less work in his analysis of the supply of labour in the economy.[12] The labouring classes should be kept poor and un-educated, he argues, for only necessity and the satisfaction of basic wants are strong enough motives to keep workers in their drudgery.[13]

Mandeville's defence of the utility of poverty thesis, along with his attack on charity schools and their sponsors, might seem in tension with the emphasis

---

Modern England, especially 298–302; idem., 'Politeness and Whiggism, 1688–1732', *The Historical Journal* 48, no. 2 (2005), especially 411–13.

10. For the argument that there are unresolved tensions between these two strands of Man-deville's thought, see Luban, 'Mandeville as Moralist and Materialist'. In the scholarship on early modern theories of sociability, the distinction is sometimes cashed out by contrasting pride with utility; see Hont, *Politics in Commercial Society*, 11–13.

11. *Fable* I, 124–28.

12. See Dew, 'Spurs to Industry', 156–64; idem., 'Labour and Wealth Creation', 198–202. Dew's work is particularly attentive to the differences between the 1714 and 1723 editions of the *Fable*, with the latter focusing a lot more on the problem of labour supply.

13. *Fable* I, 192–94, 248–49, 287–90; *Fable* II, 350–52.

he places elsewhere on pride being our dominant passion.[14] When discussing the labouring poor, he affirms that 'Human Nature is every where the same' and that there is 'no Station of Life, where Pride, Emulation, and the Love of Glory may not be displayed'.[15] Yet he does not entertain the possibility that these passions could motivate the poor to work just as (or even more) productively once their wages are raised beyond subsistence level.[16] On the contrary, he implies that the working conditions of the labouring poor are so onerous that pride-based considerations are incapable of making most toil any longer or harder than necessity demands. Pride does not always conquer other passions, especially when the rewards in terms of improved social standing are negligible.

Mandeville maintains that some of the poor will strive to raise their condition and a few will succeed if they 'come rightly to love Money and take Delight in saving it'.[17] In appealing to love of money, he suggests that it is the pursuit of material gain, more than pride and the desire for social esteem, that drives people to work beyond what their bare subsistence requires. All labourers should be paid in proportion to their diligence, rather than by regular wages, precisely because the desire to accumulate wealth can spur productivity. The 'Invention of Money', Mandeville proclaims, is 'a thing more skilfully

14. More generally on the tensions between Mandeville's account of human nature and his views on the labouring poor, see Francesca Pongiglione and Mikko Tolonen, 'Mandeville on Charity Schools: Happiness, Social Order and the Psychology of Poverty', *Erasmus Journal for Philosophy and Economics* 9, no. 1 (2016), especially 89–93.

15. *Fable* I, 275.

16. Elsewhere, however, Mandeville suggests that one of the reasons why the poor work so cheaply and are content to live in such miserable conditions is because they 'set such a small Value upon themselves and esteem the better Sort far above their own Rank', *Virgin Unmask'd*, 164–65. In this respect, Mandeville claims that the poor are better off in commonwealths like Holland—where they have a higher social standing and are proud of their liberty—and little more than slaves under absolute monarchy in France, while they occupy a middle position in England as it is a mix of commonwealth and monarchy. This suggests that the economic motivations of the poor are closely related to their political status in society, but this is not an idea that Mandeville develops in the *Fable*. See also Jonathan Israel, *Radical Enlightenment: Philosophy and the Making of Modernity 1650–1750* (Oxford: Oxford University Press, 2001), 624, who takes this discussion to indicate that Mandeville had a 'republican preference for greater equality' and that 'Dutch egalitarianism wins Mandeville's full approval'.

17. *Fable* II, 352. Mandeville adds that such success comes more to 'People of common and mean Capacities, than it does to those of brighter Parts', thereby supporting his broader argument against the supposed benefits of educating the labouring poor.

adapted to the whole Bent of our Nature, than any other human Contrivance.' Where honour holds sway only over the highest classes—and, even there, riches will often purchase, or pass for, honour—'nothing is more universally charming than Money; it suits with every Station;' amongst the poor and wealthy alike. Notice here that Mandeville does not rest his argument on the social status that wealth confers. One of the main reasons why 'Lucre is the best Restorative in the World' is simply because it 'gives Relief in Wariness, and actually supports Men in all Fatigues and Difficulties.'[18]

We should be careful not to impose too strong a distinction between pride-based considerations and the pursuit of material gain onto Mandeville's thought. He does not present them as rival explanations of any particular social phenomena, and he recognises that we sometimes love money because it allows us to purchase goods that satisfy the desires associated with our social standing—desires which increase as we become wealthier and more educated. We are often willing to undergo 'the greatest Hazards and Difficulties' to satisfy our pride and ambition, which partly explains why 'the generality of People would rather be Kings than Peasants.'[19] Nevertheless, the pride-based considerations that animate so much of Mandeville's thought are of relatively little significance when it comes to the supply of menial labour upon which he thought the material prosperity of a large and flourishing society relied.

There are two implications worth highlighting presently. First, Mandeville's discussion of the labouring poor helps us to identify some of the limits of focusing on questions of sociability. This case is particularly noteworthy because he eschews the pride-based considerations—the more *Mandevillean* considerations, it is tempting to say—that were clearly available. Second, and relatedly, Mandeville's discussion of the labouring poor counts in favour of the interpretative heuristic that I have adopted, since the 'origins of sociability' and 'private vices, public benefits' theses each draw our attention to distinct aspects of his thought. Although he accords an important role to pride in the economic sphere, particularly in relation to demand, the passion is far more prominent when it comes to analysing our social and moral norms.

18. *Fable* II, 353–55.

19. *Fable* I, 316. I say 'partly' because Mandeville also appeals to the preference we have for 'Material' rather than 'Spiritual' goods. For discussion of this passages in terms of the 'materialist' and 'moralist' strands of Mandeville's thought, see Luban, 'Mandeville as Moralist and Materialist', 852–53.

Was Mandeville right?

Throughout this book I have presented Mandeville's pride-centred theory of sociability in a sympathetic light, while considering, along the way, the extent to which it can be defended against important lines of criticism and whether apparent tensions or inconsistences can be resolved. At this stage, then, we should be well placed to briefly survey the overall merits of Mandeville's theory. Was he right about human sociability?

This question does not admit of such a pithy answer, or, if it does, then it would probably be 'yes and no': Mandeville was right about some aspects of sociability and wrong about others. One difficulty involves establishing the criteria against which the question should be answered. In parts of this book, I have evaluated Mandeville's theory in light of the considerations and objections raised by prominent eighteenth-century philosophers, placing his ideas in dialogue with those of Shaftesbury, Hume, and Smith, amongst others. In doing so, I hope to have shown that pride, as Mandeville understands it, is *more important in explaining sociability* than any of the rival theories acknowledge, which is not to say that his theory of sociability is, all things considered, superior to the alternatives. Without revisiting all my earlier arguments, two points from Chapter 1 bear emphasising.[20] First, we can accept much of Mandeville's pride-centred theory of sociability without endorsing everything he says about human nature. For example, many of his claims about the prominence of pride go through even if we find his attempts to reduce all human actions to some form of self-love unpersuasive. Second, Mandeville's theory holds that pride is the *dominant* passion in explaining sociability, not that it is the sole one. Even if it is *possible* for us to perform virtuous acts without being motivated by pride-based considerations, as many of Mandeville's critics insisted, to discredit his theory of sociability it further needs to be shown that pride is nowhere near as *prevalent* as he claims in explaining why we generally adhere to social and moral norms. With these caveats in mind, I think that Mandeville's theory of sociability stands up well against many of the criticisms it encountered in the eighteenth century. This does not establish that he was right, of course, but it strengthens the plausibility of his theory and raises the bar for showing that it is wrong.

In addition to considering criticisms and rival theories from Mandeville's contemporaries, we can also approach the 'was he right?' question by drawing

---

20. See Chapter 1, 'Criticisms of Mandeville's psychology', for the full account.

on more recent evidence that may support or undermine his theory of sociability. Again, however, this is unlikely to yield a straightforward answer either way. Many of the questions he addressed still divide scholars working on the respective topics today—topics which span various academic disciplines, from moral psychology to social anthropology and beyond. This is not the place (and I am not the person) to offer a detailed survey of the state of the relevant debates and assess Mandeville's ideas against the latest findings.[21] Nonetheless, I have occasionally drawn on evidence that corroborates some of his most important arguments. As I pointed out in Chapter 2, Mandeville's reflections on the motivational weakness of reason fit well with the evidence from social psychology documenting the pervasiveness of self-serving biases. Mandeville also articulates a version of the argument, now most famously associated with Jonathan Haidt, that moral reasoning is more often concerned with formulating post-hoc rationalisations of our conduct and views than it is with guiding our actions and shaping our ideas in the first place.[22] C. Daniel Batson's work on moral hypocrisy similarly arrives at strikingly Mandevillean conclusions. Batson argues that much of our behaviour 'that appears to be a product of moral integrity turns out on closer inspection to be a product of moral hypocrisy. And . . . we're prone to keep this truth even from ourselves.'[23] None of this is to suggest that Haidt or Batson should be read as settling matters decisively in Mandeville's favour—they have their own critics—but it does indicate that some of his most important insights are still taken seriously today, even if they are not identified as Mandevillean insights within the relevant academic fields.[24]

21. For an approach along these lines to Adam Smith's work, see Vernon L. Smith and Bart J. Wilson, *Humanomics: Moral Sentiments and the Wealth of Nations for the Twenty-First Century* (Cambridge: Cambridge University Press, 2019).

22. Haidt, 'Emotional Dog'. See Chapter 2, 'Pride vs. a well-regulated desire for esteem', for further discussion and references. As I argue more generally in Chapter 1, Mandeville's analysis of human nature owes much to a broader Augustinian tradition of moral psychology, and the considerations summarised here thus count in favour of that broader tradition too.

23. Batson, *What's Wrong with Morality*, 146.

24. Haidt draws on Hume as the most important eighteenth-century forerunner of his own position, without mentioning Mandeville; see 'Emotional Dog', especially 815–16. In his work on altruism, Batson understandably engages with Mandeville as a critical foil; see *Scientific Search for Altruism, passim*. Although Batson does not discuss Mandeville in his work on moral hypocrisy, my interpretation allows for the view that Mandeville was wrong to deny the possibility of human altruism but right to place such emphasis on hypocrisy and self-deceit when analysing moral motivation, which would fit with Batson's findings.

These examples relate to Mandeville's moral psychology, which has generally stood the test of time better than his historical narratives. Many of his speculations on the origin of society, in particular, do not seem that plausible once we take into account more recent evidence on the basis of successful human cooperation in prehistoric or stateless communities. Yet, for all the limitations of Mandeville's conjectural history, the emphasis it places on the desire of dominion (as a manifestation of pride) does find some support from the anthropological and ethnological evidence that, most famously, Christopher Boehm has adduced in arguing that there is a universal drive to dominance in human nature.[25] This is a point of no small importance, for at the heart of Mandeville's *pride-centred* theory is the claim that humans can never live together peacefully without finding ways to curb their innate desire of dominion, which, if left unchecked, would otherwise lead to conflict.

Even when the details of Mandeville's historical narratives are found wanting, something may still be said in favour of his approach. It has been noted that there 'is not much conventional political theory—as understood by the greats of the previous century—in Mandeville.'[26] To the degree that this is true, we may respond, so much the worse for conventional political theory. The political philosophy of the seventeenth and eighteenth centuries has long been associated with natural rights and social contract theory, and one of the refreshing aspects of Mandeville's thought is that it points towards a more historically and sociologically sensitive approach to theorising politics.[27] He argues that we cannot understand political authority, for instance, without considering the sources of authority found in other social groups, including families and band societies, which long predate the largescale states we now inhabit. Those who theorise political authority in terms of a transfer of rights from individuals to the state (or sovereign) are liable to downplay the importance of sources of natural authority, such as reverence, in maintaining social order. The question of in what sense humans are sociable creatures lies at the foundation of politics, for Mandeville, and answering this question takes us as much into the realms of history, psychology, and social anthropology, as it does the topics and fields more often associated with political theory today.

---

25. Boehm, *Hierarchy in the Forest*, especially 124–48. See Chapter 4, 'A theory of political authority?' for more details and further references.

26. Gunn, *Beyond Liberty and Property*, 98.

27. More generally on this point, see Sagar, 'Of Mushrooms and Method', 110–12; idem., *Opinion of Mankind*, especially 67–102.

Mandeville's theory of sociability is explanatory, first and foremost, yet it is difficult to read the *Fable* without being drawn on questions of a more evaluative character. Even if pride encompasses what we could describe as a morally neutral desire for social esteem, or recognition, the moral connotations of the term matter too: pride is 'odious to all the World'.[28] Was Mandeville right to cast pride in such a negative light? After all, we sometimes refer to pride as a positive quality. It is good to take pride in what we do, we often say, and pride is now regularly used in an emancipatory sense by social groups who have long been treated as inferior. Neither of these uses of the word, however, capture the sense in which (as a matter of definition, for Mandeville) pride involves *overvaluing* ourselves. We do not look kindly upon people who flaunt the high value they have of themselves, he observes, with such displays of pride often generating offence and conflict. Nor do we see our own pride as something to celebrate. We are typically unwilling to admit the extent to which our most esteemed deeds stem from a desire for social approval, often preferring to see ourselves as motivated by more disinterested or public-spirited principles. This is the strongest consideration in support of Mandeville's appraisal. In so far as he succeeds in uncovering the hidden depths of pride behind so much of our conduct, we should ask whether this is a side of ourselves that we are happy to acknowledge. Mandeville thought not and I am inclined to agree, for nothing humbles our pride as much as seeing that passion in its true colours.

28. *Fable* I, 124.

BIBLIOGRAPHY

Primary Sources

Anon. *The True Meaning of the Fable of the Bees: In a Letter, &c.* (London, 1726).

Augustine, St. *The City of God against the Pagans*, ed. and trans. R. W. Dyson (Cambridge: Cambridge University Press, 1998).

Bacon, Francis. *The Advancement of Learning*, ed. Joseph Devy (New York: P. F. Collier and Son, 1901).

Bayle, Pierre. *Various Thoughts on the Occasion of a Comet*, trans. Robert C. Bartlett (New York: State University of New York, 2000).

Berkeley, George. *Alciphron, or the Minute Philosopher* (London, 1732).

Bluet [or Blewitt], George. *An Enquiry whether A general Practice of Virtue tends to the Wealth or Poverty, Benefit or Disadvantage of a People?* (London, 1725).

Boswell, James. *Life of Johnson*, ed. R. W. Chapman (Oxford: Oxford University Press, 2008).

Brown, John. *Essays on the Characteristics* (London, 1751).

Brown, John. *Thoughts on Civil Liberty, on Licentiousness, and Faction* (London, 1765).

Burrow, Robert. *Civil Society and Government vindicated from the Charge of being Founded on, and Preserv'd by, Dishonest Arts* (London, 1723).

Butler, Joseph. *Fifteen Sermons Preached on the Rolls Chapel and Other Writings on Ethics*, ed. David McNaughton (Oxford: Oxford University Press, 2017).

Campbell, Archibald. *An Enquiry Into the Original of Moral Virtue* (Edinburgh, 1733).

Charleton, Walter. *Epicurus's Morals, Collected Partly out of his owne Greek Text, and Diogenes Laertius, And Partly out of the Rhapsodies of Marcus Antonius, Plutarch, Cicero, & Seneca* (London, 1656).

Cockburn, John. *The History and Examination of Duels, shewing Their Heinous Nature and the Necessity of Suppressing them* (London, 1720).

Dennis, John. *Vice and Luxury, Public Mischiefs: or, Remarks On a Book Intituled, The Fable of the Bees; or, Private Vices Publick Benefits* (London, 1724).

Digby, John. *Epicurus's Morals, Translated from the Greek by John Digby, Esq. with Comments and Reflections Taken out of several Authors* (London, 1712).

Disney, John. *A View of Ancient Laws against Immorality and Profaneness* (Cambridge, 1729).

Du Châtelet, Emilie. 'Translator's Preface for The Fable of the Bees', in her *Selected Philosophical and Scientific Writings*, ed. Judith P. Zinsser (Chicago and London: The University of Chicago Press, 2009), 44–51.

Esprit, Jacques. *The Falsehood of Moral Virtue: A Moral Essay* (London, 1691).

Ferguson, Adam. *Institutes of Moral Philosophy* (Edinburgh, 1769).

Ferguson, Adam. *An Essay on the History of Civil Society*, ed. Duncan Forbes (Edinburgh: Edinburgh University Press, 1966).

Fiddes, Richard. *A General Treatise of Morality, Form'd upon the Principles of Natural Reason only* (London, 1724).

Hawkins, John. *Life of Samuel Johnson, LL.D.* (London, 1787).

Hervey, John. *Some Remarks on the Minute Philosopher. In a Letter from a Country Clergyman to his Friend in London* (London, 1732).

Hobbes, Thomas. *On the Citizen*, ed. and trans. Richard Tuck and Michael Silverthorne (Cambridge: Cambridge University Press, 1998).

Hobbes, Thomas. *Leviathan: The English and Latin Texts*, ed. Noel Malcolm (Oxford: Clarendon Press, 2012).

Hume, David. *The Letters of David Hume*, ed. J.Y.T. Greig (Oxford: Clarendon Press, 1932).

Hume, David. *Essays: Moral, Political, and Literary*, ed. Eugene F. Miller (Indianapolis: Liberty Fund, 1985).

Hume, David. *An Enquiry concerning the Principles of Morals*, ed. Tom L. Beauchamp (Oxford: Oxford University Press, 1998).

Hume, David. *An Enquiry concerning Human Understanding*, ed. Tom L. Beauchamp (Oxford: Oxford University Press, 1999).

Hume, David. *A Treatise of Human Nature*, ed. David Fate Norton and Mary J. Norton (Oxford: Oxford University Press, 2000).

Hutcheson, Francis. *Reflections upon Laughter and Remarks upon The Fable of the Bees* (Glasgow, 1750).

Hutcheson, Francis. *An Essay on the Nature and Conduct of the Passions and Affections, with Illustrations on the Moral Sense*, ed. Aaron Garrett (Indianapolis: Liberty Fund, 2002).

Hutcheson, Francis. *An Inquiry into the Original of Our Ideas of Beauty and Virtue in Two Treatises*, ed. Wolfgang Leidhold (Indianapolis: Liberty Fund, 2004).

Hutcheson, Francis. 'On the Natural Sociability of Mankind', in *Logic, Metaphysics and the Natural Sociability of Mankind*, ed. James Moore and Michael Silverthorne (Indianapolis: Liberty Fund, 2006), 189–216.

Innes, Alexander. 'A Prefatory Introduction', to [Archibald Campbell] *Aretē-logia, Or, An Enquiry Into the Original of Moral Virtue* (Westminster, 1728).

La Rochefoucauld, François de. *Moral Maxims and Reflections* (London 1694).

La Rochefoucauld, François de. *Collected Maxims and Other Reflections*, trans. E. H. and A. M. Blackmore, and Francine Giguère (Oxford: Oxford University Press, 2007).

Law, William. *Remarks upon A Late Book, entituled, The Fable of the Bees, or Private Vices, Publick Benefits* (London, 1724).

Lucretius. *On the Nature of the Universe*, trans. Ronald Melville (Oxford: Oxford University Press, 1997).

Mandeville, Bernard. *The Pamphleteers: A Satyr* (London, 1703).

Mandeville, Bernard. *The Virgin Unmask'd: or Female Dialogues Betwixt an Elderly Maiden Lady, and her Niece, On Several Diverting Discourses on Love, Marriage, Memoirs, Morals, &c. of the Times* (London: J. Morphew and J. Woodward, 1709).

Mandeville, Bernard. *The Mischiefs that ought Justly to be Apprehended from a Whig-Government* (London, 1714).

Mandeville, Bernard. *An Enquiry into the Causes of the Frequent Executions at Tyburn: and A Proposal for some Regulations concerning Felons in Prison, and the good Effects to be Expected from them* (London: J. Roberts, 1725).

Mandeville, Bernard. *An Enquiry into the Origin of Honour, and the Usefulness of Christianity in War* (London, 1732).

Mandeville, Bernard. *A Letter to Dion, Occasion'd by his Book call'd Alciphron, or The Minute Philosopher* (London: J. Roberts, 1732).

Mandeville, Bernard. *The Fable of the Bees: or, Private Vices, Publick Benefits*, ed. F. B. Kaye in 2 vols. (Indianapolis: Liberty Fund, 1988).

Mandeville, Bernard. *By a Society of Ladies: Essays in the Female Tatler*, ed. Maurice M. Goldsmith (Bristol: Thoemmes Press, 1999).

Mandeville, Bernard. *Bernard Mandeville's "A Modest Defence of Publick Stews": Prostitution and Its Discontents in Early Georgian England*, ed. Irwin Primer (New York: Palgrave Macmillan, 2006).

Mandeville, Bernard. *A Treatise of the Hypochondriack and Hysterick Diseases (1730)*, ed. Sylvie Kleiman-Lafon (Cham: Springer, 2017).

Mandeville, Bernard. *Free Thoughts on Religion, the Church, and National Happiness*, ed. Irwin Primer (London and New York: Routledge, 2017).

Mill, James. *A Fragment on Mackintosh* (London, 1835).

Nicole, Pierre. 'Of Charity, and Self-Love', in his *Moral Essays, Contain'd in several Treatises on many Important Duties*, vol. 3 (London, 1696), 179–206.

Nihell, Laurence. *Rational Self-Love; or, a Philosophical and Moral Essay on the Natural Principles of Happiness and Virtue* (London, 1773).

Pascal, Blaise. *Pensées and Other Writings*, trans. Honor Levi, ed. Anthony Levi (Oxford: Oxford University Press, 1995).

Rochester, John Wilmot, Earl of. *A Satyr Against Mankind*, in *The Poems and Lucina's Rape*, ed. Keith Walker and Nicholas Fisher (Chichester: Wiley-Blackwell, 2010), 88–97.

Rousseau, Jean-Jacques. *Discourse on the Origin and Foundations of Inequality among Men*, in *The Collected Writings of Rousseau*, vol. 3, ed. Christopher Kelly and Roger D. Masters (Hanover, NH: University Press of New England, 1992).

Sandeman, Robert. *Letters on Theron and Aspasio. Addressed to the Author*, vol. 1 (Edinburgh, 1757).

Shaftesbury, Anthony Ashley Cooper, Third Earl of. *Characteristicks of Men, Manners, Opinions, Times*, ed. Douglas Den Uyl in 3 vols. (Indianapolis: Liberty Fund, 2001).

Skelton, Philip. *Deism Revealed, or, the Attack on Christianity Candidly Reviewed In its real Merits*, vol. 2 (London, 1751).

Smith, Adam. *An Inquiry into the Nature and Causes of the Wealth of Nations*, ed. R. H. Campbell and A. S. Skinner (Indianapolis: Liberty Fund, 1981).

Smith, Adam. 'Letter to the *Edinburgh Review*', in his *Essays on Philosophical Subjects*, ed. W.P.D. Wightman and J. C. Bryce (Indianapolis: Liberty Fund, 1982), 242–56.

Smith, Adam. *The Theory of Moral Sentiments*, ed. D. D. Raphael and A. L. Macfie (Indianapolis: Liberty Fund, 1982).

Stephen, Leslie. *Essays on Freethinking and Plainspeaking* (London: Longmans, Green, and Co., 1873).

Stephen, Leslie. *History of English Thought in the Eighteenth Century*, vol. 2 (London: Smith, Elder, and Co., 1876).

Stewart, Dugald. 'Account of the Life and Writings of Adam Smith, L.L.D.', in Adam Smith, *Essays on Philosophical Subjects*, ed. W.P.D. Wightman and J. C. Bryce (Indianapolis: Liberty Fund, 1982), 269–332.

Temple, William. *An Essay upon the Original and Nature of Government*, in *The Works of Sir William Temple Bart*, vol. 1 (London, 1757).

Thorold, John. *A Short Examination of The Notions Advanc'd In a (late) Book, intituled, The Fable of the Bees, or Private Vices, Publick Benefits* (London, 1726).

Warburton, William. *A Critical and Philosophical Enquiry into the Causes of Prodigies and Miracles, as related by Historians* (London, 1727).

Warburton, William. *The Divine Legation of Moses Demonstrated*, vol. 1 (London, 1738).

Secondary Sources

Abizadeh, Arash. *Hobbes and the Two Faces of Ethics* (Cambridge: Cambridge University Press, 2019).

Alicke, Mark D. and Constantine Sedikides. 'Self-enhancement and Self-protection: What they are and what they do', *European Review of Social Psychology* 20, no. 1 (2009): 1–48.

Andrew, Donna T. 'The Code of Honour and Its Critics: The Opposition to Duelling in England, 1700–1850', *Social History* 5, no. 3 (1980): 409–34.

Appiah, Kwame Anthony. *The Honor Code: How Moral Revolutions Happen* (New York and London: W. W Norton, 2010).

Baggini, Julian. 'The radical wrongness of Bernard Mandeville: the free marketeer whose bee analogy came back to sting him', *Prospect*, May 10 2020: https://www.prospectmagazine.co.uk/philosophy/bernard-mandeville-free-market-economics-fable-bees (accessed May 27, 2022).

Batson, C. Daniel. *What's Wrong with Morality: A Social-Psychological Perspective* (Oxford: Oxford University Press, 2016).

Batson, C. Daniel. *A Scientific Search for Altruism: Do We Care Only About Ourselves?* (New York: Oxford University Press, 2019).

Baumgold, Deborah. 'The Difficulties of Hobbes Interpretation', *Political Theory* 36, no. 6 (2008): 827–55.

Berkovski, Sandy. 'Mandeville on Self-liking, Morality, and Hypocrisy', *Intellectual History Review* 32, no. 1 (2022): 157–78.

Bick, Alexander. 'Bernard Mandeville and the "Economy" of the Dutch', *Erasmus Journal for Philosophy and Economics* 1, no. 1 (2008): 87–106.

Billacois, François. *The Duel: Its Rise and Fall in Early Modern France*, trans. Trista Selous (New Haven: Yale University Press, 1990).

Blank, Andreas. 'Esteem and Self-Esteem in Early Modern Ethics and Politics. An Overview', *Intellectual History Review* 32, no. 1 (2022): 1–14.

Blom, Hans. 'Decay and the Political Gestalt of Decline in Bernard Mandeville and his Dutch Contemporaries', *History of European Ideas* 36, no. 2 (2010): 153–66.

Boehm, Christopher. *Hierarchy in the Forest: The Evolution of Egalitarian Behavior* (Cambridge MA and London: Harvard University Press, 1999).

Braga, Joaquim. 'Simulation and Dissimulation. Mandeville's Satiric View of Commercial Society', in *Bernard de Mandeville's Tropology of Paradoxes: Morals, Politics, Economics, and Therapy*, ed. Edmund Balsemão Pires and Joaquim Braga (New York, Dordrecht, and London: Springer, 2015), 243–55.

Braga, Joaquim. 'Hypothetical Thought in Mandeville's Deconstructive Genealogy of Sociability', *I castelli di Yale* 4, no. 2 (2016): 145–59.

Branchi, Andrea. 'Vanity, Virtue and the Duel: The Scottish Response to Mandeville', *Journal of Scottish Philosophy* 12, no. 1 (2014): 71–93.

Branchi, Andrea. 'Courage and Chastity in Commercial Society: Mandeville's Point on Male and Female Honour', in *Bernard de Mandeville's Tropology of Paradoxes: Morals, Politics, Economics, and Therapy*, ed. Edmund Balsemão Pires and Joaquim Braga (New York, Dordrecht, and London: Springer, 2015), 199–211.

Branchi, Andrea. 'Honour and the Art of Politics', *I castelli di Yale* 6, no. 2 (2018): 29–43.

Branchi, Andrea. *Pride, Manners, and Morals: Bernard Mandeville's Anatomy of Honour* (Leiden and Boston: Brill, 2022).

Brennan, Geoffrey and Philip Pettit, *The Economy of Esteem: An Essay on Civil and Political Society* (Oxford: Oxford University Press, 2004).

Broad, C. D. 'Egoism as a Theory of Human Motives', in his *Ethics and the History of Philosophy: Selected Essays* (London: Routledge and Kegan Paul, 1952), 218–31.

Brooke, Christopher. *Philosophic Pride: Stoicism and Political Thought from Lipsius to Rousseau* (Princeton and Oxford: Princeton University Press, 2012).

Burtt, Shelley. *Virtue Transformed: Political Argument in England, 1688–1740* (Cambridge: Cambridge University Press, 1992).

Callanan, John J. 'Mandeville on Pride and Animal Nature', in *Bernard de Mandeville's Tropology of Paradoxes: Morals, Politics, Economics, and Therapy*, ed. Edmund Balsemão Pires and Joaquim Braga (New York, Dordrecht, and London: Springer, 2015), 125–36.

Carey, Daniel. *Locke, Shaftesbury, and Hutcheson: Contesting Diversity in the Enlightenment and Beyond* (Cambridge: Cambridge University Press, 2005).

Carrive, Paulette. *Bernard Mandeville: Passions, vices, vertus* (Paris: Vrin, 1980).

Carroll, Ross. *Uncivil Mirth: Ridicule in Enlightenment Britain* (Princeton and Oxford: Princeton University Press, 2021).

Castiglione, Dario. 'Mandeville Moralized', *Annali Della Fondazione Luigi Einaudi* 17 (1983): 239–90.

Castiglione, Dario. 'Considering Things Minutely: Reflections on Mandeville and the Eighteenth-Century Science of Man', *History of Political Thought* 7, no. 3 (1986): 463–88.

Castiglione, Dario. 'Excess Frugality and the Spirit of Capitalism: Readings of Mandeville on Commercial Society', in *Culture in History: Production, Consumption and Values in Historical Perspective*, ed. Joseph Melling and Jonathan Barry (Exeter: University of Exeter, 1992), 155–79.

Cheney, Paul. 'István Hont, the Cosmopolitan Theory of Commercial Globalization, and Twenty-First-Century Capitalism', *Modern Intellectual History* 19, no. 3 (2022): 883–911.

Chiasson, Elias J. 'Bernard Mandeville: A Reappraisal', *Philological Quarterly* 49, no. 4 (1970): 489–519.

Colman, John. 'Bernard Mandeville and the Reality of Virtue', *Philosophy* 47 (1972): 125–39.

Cook, Harold J. 'Bernard Mandeville', in *A Companion to Early Modern Philosophy*, ed. Steven Nadler (Malden, MA: Blackwell, 2002), 469–82.

Cook, Harold J. 'Treating of Bodies Medical and Political: Dr. Mandeville's Materialism', *Erasmus Journal for Philosophy and Economics* 9, no. 1 (2016): 1–31.

Cook, Richard I. *Bernard Mandeville* (New York: Twayne, 1974).

Cook, Richard I. '"The Great Leviathan of Leachery": Mandeville's *Modest Defence of Publick Stews* (1724)', in *Mandeville Studies: New Explorations in the Art and Thought of Dr. Bernard Mandeville (1670–1733)*, ed. Irwin Primer (The Hague: Martinus Nijhoff, 1975), 21–33.

Crisp, Roger. *Sacrifice Regained: Morality and Self-Interest in British Moral Philosophy from Hobbes to Bentham* (Oxford: Oxford University Press, 2019).

Daniel, Stephen H. 'Myth and Rationality in Mandeville', *Journal of the History of Ideas* 47, no. 4 (1986): 595–609.

Darwall, Stephen L. 'Two Kinds of Respect', *Ethics* 88, no. 1 (1977): 36–49.

Davidson, Jenny. *Hypocrisy and the Politics of Politeness: Manners and Morals from Locke to Austen* (Cambridge: Cambridge University Press, 2004).

Dawson, Hannah. 'Shame in Early Modern Thought: From Sin to Sociability', *History of European Ideas* 45, no. 3 (2019): 377–98.

Dekker, Rudolph. '"Private Vices, Public Virtues" Revisited: The Dutch Background of Bernard Mandeville', trans. Gerard T. Moran, *History of European Ideas* 14, no. 4 (1992): 481–98.

Den Uyl, Douglas J. 'Passion, State, and Progress: Spinoza and Mandeville on the Nature of Human Association', *Journal of the History of Philosophy* 25, no. 3 (1987): 369–95.

Dew, Ben. 'Spurs to Industry in Bernard Mandeville's *Fable of the Bees*', *British Journal for Eighteenth-Century Studies* 28, no. 2 (2005): 151–65.

Dew, Ben. '"Damn'd to Sythes and Spades": Labour and Wealth Creation in the Writings of Bernard Mandeville', *Intellectual History Review* 23, no. 2 (2013): 187–205.

Dickey, Laurence. 'Pride, Hypocrisy and Civility in Mandeville's Social and Historical Theory', *Critical Review* 4, no. 3 (1990): 387–431.

Dickinson, H. T. 'The Politics of Bernard Mandeville', in *Mandeville Studies: New Explorations in the Art and Thought of Dr. Bernard Mandeville (1670–1733)*, ed. Irwin Primer (The Hague: Martinus Nijhoff, 1975), 80–97.

Douglass, Robin. *Rousseau and Hobbes: Nature, Free Will, and the Passions* (Oxford: Oxford University Press, 2015).

Douglass, Robin. 'What's Wrong with Inequality? Some Rousseauian Perspectives', *European Journal of Political Theory* 14, no. 3 (2015): 368–77.

Douglass, Robin. 'Morality and Sociability in Commercial Society: Smith, Rousseau—and Mandeville', *The Review of Politics* 79, no. 4 (2017): 597–620.

Douglass, Robin. 'Theorising Commercial Society: Rousseau, Smith and Hont', *European Journal of Political Theory* 17, no. 4 (2018): 501–11.

Douglass, Robin. 'Mandeville on the Origins of Virtue', *British Journal for the History of Philosophy* 28, no. 2 (2020): 276–95.

Douglass, Robin. 'The Dark Side of Recognition: Bernard Mandeville and the Morality of Pride', *British Journal for the History of Philosophy* (2021), online first.

Douglass, Robin. 'Bernard Mandeville on the Use and Abuse of Hypocrisy', *Political Studies* 70, no. 2 (2022): 465–82.

Douglass, Robin and Johan Olsthoorn. 'Introduction', to *Hobbes's On the Citizen: A Critical Guide*, ed. Robin Douglass and Johan Olsthoorn (Cambridge: Cambridge University Press, 2020), 1–11.

Dykstal, Timothy. *The Luxury of Skepticism: Politics, Philosophy and Dialogue in the English Public Sphere, 1660–1740* (Charlottesville: University Press of Virginia, 2001).

Edwards Jr., Thomas R. 'Mandeville's Moral Prose', *ELH* 31, no. 2 (1964): 195–212.

Elster, Jon. *Sour Grapes: Studies in the Subversion of Rationality* (Cambridge: Cambridge University Press, 1983).

Elster, Jon. *The Cement of Society: A Study of Social Order* (Cambridge: Cambridge University Press, 1989).

Faas, Ekbert. *The Genealogy of Aesthetics* (Cambridge: Cambridge University Press, 2002).

Force, Pierre. *Self-Interest before Adam Smith: A Genealogy of Economic Science* (Cambridge: Cambridge University Press, 2003).

Francesconi, Daniele. 'Mandeville sull'origine della società', *Il pensiero politico* 28, no. 3 (1995): 407–34.

Frykholm, Erin. 'Hume, Mandeville, Butler, and "that Vulgar Dispute"', *Archiv für Geschichte der Philosophie* 101, no. 2 (2019): 280–309.

Gaus, Gerald. 'The Egalitarian Species', *Social Philosophy and Policy* 31, no. 2 (2015): 1–27.

Gibbs, John C. *Moral Development and Reality: Beyond the Theories of Kohlberg, Hoffman, and Haidt*, 3rd ed. (New York: Oxford University Press, 2014).

Gill, Michael B. *The British Moralists on Human Nature and the Birth of Secular Ethics* (Cambridge: Cambridge University Press, 2006).

Goldsmith, Maurice M. *Private Vices, Public Benefits: Bernard Mandeville's Social and Political Thought* (Cambridge: Cambridge University Press, 1985).

Goldsmith, Maurice M. '"The Treacherous Arts of Mankind": Bernard Mandeville and Female Virtue', *History of Political Thought* 7, no. 1 (1986): 93–114.

Goldsmith, Maurice M. 'Regulating Anew the Moral and Political Sentiments of Mankind: Bernard Mandeville and the Scottish Enlightenment', *Journal of the History of Ideas* 49, no. 4 (1988): 587–606.

Goldsmith, Maurice M. 'Introduction', to *By a Society of Ladies: Essays in the Female Tatler*, ed. Maurice M. Goldsmith (Bristol: Thoemmes Press, 1999), 11–74.

Goldsmith, Maurice M. 'Mandeville's Pernicious System', in *Mandeville and Augustan Ideas: New Essays*, ed. Charles W. A. Prior (University of Victoria: ELS Editions, 2000), 71–84.

Gomes, Bjorn Wee. 'The Desire and Struggle for Recognition' (Columbia University PhD thesis, 2017).

Gooding, Nicholas and Kinch Hoekstra. 'Hobbes and Aristotle on the Foundation of Political Science', in *Hobbes's On the Citizen: A Critical Guide*, ed. Robin Douglass and Johan Olsthoorn (Cambridge: Cambridge University Press, 2020), 31–50.

Gottmann, Felicia. 'Du Châtelet, Voltaire, and the Transformation of Mandeville's *Fable*', *History of European Ideas* 38, no. 2 (2012): 218–32.

Greco, Lorenzo. 'On Pride', *HUMANA.MENTE Journal of Philosophical Studies* 12, no. 35 (2019): 101–23.

Griswold, Charles. 'Genealogical Narrative and Self-Knowledge in Rousseau's *Discourse on the Origin and Foundations of Inequality among Men*', *History of European Ideas* 42, no. 2 (2016): 276–301.

Guion, Béatrice. 'The Fable of the Bees: *proles sine matre?*', in *Bernard de Mandeville's Tropology of Paradoxes: Morals, Politics, Economics, and Therapy*, ed. Edmund Balsemão Pires and Joaquim Braga (New York, Dordrecht, and London: Springer, 2015), 91–104.

Gunn, J.A.W. 'Mandeville and Wither: Individualism and the Workings of Providence', in *Mandeville Studies: New Explorations in the Art and Thought of Dr. Bernard Mandeville (1670–1733)*, ed. Irwin Primer (The Hague: Martinus Nijhoff, 1975), 98–118.

Gunn, J.A.W. *Beyond Liberty and Property: The Process of Self-Recognition in Eighteenth-Century Political Thought* (Kingston: McGill-Queen's University Press, 1983).

Gunn, J.A.W. '"State Hypochondriacks" Dispraised: Mandeville versus the Active Citizen', in *Mandeville and Augustan Ideas: New Essays*, ed. Charles W. A. Prior (University of Victoria: ELS Editions, 2000), 16–34.

Haara, Heikki. *Pufendorf's Theory of Sociability: Passions, Habits and Social Order* (Cham: Springer, 2018).

Haara, Heikki and Tim Stuart-Buttle. 'Beyond Justice: Pufendorf and Locke on the Desire for Esteem', *Political Theory* 74, no. 5 (2019): 699–723.

Haidt, Jonathan. 'The Emotional Dog and Its Rational Tail: A Social Intuitionist Approach to Moral Judgment', *Psychological Review* 108, no. 4 (2001): 814–34.

Hamowy, Ronald. *The Scottish Enlightenment and the Theory of Spontaneous Order* (Carbondale and Edwardsville: Southern Illinois University Press, 1987).

Harris, James A. 'The Government of the Passions', in *The Oxford Handbook of British Philosophy in the Eighteenth Century*, ed. James A. Harris (Oxford: Oxford University Press, 2013), 270–88.

Harth, Phillip. 'The Satiric Purpose of the *Fable of the Bees*', *Eighteenth-Century Studies* 2, no. 4 (1969): 321–40.

Haydon, Colin. *Anti-Catholicism in Eighteenth-Century England: A Political and Social Study, c. 1714–80* (Manchester and New York: Manchester University Press, 1993).

Haydon, Colin. 'Eighteenth-Century English Anti-Catholicism: Contexts, Continuity, and Dissimulation', in *Protestant-Catholic Conflict from the Reformation to the Twenty-first Century: The Dynamics of Religious Difference*, ed. John Wolffe (New York: Palgrave Macmillan, 2013), 46–70.

Hayek, F. A. 'Lecture on a Master Mind: Dr. Bernard Mandeville', *Proceedings of the British Academy* 52 (1966): 125–41.

Heath, Eugene. 'Mandeville's Bewitching Engine of Praise', *History of Philosophy Quarterly* 15, no. 2 (1998): 205–26.

Heath, Eugene. 'Carrying Matters Too Far? Mandeville and the Eighteenth-Century Scots on the Evolution of Morals', *Journal of Scottish Philosophy* 12, no. 1 (2014): 95–119.

Hengstmengel, Joost W. 'Augustinian Motifs in Mandeville's Theory of Society', *Journal of Markets and Morality* 19, no. 2 (2016): 317–38.

Herdt, Jennifer A. *Putting On Virtue: The Legacy of the Splendid Vices* (Chicago and London: The University of Chicago Press, 2008).

Heydt, Colin. *Moral Philosophy in Eighteenth-Century Britain: God, Self, and Other* (Cambridge: Cambridge University Press, 2018).

Hilton, Phillip. *Bitter Honey: Recuperating the Medical and Scientific Context of Bernard Mandeville* (Bern: Peter Lang, 2010).

Hirschman, Albert O. *The Passions and the Interests: Political Arguments for Capitalism before Its Triumph* (Princeton: Princeton University Press, 1977).

Hollander, Samuel. *A History of Utilitarian Ethics: Studies in Private Motivation and Distributive Justice, 1700–1875* (London and New York: Routledge, 2020).

Honneth, Alex. *The Struggle for Recognition: The Moral Grammar of Social Conflicts*, trans. Joel Anderson (Cambridge: Polity Press, 1995).

Honneth, Alex. 'The Depths of Recognition: The Legacy of Jean-Jacques Rousseau', in *Engaging with Rousseau: Reaction and Interpretation from the Eighteenth Century to the Present*, ed. Avi Lifschitz (Cambridge: Cambridge University Press, 2016), 189–206.

Honneth, Alex. *Recognition: A Chapter in the History of European Ideas*, trans. Joseph Ganahl (Cambridge: Cambridge University Press, 2021).

Hont, István. *Jealousy of Trade: International Competition and the Nation-State in Historical Perspective* (Cambridge, MA and London: Belknap Press of Harvard University Press, 2005).

Hont, István. 'The Early Enlightenment Debate on Commerce and Luxury', in *The Cambridge History of Eighteenth-Century Political Thought*, ed. Mark Goldie and Robert Wokler (Cambridge: Cambridge University Press, 2006), 379–418.

Hont, István. *Politics in Commercial Society: Jean-Jacques Rousseau and Adam Smith*, ed. Béla Kapossy and Michael Sonenscher (Cambridge MA and London: Harvard University Press, 2015).

Horne, Thomas A. *The Social Thought of Bernard Mandeville: Virtue and Commerce in Early Eighteenth-Century England* (London: Macmillan, 1978).

Horne, Thomas A. 'Envy and Commercial Society: Mandeville and Smith on "Private Vices, Public Benefits"', *Political Theory* 9, no. 4 (1981): 551–69.

Hundert, Edward J. *The Enlightenment's Fable: Bernard Mandeville and the Discovery of Society* (Cambridge: Cambridge University Press, 1994).

Hundert, Edward J. 'Mandeville, Rousseau and the Political Economy of Fantasy', in *Luxury in the Eighteenth-Century: Debates, Desires and Delectable Goods*, ed. Maxine Berg and Elizabeth Elgar (Basingstoke: Palgrave, 2002), 28–40.

Hurtado Prieto, Jimena. 'Bernard Mandeville's Heir: Adam Smith or Jean Jacques Rousseau on the Possibility of Economic Analysis', *The European Journal of the History of Economic Thought* 11, no. 1 (2004): 1–31.

Iser, Mattias. 'Recognition', *Stanford Encyclopedia of Philosophy*, ed. Edward N. Zalta (2019): https://plato.stanford.edu/archives/sum2019/entries/recognition/ (accessed May 27, 2022).

Israel, Jonathan. *Radical Enlightenment: Philosophy and the Making of Modernity 1650–1750* (Oxford: Oxford University Press, 2001).

Jack, Malcolm. 'Religion and Ethics in Mandeville', in *Mandeville Studies: New Explorations in the Art and Thought of Dr. Bernard Mandeville (1670–1733)*, ed. Irwin Primer (The Hague: Martinus Nijhoff, 1975), 34–42.

Jack, Malcolm. 'One State of Nature: Mandeville and Rousseau', *Journal of the History of Ideas* 39, no. 1 (1978): 119–24.

Jack, Malcolm. *The Social and Political Thought of Bernard Mandeville* (New York and London: Garland, 1987).

Jack, Malcolm. 'Men Become Sociable by Living Together in Society: Re-assessing Mandeville's Social Theory', in *Bernard de Mandeville's Tropology of Paradoxes: Morals, Politics, Economics, and Therapy*, ed. Edmund Balsemão Pires and Joaquim Braga (New York, Dordrecht, and London: Springer, 2015), 1–13.

James, E. D. *Pierre Nicole, Jansenist and Humanist: A Study of his Thought* (The Hague: Martinus Nijhoff, 1972).

James, E. D. 'Faith, Sincerity and Morality: Mandeville and Bayle', in *Mandeville Studies: New Explorations in the Art and Thought of Dr. Bernard Mandeville (1670–1733)*, ed. Irwin Primer (The Hague: Martinus Nijhoff, 1975), 43–65.

Kapust, Daniel J. *Flattery and the History of Political Thought: That Glib and Oily Art* (Cambridge: Cambridge University Press, 2018).

Kaye, F. B. 'Mandeville on the Origin of Language', *Modern Language Notes* 39, no. 3 (1924): 136–42.

Kaye, F. B. 'Introduction', to *The Fable of the Bees: or, Private Vices, Publick Benefits*, ed. F. B. Kaye in 2 vols. (Indianapolis: Liberty Fund, 1988), xvii–cxlvi.

Kerkhof, Bert. 'A Fatal Attraction? Smith's "Theory of Moral Sentiments" and Mandeville's "Fable"', *History of Political Thought* 16, no. 2 (1995): 219–33.

Kleiman-Lafon, Sylvie. 'Introduction', to Bernard Mandeville, *A Treatise of the Hypochondriack and Hysterick Diseases (1730)*, ed. Sylvie Kleiman-Lafon (Cham: Springer, 2017), 1–13.

Klein, Lawrence E. *Shaftesbury and the Culture of Politeness: Moral Discourse and Cultural Politics in Early Eighteenth-Century England* (Cambridge: Cambridge University Press, 1994).

Kow, Simon. 'Rousseau's Mandevillean Conception of Desire and Modern Society', in *Rousseau and Desire*, ed. Mark Blackell, John Duncan, and Simon Kow (Toronto: University of Toronto Press, 2009), 62–81.

Kristjánsson, Kristján. *Justifying Emotions: Pride and Jealousy* (London and New York: Routledge, 2002).

Lafond, Jean. *L'homme et son image: Morales et littérature de Montaigne à Mandeville* (Paris: Champion, 1996).

Lamprecht, Sterling P. 'The Fable of the Bees', *The Journal of Philosophy* 23 (1926): 561–79.

Landreth, Harry. 'The Economic Thought of Bernard Mandeville', *History of Political Economy* 7, no. 2 (1975): 193–208.

Launay, Robert. *Savages, Romans, and Despots: Thinking about Others from Montaigne to Herder* (Chicago and London: The University of Chicago Press, 2018).

Lifschitz, Avi. *Language and Enlightenment: The Berlin Debates of the Eighteenth Century* (Oxford: Oxford University Press, 2012).

Liu, Antong. 'The Tragedy of Honor in Early Modern Political Thought: Hobbes, Mandeville, Montesquieu, and Rousseau', *History of European Ideas* 47, no. 8 (2021): 1243–61.

Lloyd, S. A. 'All the Mind's Pleasure: Glory, Self-Admiration, and Moral Motivation', in *Hobbes's On the Citizen: A Critical Guide*, ed. Robin Douglass and Johan Olsthoorn (Cambridge: Cambridge University Press, 2020), 51–70.

Lovejoy, Arthur O. '"Pride" in Eighteenth-Century Thought', in his *Essays in the History of Ideas* (Baltimore: John Hopkins University Press, 1948), 62–68.

Lovejoy, Arthur O. *Reflections on Human Nature* (Baltimore: The John Hopkins Press, 1961).

Luban, Daniel. 'Adam Smith on Vanity, Domination, and History', *Modern Intellectual History* 9, no. 2 (2012): 275–302.

Luban, Daniel. 'Bernard Mandeville as Moralist and Materialist', *History of European Ideas* 41, no. 7 (2015): 831–57.

Luban, Daniel. 'What is Spontaneous Order?', *American Political Science Review* 114, no. 1 (2020): 68–80.

Maurer, Christian. 'Archibald Campbell's Views of Self-Cultivation and Self-Denial in Context', *Journal of Scottish Philosophy* 10, no. 1 (2012): 13–27.

Maurer, Christian. 'Self-Interest and Sociability', in *The Oxford Handbook of British Philosophy in the Eighteenth Century*, ed. James A. Harris (Oxford: Oxford University Press, 2013), 291–314.

Maurer, Christian. 'What Can an Egoist say to an Egoist? On Archibald Campbell's Criticisms of Bernard Mandeville', *Journal of Scottish Philosophy* 12, no. 1 (2014): 1–18.

Maurer, Christian. *Self-love, Egoism and the Selfish Hypothesis: Key Debates from Eighteenth-Century British Moral Philosophy* (Edinburgh: Edinburgh University Press, 2019).

Maxwell, J. C. 'Ethics and Politics in Mandeville', *Philosophy* 26 (1951): 242–52.

McBride, Cillian. *Recognition* (Cambridge: Polity Press, 2013).

McKinnon, Christine. 'Hypocrisy, with a Note on Integrity', *American Philosophical Quarterly* 28, no. 4 (1991): 321–30.

McLendon, Michael Locke. *The Psychology of Inequality: Rousseau's Amour-Propre* (Philadelphia: University of Pennsylvania Press, 2019).

Mercer, Hugo and Dan Sperber, *The Enigma of Reason* (Cambridge, MA: Harvard University Press, 2017).

Mitchell, Annie. 'Character of an Independent Whig—"Cato" and Bernard Mandeville', *History of European Ideas* 29, no. 3 (2003): 291–311.

Monro, Hector. *The Ambivalence of Bernard Mandeville* (Oxford: Clarendon Press, 1975).

Moriarty, Michael. *Fallen Nature, Fallen Selves: Early Modern French Thought II* (Oxford: Oxford University Press, 2006).

Moriarty, Michael. *Disguised Vices: Theories of Virtue in Early Modern French Thought* (Oxford: Oxford University Press, 2011).

Muceni, Elena. *Apologia della virtù sociale: L'ascesa dell'amor proprio nella crisi della coscienza europea* (Milan: Mimesis, 2018).

Muthu, Sankar. *Enlightenment Against Empire* (Princeton and Oxford: Princeton University Press, 2003).

Myers, David G. and Jean M. Twenge, *Exploring Social Psychology*, 8th ed. (New York: McGraw Hill Education, 2018).

Nacol, Emily C. 'The Beehive and the Stew: Prostitution and the Politics of Risk in Bernard Mandeville's Political Thought', *Polity* 47, no. 1 (2015): 61–83.

Neuhouser, Frederick. *Rousseau's Theodicy of Self-Love: Evil, Rationality, and the Drive for Recognition* (Oxford: Oxford University Press, 2008).

Neuhouser, Frederick. 'Rousseau and the Human Desire for Recognition (*Amour Propre*)', in *The Philosophy of Recognition: Historical and Contemporary Perspectives*, ed. Hans-Christoph Schmidt am Busch and Christopher F. Zurn (Lanham, MA and Plymouth: Lexington Books, 2010), 21–46.

Neuhouser, Frederick. *Rousseau's Critique of Inequality: Reconstructing the Second Discourse* (Cambridge: Cambridge University Press, 2014).

Nieli, Russell. 'Commercial Society and Christian Virtue: The Mandeville-Law Dispute', *The Review of Politics* 51, no. 4 (1989): 581–610.

Nolan, Mark Charles. 'Paul Sakmann's and Albert Schatz's Mandeville Studies: Their Link to Hayek's "Spontaneous Order" Theory', *Journal of the History of Economic Thought* 38, no. 4 (2016): 485–506.

Olsthoorn, Peter. *Honor in Political and Moral Philosophy* (Albany, NY: SUNY Press, 2015).

Olsthoorn, Peter. 'Bernard Mandeville on Honor, Hypocrisy, and War', *The Heythrop Journal* 60, no. 2 (2019): 205–18.

Origgi, Gloria. *Reputation: What It Is and Why It Matters*, trans. Stephen Holmes and Noga Arikha (Princeton and Oxford: Princeton University Press, 2018).

Otero Knott, Martin. 'Mandeville on Governability', *Journal of Scottish Philosophy* 12, no. 1 (2014): 19–49.

Palmeri, Frank. 'Bernard de Mandeville and the Shaping of Conjectural History', in *Bernard de Mandeville's Tropology of Paradoxes: Morals, Politics, Economics, and Therapy*, ed. Edmund Balsemão Pires and Joaquim Braga (New York, Dordrecht, and London: Springer, 2015), 15–24.

Parrish, John M. *Paradoxes of Political Ethics: From Dirty Hands to the Invisible Hand* (Cambridge: Cambridge University Press, 2007).

Peltonen, Markku. *The Duel in Early Modern England: Civility, Politeness and Honour* (Cambridge: Cambridge University Press, 2003).

Peltonen, Markku. 'Politeness and Whiggism, 1688–1732', *The Historical Journal* 48, no. 2 (2005): 391–414.

Petsoulas, Christina. *Hayek's Liberalism and its Origins: His Idea of Spontaneous Order and the Scottish Enlightenment* (London and New York: Routledge, 2001).

Phillipson, Nicholas. *Adam Smith: An Enlightened Life* (London: Penguin, 2011).

Pinkus, Philip. 'Mandeville's Paradox', in *Mandeville Studies: New Explorations in the Art and Thought of Dr. Bernard Mandeville (1670–1733)*, ed. Irwin Primer (The Hague: Martinus Nijhoff, 1975), 193–211.

Pocock, J.G.A. *Barbarism and Religion, Volume Four: Barbarians, Savages, and Empires* (Cambridge: Cambridge University Press, 2005).

Pongiglione, Francesca and Mikko Tolonen. 'Mandeville on Charity Schools: Happiness, Social Order and the Psychology of Poverty', *Erasmus Journal for Philosophy and Economics* 9, no. 1 (2016): 82–100.

Prendergast, Renee. 'Knowledge, Innovation and Emulation in the Evolutionary Thought of Bernard Mandeville', *Cambridge Journal of Economics* 38, no. 1 (2014): 87–107.

Prendergast, Renee. 'Mandeville and the Doctrine of Laissez-faire', *Erasmus Journal for Philosophy and Economics* 9, no. 1 (2016): 101–23.

Primer, Irwin. 'Introduction', to Bernard Mandeville, *The Fable of the Bees*, ed. Irwin Primer (New York: Capricorn Books, 1962), 1–17.

Primer, Irwin. 'Mandeville and Shaftesbury: Some Facts and Problems', in *Mandeville Studies: New Explorations in the Art and Thought of Dr. Bernard Mandeville (1670–1733)*, ed. Irwin Primer (The Hague: Martinus Nijhoff, 1975), 126–141.

Primer, Irwin. 'Mandeville on War', in *Mandeville and Augustan Ideas: New Essays*, ed. Charles W. A. Prior (University of Victoria: ELS Editions, 2000), 117–140.

Primer, Irwin. 'Introduction', to *Bernard Mandeville's "A Modest Defence of Publick Stews": Prostitution and Its Discontents in Early Georgian England*, ed. Irwin Primer (New York: Palgrave Macmillan, 2006), 1–25.

Prince, Michael. *Philosophical Dialogue in the British Enlightenment: Theology, Aesthetics, and the Novel* (Cambridge: Cambridge University Press, 1994).

Prior, Charles W. A. '"Then Leave Complaints": Mandeville, Anti-Catholicism, and English Orthodoxy', in *Mandeville and Augustan Ideas: New Essays*, ed. Charles W. A. Prior (University of Victoria: ELS Editions, 2000), 51–70.

Rashid, Salim. 'Mandeville's *Fable*: Laissez-Faire or Libertinism?', *Eighteenth-Century Studies* 18, no. 3 (1985): 313–30.

Rivers, Isabel. *Reason, Grace, and Sentiment: A Study of the Language of Religion and Ethics in England 1660–1780, Volume 2: Shaftesbury to Hume* (Cambridge: Cambridge University Press, 2000).

Robertson, John. *The Case for the Enlightenment: Scotland and Naples 1680–1760* (Cambridge: Cambridge University Press, 2005).

Robertson, John. *The Enlightenment: A Very Short Introduction* (Oxford: Oxford University Press, 2015).

Rogers, A. K. 'The Ethics of Mandeville', *International Journal of Ethics* 36, no. 1 (1925): 1–17.

Rosenberg, Nathan. 'Mandeville and Laissez-Faire', *Journal of the History of Ideas* 24, no. 2 (1963): 183–96.

Rosenblatt, Helena. *Rousseau and Geneva: From the First Discourse to the Social Contract, 1749–1762* (Cambridge: Cambridge University Press, 1997).

Rosenthal, Laura J. *Infamous Commerce: Prostitution in Eighteenth-Century British Literature and Culture* (Ithaca and London: Cornell University Press, 2006).

Rossi, Paolo. *The Dark Abyss of Time: The History of the Earth and the History of Nations from Hooke to Vico*, trans. Lydia G. Cochrane (Chicago and London: The University of Chicago Press, 1984).

Runciman, David. *Political Hypocrisy: The Mask of Power, from Hobbes to Orwell and Beyond* (Princeton and Oxford: Princeton University Press, 2008).

Sagar, Paul. 'Sociability, Luxury and Sympathy: The Case of Archibald Campbell', *History of European Ideas* 39, no. 6 (2013): 791–814.

Sagar, Paul. 'Of Mushrooms and Method: History and the Family in Hobbes's Science of Politics', *European Journal of Political Theory* 14, no. 1 (2015): 98–117.

Sagar, Paul. *The Opinion of Mankind: Sociability and the Theory of the State from Hobbes to Smith* (Princeton and Oxford: Princeton University Press, 2018).

Sagar, Paul. *Adam Smith Reconsidered: History, Liberty, and the Foundations of Modern Politics* (Princeton and Oxford: Princeton University Press, 2022).

Schneider, Louis. 'Mandeville as a Forerunner of Modern Sociology', *Journal of the History of Behavioral Science* 6, no. 3 (1970): 219–30.

Schneider, Louis. *Paradox and Society: The Work of Bernard Mandeville* (New Brunswick and Oxford: Transaction Books, 1987).

Schreyer, Rüdiger. 'Condillac, Mandeville and the Origin of Language', *Historiographia Linguistica* 1, no. 2 (1978): 15–43.

Scott, Kyle. 'Mandeville's Paradox as Satire: The Moral Consequences of Being a Good Citizen in a Commercial Society', *Politics and Policy* 37, no. 2 (2009): 369–94.

Scribano, Maria Emanuela. *Natura umana e società competitiva: studio su Mandeville* (Milan: Feltrinelli, 1980).

Sebastiani, Silvia. *The Scottish Enlightenment: Race, Gender, and the Limits of Progress*, trans. Jeremy Carden (New York: Palgrave Macmillan, 2013).

Sedlacek, Tomas. *Economics of Good and Evil: The Quest for Economic Meaning from Gilgamesh to Wall Street* (New York: Oxford University Press, 2011).

Seigel, Jerrold. *The Idea of the Self: Thought and Experience in Western Europe since the Seventeenth Century* (Cambridge: Cambridge University Press, 2005).

Selby-Bigge, L. A. 'Introduction', to *British Moralists, being Selections from Writers Principally of the Eighteenth Century*, ed. L. A. Selby-Bigge (Indianapolis: Bobbs Merrill, 1964), xxxiii–xcii.

Shaver, Robert. 'Egoism', *Stanford Encyclopedia of Philosophy*, ed. Edward N. Zalta (2019): https://plato.stanford.edu/archives/spr2019/entries/egoism/ (accessed May 27, 2022).

Sheridan, Patricia. 'Parental Affection and Self-Interest: Mandeville, Hutcheson, and the Question of Natural Benevolence', *History of Philosophy Quarterly* 24, no. 4 (2007): 377–92.

Shklar, Judith N. *Ordinary Vices* (Cambridge, MA and London: The Belknap Press of Harvard University Press, 1984).

Simonazzi, Mauro. 'Self-liking, onore e religione nella *Ricerca sull'origine dell'onore e sull'utilità del cristianesimo in guerra* di Bernard Mandeville', *Il pensiero politico: rivista di storia delle idee politiche e sociali* 32, no. 3 (1999): 352–82.

Simonazzi, Mauro. *Le favole della filosofia: Saggio su Bernard Mandeville* (Milan: Franco Angeli, 2008).

Simonazzi, Mauro. 'Bernard Mandeville e Jean-Jacques Rousseau', in *La filosofia politica di Rousseau*, ed. Giulio M. Chiode and Roberto Gatti (Milan: Franco Angeli, 2012), 231–37.

Simonazzi, Mauro. 'Atheism, Religion and Society in Mandeville's Thought', in *Bernard de Mandeville's Tropology of Paradoxes: Morals, Politics, Economics, and Therapy*, ed. Edmund Balsemão Pires and Joaquim Braga (New York, Dordrecht, and London: Springer, 2015), 221–42.

Simonazzi, Mauro. 'Bernard Mandeville on Hypochondria and Self-liking', *Erasmus Journal for Philosophy and Economics* 9, no. 1 (2016): 62–81.

Simonazzi, Mauro. 'Reconnaissance, *Self-liking* et contrôle social chez Mandeville', in *La reconnaissance avant la reconnaissance: Archéologie d'une problématique moderne*, ed. Francesco Toto, Théophile Pénigaud de Mourgues and Emmanuel Renault (Lyon: ENS Éditions, 2017), 127–44.

Simonazzi, Mauro. 'Common Law, Mandeville and the Scottish Enlightenment: At the Origin of the Evolutionary Theory of Historical Development', *Storia del pensiero politico* 7, no. 1 (2018): 107–26.

Simpson, James. *Permanent Revolution: The Reformation and the Illiberal Roots of Liberalism* (Cambridge, MA and London: The Belknap Press of Harvard University Press, 2019).

Skarbek, Emily. 'F. A. Hayek and the Early Foundations of Spontaneous Order', in *F. A. Hayek and the Modern Economy: Economic Organization and Activity*, ed. Sandra J. Peart and David M. Levy (New York: Palgrave Macmillan, 2013), 101–117.

Skinner, Quentin. 'Meaning and Understanding in the History of Ideas', *History and Theory* 8, no. 1 (1969): 3–53.

Smith, Vernon L. and Bart J. Wilson. *Humanomics: Moral Sentiments and the Wealth of Nations for the Twenty-First Century* (Cambridge: Cambridge University Press, 2019).

Speck, W. A. 'Mandeville and the Eutopia Seated in the Brain', in *Mandeville Studies: New Explorations in the Art and Thought of Dr. Bernard Mandeville (1670–1733)*, ed. Irwin Primer (The Hague: Martinus Nijhoff, 1975), 66–79.

Stafford, J. Martin. 'General Introduction', to *Private Vices, Publick Benefits? The Contemporary Reception of Bernard Mandeville*, ed. J. Martin Stafford (Solihull: Ismeron, 1997), xi–xxiv.

Starkie, Andrew. 'William Law and *The Fable of the Bees*', *Journal for Eighteenth-Century Studies* 32, no. 3 (2009): 307–19.

Statman, Daniel. 'Hypocrisy and Self-deception', *Philosophical Psychology* 10, no. 1 (1997): 57–75.

Stiker-Métral, Charles-Olivier. *Narcisse contrarié: l'amour propre dans le discours moral en France (1650–1715)* (Paris: Champion, 2007).

Stuart-Buttle, Tim. '"A Burthen too heavy for humane Sufferance": Locke on Reputation', *History of Political Thought* 38, no. 4 (2017): 644–80.

Stuart-Buttle, Tim. *From Moral Theology to Moral Philosophy: Cicero and Visions of Humanity from Locke to Hume* (Oxford: Oxford University Press, 2019).

Stuart-Buttle, Tim. 'Recognition, Sociability and Intolerance: A Study of Archibald Campbell (1691–1756)', *Global Intellectual History* 5, no. 2 (2020): 231–46.

Stumpf, Thomas. 'Mandeville, Asceticism, and the Spare Diet of the Golden Age', in *Mandeville and Augustan Ideas: New Essays*, ed. Charles W. A. Prior (University of Victoria: ELS Editions, 2000), 97–116.

Szabados, Béla and Eldon Soifer. *Hypocrisy: Ethical Investigations* (Peterborough, ON: Broadview Press, 2004).

Taylor, Jacqueline. *Reflecting Subjects: Passion, Sympathy, and Society in Hume's Philosophy* (Oxford: Oxford University Press, 2015).

Tolonen, Mikko. *Mandeville and Hume: Anatomists of Civil Society* (Oxford: Voltaire Foundation, 2013).

Tolonen, Mikko. 'The Gothic Origin of Modern Civility: Mandeville and the Scots on Courage', *The Journal of Scottish Philosophy* 12, no. 1 (2014): 51–69.

Tracy, Jessica L., Azim F. Shariff, and Joey T. Cheng. 'A Naturalist's View of Pride', *Emotion Review* 2, no. 2 (2010): 163–77.

Trivers, Robert. *Natural Selection and Social Theory: Selected Papers of Robert Trivers* (New York: Oxford University Press, 2002).

Turner, Brandon P. 'Mandeville against Luxury', *Political Theory* 44, no. 1 (2016): 26–52.

Verburg, Rudi. 'Bernard Mandeville's Vision of the Social Utility of Pride and Greed', *The European Journal of the History of Economic Thought* 22, no. 4 (2015): 662–91.

Verburg, Rudi. 'The Dutch Background of Mandeville's Thought: Escaping the Procrustean Bed of Neo-Augustinianism', *Erasmus Journal for Philosophy and Economics* 9, no. 1 (2016): 32–61.

Viner, Jacob. *Essays on the Intellectual History of Economics*, ed. Douglas A. Irwin (Princeton: Princeton University Press, 1991).

Wallmann, Elisabeth. 'The Human-Animal Debate and the Enlightenment Body Politic: Emile Du Châtelet's Reading of Mandeville's *Fable of the Bees*', *Early Modern French Studies* 42, no. 1 (2020): 86–103.

Welchman, Jennifer. 'Who Rebutted Bernard Mandeville?', *History of Philosophy Quarterly* 24, no. 1 (2007): 57–74.

Welsh, Alexander. *What is Honor? A Question of Moral Imperatives* (New Haven and London: Yale University Press, 2008).

Wilde, Norman. 'Mandeville's Place in English Thought', *Mind* 7 (1898): 219–32.

Wilderquist, Karl and Grant S. McCall. *Prehistoric Myths in Modern Political Philosophy* (Edinburgh: Edinburgh University Press, 2017).

Williams, Callum. *The Classical School: The Turbulent Birth of British Economics in Twenty Extraordinary Lives* (London: Profile Books, 2020).

Wootton, David. *Power, Pleasure, and Profit: Insatiable Appetites from Machiavelli to Madison* (Cambridge, MA and London: The Belknap Press of Harvard University Press, 2018).

Wright, John P. 'Hume on the Origin of "modern honour": A Study in Hume's Philosophical Development', in *Philosophy and Religion in Enlightenment Britain: New Case Studies*, ed. Ruth Savage (Oxford: Oxford University Press, 2012), 187–209.

Zinsser, Judith P. 'Entrepreneur of the "Republic of Letters": Emile de Breteuil, Marquise Du Châtelet, and Bernard Mandeville's *Fable of the Bees*', *French Historical Studies* 25, no. 4 (2002): 595–624.

INDEX

Addison, Joseph, 96

anger, 34, 50, 60, 99, 143–44, 152, 160, 170, 189n31, 209–10, 213

Augustine, St., 31n23, 70, 72–73

Augustinianism, 6, 23, 31, 58, 59, 63, 69–75, 81, 85, 227n22

authority: of the church and clergy, 118, 201–203; civil or political, 24, 67, 138, 158–59, 161–62, 168, 175, 179–80, 201, 228; natural or parental, 115, 146–47, 158–60, 167, 180

Bacon, Francis, 14

Batson, C. Daniel, 45n88, 55n126, 122n113, 227

Bayle, Pierre, 7–8, 166n120, 173n146

Berkeley, George, 124n120, 125

Bluet, George, 1, 24, 61n16, 71n57, 78n83, 84, 143nn34 and 36, 148, 159, 193n48, 206–10

Boehm, Christopher, 182n182, 228

Brown, John, 84, 102n48, 129n143

Butler, Joseph, 37–38, 42–45, 47, 54n123, 60

Campbell, Archibald, 83–84, 125, 155n76, 163n109, 166n119, 171n140

Cato, Marcus Porcius, 104–105, 112–13

Charleton, Walter, 141n27

chastity, 40n67, 184, 193–94

Christianity, 6, 8, 31, 59, 69n45, 71, 76, 97, 123, 126n131, 156, 172–75, 206; relation to honour, 183, 185–86, 195–99, 203, 205–206, 209–10, 218; use in war, 117, 199, 203, 211, 213–16. See also virtue: Christian

Church of Rome, 197, 198–203; political wisdom compared with Oliver Cromwell's, 215–16, 218, 220

Cicero, Marcus Tullius, 33, 81n93, 104–105, 112–13, 142n27, 188, 193n48

clergy: criticisms of, 74, 76, 117–18, 201–202.

Cockburn, John, 206n98, 207n104, 208n106

commercial society (or modernity), 218–19; commercial sociability, 9

conjectural history, 8, 23–24, 28, 149–52, 174, 181, 183, 199–200, 211, 217–19, 228

courage, 104, 143–44, 166, 184, 186n14, 187–89, 191–93, 198, 214

Cromwell, Oliver, 117–18, 203, 214–18, 220

cultural relativism, 102–103

deism, 129, 172, 174–75

Dennis, John, 1, 156, 171n140

Digby, John, 141n27

Disney, John, 205n96

division of labour, 169; as key to the success of the Church of Rome, 200–202

dominion: desire of, 24, 137–38, 161–64, 166, 168, 175, 182, 228. See also sovereignty: instinct of

Du Châtelet, Emilie, 1–2

duelling, 33, 53–54, 104, 185, 193n48, 203–10, 212, 218, 222; Louis XIV's edicts against, 207–210. See also honour

egoism. See psychological egoism

envy, 18, 39, 55, 60, 65, 104, 112, 143, 155

Epicureanism, 136n6, 141–42, 164n112, 165n116, 170n134, 172

equality, 31, 152, 210, 224n16

Esprit, Jacques, 7–8, 78n83, 97n23

esteem: desire for, 5–7, 9, 11, 29–32, 35–39, 41, 44, 49n100, 58, 60–61, 66, 82–90, 105, 121–22, 189, 191, 197, 221, 224, 229; involved in reverence, 160, 162, 180 (*see also* reverence)

evolution, 55n125, 86n115; evolutionary explanations of social phenomena, 136, 138–40, 151, 175–79

fear: of death (and overcoming it), 33, 40, 104, 143–44, 187–89, 193, 197, 214; of God or an invisible cause, 147, 161–62, 167, 185, 194–95, 197–99, 203, 214, 215, 217, 218; involved in reverence, 146–47, 160, 162, 179–80, 197 (*see also* reverence); relation to pride and shame, 7, 32–34, 39–40, 45, 54, 65–66, 104, 184, 197–98, 206–207; of temporal punishment, 143–45, 195, 205, 207

Fénelon, François, 96

Ferguson, Adam, 42n78, 48n97, 181

Fiddes, Richard, 48, 52, 156

glory, 7, 32, 49, 52–53, 75–76, 199, 211–12, 215, 224

golden age, 115, 146, 171–72

Haidt, Jonathan, 86n114, 227

Hayek, F. A., 140n24, 169n132, 176–78

Hervey, John, 124

Hobbes, Thomas, 4, 6–7, 14, 16, 28, 31, 33, 72, 81n94, 84n108, 154–55, 158, 159, 163nn109 and 110, 165n119; Shaftesbury's criticisms of, 96–98

honour, 11, 67, 70, 92, 131, 141, 167, 180, 183–85, 200, 204–11, 213, 216, 225; distinction between ancient and modern, 191–94; female, 40n67, 184, 193–94; origin of, 23–24, 137, 143–45, 147, 149, 151, 153, 159, 178–79, 185–91, 195–99, 203, 217–19, 223; relation to virtue, 53, 187–90, 203, 205–206, 209, 217

Hume, David, 2, 8–9, 10n33, 20nn75 and 76, 23, 42–3, 67–68, 80–83, 87, 127–28, 179, 226, 227n24

Hutcheson, Francis, 10, 21n78, 45, 46n93, 47, 49n100, 68, 127–29

hypocrisy, xii, 23, 91, 92–94, 106–109, 125, 215, 227; distinction between fashionable and malicious, 116–18; of Mandeville's adversaries, 13, 76, 93, 198; and self-deception, 55n126, 93, 103, 106–109, 123, 130, 227n24 (*see also* self-deception); of Shaftesbury, 103–105, 109; social utility of, 110, 113–16, 122–23, 126, 128, 130–31, 222

idolatry, 197–98, 200n80, 204, 214

La Rochefoucauld, François de, 7–8, 69n47, 71, 78n83, 83n102, 92,

labouring poor, 95n16, 223–25

language: origin of, 137, 155, 168–71, 176–78

Law, William, 1, 24, 74n67, 80n90, 107n64, 147–49, 162, 165n116, 173–74

Locke, John, 11, 96–97

luxury, 11, 18, 27, 59, 73, 76, 96, 216n145, 219, 223; and politeness, 153, 205, 210, 218, 222

Mill, James, 68n40

Montesquieu, Charles-Louis de Secondat Baron de, 11

Moses, 149n54, 165n119, 172

Nicole, Pierre, 9n30, 72n60

Original Sin (and the fallen condition), 6, 7, 59, 63n22, 69–72, 74–75, 85, 90, 115, 122–23, 146, 174, 165n117

parental affection, 38n58, 46–47, 98–99, 159–60, 165

Pascal, Blaise, 85

pity, 45, 62n20, 120, 160

politeness (and good manners), 14n51, 27, 38–39, 53, 55, 64, 67, 70, 79, 95, 100, 104, 107–108, 111, 113, 116–19, 174–75, 177; origin

of, 23, 63, 137, 149, 152–53, 170–71, 177,
    187n205, 210, 222; relation to honour and
    duelling, 185–87, 203–207, 210–11, 216–18
providence, 70, 74n67, 147, 156, 164–66, 172–73
psychological egoism, 28–29, 37, 41–47, 56.
    See also self-love
Pufendorf, Samuel, 9n30, 11

reason, 19, 47, 60, 78n83, 99, 111n81, 155, 159,
    162–64, 170, 172, 201, 206–207; motivational
    weakness of, 50, 74, 85–86, 175, 227
recognition theory, 5–6, 10, 22, 30–31, 189, 229.
    See also esteem: desire for
religion, 24, 51, 71, 75, 84n108, 95n14, 100, 102,
    107, 118, 123, 142, 147, 167, 173–75, 189n27, 191,
    209, 219; origin of, 137, 153, 161–62, 194;
    religious enthusiasm, 117–18, 185, 212–17,
    218; temporal benefits of, 194–95, 198, 200–203
reverence, 146–47, 149, 160–62, 168, 179–80,
    197–98, 228
Rochester, John Wilmot Earl of, 78n83
Rousseau, Jean-Jacques, 5, 6, 10–11, 15, 36,
    163n109, 181

Sandeman, Robert, 68
satire, 4, 12–14, 69, 75, 78, 106n61, 123n118
self-deception, 54–55, 74, 85, 93, 103, 106–109,
    122–23, 130, 227n24
self-liking, 32, 40, 42, 50n106, 56, 83, 152, 191,
    197n71; compared with self-love, 35–38,
    44, 57n2, 63–65; moral status of, 62–67, 86
self-love, 8, 10, 22, 32, 39, 41–47, 54n123, 55–56,
    60, 69, 84n108, 85, 97, 109, 114, 115–16,
    121–22, 129, 130, 226; compared with self-
    liking, 35–38, 44, 57n2, 63–65
self-preservation, 32–37, 40, 45, 63–64, 143,
    195n61
Shaftesbury, Anthony Ashley Cooper Third
    Earl of, 10, 14nn50 and 51, 21, 96–101, 156n81,
    221n4, 226; Mandeville's opposition to,
    21, 23, 40, 63n25, 93–95, 101–15, 118–19,
    125–27, 129–30, 145, 154, 158–59, 174–75
shame, 5, 20, 32, 34, 36, 53, 54nn121 and 122,
    61, 76, 93, 114, 120–21, 130, 141–44, 156,

    184, 188–89, 191, 193, 197–98, 206, 212;
    relation to pride, 38–41, 79, 191
Skelton, Philip, 129n143
Smith, Adam, xi, 2, 6, 8–9, 10n33, 15n33, 23,
    45n89, 49–52, 54n123, 56, 68, 84, 87, 116,
    127–28, 170n134, 219n153, 226
sovereignty: instinct of, 137, 152n63, 168–69,
    180–81, 198, 208–209. See also dominion:
    desire of
Spinoza, Baruch (and Spinozism), 15, 16,
    84n102, 172
Steele, Richard, 19n69, 33n35, 96
Stephen, Leslie, 48n97, 129
Stewart, Dugald, 150
Stoicism: criticisms of, 72–74, 85, 123

Temple, William, 157–60, 162, 164, 167, 179,
    181n180
Ten Commandments, 32n28, 162, 168–69, 172
Thorold, John, 205–206

valour, 144, 148, 158, 178, 186n14, 188–89,
    193n50, 199
vanity, 18, 32, 33, 48–49, 51–52, 82, 104, 112,
    124, 146, 196, 216
virtue 1, 5, 8, 19, 34, 40, 49–56, 60–62, 67–68,
    71, 73–74, 77n80, 78, 80, 84, 92–94, 118, 126,
    128, 191, 196; Christian, 71n54, 97, 111–12n83,
    123, 199–203, 205–206, 213, 218 (see also
    Christianity); distinction between coun-
    terfeited and real, 63–64, 94, 110–13, 118–23,
    130–31, 189; origin of, 20, 23, 27, 85, 109–10,
    119–21, 125n128, 137, 139–40, 141–42,
    145–47, 151, 153, 156, 159, 162–64, 178–79,
    185–90, 193, 217; (Mandeville's criticisms
    of) Shaftesbury's notions of, 97–108,
    112–13, 174–75

war, 98, 115, 117, 147, 152, 158, 164, 165, 187–88,
    195, 196, 211–13; relation to honour, 24, 144,
    184–85, 188–92, 199, 203, 207–17, 218–19
women: differences from men explained by
    socialisation rather than nature, 39–40,
    184, 193–94; enslaved by men, 117n101

A NOTE ON THE TYPE

This book has been composed in Arno, an Old-style serif typeface in the
classic Venetian tradition, designed by Robert Slimbach at Adobe.

CPSIA information can be obtained
at www.ICGtesting.com
Printed in the USA
JSHW081002080323
38610JS00004B/5